Kakuriyo
Bed & Breakfast for Spirits

1

Art by

Waco Ioka

Original Story by **Midori Yuma**
Character Design by **Laruha**

CONTENTS

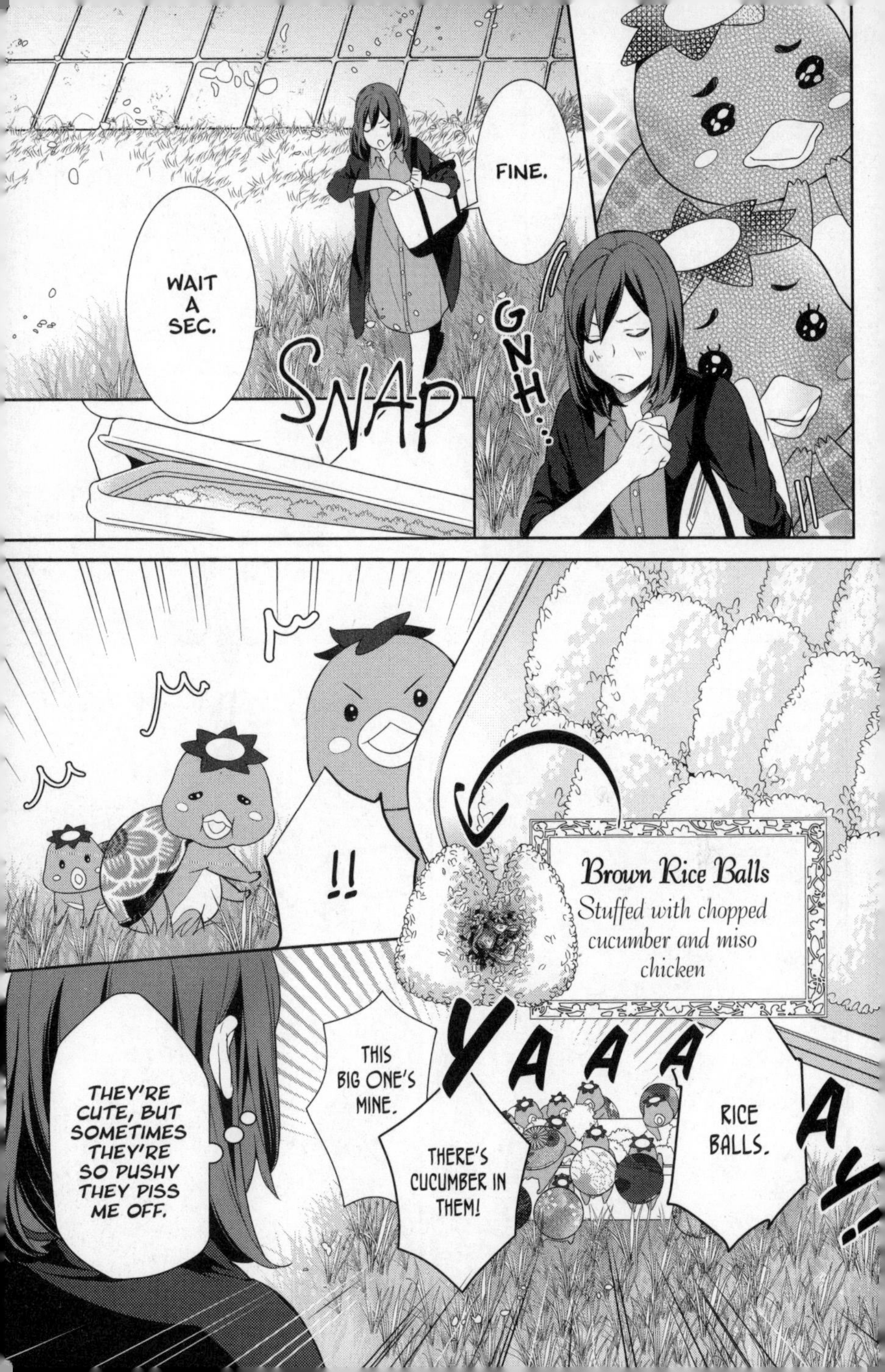
GNH..
FINE.
WAIT A SEC.
SNAP
Brown Rice Balls
Stuffed with chopped cucumber and miso chicken
!!
YAAAAY!!
RICE BALLS.
THERE'S CUCUMBER IN THEM!
THIS BIG ONE'S MINE.
THEY'RE CUTE, BUT SOMETIMES THEY'RE SO PUSHY THEY PISS ME OFF.

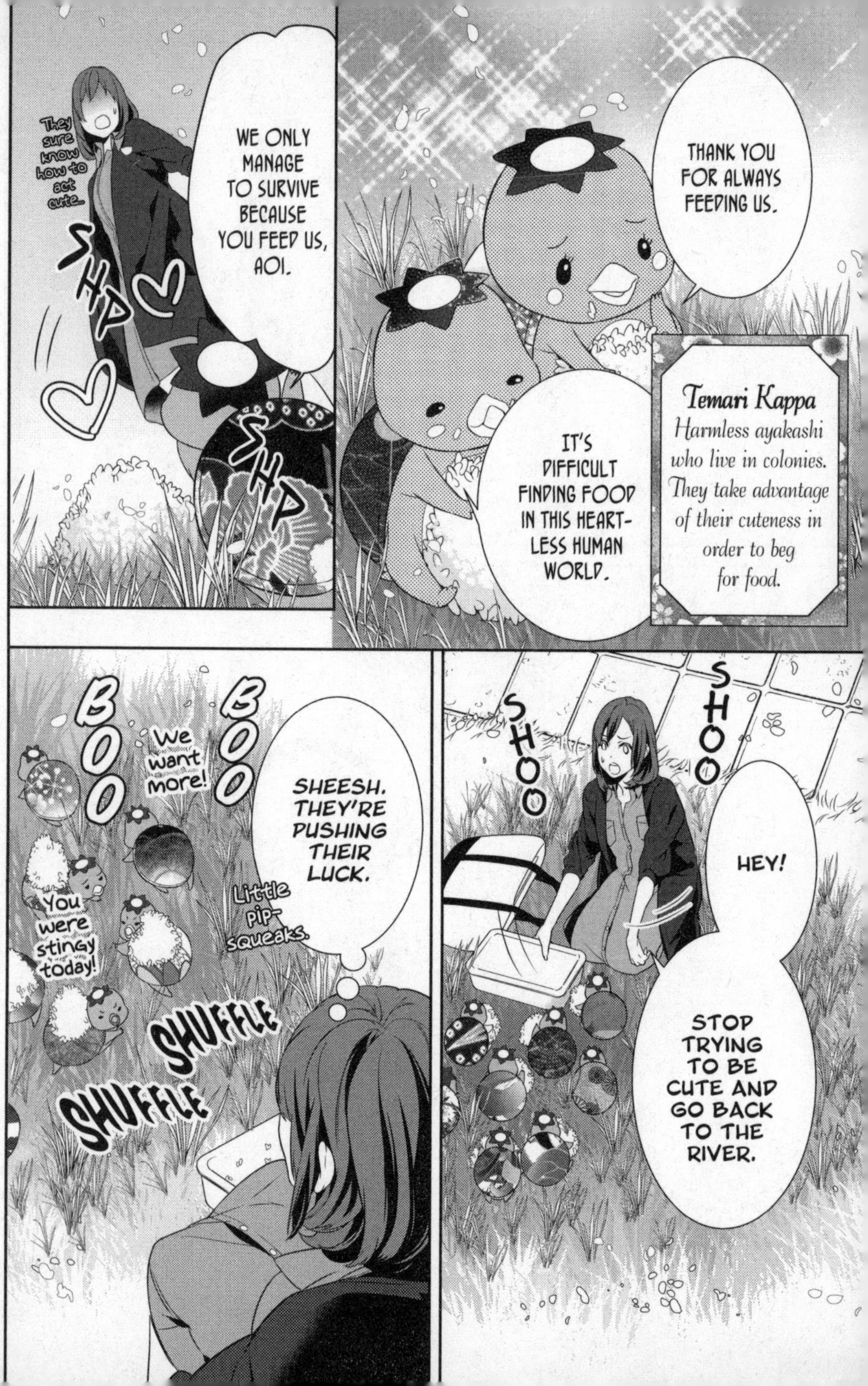
THANK YOU FOR ALWAYS FEEDING US.
IT'S DIFFICULT FINDING FOOD IN THIS HEART-LESS HUMAN WORLD.
Temari Kappa
Harmless ayakashi who live in colonies. They take advantage of their cuteness in order to beg for food.
WE ONLY MANAGE TO SURVIVE BECAUSE YOU FEED US, AOI.
They sure know how to act cute...
SHP
SHP
SHOO
SHOO
HEY!
STOP TRYING TO BE CUTE AND GO BACK TO THE RIVER.
BOO
BOO
We want more!
SHEESH. THEY'RE PUSHING THEIR LUCK.
Little pip-squeaks.
You were stingy today!
SHUFFLE
SHUFFLE

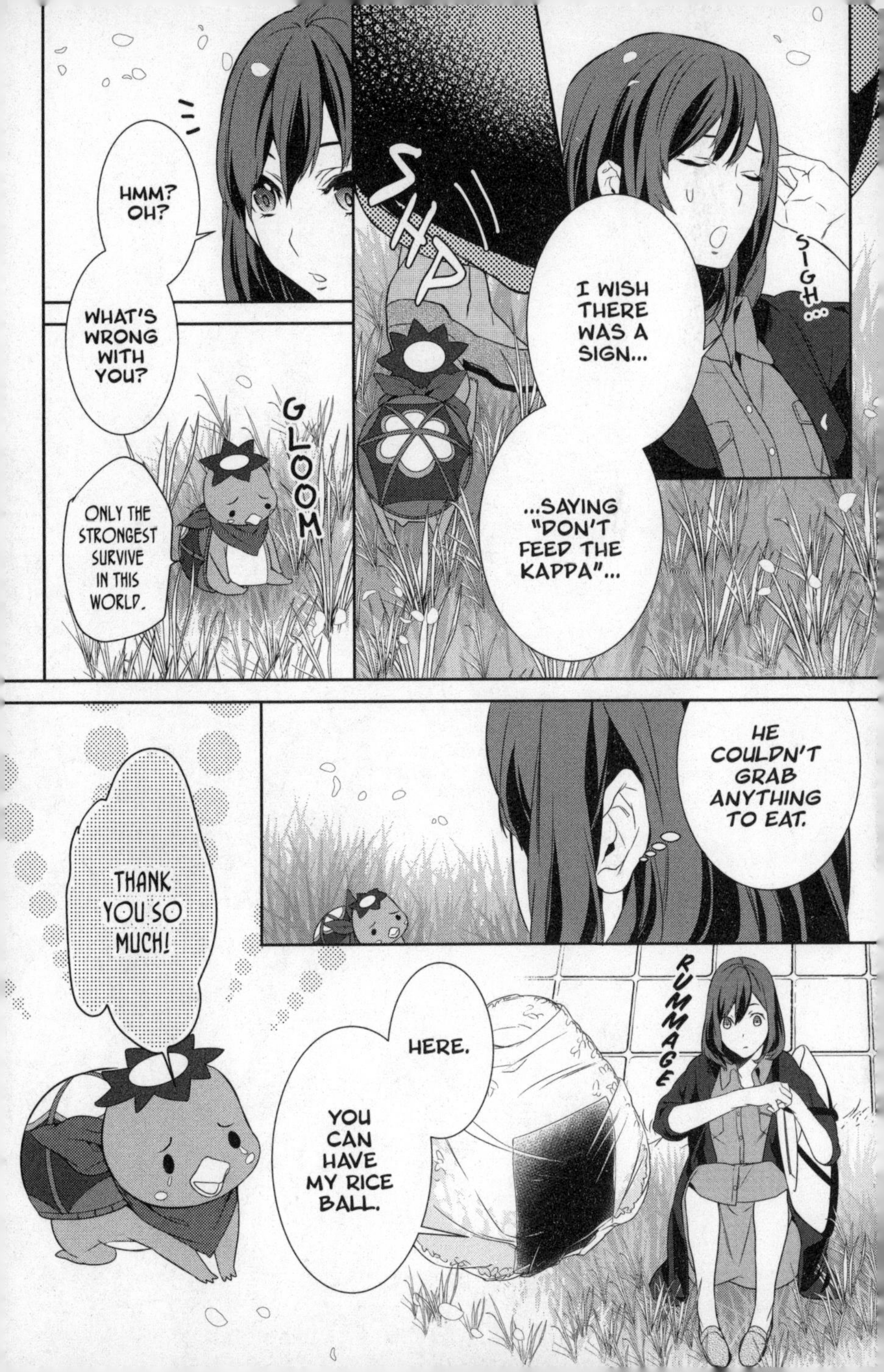
SIGH...
I WISH THERE WAS A SIGN...
...SAYING "DON'T FEED THE KAPPA"...
SHP
HMM? OH?
WHAT'S WRONG WITH YOU?
GLOOM
ONLY THE STRONGEST SURVIVE IN THIS WORLD.
HE COULDN'T GRAB ANYTHING TO EAT.
RUMMAGE
HERE.
YOU CAN HAVE MY RICE BALL.
THANK YOU SO MUCH!

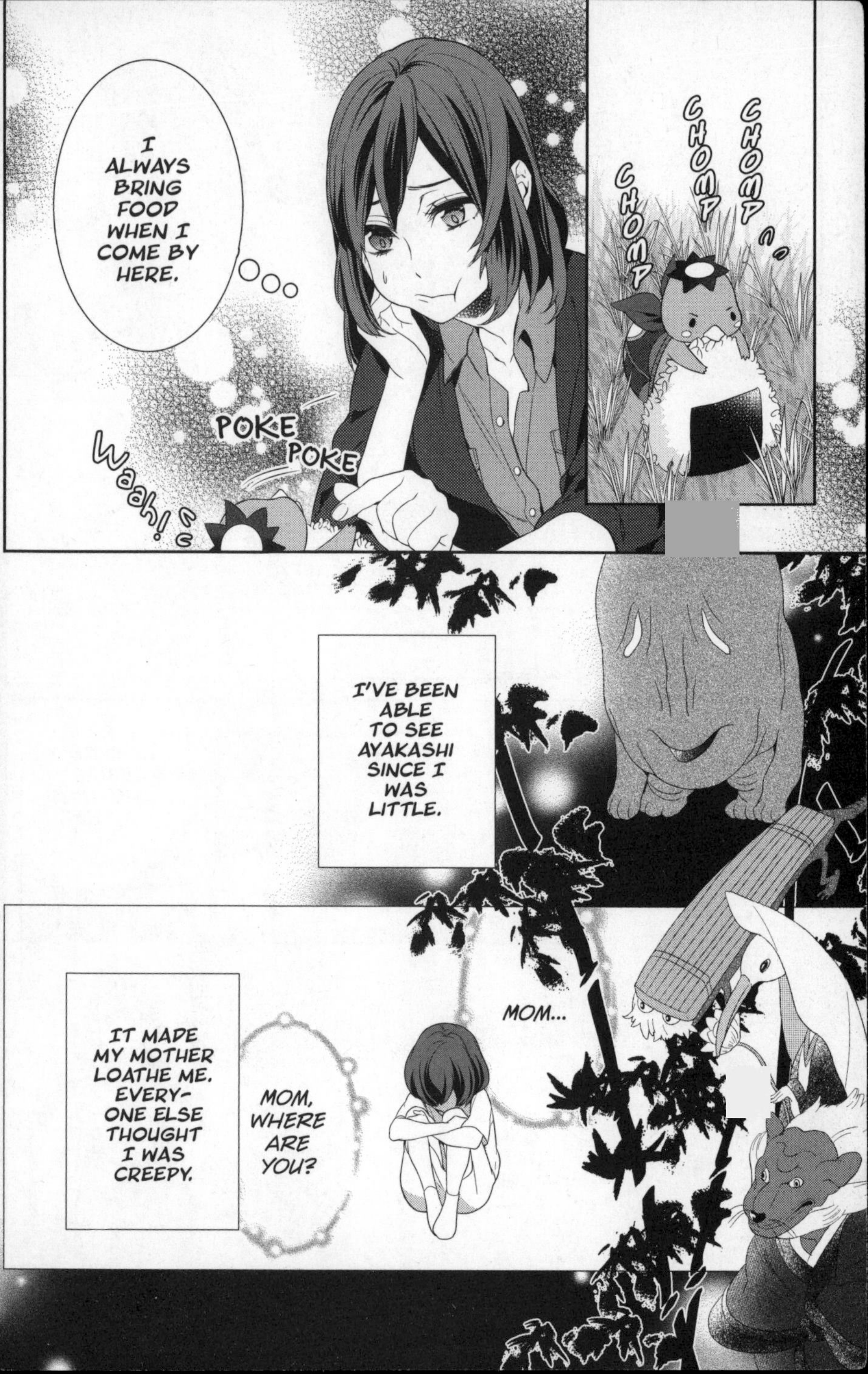
CHOMP
CHOMP
CHOMP
I ALWAYS BRING FOOD WHEN I COME BY HERE.
POKE POKE
Waah!
I'VE BEEN ABLE TO SEE AYAKASHI SINCE I WAS LITTLE.
MOM...
MOM, WHERE ARE YOU?
IT MADE MY MOTHER LOATHE ME. EVERY-ONE ELSE THOUGHT I WAS CREEPY.

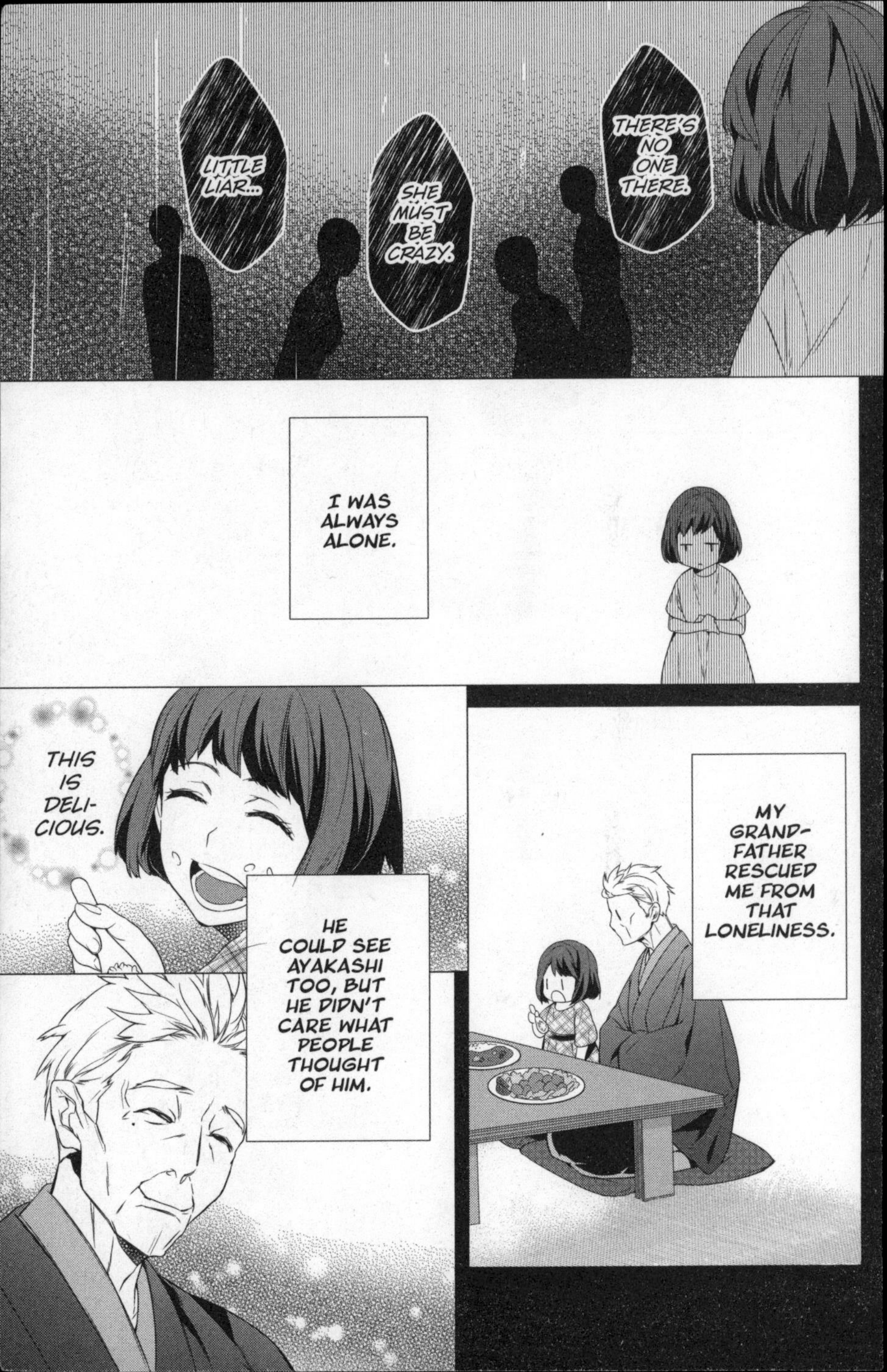
THERE'S NO ONE THERE.
SHE MUST BE CRAZY.
LITTLE LIAR...
I WAS ALWAYS ALONE.
MY GRAND-FATHER RESCUED ME FROM THAT LONELINESS.
THIS IS DELI-CIOUS.
HE COULD SEE AYAKASHI TOO, BUT HE DIDN'T CARE WHAT PEOPLE THOUGHT OF HIM.

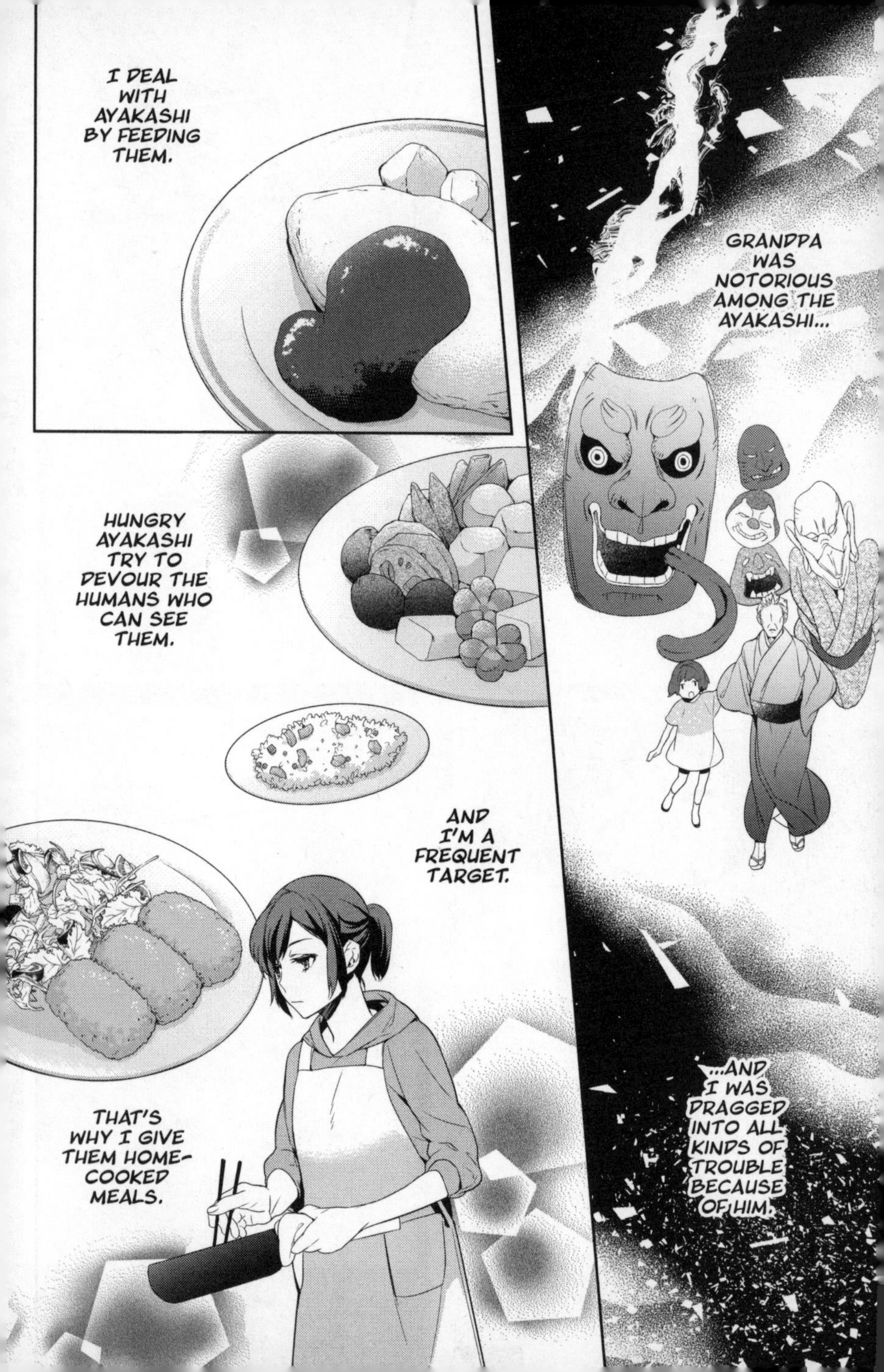
GRANDPA WAS NOTORIOUS AMONG THE AYAKASHI...
...AND I WAS DRAGGED INTO ALL KINDS OF TROUBLE BECAUSE OF HIM.
I DEAL WITH AYAKASHI BY FEEDING THEM.
HUNGRY AYAKASHI TRY TO DEVOUR THE HUMANS WHO CAN SEE THEM.
AND I'M A FREQUENT TARGET.
THAT'S WHY I GIVE THEM HOME-COOKED MEALS.

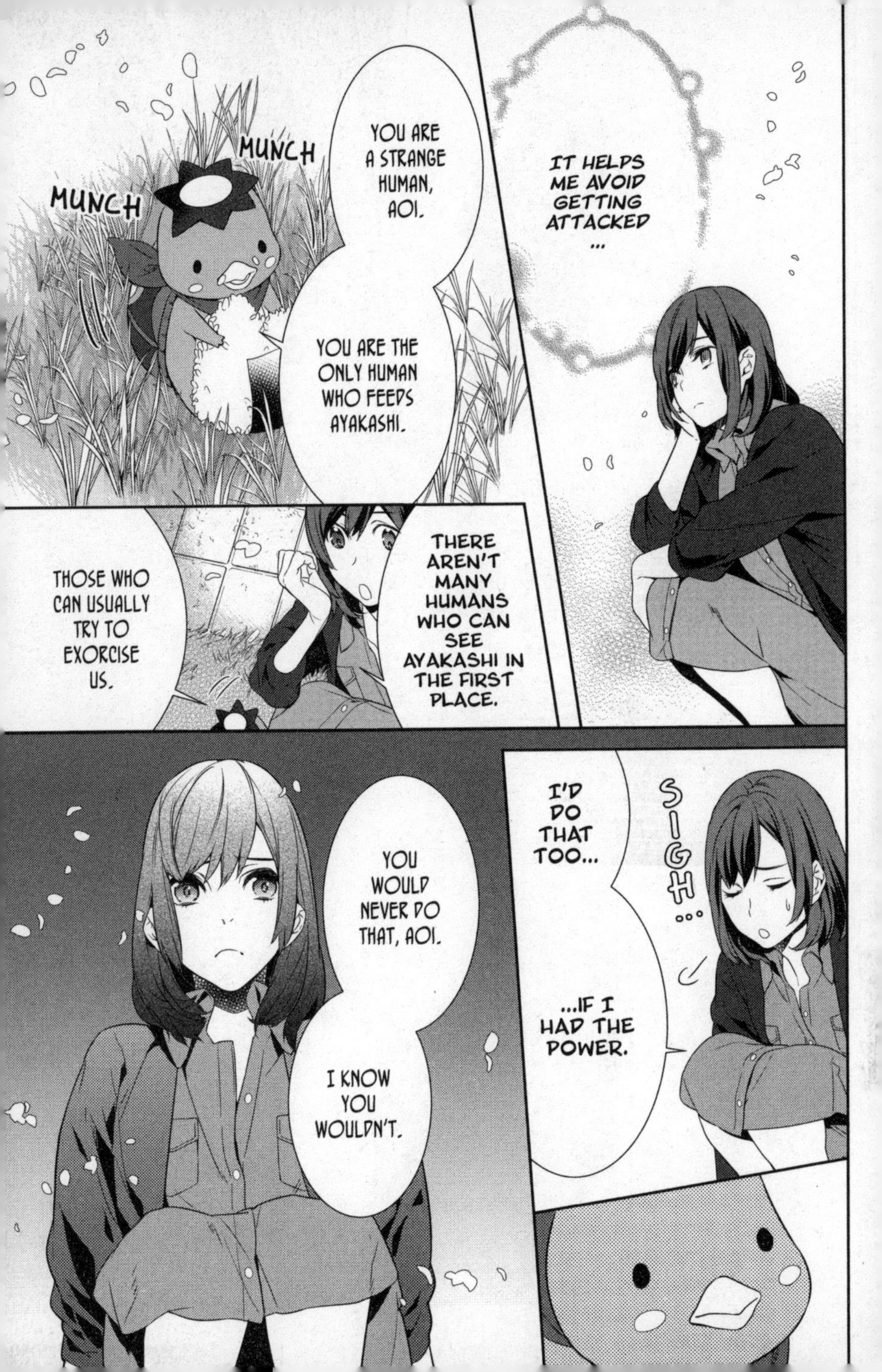
IT HELPS ME AVOID GETTING ATTACKED...
YOU ARE A STRANGE HUMAN, AOI.
YOU ARE THE ONLY HUMAN WHO FEEDS AYAKASHI.
MUNCH
MUNCH
THERE AREN'T MANY HUMANS WHO CAN SEE AYAKASHI IN THE FIRST PLACE.
THOSE WHO CAN USUALLY TRY TO EXORCISE US.
SIGH...
I'D DO THAT TOO...
...IF I HAD THE POWER.
YOU WOULD NEVER DO THAT, AOI.
I KNOW YOU WOULDN'T.

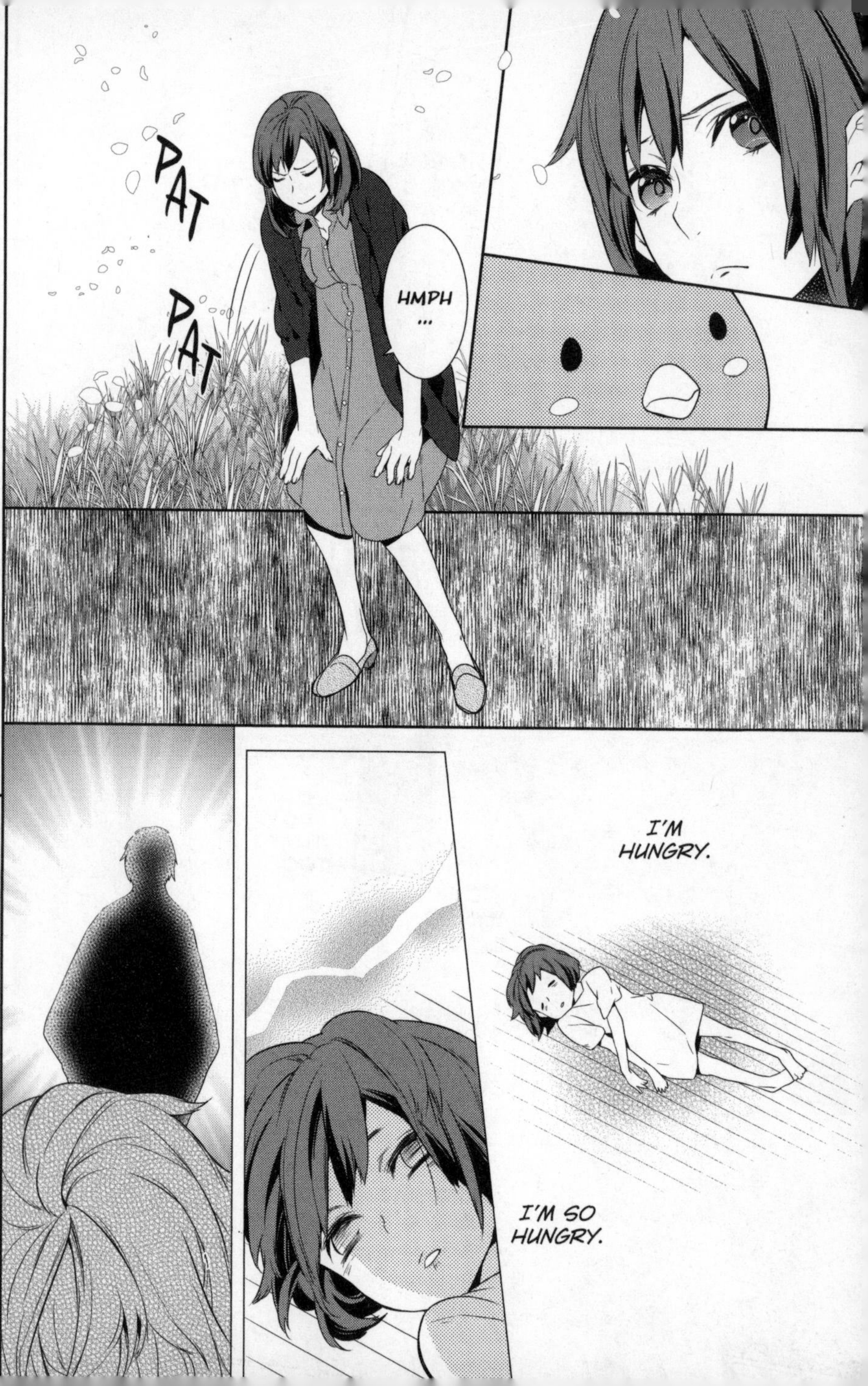
PAT PAT
HMPH...
I'M HUNGRY.
I'M SO HUNGRY.

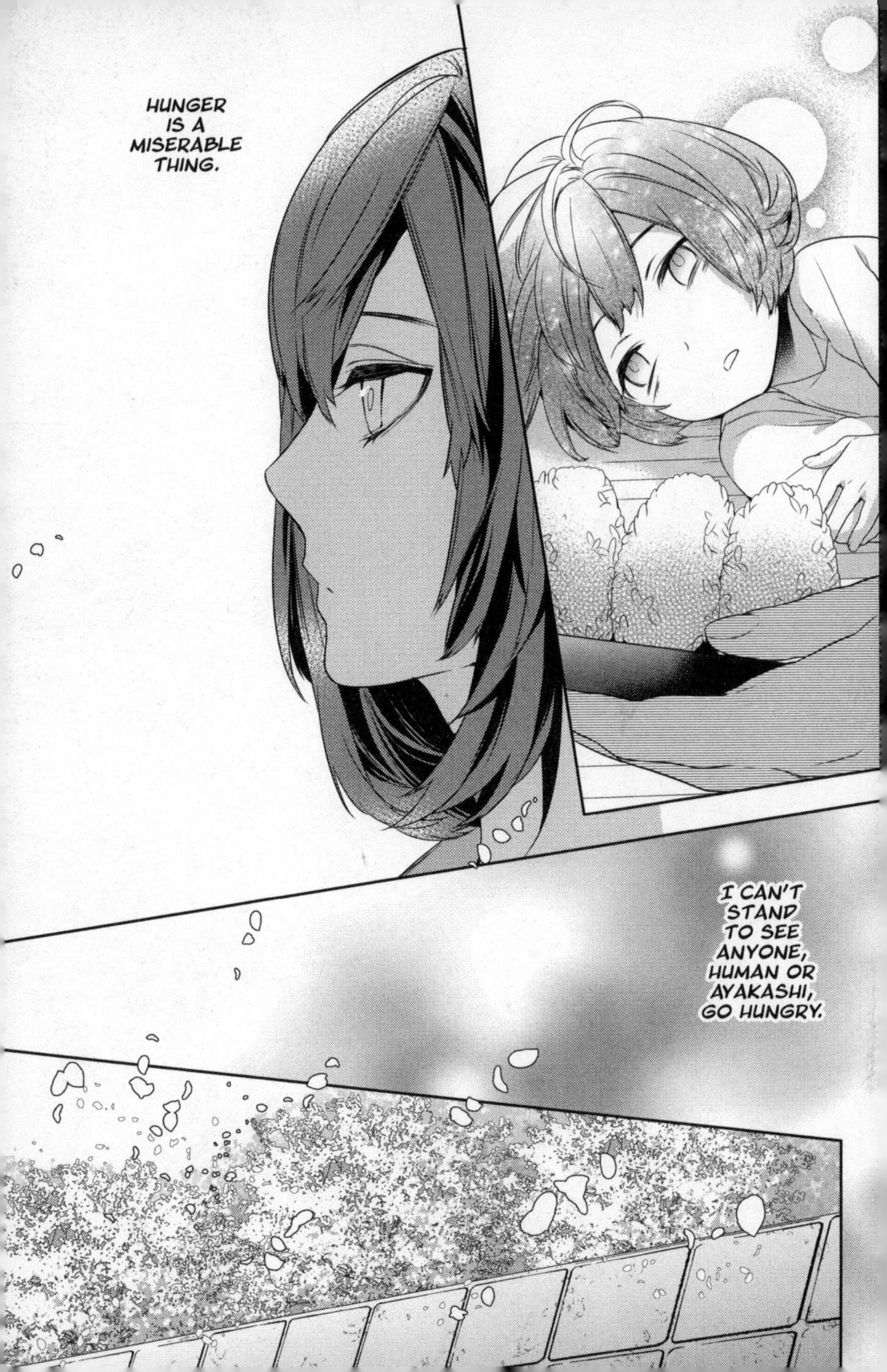
HUNGER IS A MISERABLE THING.
I CAN'T STAND TO SEE ANYONE, HUMAN OR AYAKASHI, GO HUNGRY.

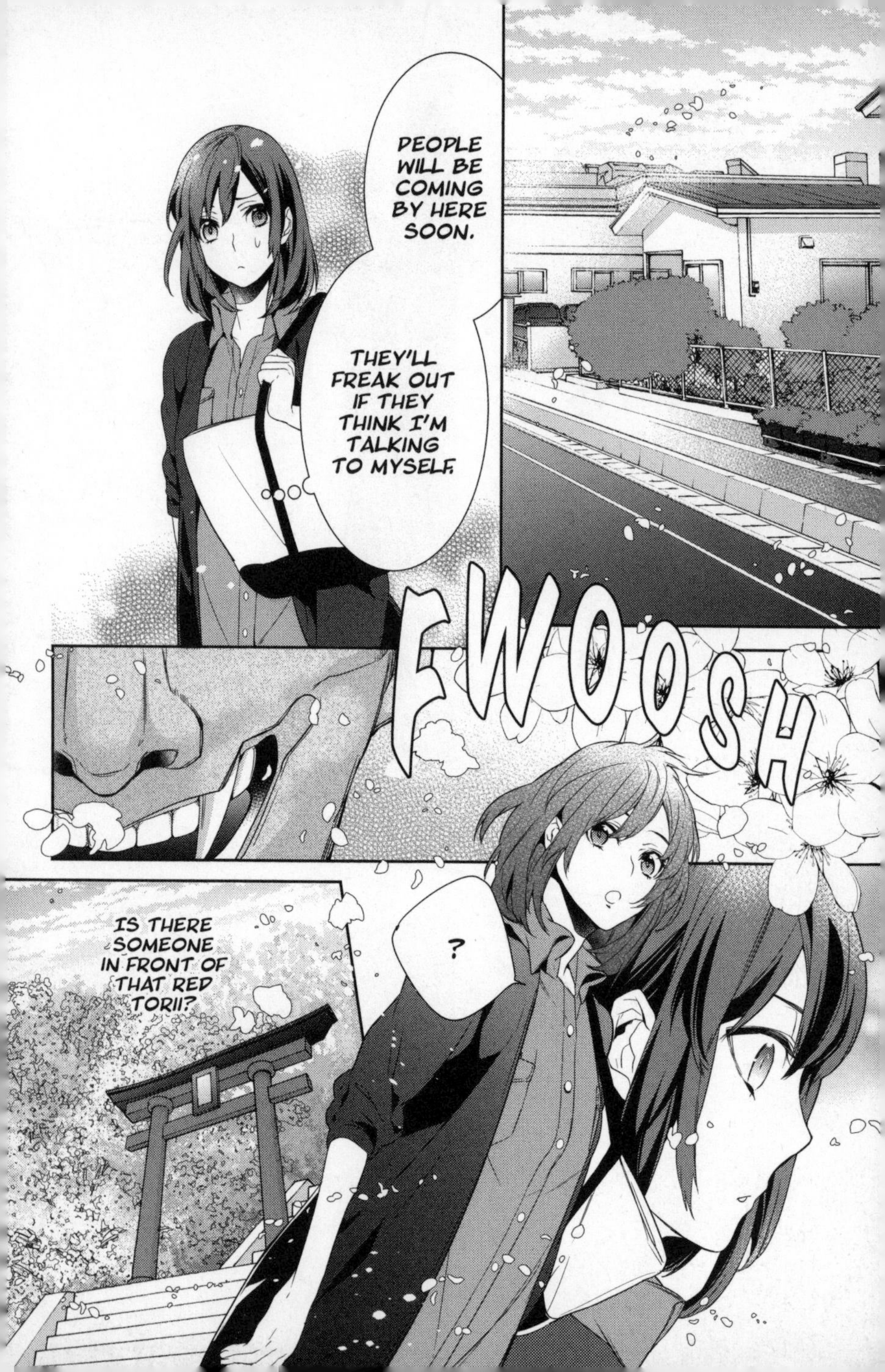
PEOPLE WILL BE COMING BY HERE SOON.
THEY'LL FREAK OUT IF THEY THINK I'M TALKING TO MYSELF.
FWOOSH
?
IS THERE SOMEONE IN FRONT OF THAT RED TORII?

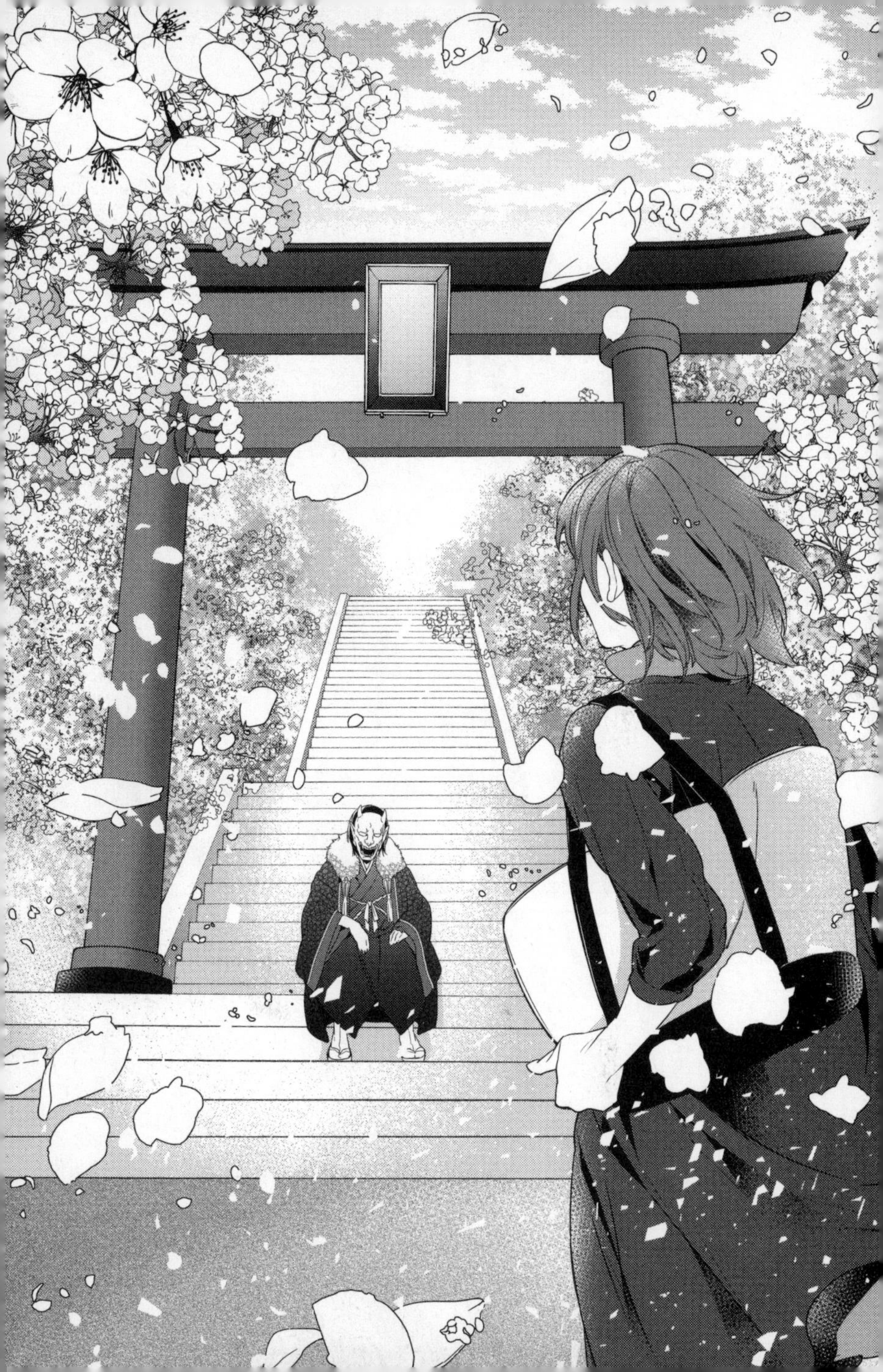

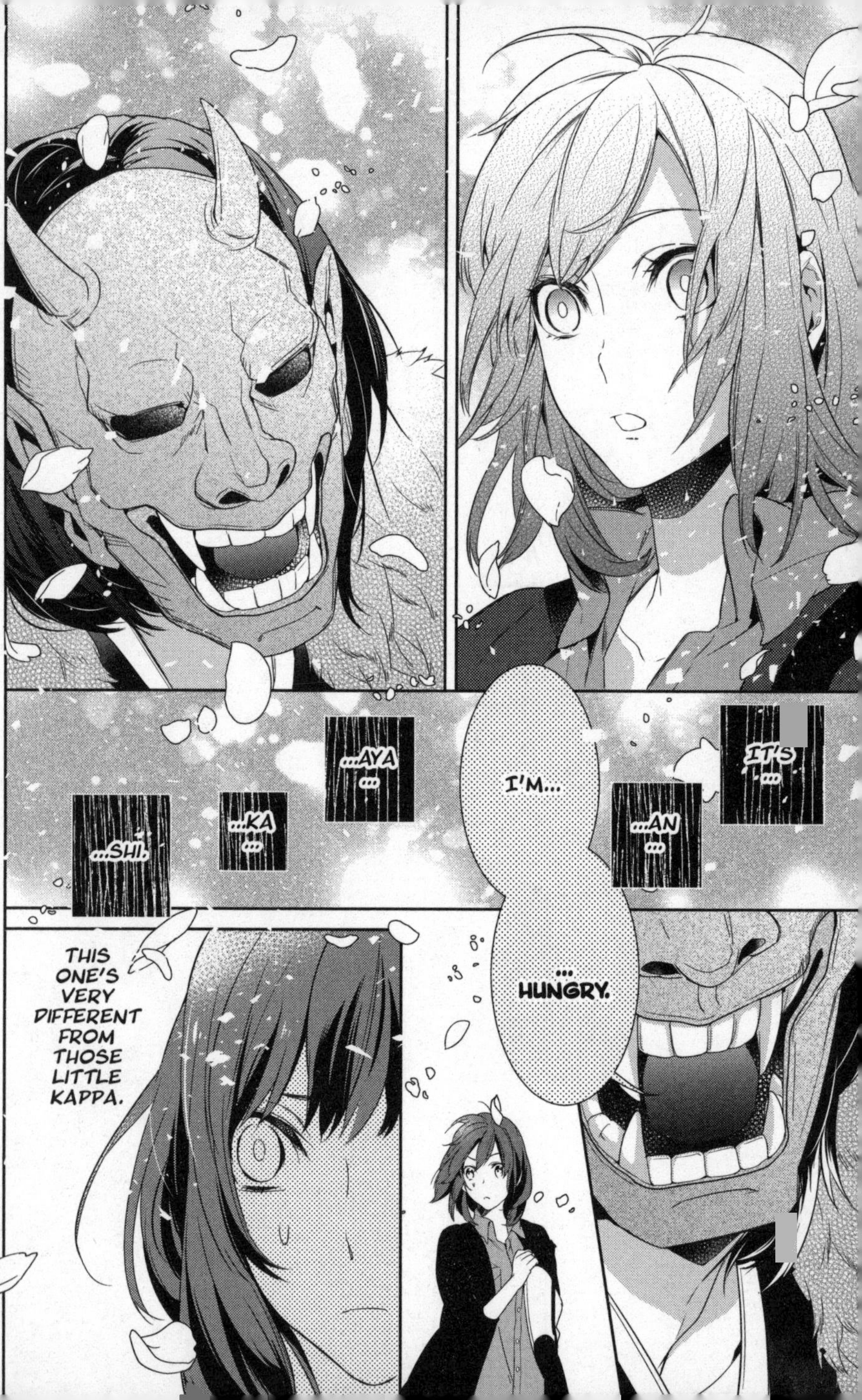
IT'S ...
...AN ...
...AYA ...
...KA ...
...SHI.
I'M... ...HUNGRY.
THIS ONE'S VERY DIFFERENT FROM THOSE LITTLE KAPPA.

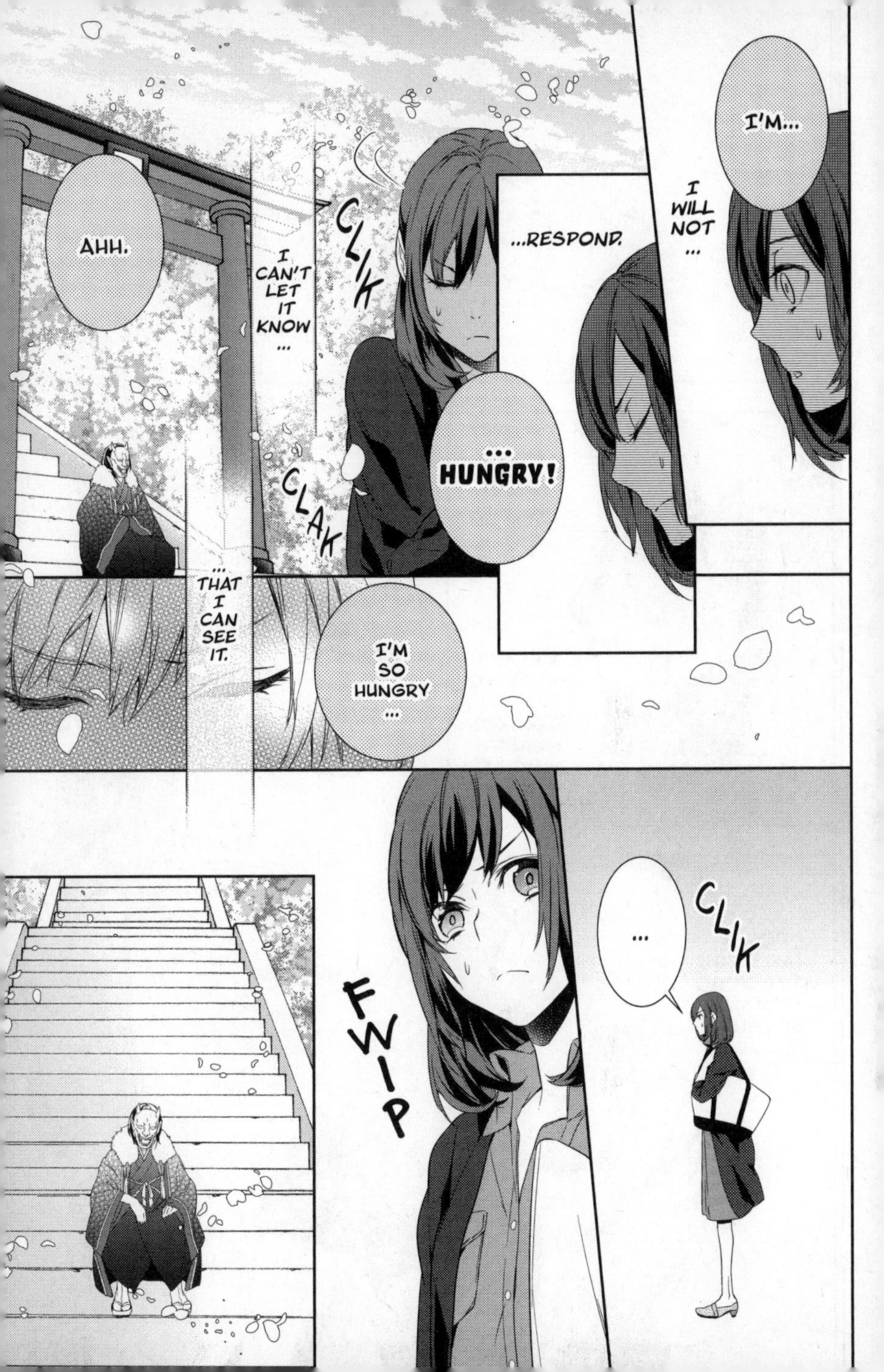

I'M...
I WILL NOT ...
...RESPOND.
CLIK
I CAN'T LET IT KNOW ...
AHH.
... HUNGRY!
CLAK
... THAT I CAN SEE IT.
I'M SO HUNGRY ...
CLIK
...
FWIP

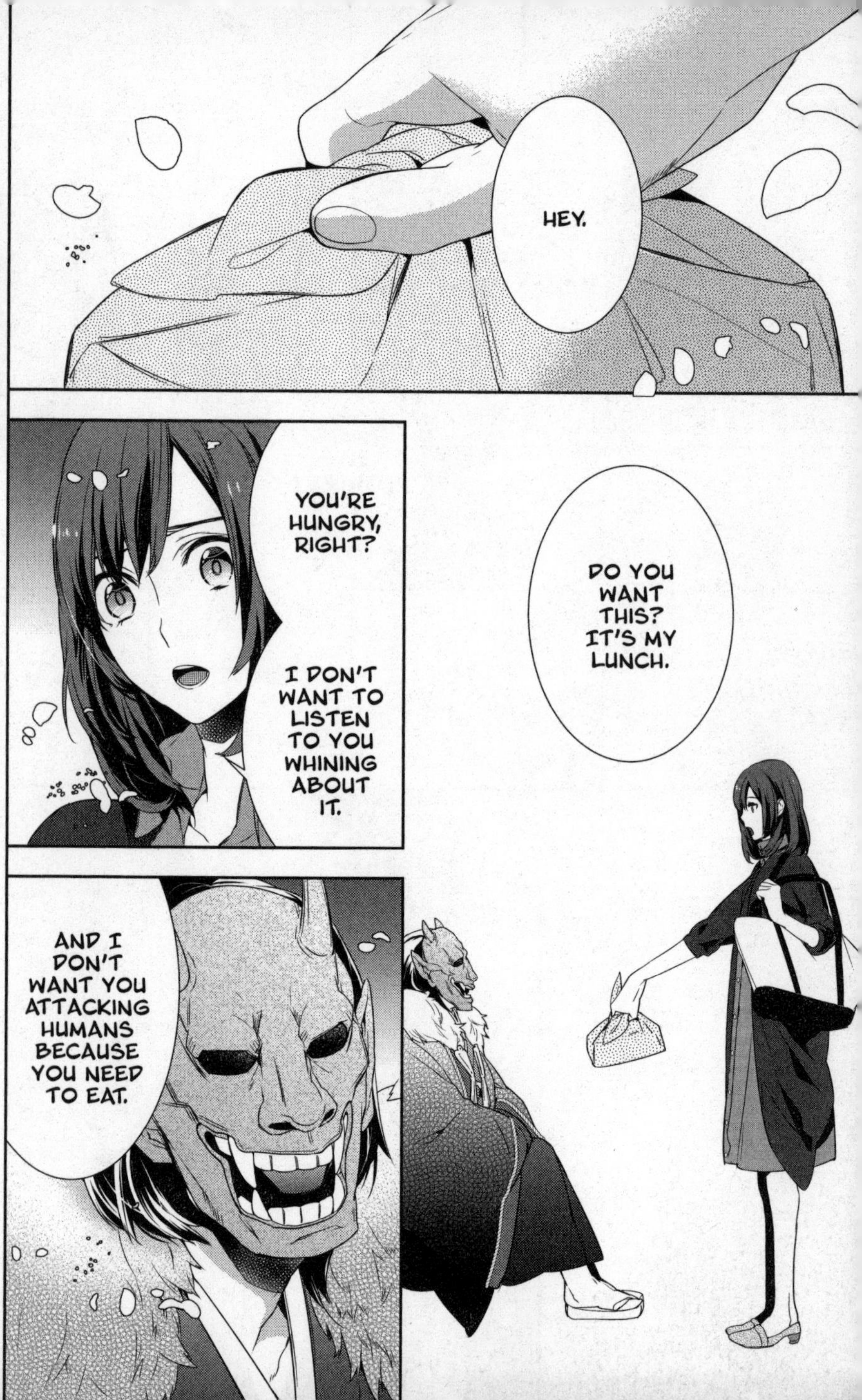
HEY.
DO YOU WANT THIS? IT'S MY LUNCH.
YOU'RE HUNGRY, RIGHT?
I DON'T WANT TO LISTEN TO YOU WHINING ABOUT IT.
AND I DON'T WANT YOU ATTACKING HUMANS BECAUSE YOU NEED TO EAT.

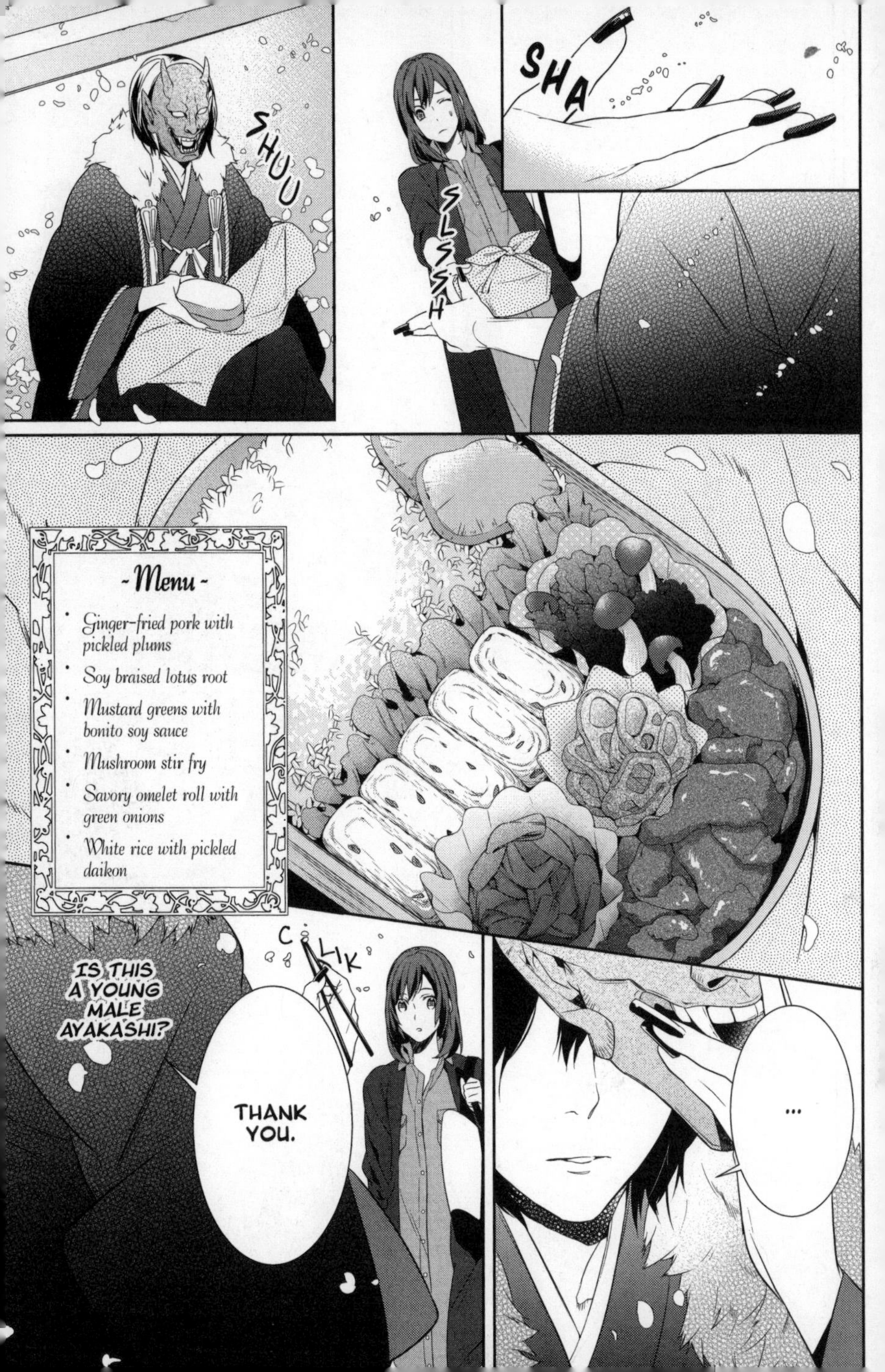
SHA
SLSSH
SHUU
-Menu-
• Ginger-fried pork with pickled plums
• Soy braised lotus root
• Mustard greens with bonito soy sauce
• Mushroom stir fry
• Savory omelet roll with green onions
• White rice with pickled daikon
...
CLIK
IS THIS A YOUNG MALE AYAKASHI?
THANK YOU.

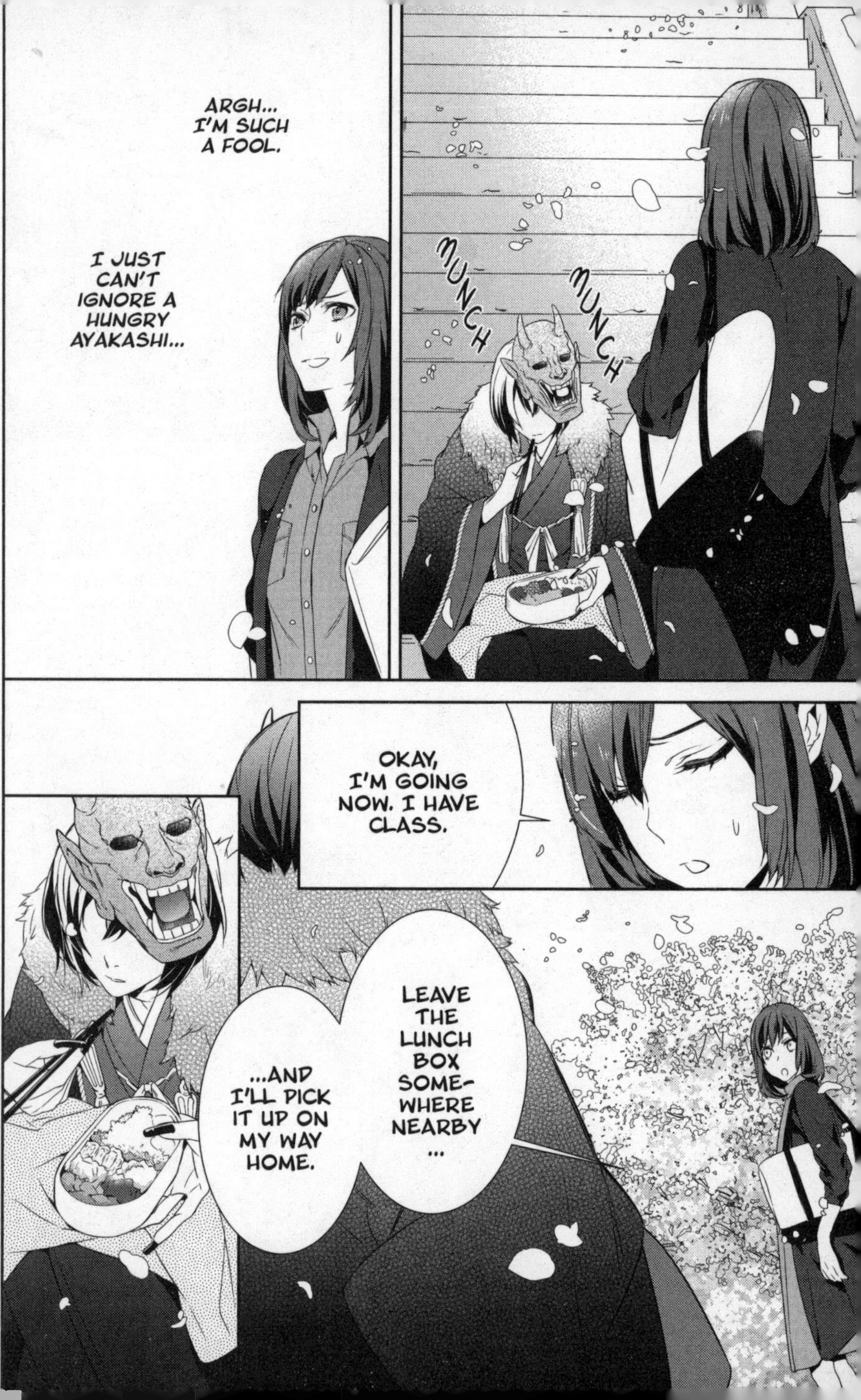
MUNCH
MUNCH
ARGH... I'M SUCH A FOOL.
I JUST CAN'T IGNORE A HUNGRY AYAKASHI...
OKAY, I'M GOING NOW. I HAVE CLASS.
LEAVE THE LUNCH BOX SOME-WHERE NEARBY ...
...AND I'LL PICK IT UP ON MY WAY HOME.

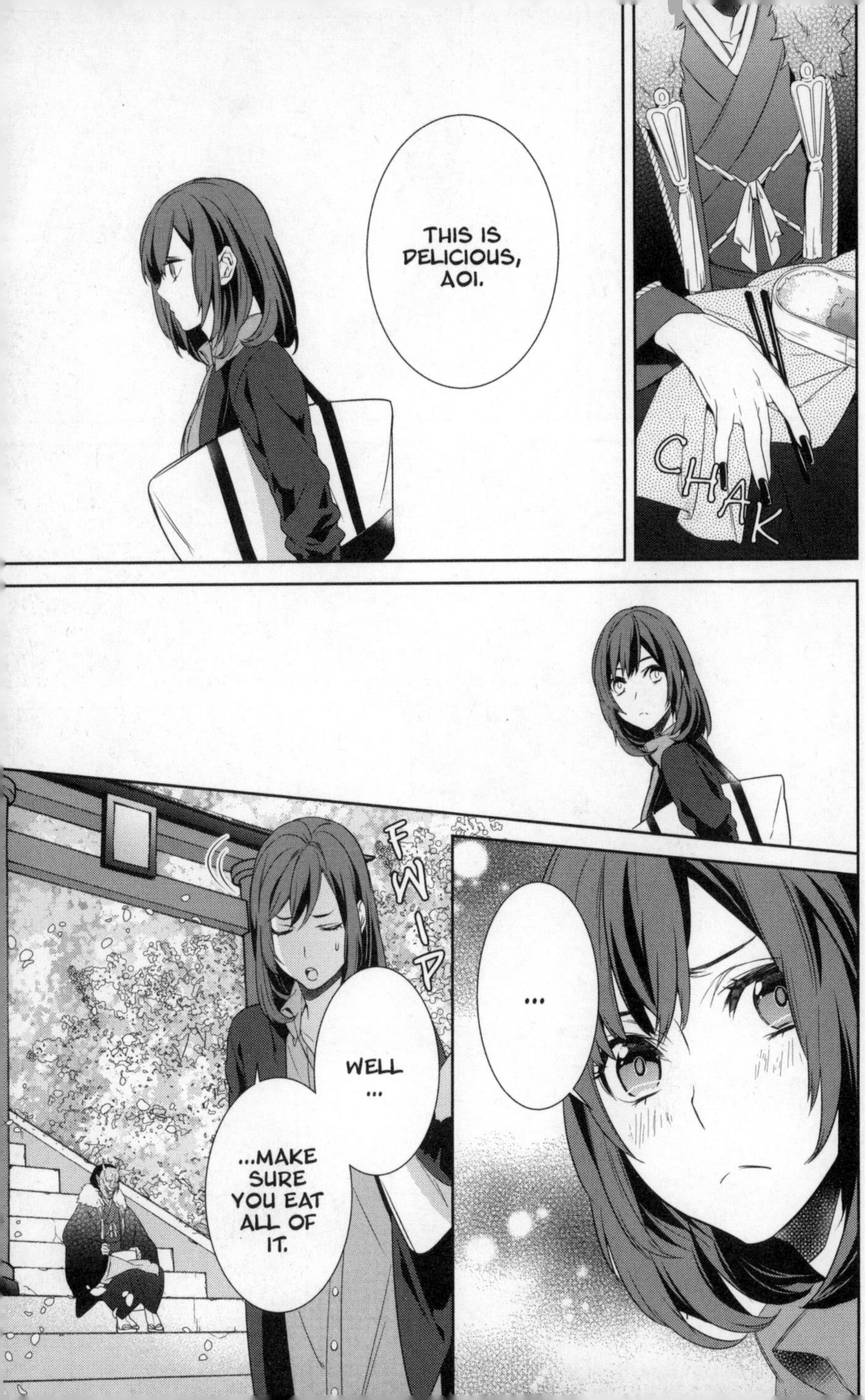
CHAK
THIS IS DELICIOUS, AOI.
...
FWIP
WELL ...
...MAKE SURE YOU EAT ALL OF IT.

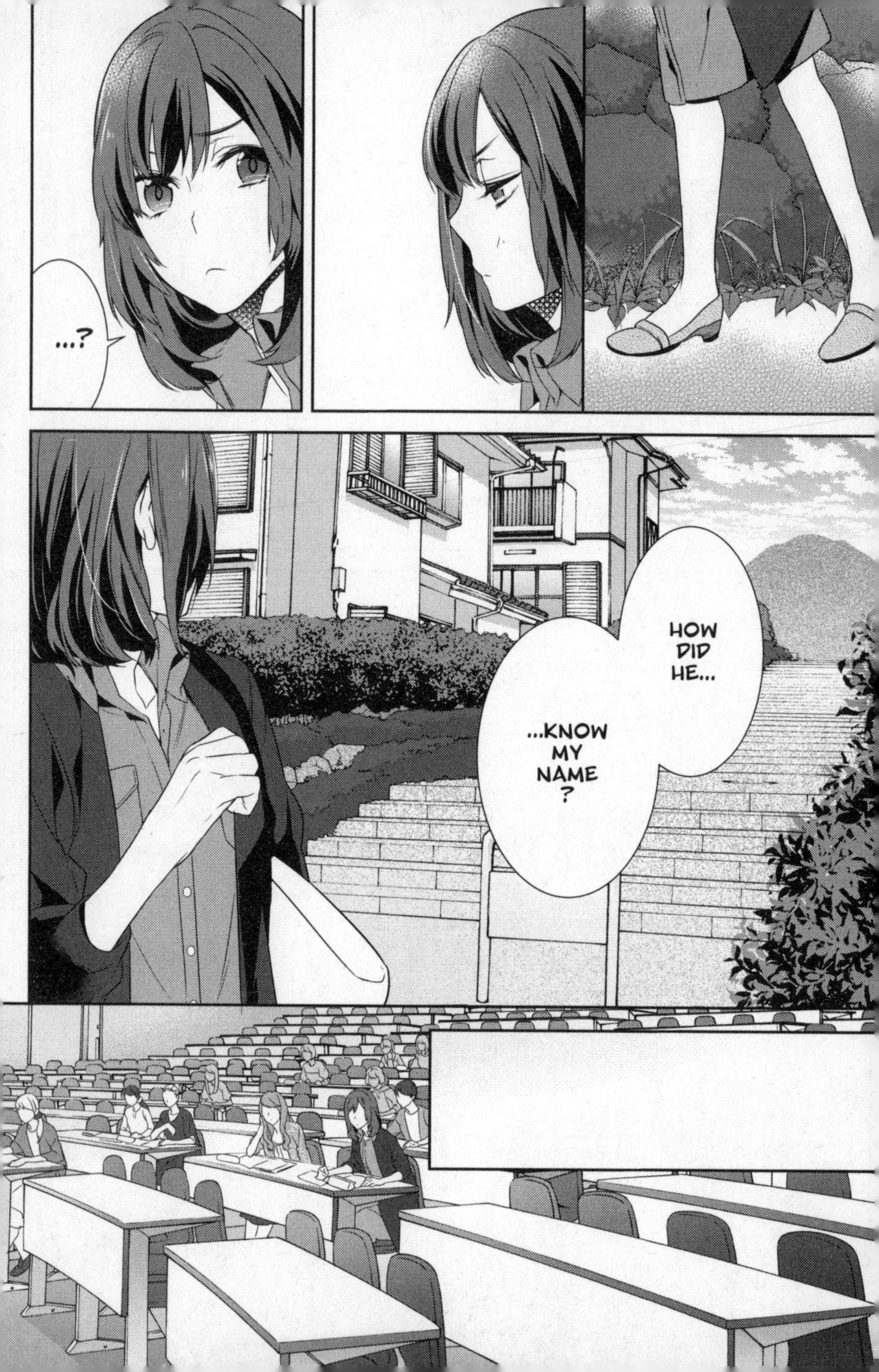
...?
HOW DID HE...
...KNOW MY NAME?

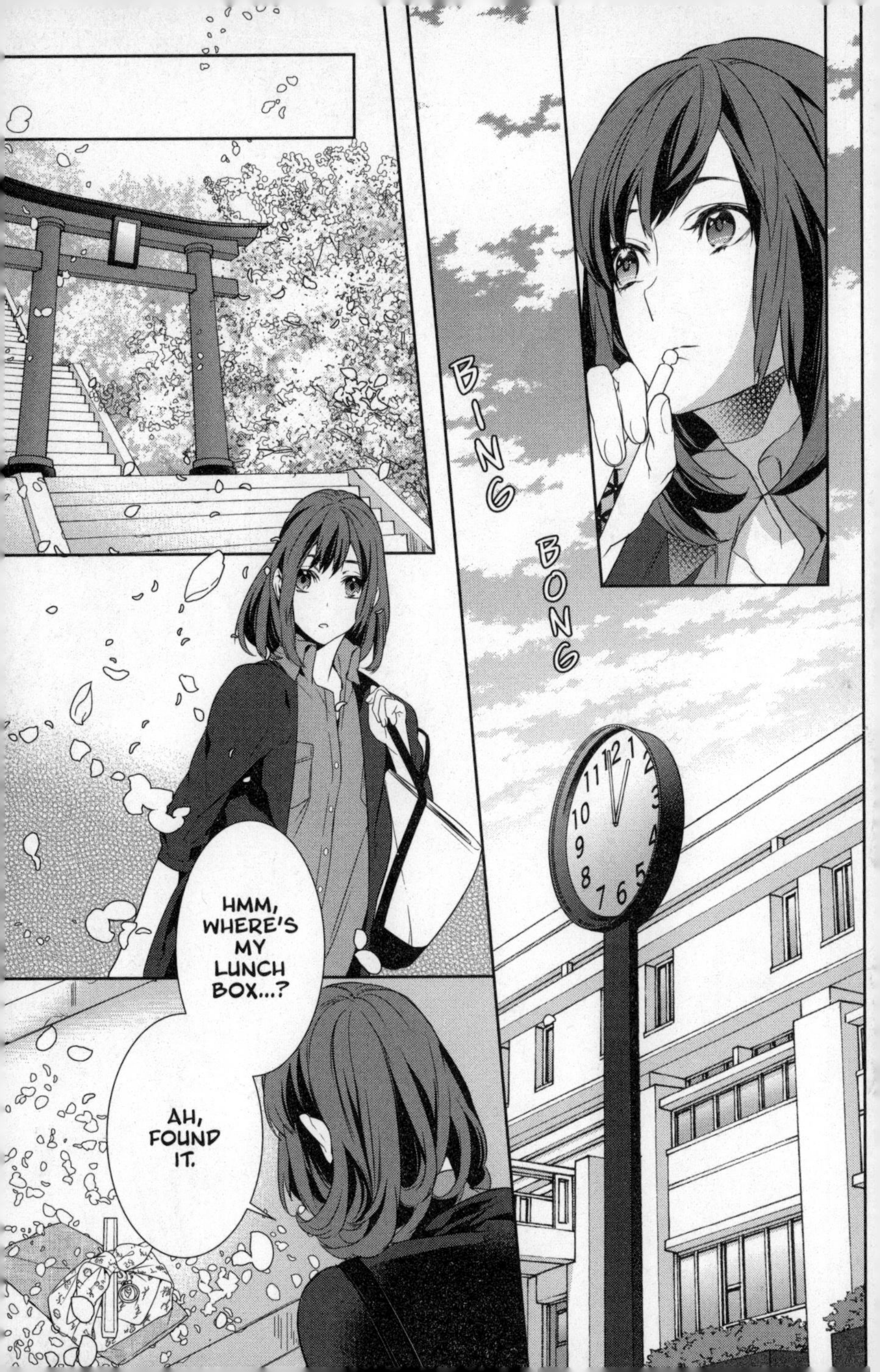
BING
BONG
HMM, WHERE'S MY LUNCH BOX...?
AH, FOUND IT.

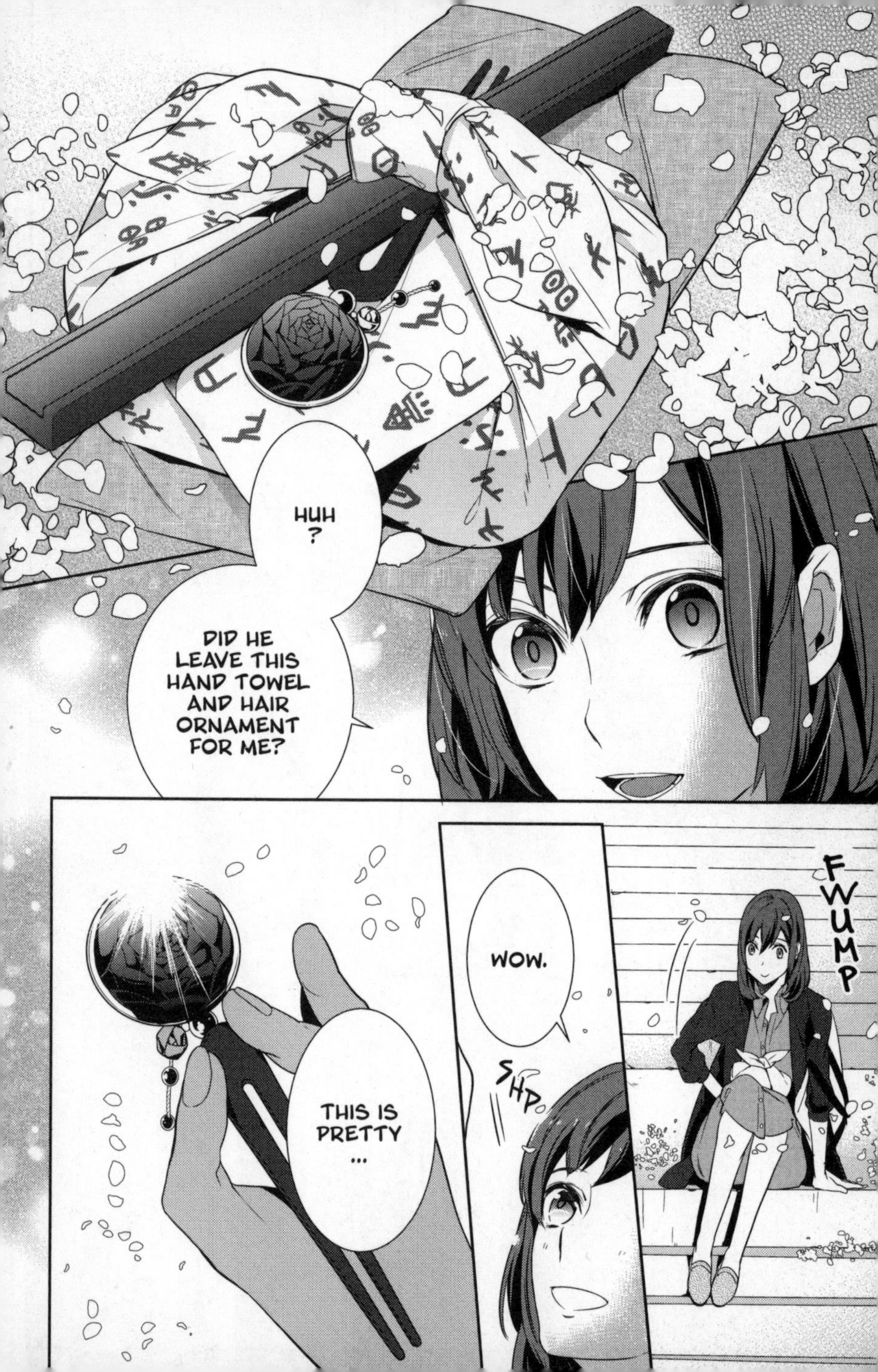
HUH?
DID HE LEAVE THIS HAND TOWEL AND HAIR ORNAMENT FOR ME?
FWUMP
WOW.
SHP
THIS IS PRETTY...

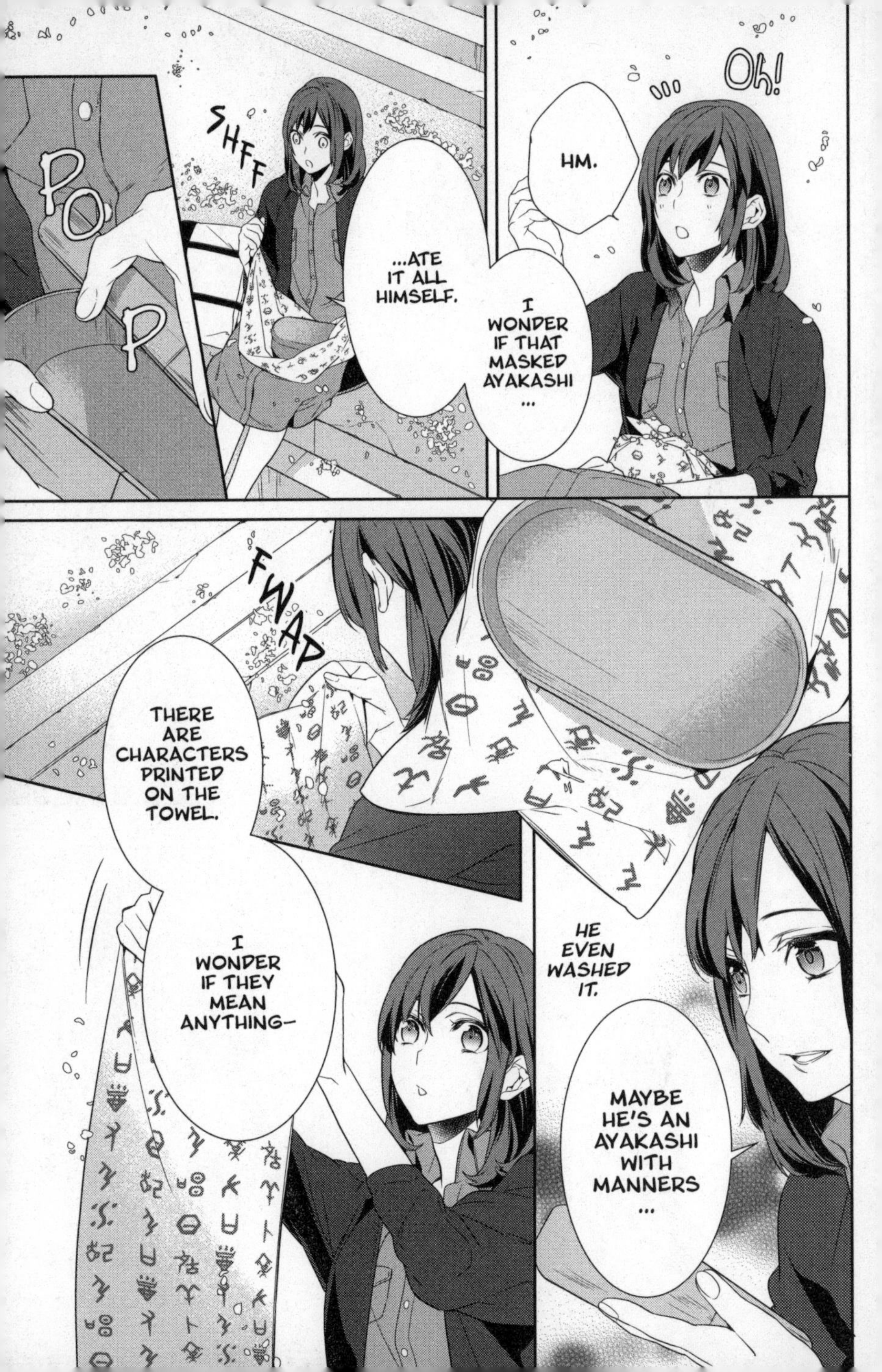
Oh!
HM.
I WONDER IF THAT MASKED AYAKASHI ...
...ATE IT ALL HIMSELF.
SHFF
POP
FWAP
THERE ARE CHARACTERS PRINTED ON THE TOWEL.
I WONDER IF THEY MEAN ANYTHING—
HE EVEN WASHED IT.
MAYBE HE'S AN AYAKASHI WITH MANNERS ...

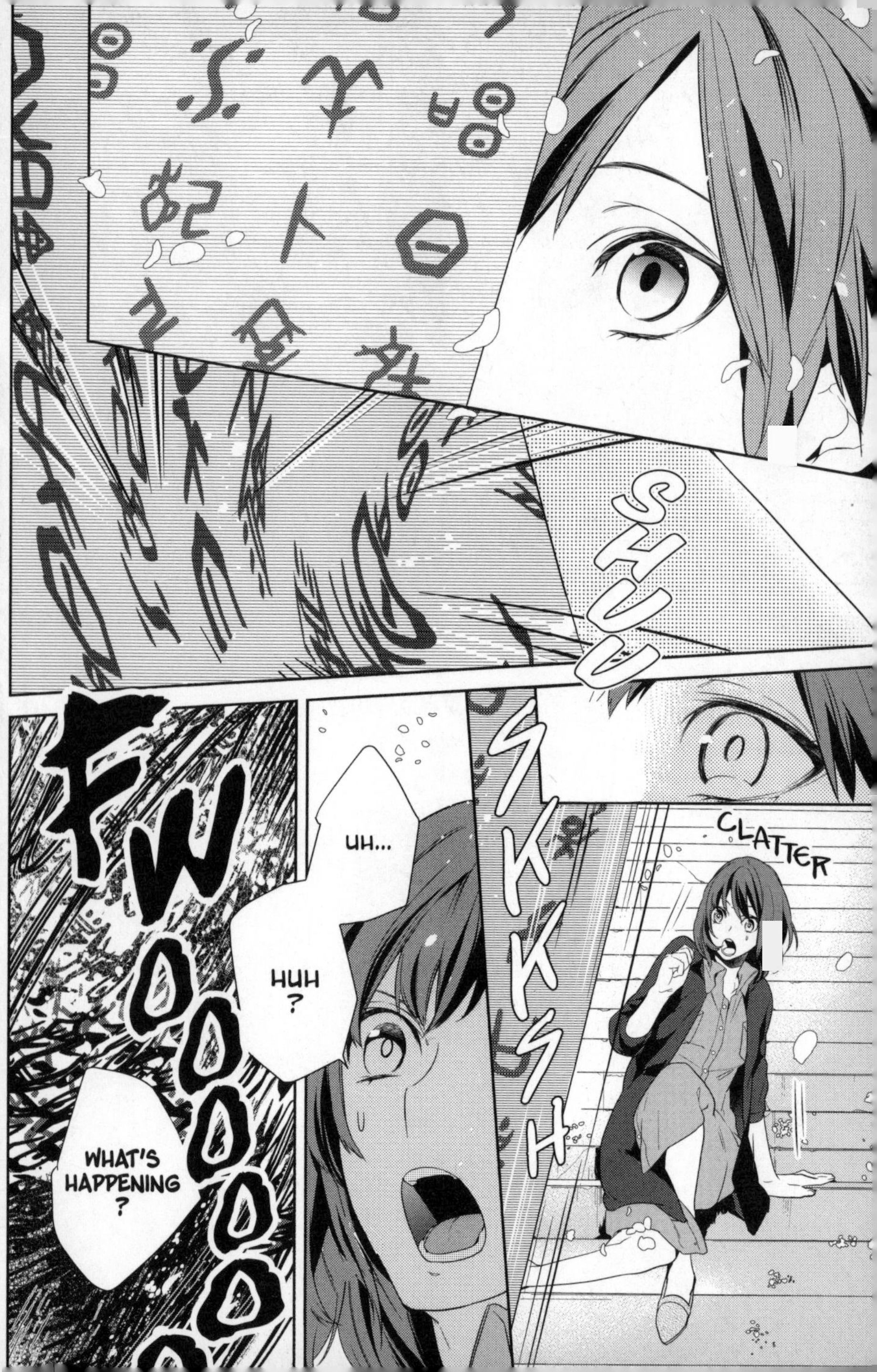
SHUU
CLATTER
SKKSH
UH...
HUH?
WHAT'S HAPPENING?
FWOOOOOO

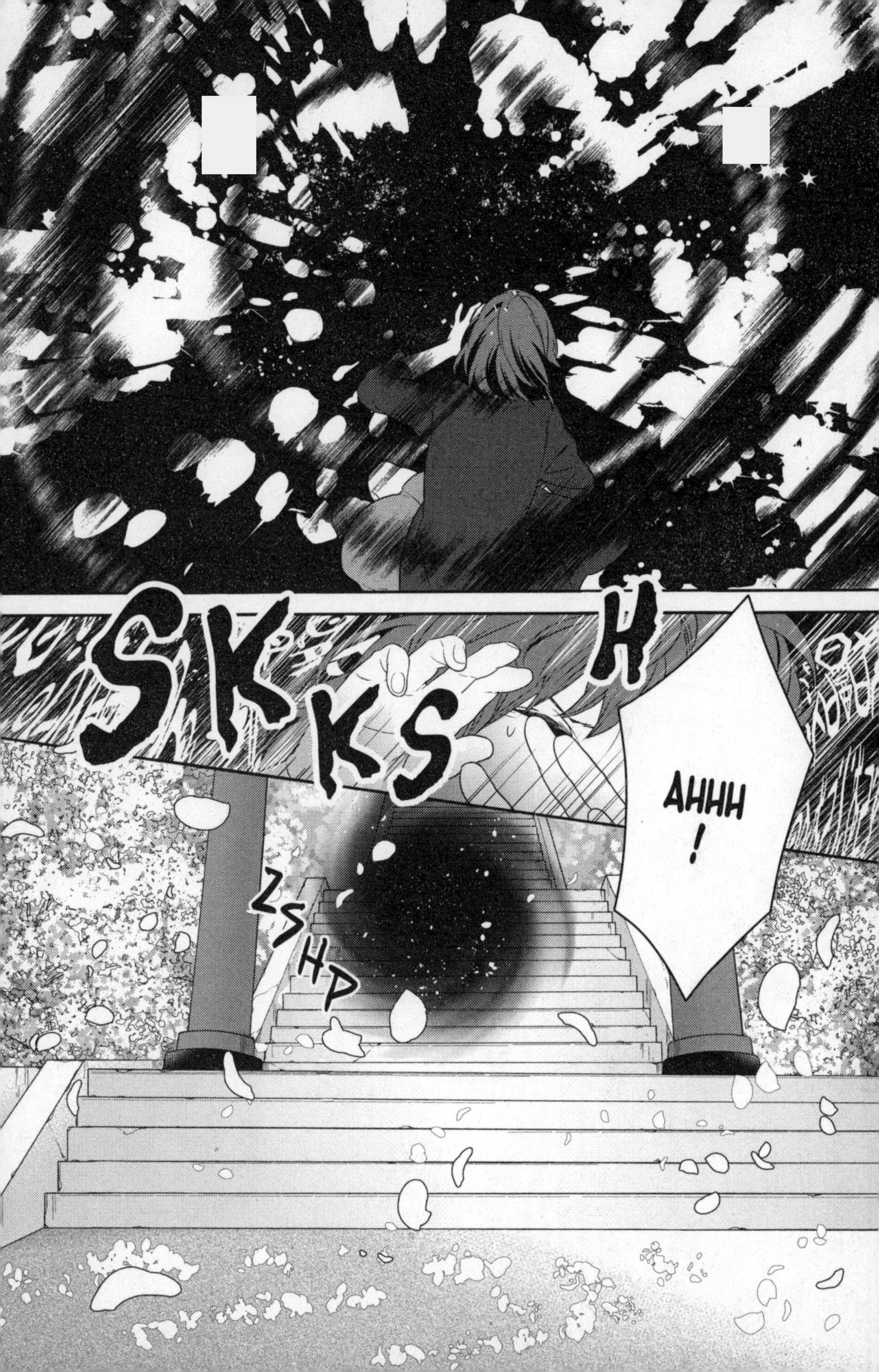
AHHH!
SKKSH
ZSHP

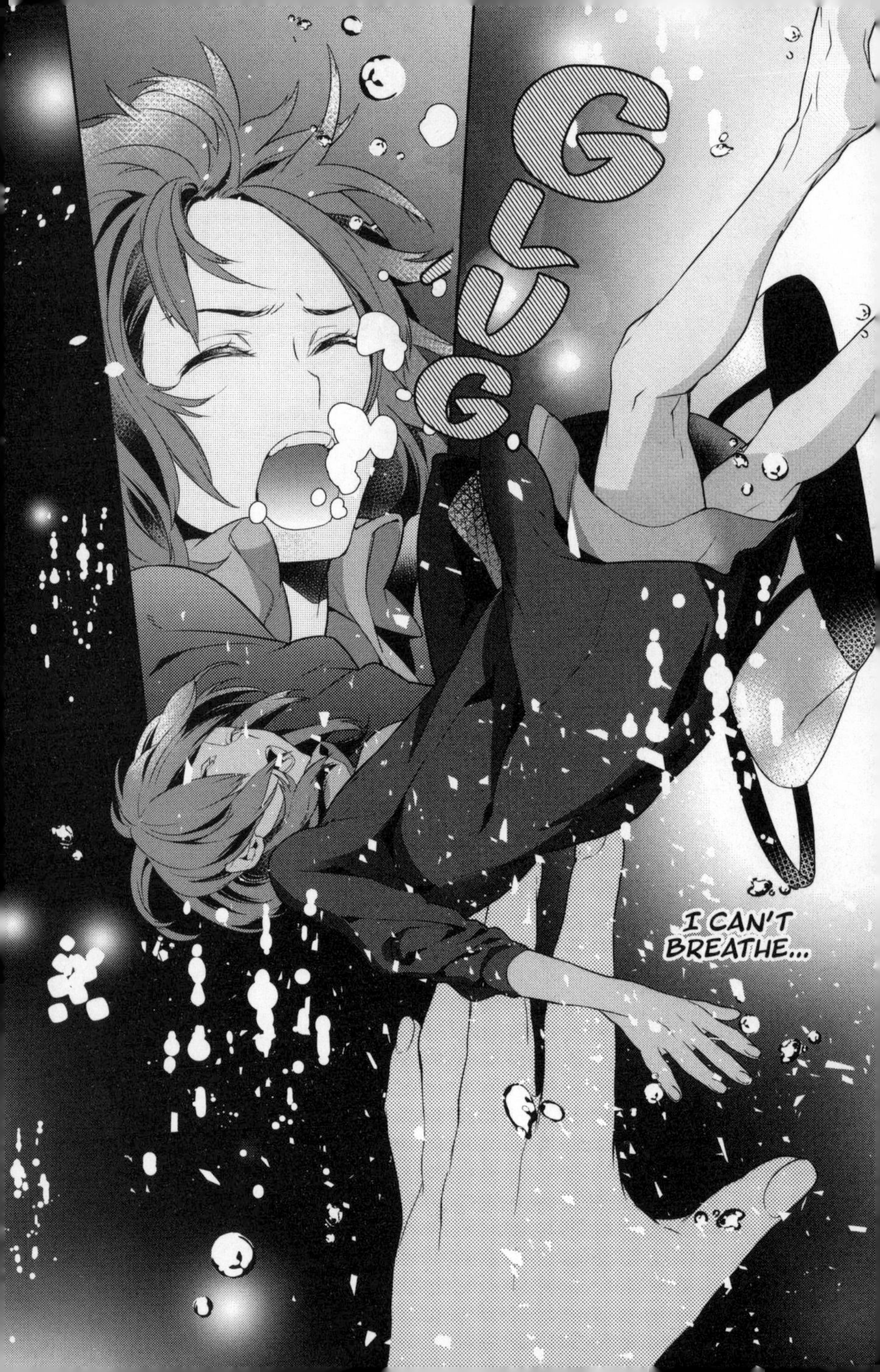
GLUG
I CAN'T BREATHE...

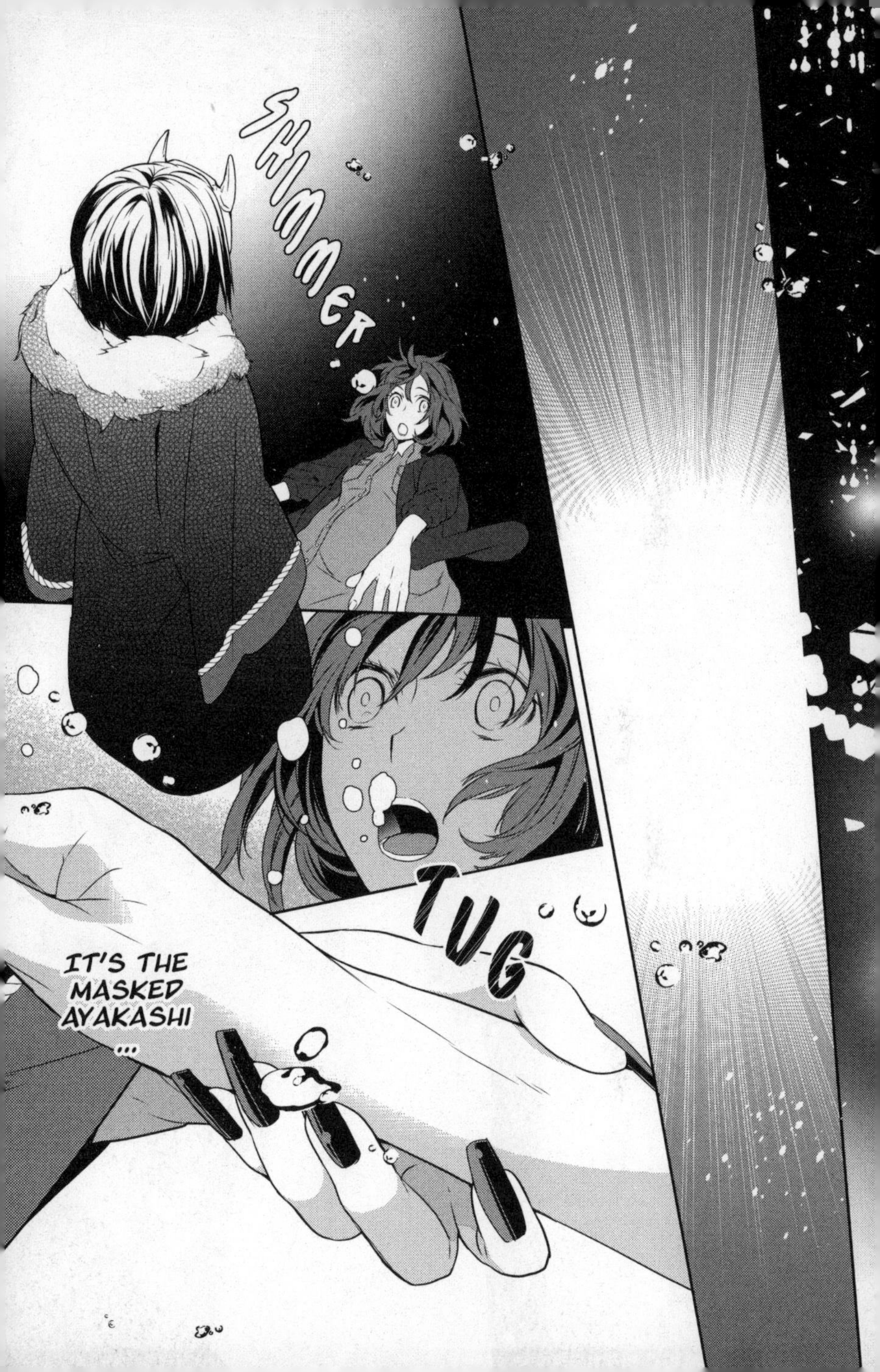
SHIMMER
TUG
IT'S THE MASKED AYAKASHI ...

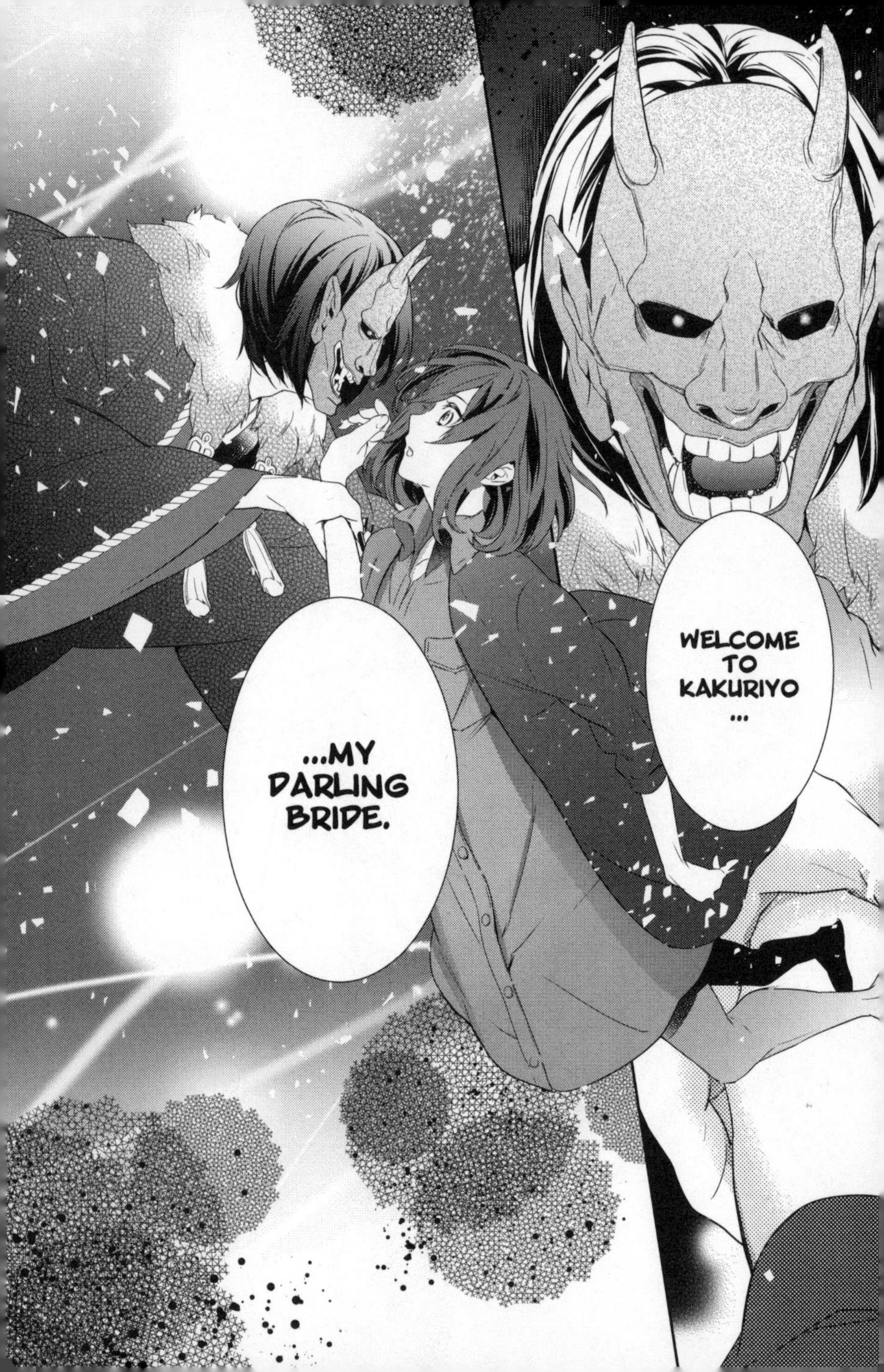
WELCOME TO KAKURIYO ...
...MY DARLING BRIDE.

Kakuriyo
Bed & Breakfast for Spirits

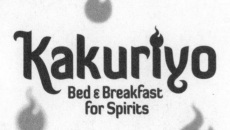

Kakuriyo
Bed & Breakfast
for Spirits

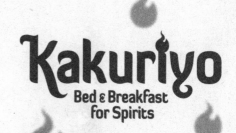

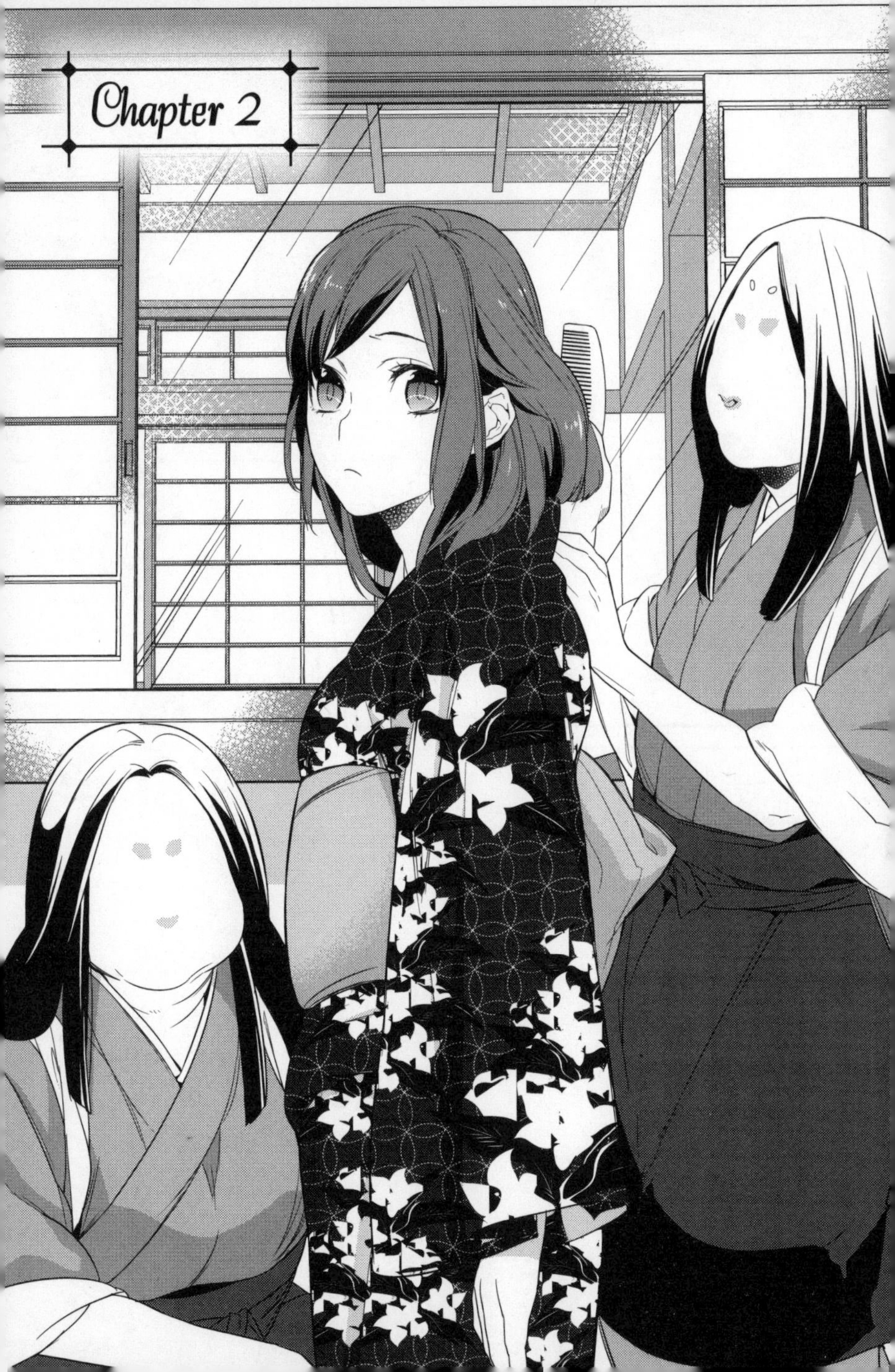
Chapter 2

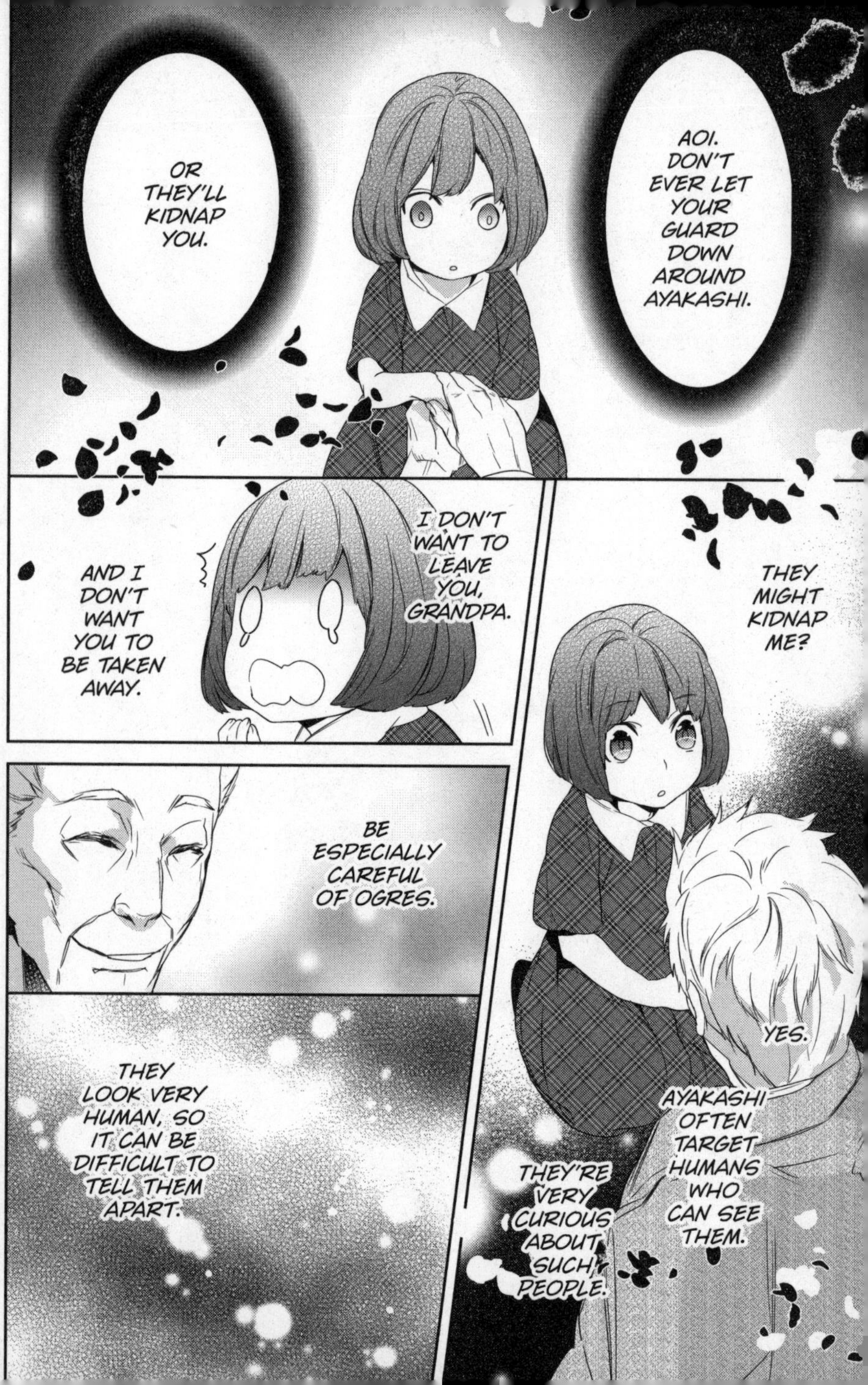
AOI. DON'T EVER LET YOUR GUARD DOWN AROUND AYAKASHI.
OR THEY'LL KIDNAP YOU.
THEY MIGHT KIDNAP ME?
YES.
AYAKASHI OFTEN TARGET HUMANS WHO CAN SEE THEM.
THEY'RE VERY CURIOUS ABOUT SUCH PEOPLE.
I DON'T WANT TO LEAVE YOU, GRANDPA.
AND I DON'T WANT YOU TO BE TAKEN AWAY.
BE ESPECIALLY CAREFUL OF OGRES.
THEY LOOK VERY HUMAN, SO IT CAN BE DIFFICULT TO TELL THEM APART.

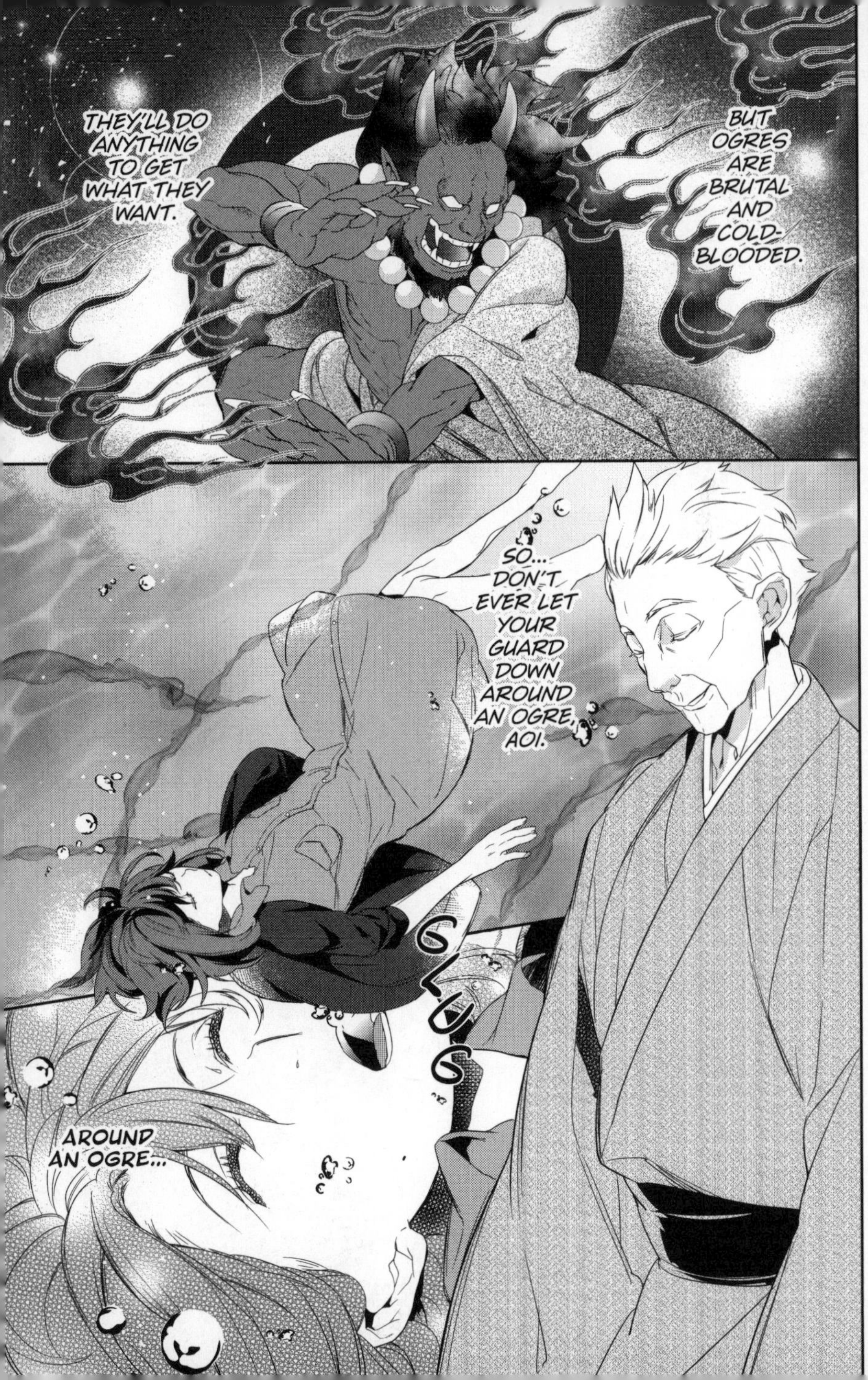
BUT OGRES ARE BRUTAL AND COLD-BLOODED.
THEY'LL DO ANYTHING TO GET WHAT THEY WANT.
SO... DON'T EVER LET YOUR GUARD DOWN AROUND AN OGRE, AOI.
GLUG
AROUND AN OGRE...

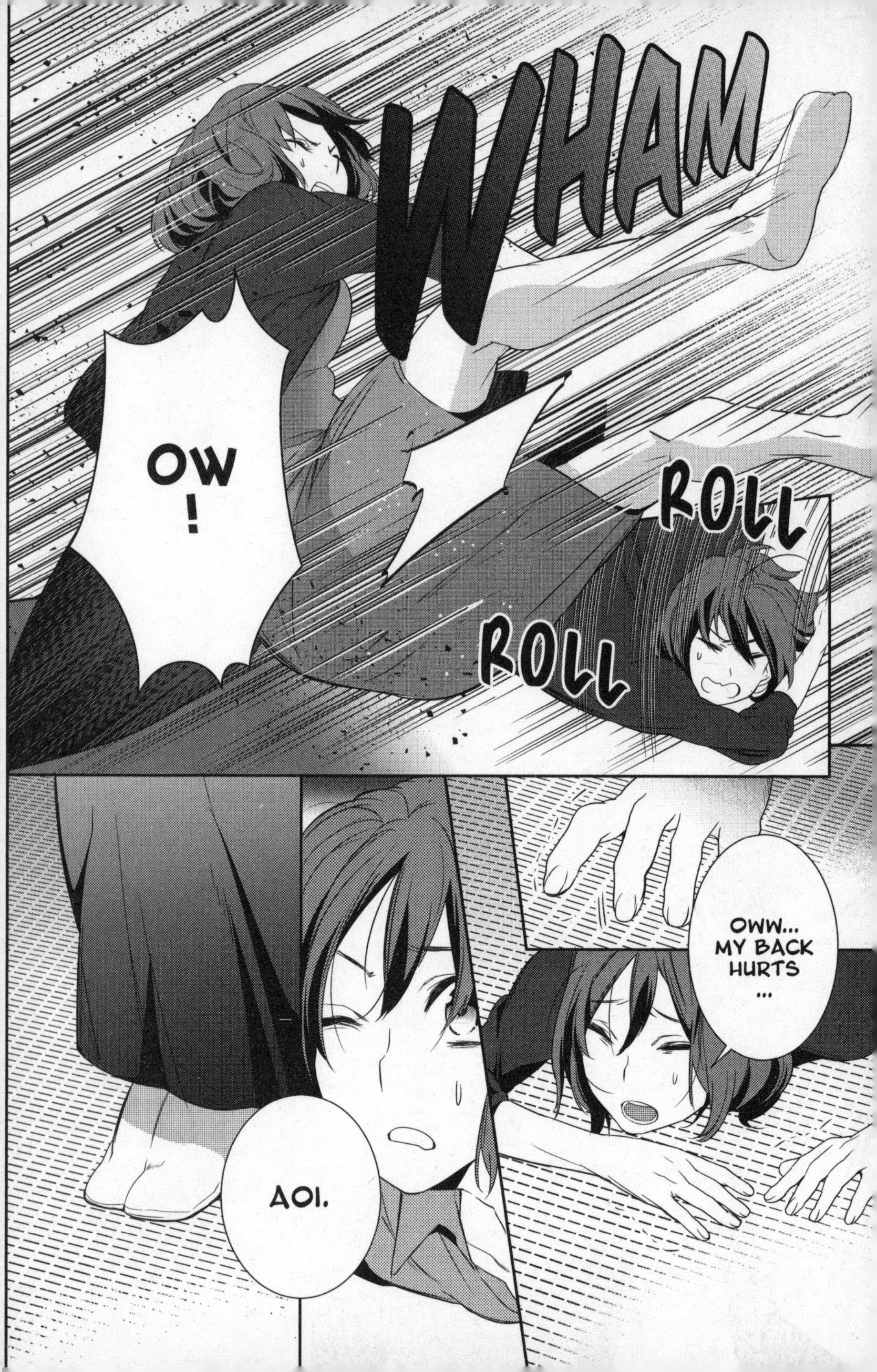
WHAM
OW!
ROLL
ROLL
OWW... MY BACK HURTS...
AOI.

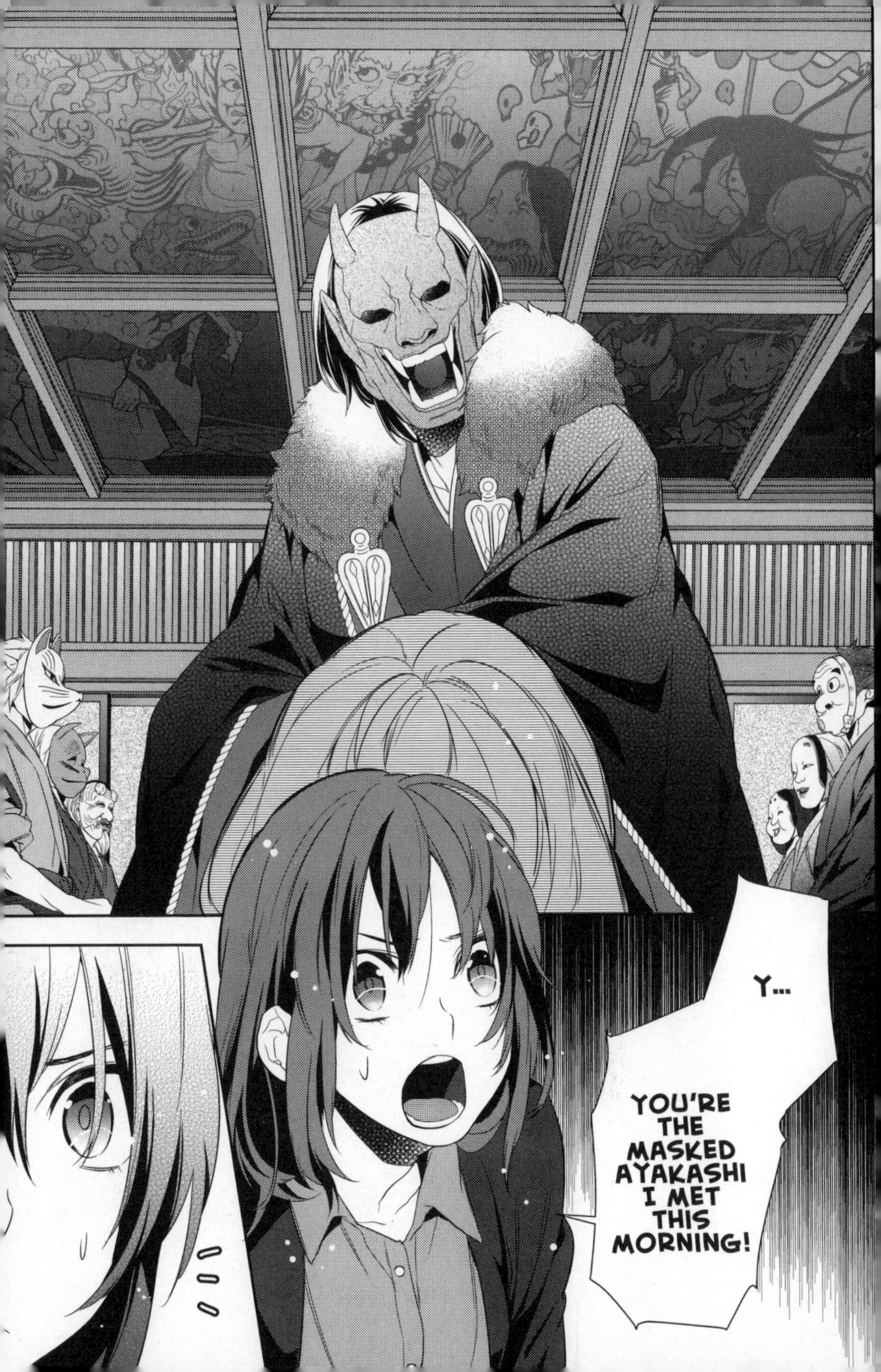
Y...
YOU'RE THE MASKED AYAKASHI I MET THIS MORNING!

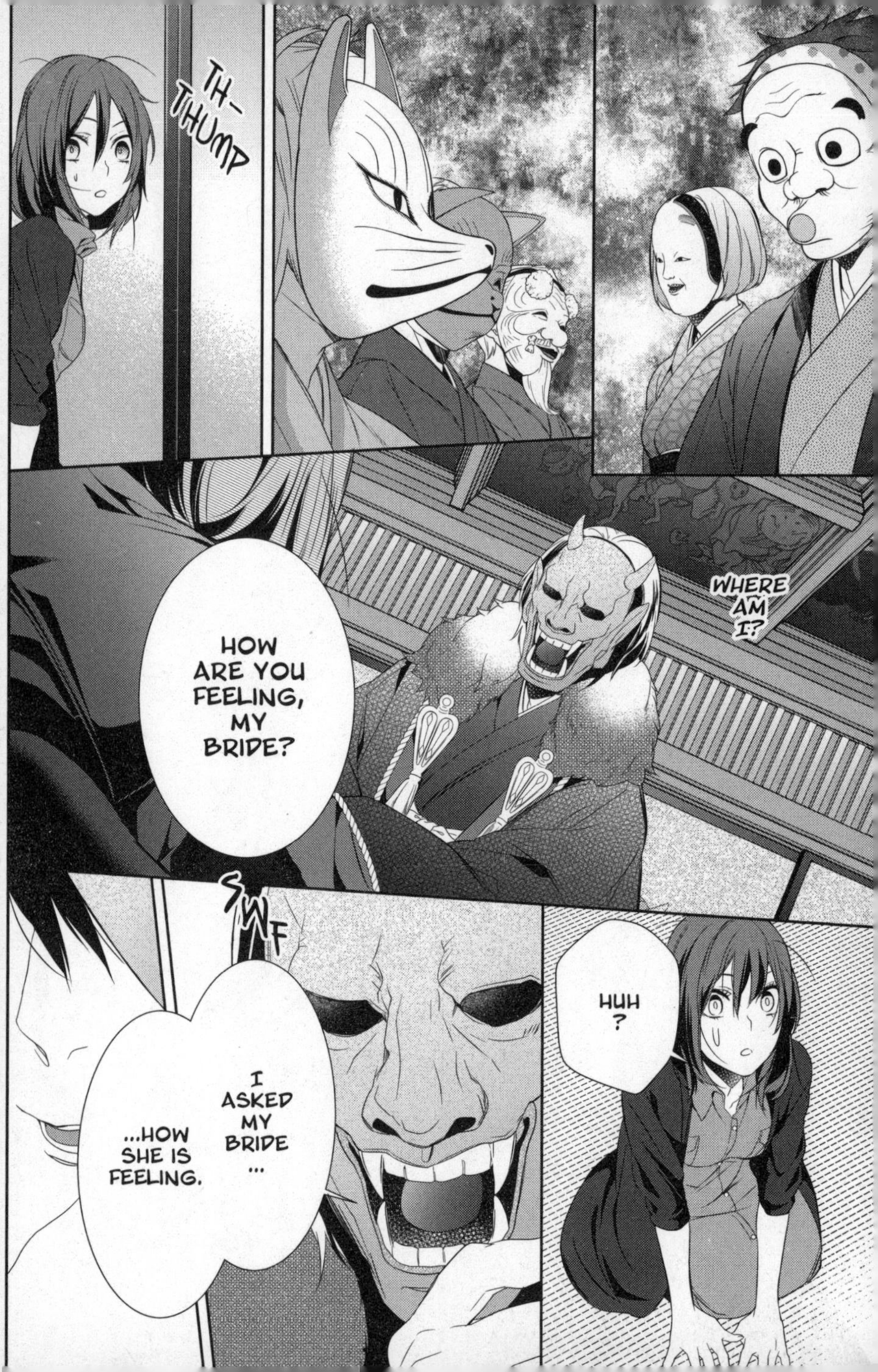
TH-THUMP
WHERE AM I?
HOW ARE YOU FEELING, MY BRIDE?
HUH?
SWF
I ASKED MY BRIDE...
...HOW SHE IS FEELING.

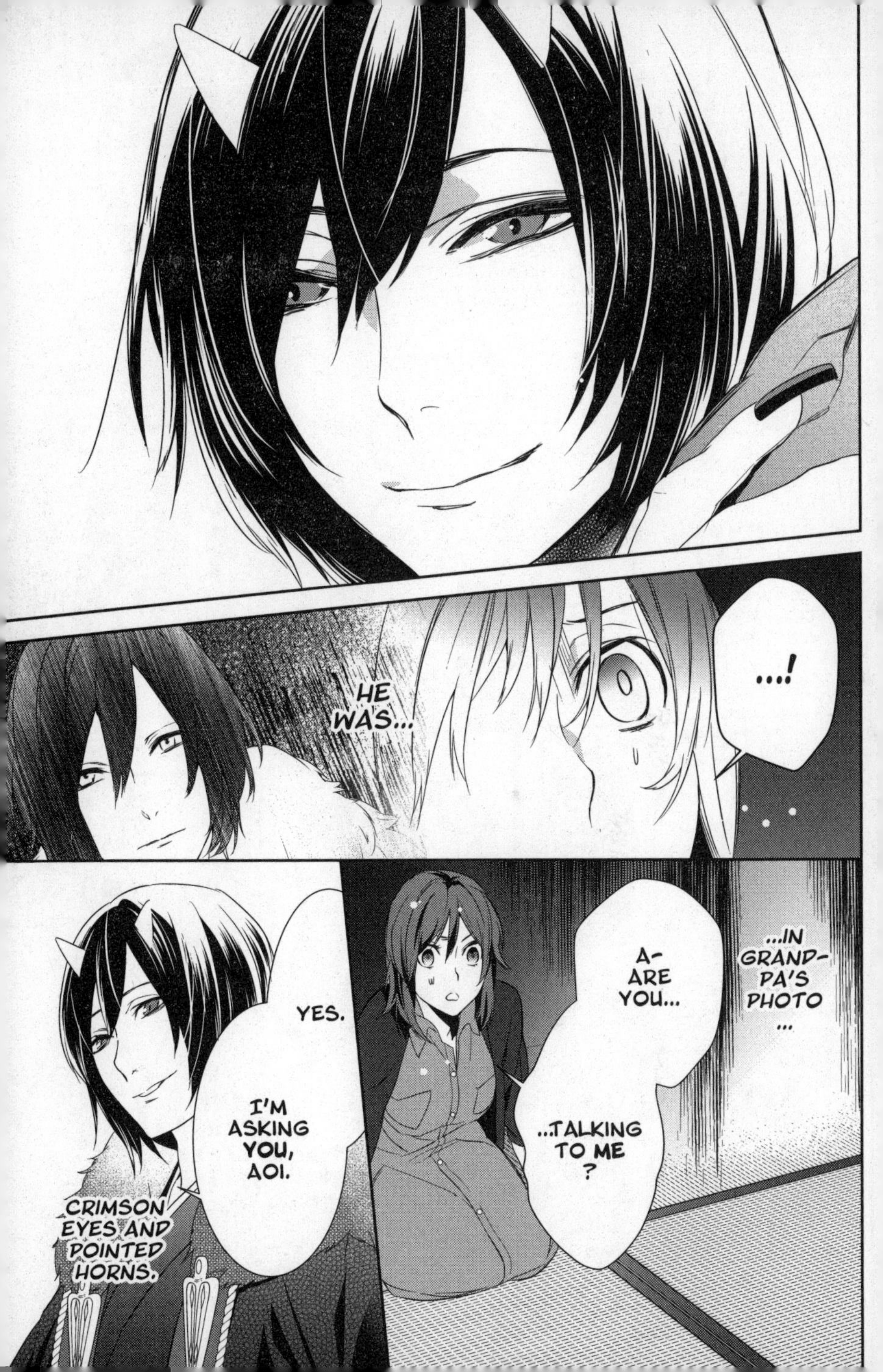
...!
HE WAS...
...IN GRAND-PA'S PHOTO...
A-ARE YOU...
...TALKING TO ME?
YES.
I'M ASKING YOU, AOI.
CRIMSON EYES AND POINTED HORNS.

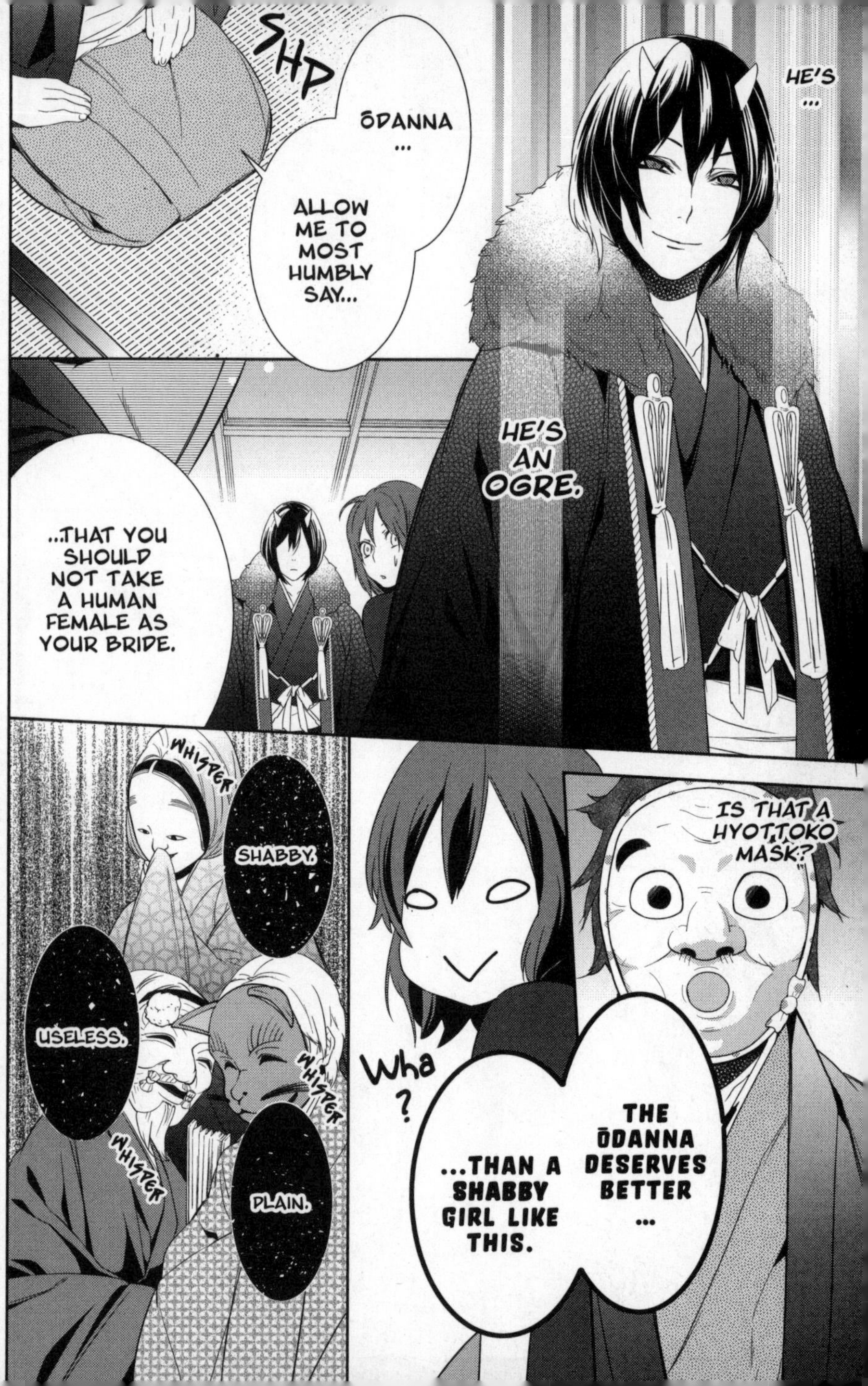
HE'S ...
HE'S AN OGRE.
SHP
ŌDANNA ...
ALLOW ME TO MOST HUMBLY SAY...
...THAT YOU SHOULD NOT TAKE A HUMAN FEMALE AS YOUR BRIDE.
IS THAT A HYOTTOKO MASK?
Wha ?
THE ŌDANNA DESERVES BETTER ...
...THAN A SHABBY GIRL LIKE THIS.
WHISPER
SHABBY.
USELESS.
WHISPER
WHISPER
PLAIN.

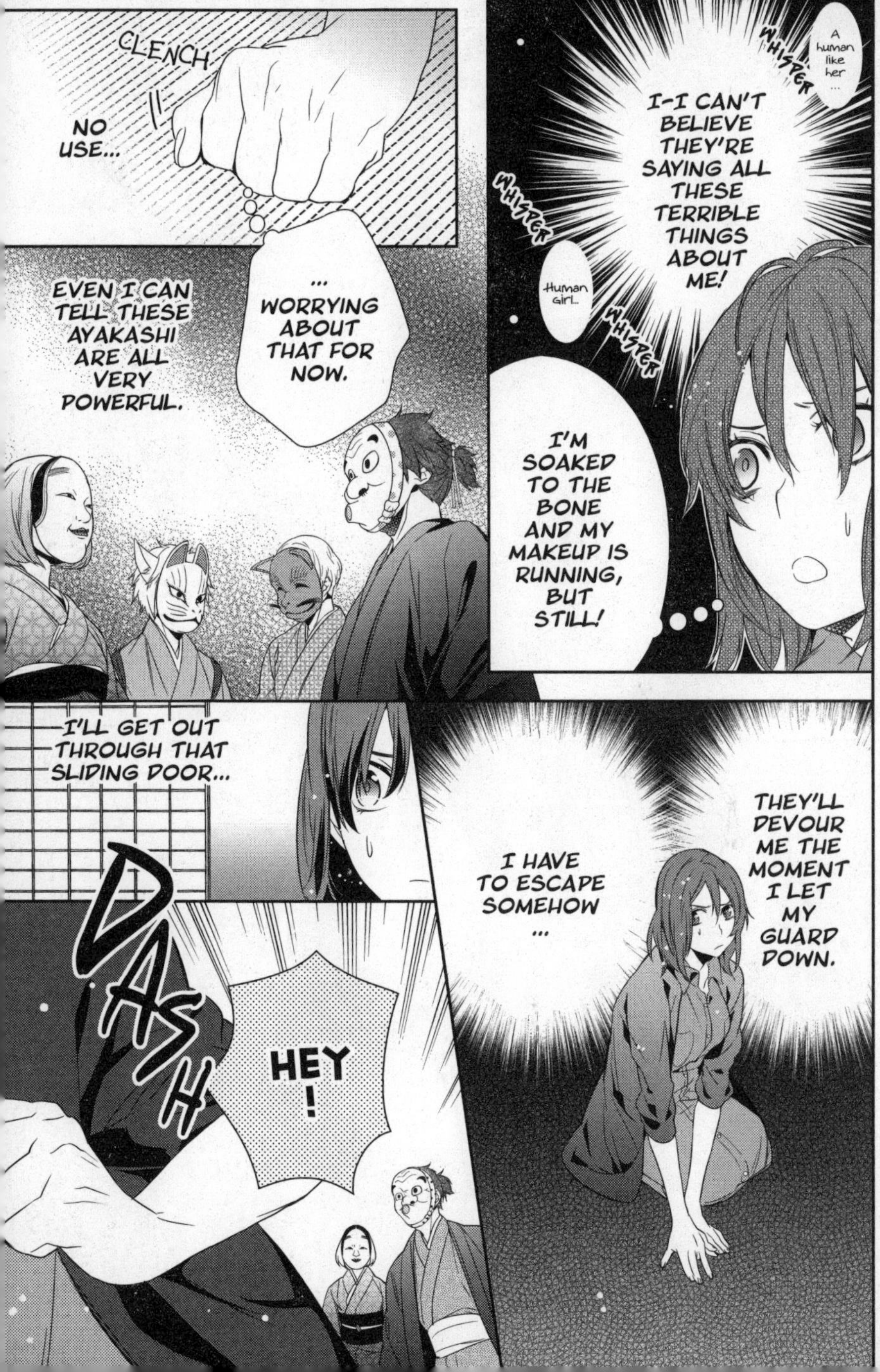
A human like her...
WHISPER
I-I CAN'T BELIEVE THEY'RE SAYING ALL THESE TERRIBLE THINGS ABOUT ME!
WHISPER
Human girl...
WHISPER
I'M SOAKED TO THE BONE AND MY MAKEUP IS RUNNING, BUT STILL!
CLENCH
NO USE...
... WORRYING ABOUT THAT FOR NOW.
EVEN I CAN TELL THESE AYAKASHI ARE ALL VERY POWERFUL.
THEY'LL DEVOUR ME THE MOMENT I LET MY GUARD DOWN.
I HAVE TO ESCAPE SOMEHOW ...
I'LL GET OUT THROUGH THAT SLIDING DOOR...
DASH
HEY!

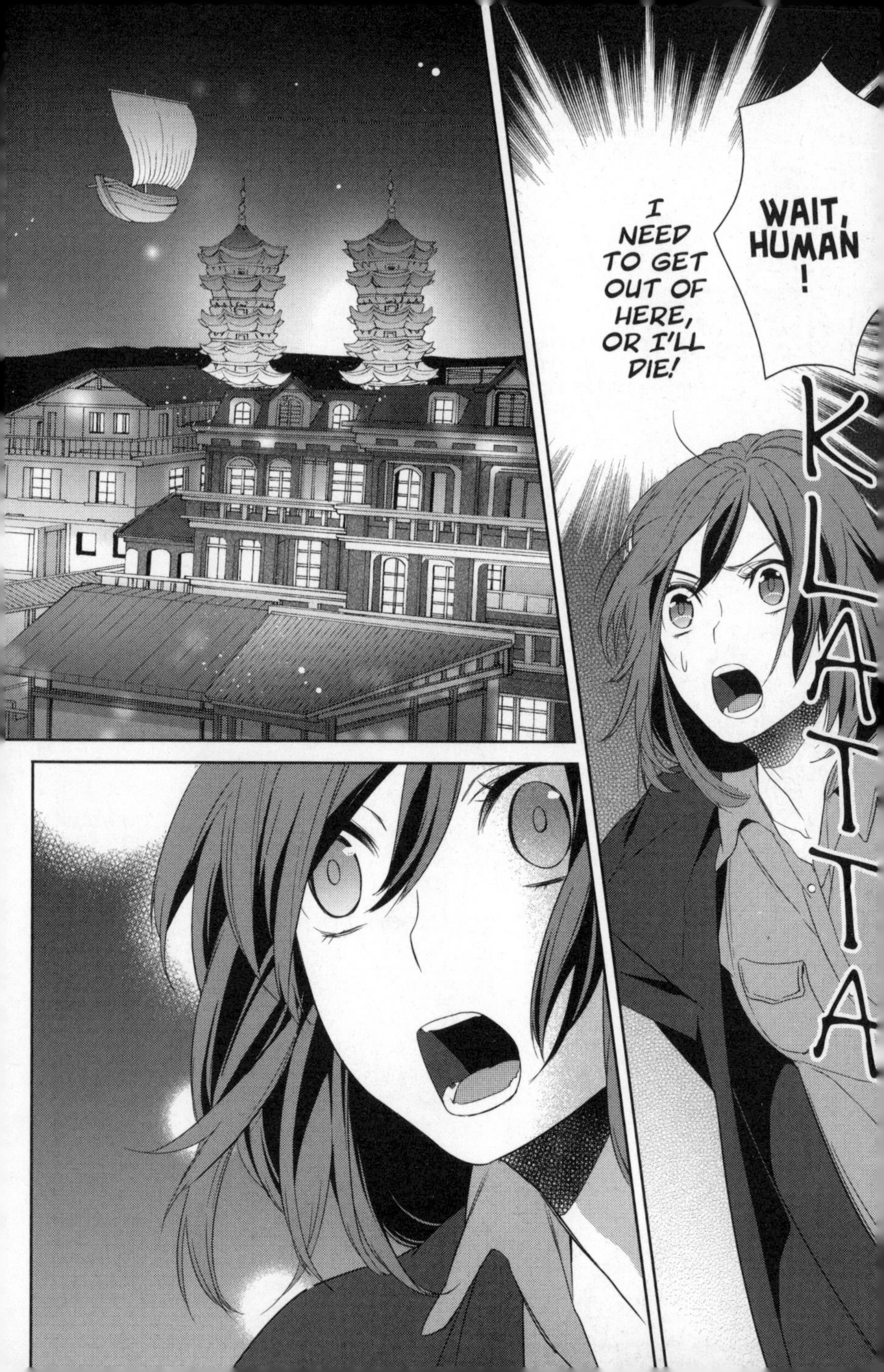
WAIT, HUMAN!
I NEED TO GET OUT OF HERE, OR I'LL DIE!
KLATTA

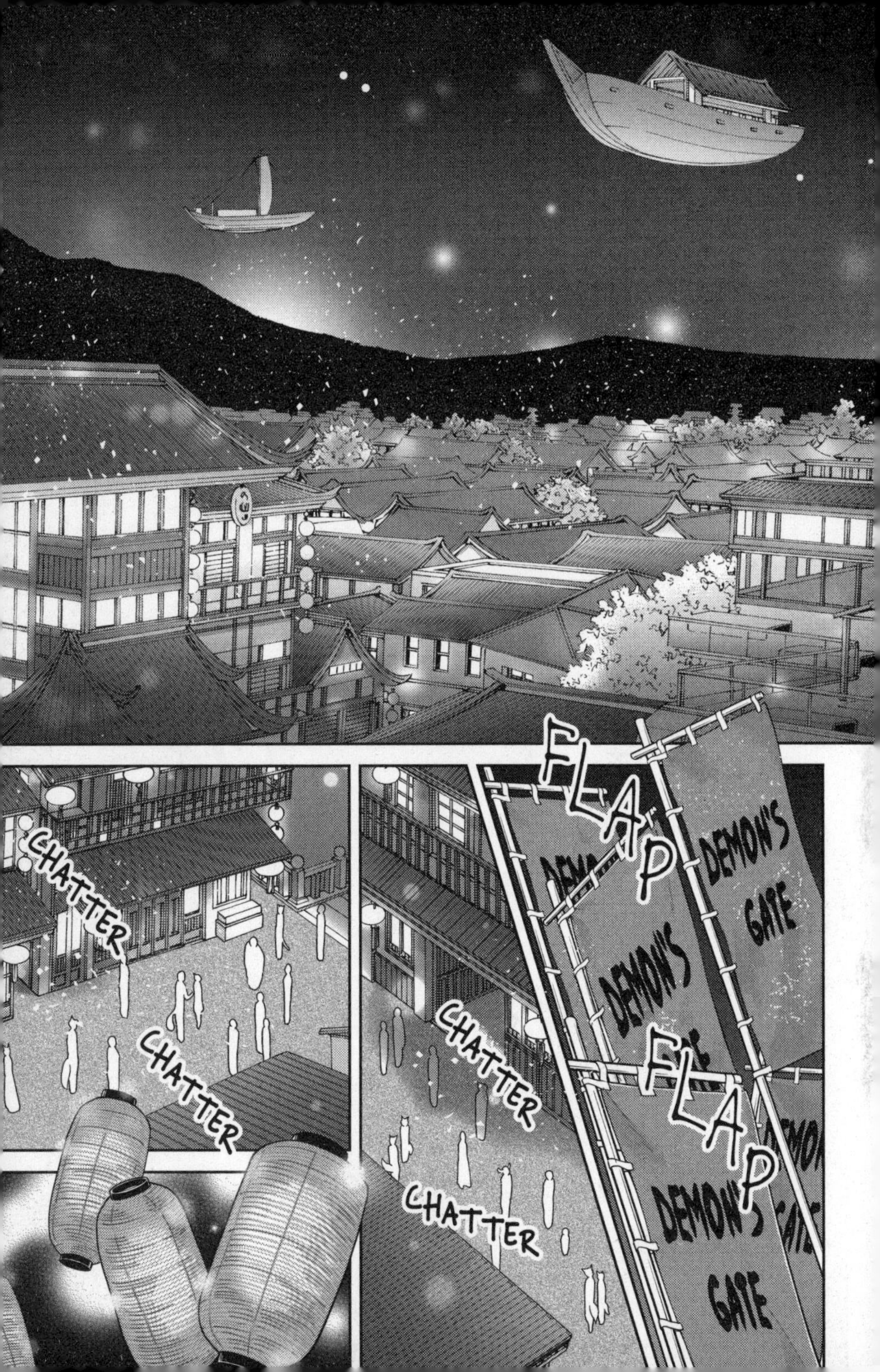
FLAP
FLAP
DEMON'S GATE
DEMON'S
DEMON'S GATE
CHATTER
CHATTER
CHATTER
CHATTER

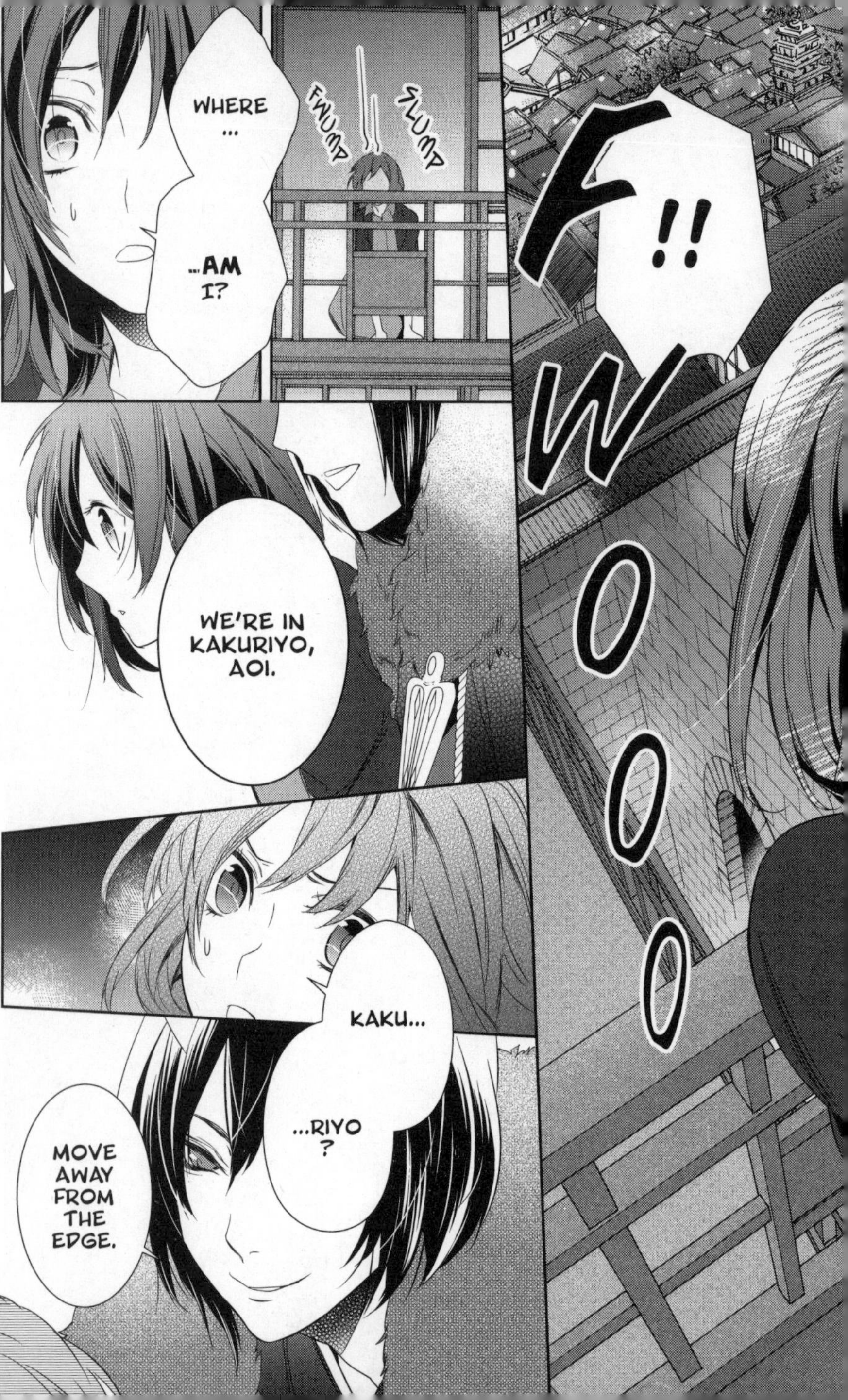
!!
WOOO
FWUMP
SLUMP
WHERE ...
...AM I?
WE'RE IN KAKURIYO, AOI.
KAKU...
...RIYO ?
MOVE AWAY FROM THE EDGE.

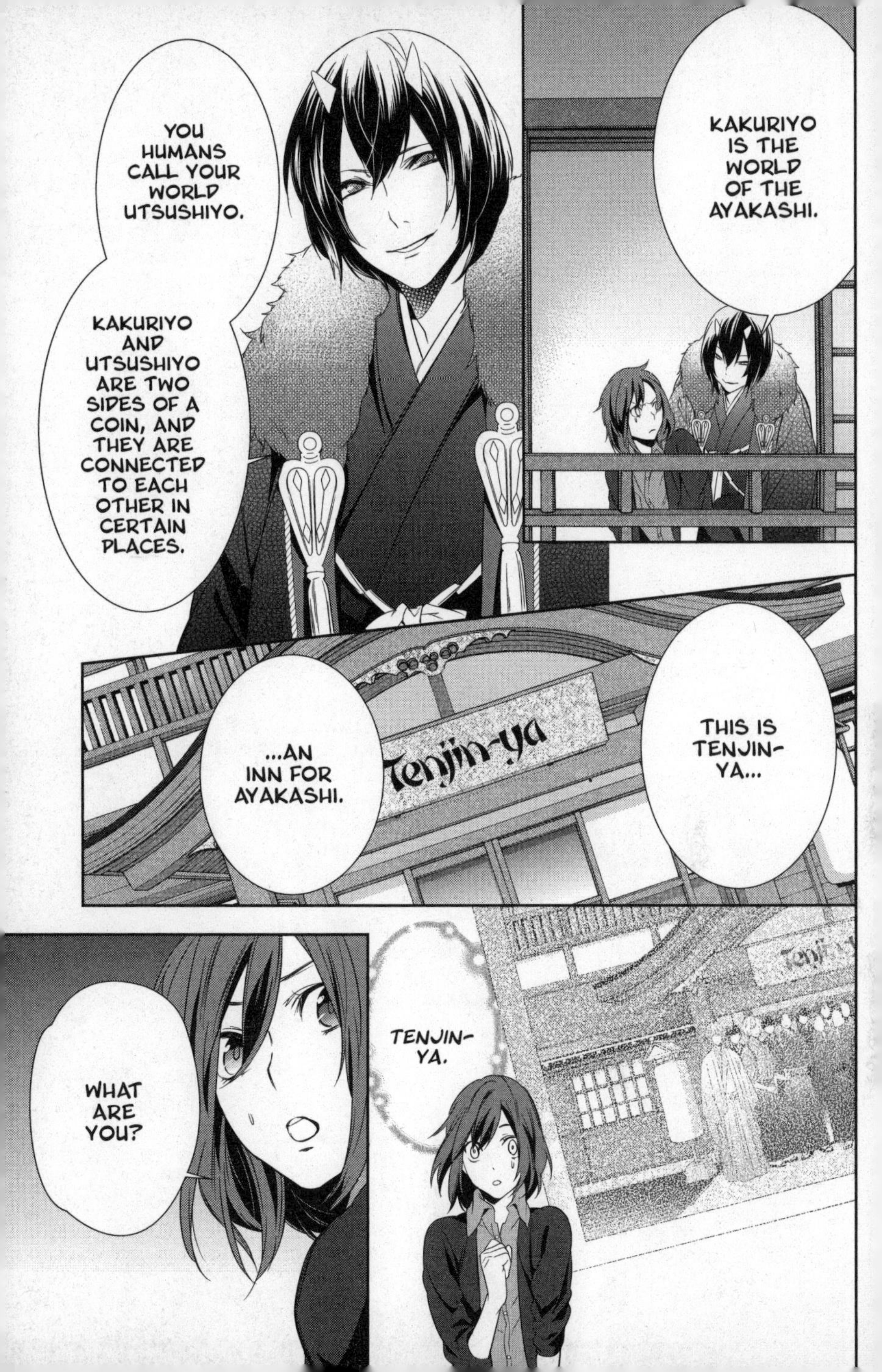
KAKURIYO IS THE WORLD OF THE AYAKASHI.
YOU HUMANS CALL YOUR WORLD UTSUSHIYO.
KAKURIYO AND UTSUSHIYO ARE TWO SIDES OF A COIN, AND THEY ARE CONNECTED TO EACH OTHER IN CERTAIN PLACES.
THIS IS TENJIN-YA...
Tenjin-ya
...AN INN FOR AYAKASHI.
TENJIN-YA.
WHAT ARE YOU?

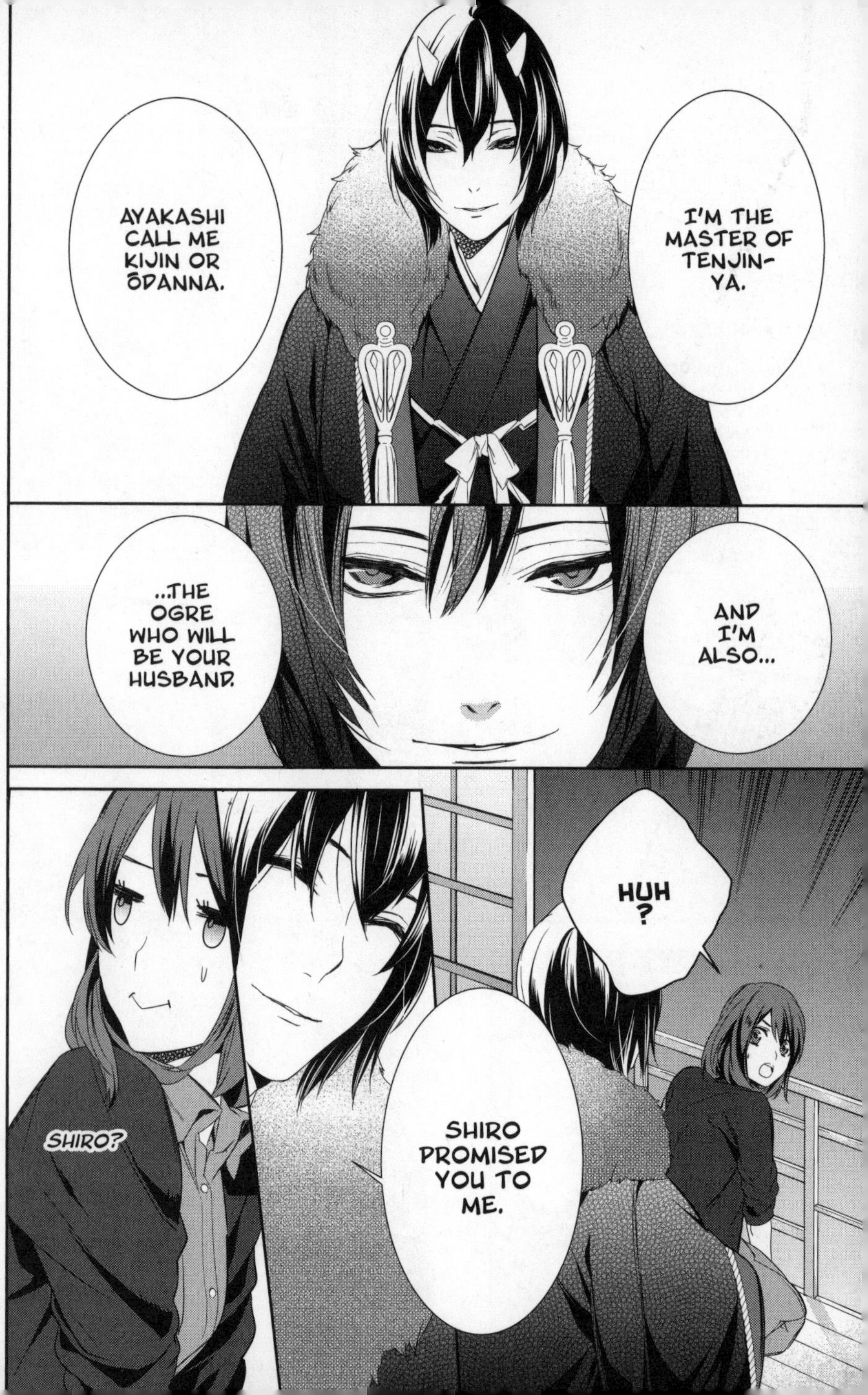
I'M THE MASTER OF TENJIN-YA.
AYAKASHI CALL ME KIJIN OR ŌDANNA.
AND I'M ALSO...
...THE OGRE WHO WILL BE YOUR HUSBAND.
HUH?
SHIRO PROMISED YOU TO ME.
SHIRO?

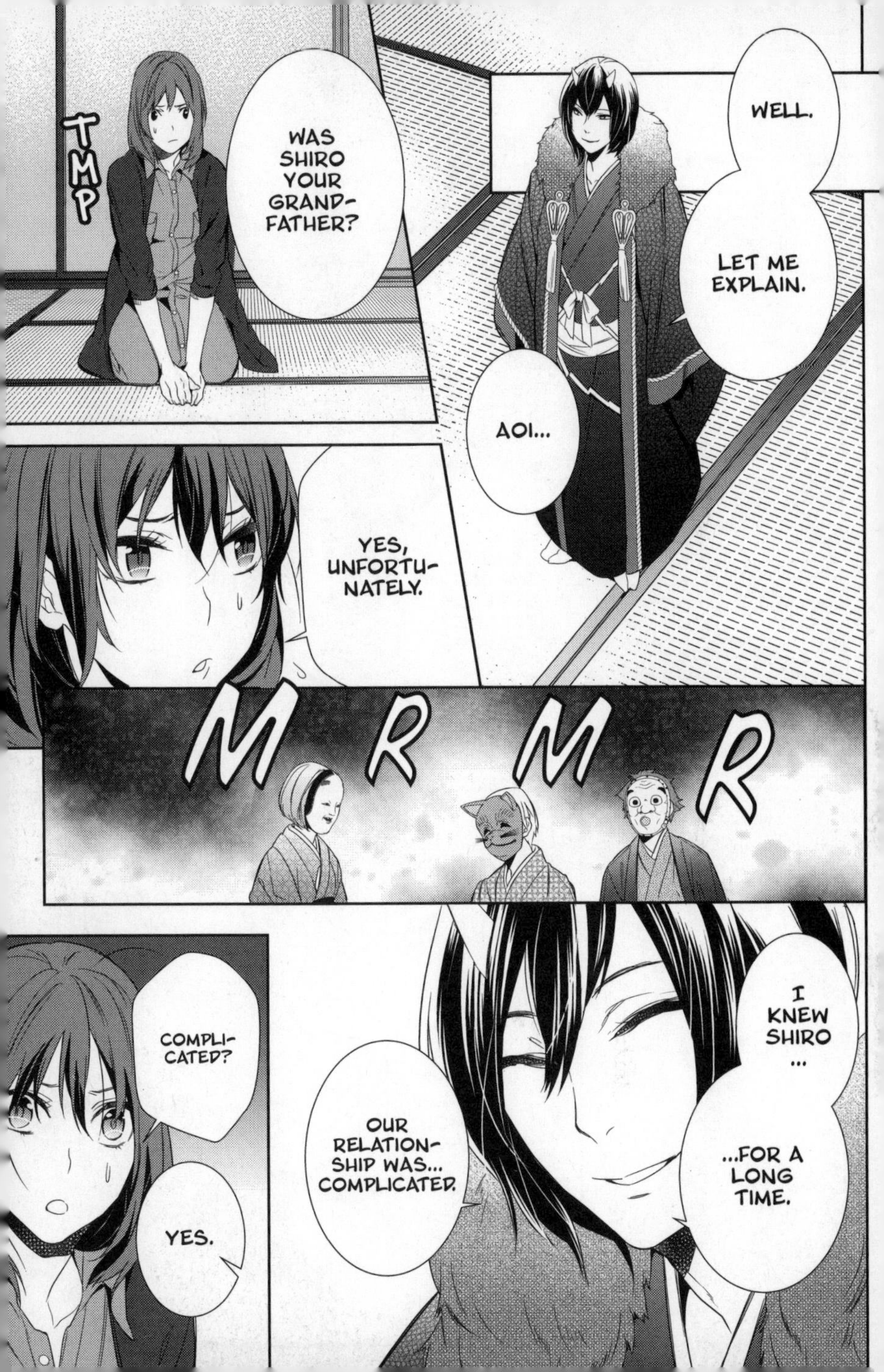
WELL.
LET ME EXPLAIN.
AOI...
TMP
WAS SHIRO YOUR GRAND-FATHER?
YES, UNFORTU-NATELY.
MRMR
I KNEW SHIRO ...
...FOR A LONG TIME.
OUR RELATION-SHIP WAS... COMPLICATED.
COMPLI-CATED?
YES.

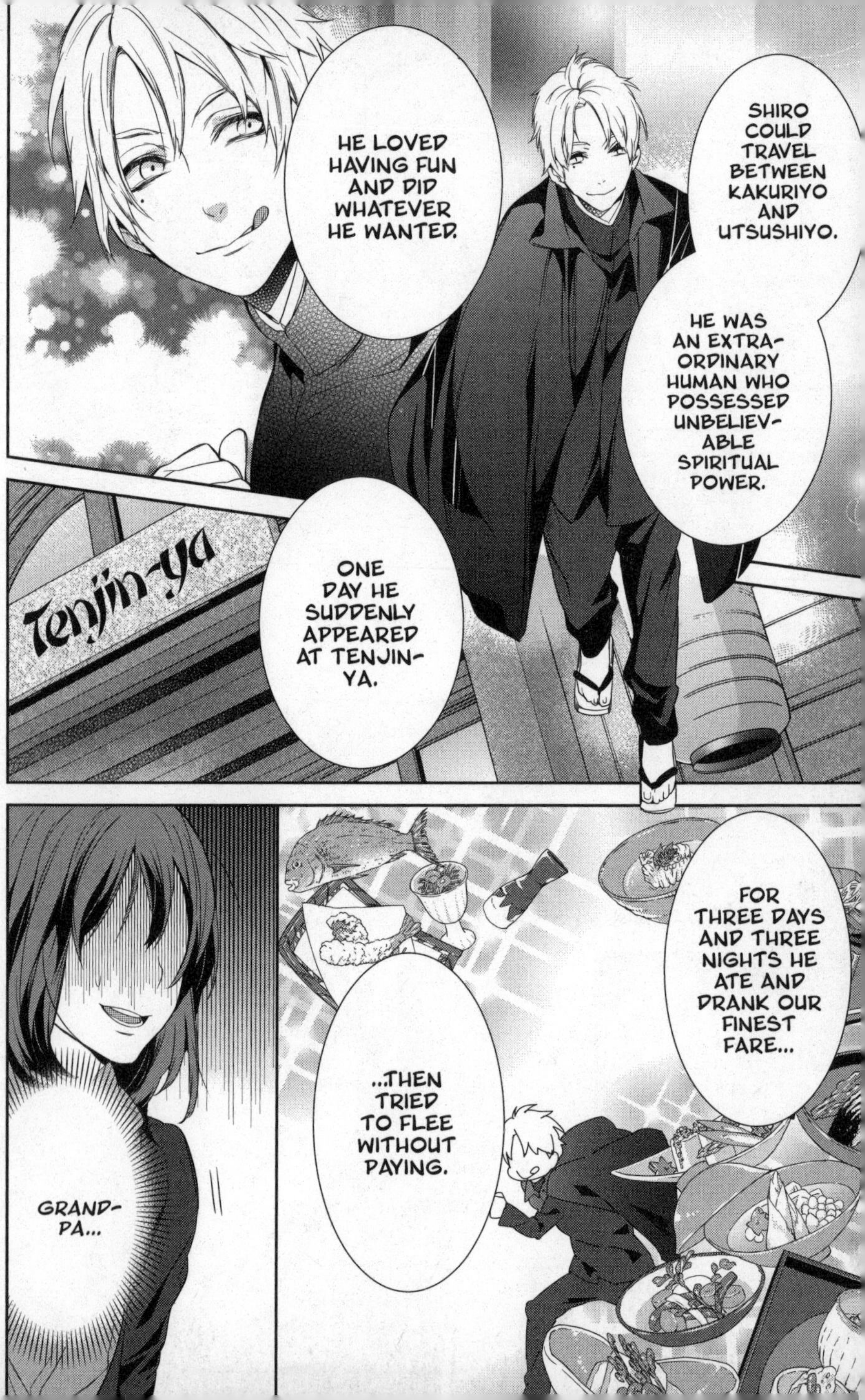
SHIRO COULD TRAVEL BETWEEN KAKURIYO AND UTSUSHIYO.
HE WAS AN EXTRA-ORDINARY HUMAN WHO POSSESSED UNBELIEV-ABLE SPIRITUAL POWER.
HE LOVED HAVING FUN AND DID WHATEVER HE WANTED.
ONE DAY HE SUDDENLY APPEARED AT TENJIN-YA.
Tenjin-ya
FOR THREE DAYS AND THREE NIGHTS HE ATE AND DRANK OUR FINEST FARE...
...THEN TRIED TO FLEE WITHOUT PAYING.
GRAND-PA...

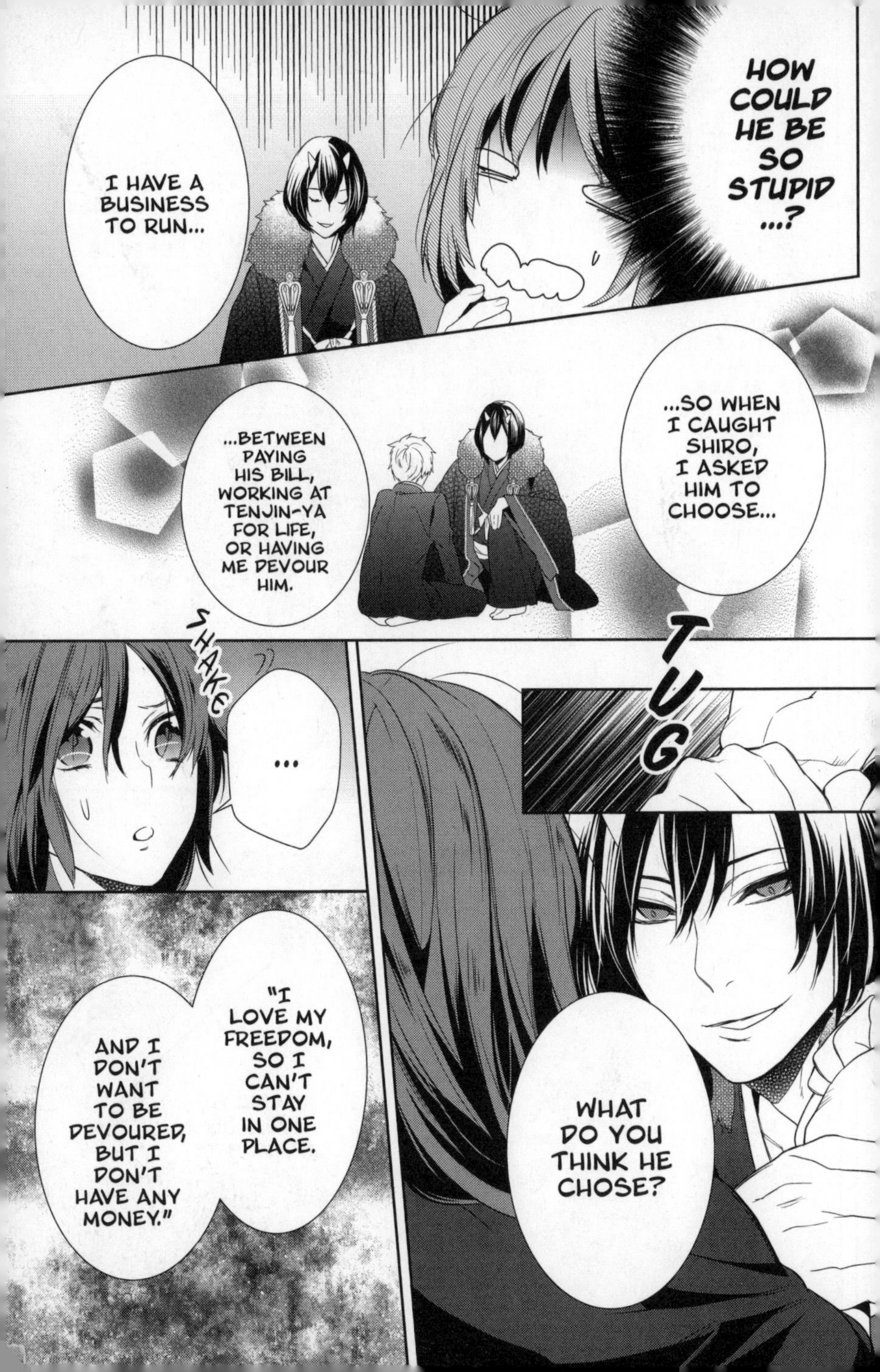
HOW COULD HE BE SO STUPID ...?
I HAVE A BUSINESS TO RUN...
...SO WHEN I CAUGHT SHIRO, I ASKED HIM TO CHOOSE...
...BETWEEN PAYING HIS BILL, WORKING AT TENJIN-YA FOR LIFE, OR HAVING ME DEVOUR HIM.
TUG
WHAT DO YOU THINK HE CHOSE?
SHAKE
...
"I LOVE MY FREEDOM, SO I CAN'T STAY IN ONE PLACE.
AND I DON'T WANT TO BE DEVOURED, BUT I DON'T HAVE ANY MONEY."

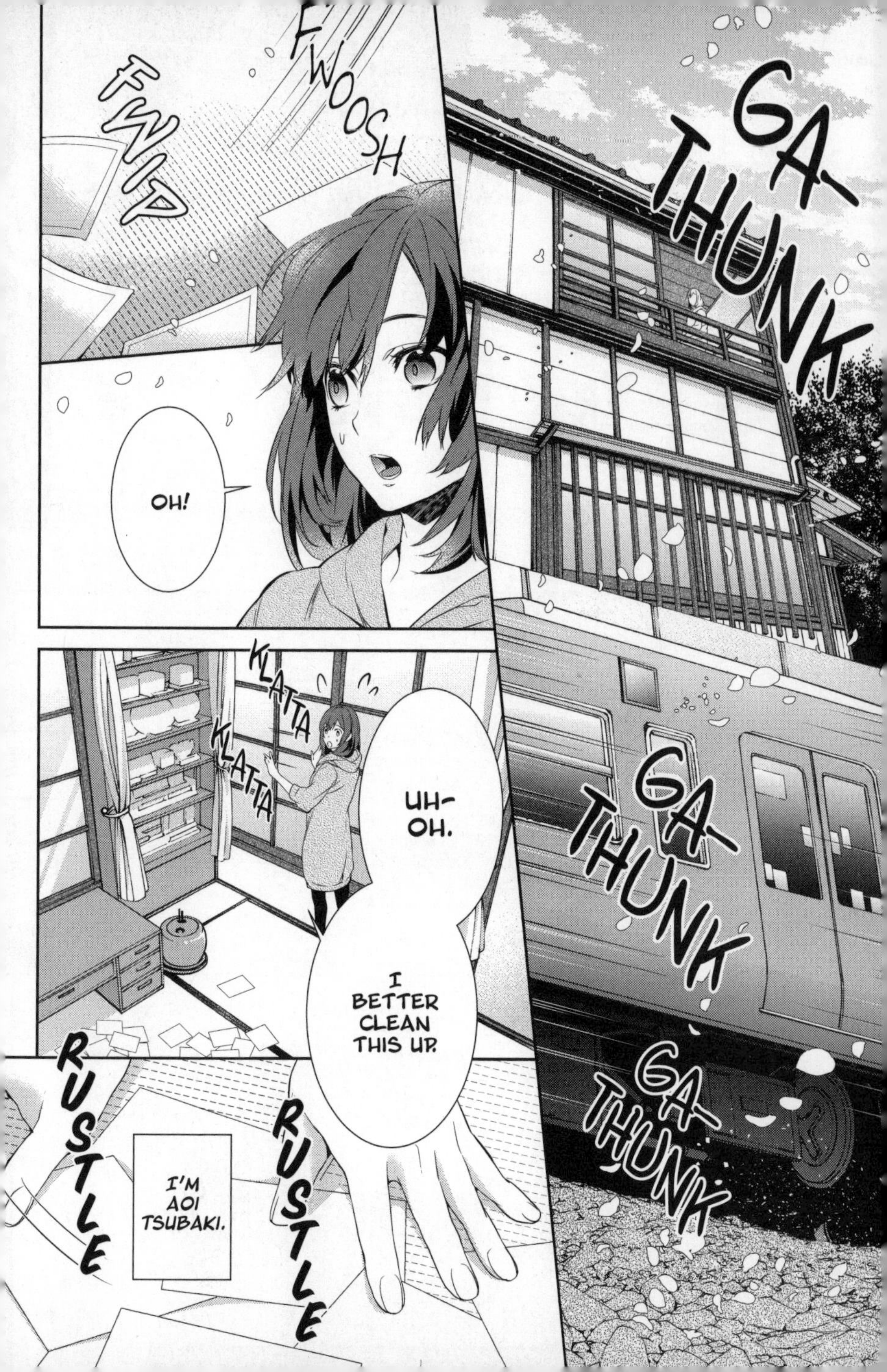
GA THUNK
GA THUNK
GA THUNK
FWOOSH
FWIP
OH!
KLATTA
KLATTA
UH-OH.
I BETTER CLEAN THIS UP.
RUSTLE
RUSTLE
I'M AOI TSUBAKI.

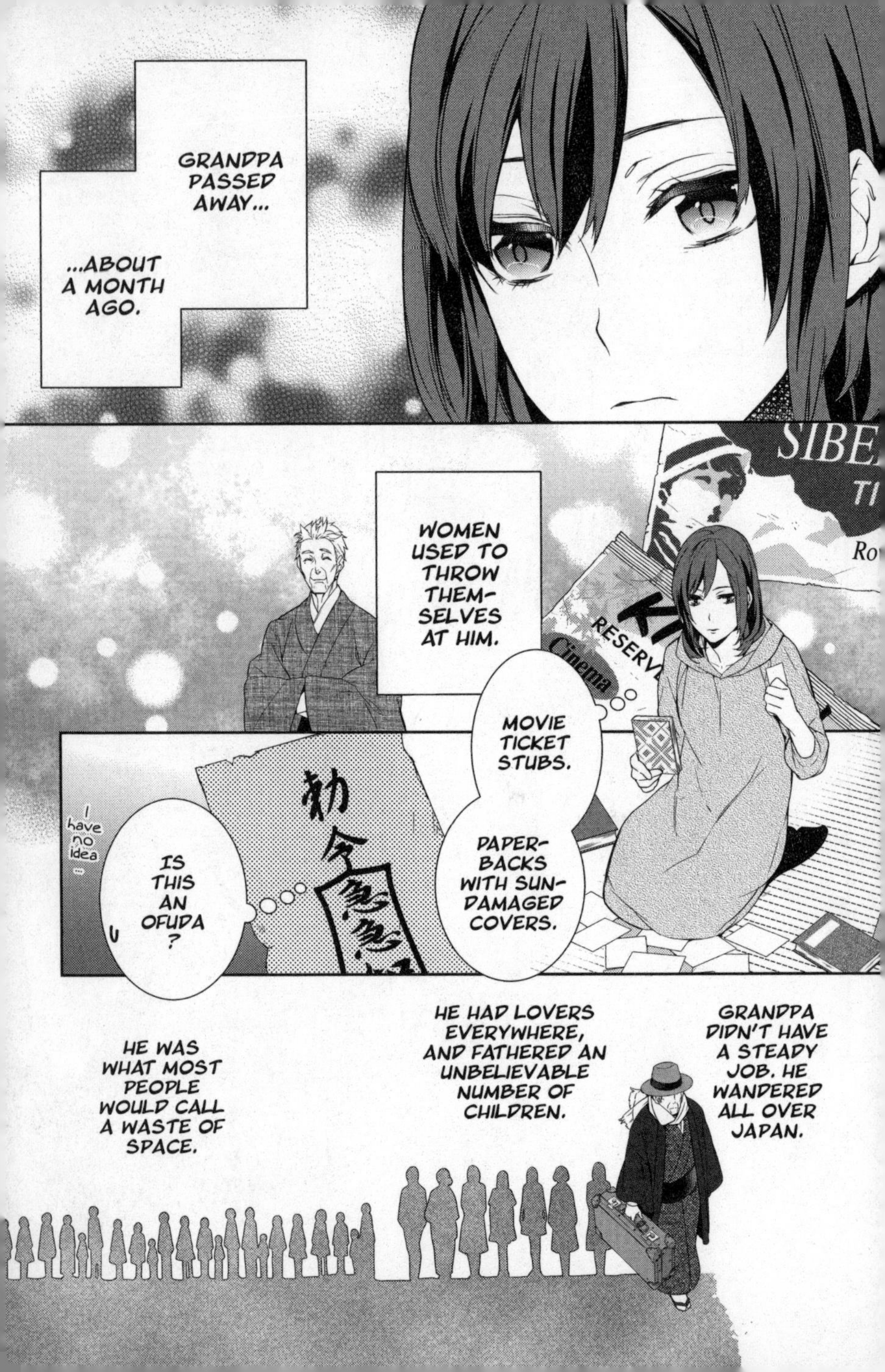
GRANDPA PASSED AWAY...
...ABOUT A MONTH AGO.
WOMEN USED TO THROW THEM-SELVES AT HIM.
Cinema
MOVIE TICKET STUBS.
PAPER-BACKS WITH SUN-DAMAGED COVERS.
IS THIS AN OFUDA?
I have no idea...
GRANDPA DIDN'T HAVE A STEADY JOB. HE WANDERED ALL OVER JAPAN.
HE HAD LOVERS EVERYWHERE, AND FATHERED AN UNBELIEVABLE NUMBER OF CHILDREN.
HE WAS WHAT MOST PEOPLE WOULD CALL A WASTE OF SPACE.

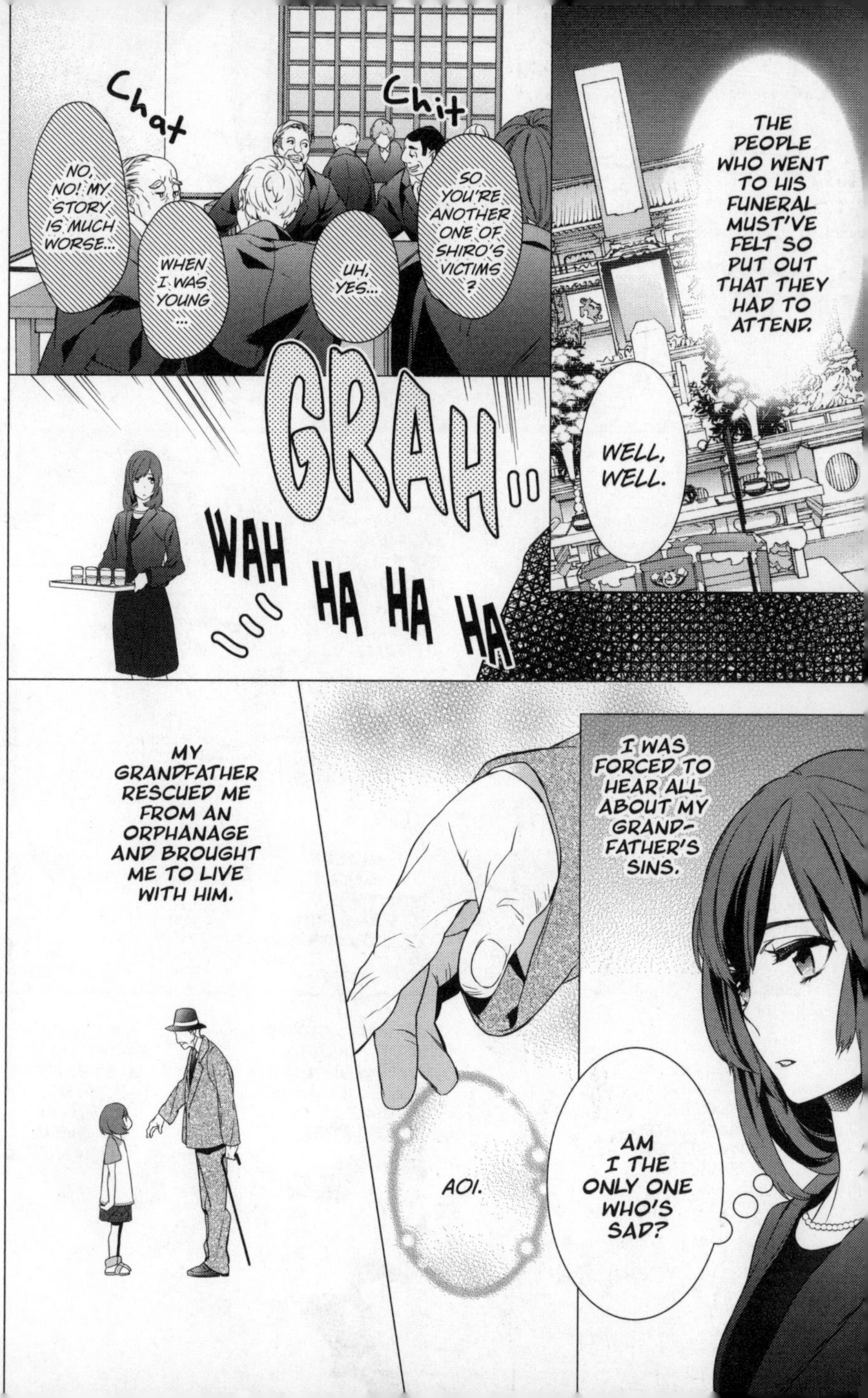
THE PEOPLE WHO WENT TO HIS FUNERAL MUST'VE FELT SO PUT OUT THAT THEY HAD TO ATTEND.
WELL, WELL.
Chit
SO YOU'RE ANOTHER ONE OF SHIRO'S VICTIMS?
UH, YES...
WHEN I WAS YOUNG...
Chat
NO, NO! MY STORY IS MUCH WORSE...
GRAH
WAH HA HA HA
I WAS FORCED TO HEAR ALL ABOUT MY GRAND-FATHER'S SINS.
AM I THE ONLY ONE WHO'S SAD?
AOI.
MY GRANDFATHER RESCUED ME FROM AN ORPHANAGE AND BROUGHT ME TO LIVE WITH HIM.

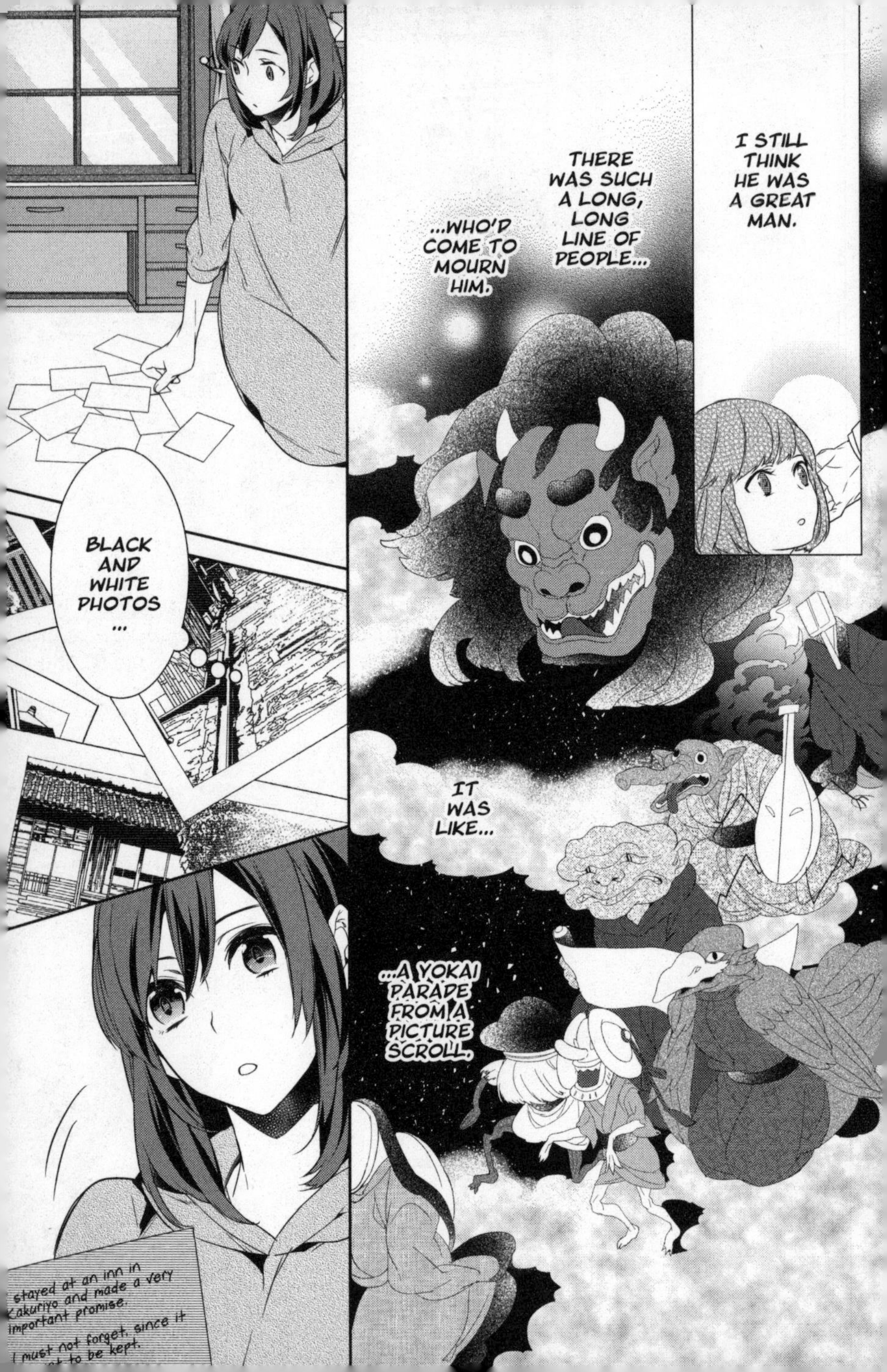
I STILL THINK HE WAS A GREAT MAN.
THERE WAS SUCH A LONG, LONG LINE OF PEOPLE...
...WHO'D COME TO MOURN HIM.
IT WAS LIKE...
...A YOKAI PARADE FROM A PICTURE SCROLL.
BLACK AND WHITE PHOTOS ...
stayed at an inn in Kakuriyo and made a very important promise.
I must not forget, since it
to be kept.

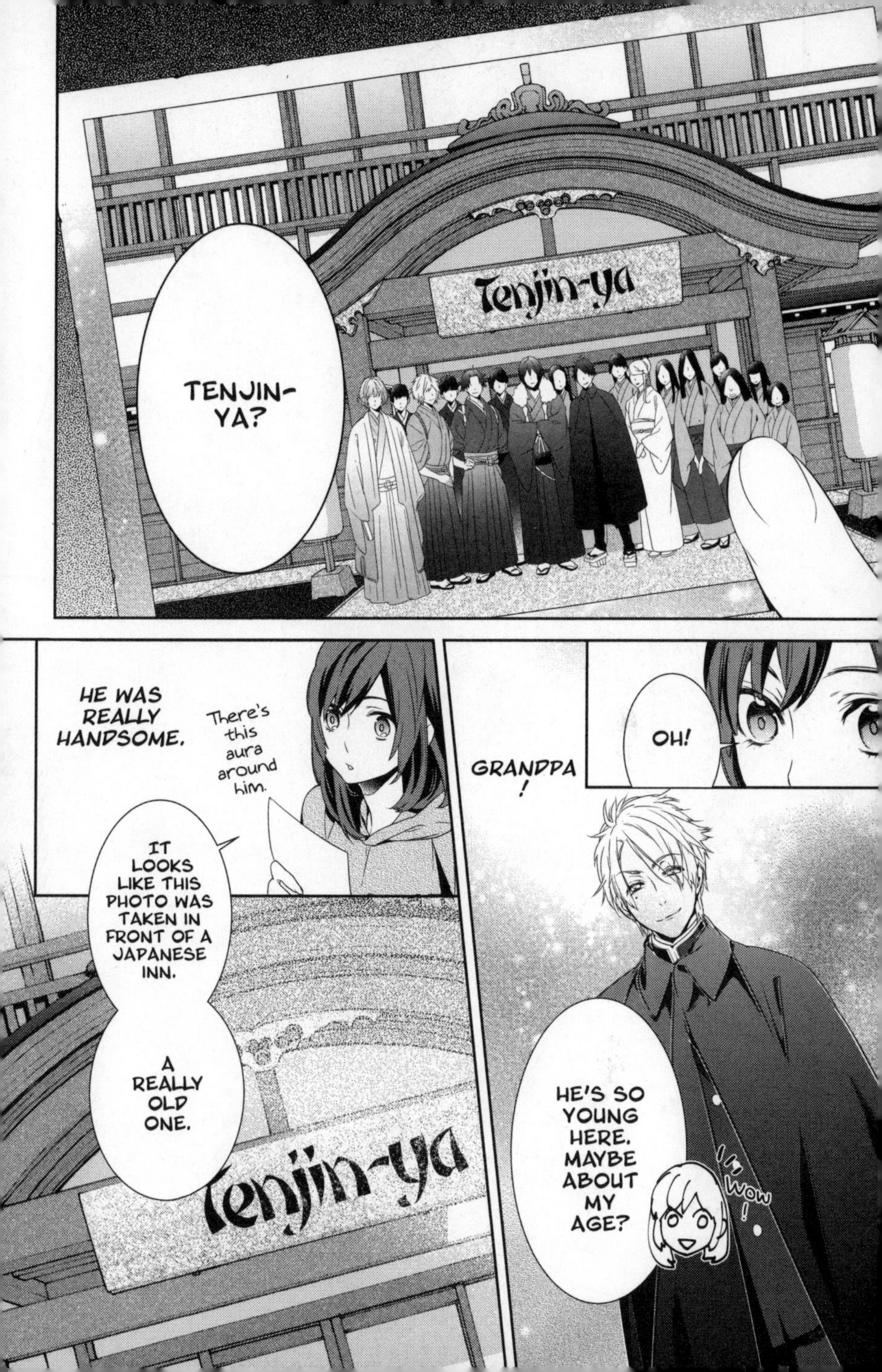
TENJIN-YA?
Tenjin-ya
OH!
GRANDPA!
HE'S SO YOUNG HERE. MAYBE ABOUT MY AGE?
Wow!
HE WAS REALLY HANDSOME.
There's this aura around him.
IT LOOKS LIKE THIS PHOTO WAS TAKEN IN FRONT OF A JAPANESE INN.
A REALLY OLD ONE.
Tenjin-ya

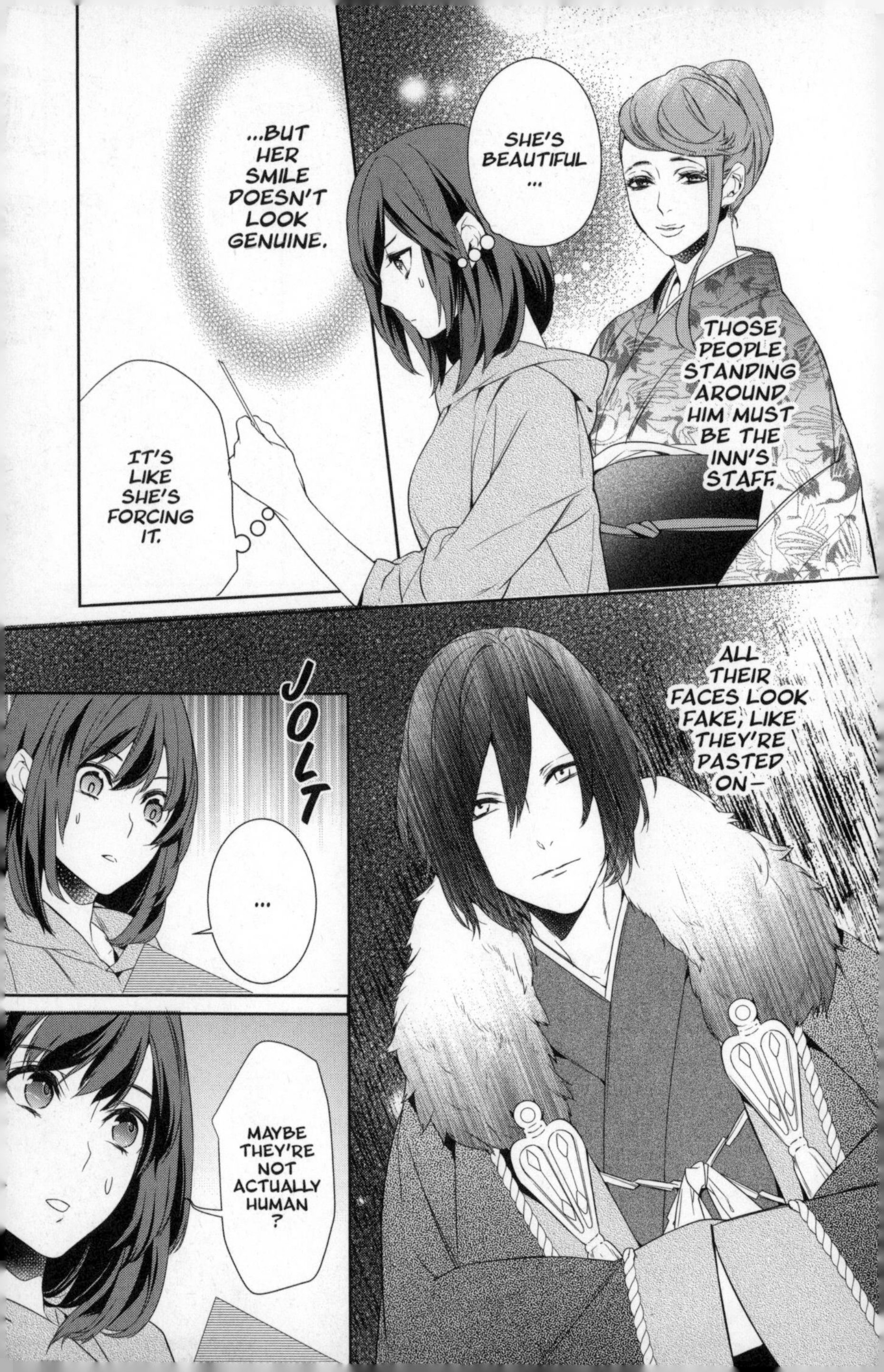
SHE'S BEAUTIFUL ...
...BUT HER SMILE DOESN'T LOOK GENUINE.
IT'S LIKE SHE'S FORCING IT.
THOSE PEOPLE STANDING AROUND HIM MUST BE THE INN'S STAFF.
ALL THEIR FACES LOOK FAKE, LIKE THEY'RE PASTED ON—
JOLT
...
MAYBE THEY'RE NOT ACTUALLY HUMAN ?

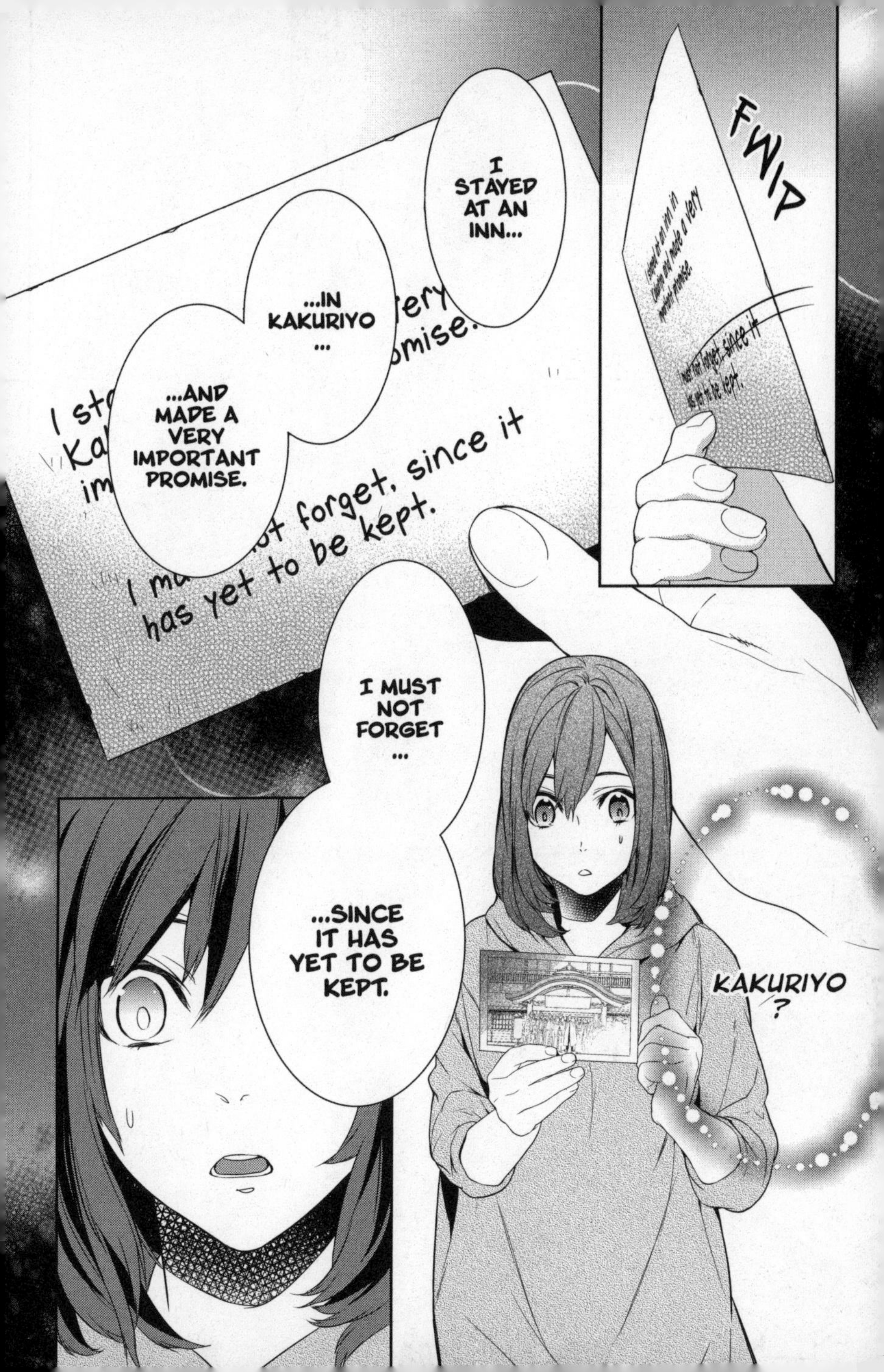
FWIP
I STAYED AT AN INN...
...IN KAKURIYO...
...AND MADE A VERY IMPORTANT PROMISE.
forget, since it
has yet to be kept.
I MUST NOT FORGET...
...SINCE IT HAS YET TO BE KEPT.
KAKURIYO?

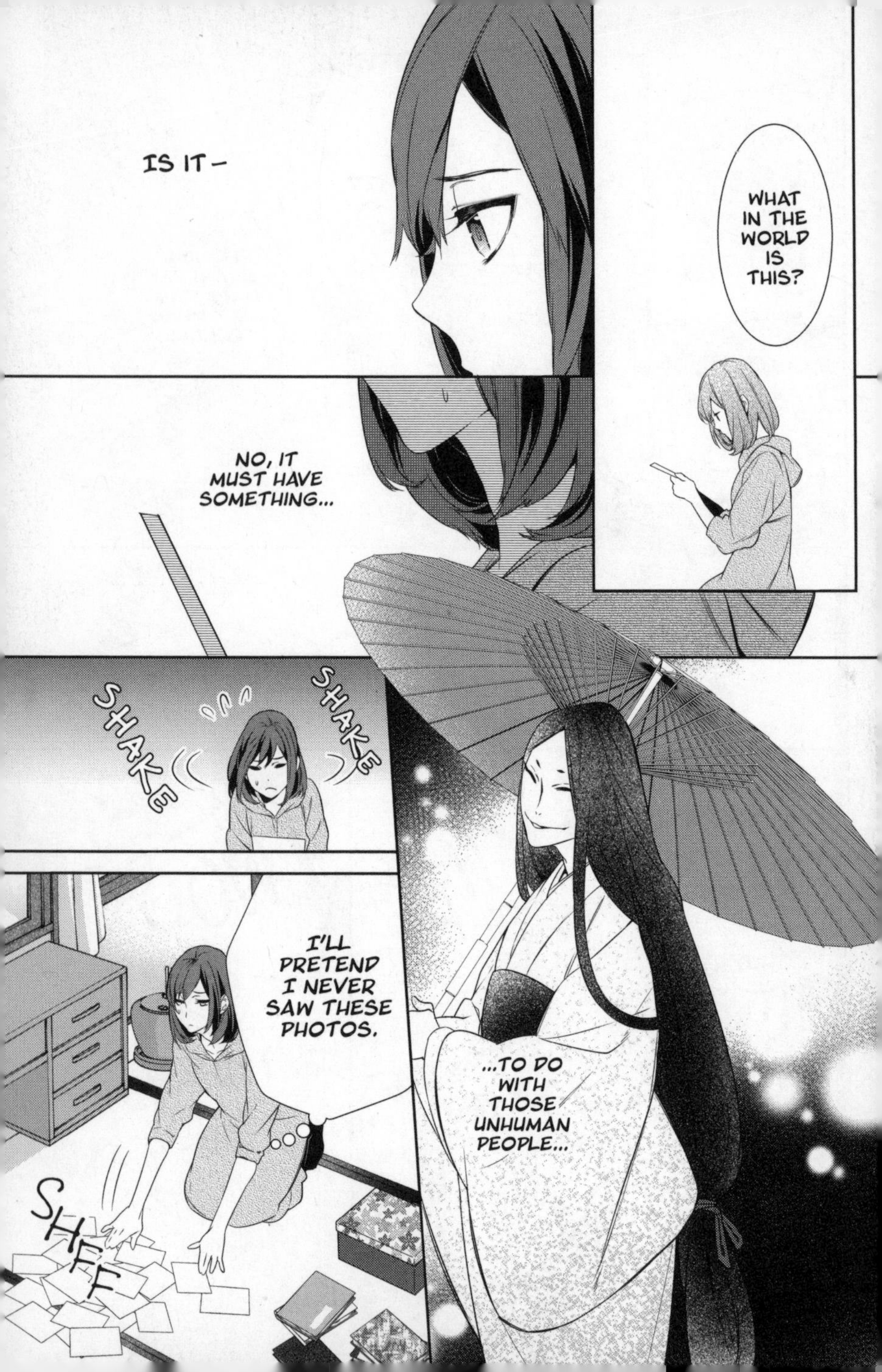
WHAT IN THE WORLD IS THIS?
IS IT—
NO, IT MUST HAVE SOMETHING...
...TO DO WITH THOSE UNHUMAN PEOPLE...
SHAKE
SHAKE
I'LL PRETEND I NEVER SAW THESE PHOTOS.
SHFF

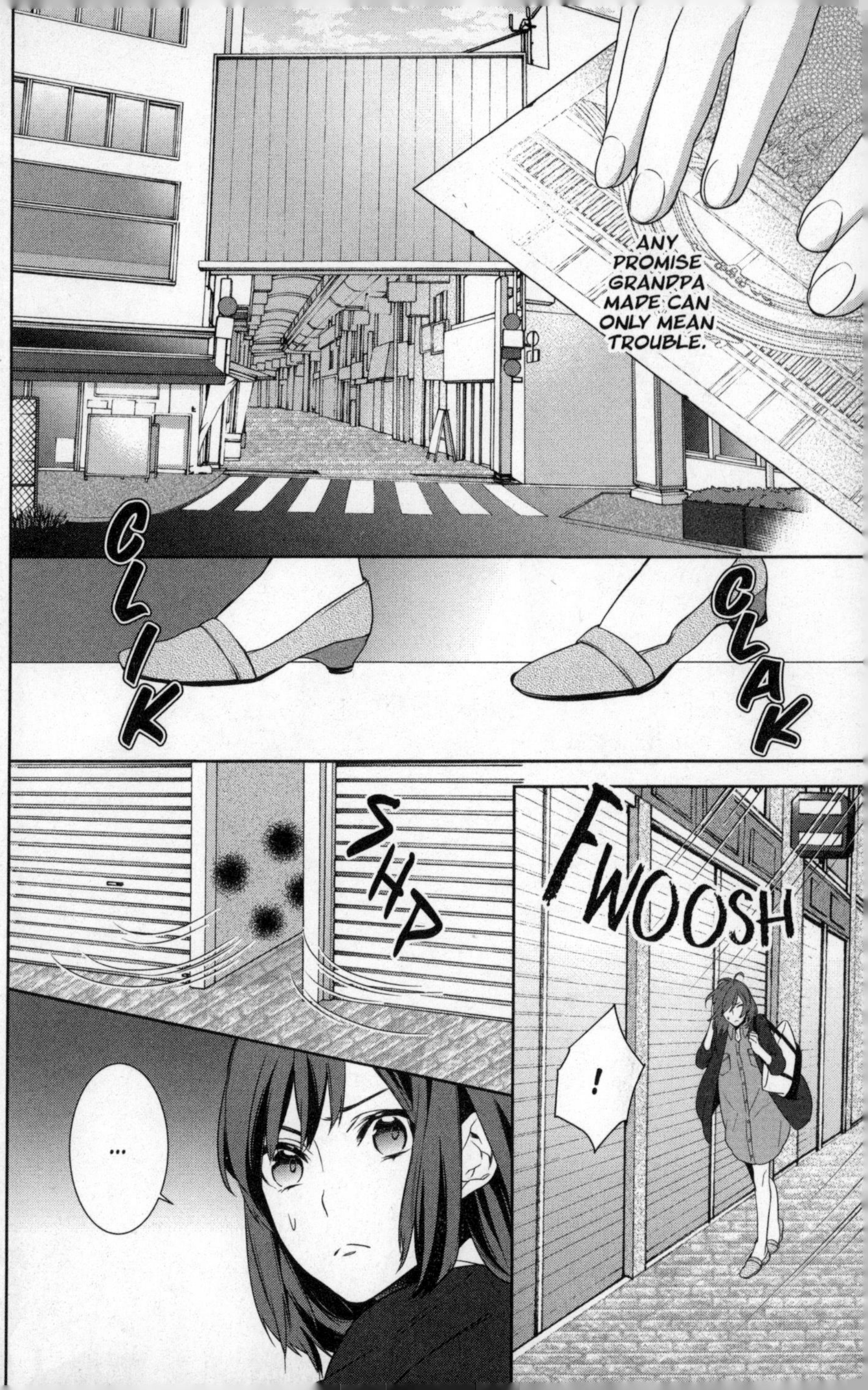
ANY PROMISE GRANDPA MADE CAN ONLY MEAN TROUBLE.
CLAK
CLIK
FWOOSH
!
SHP
...

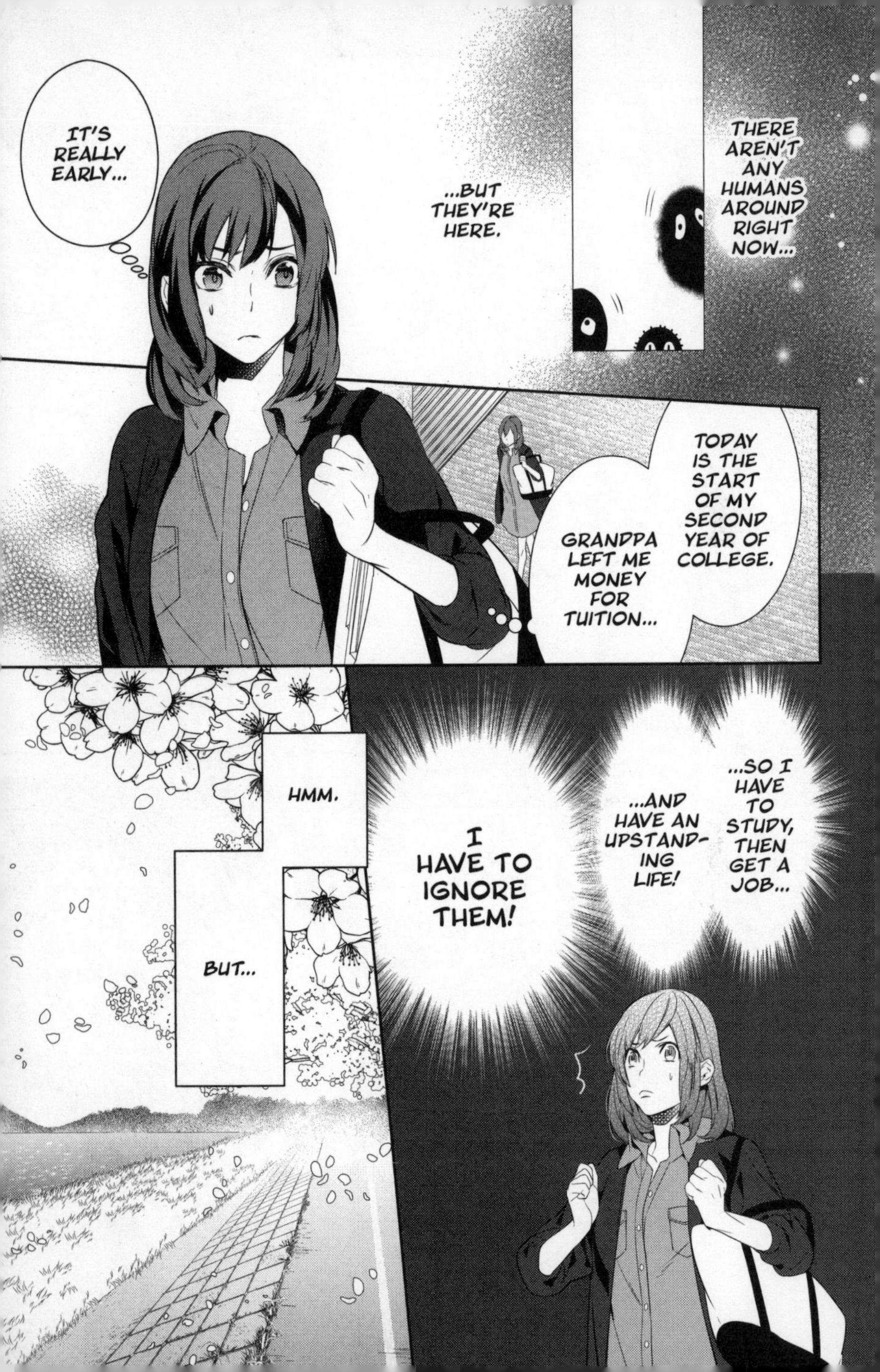
THERE AREN'T ANY HUMANS AROUND RIGHT NOW...
...BUT THEY'RE HERE.
IT'S REALLY EARLY...
TODAY IS THE START OF MY SECOND YEAR OF COLLEGE.
GRANDPA LEFT ME MONEY FOR TUITION...
...SO I HAVE TO STUDY, THEN GET A JOB...
...AND HAVE AN UPSTAND-ING LIFE!
I HAVE TO IGNORE THEM!
HMM.
BUT...

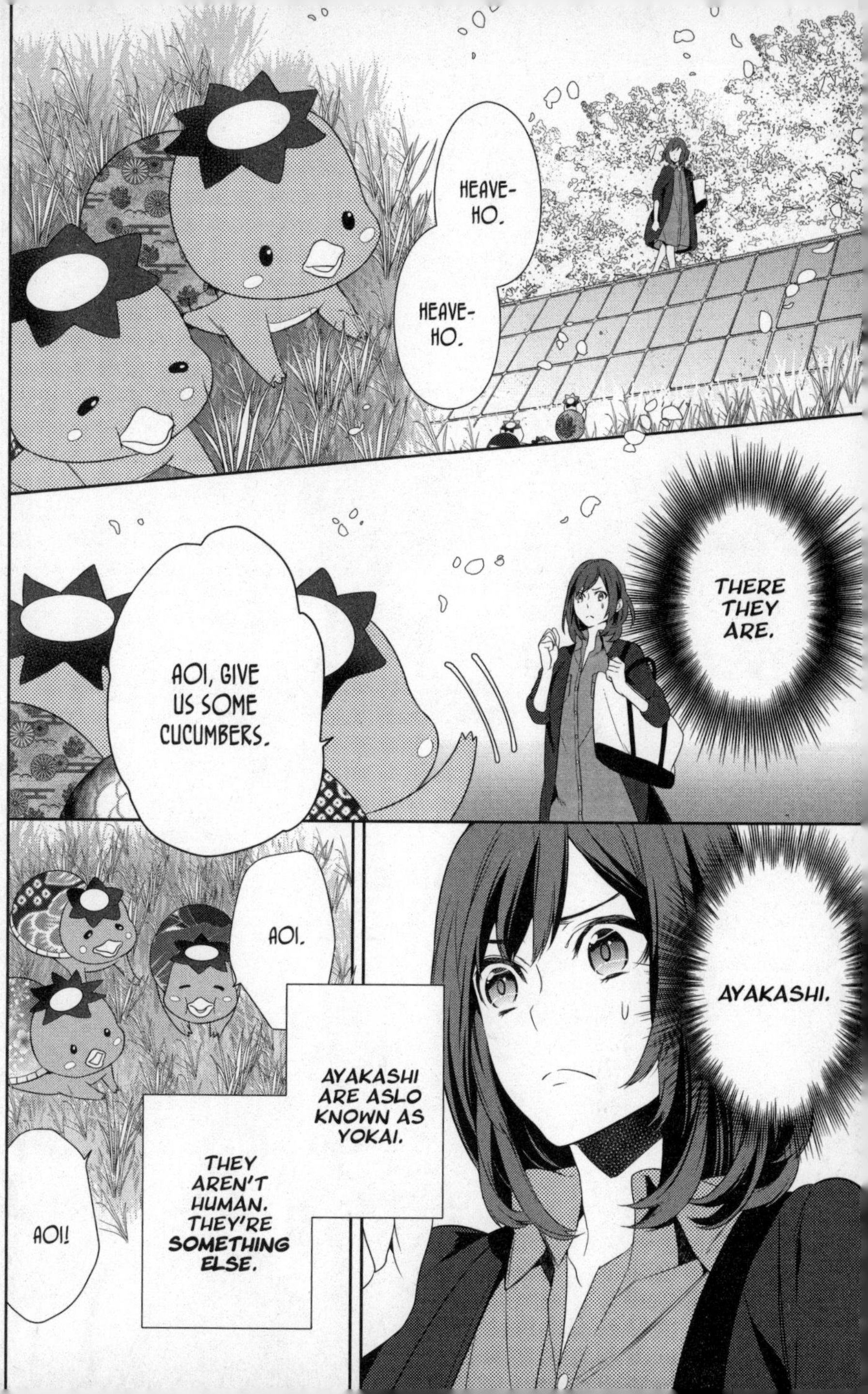
HEAVE-HO.
HEAVE-HO.
THERE THEY ARE.
AOI, GIVE US SOME CUCUMBERS.
AYAKASHI.
AYAKASHI ARE ASLO KNOWN AS YOKAI.
THEY AREN'T HUMAN. THEY'RE SOMETHING ELSE.
AOI.
AOI!

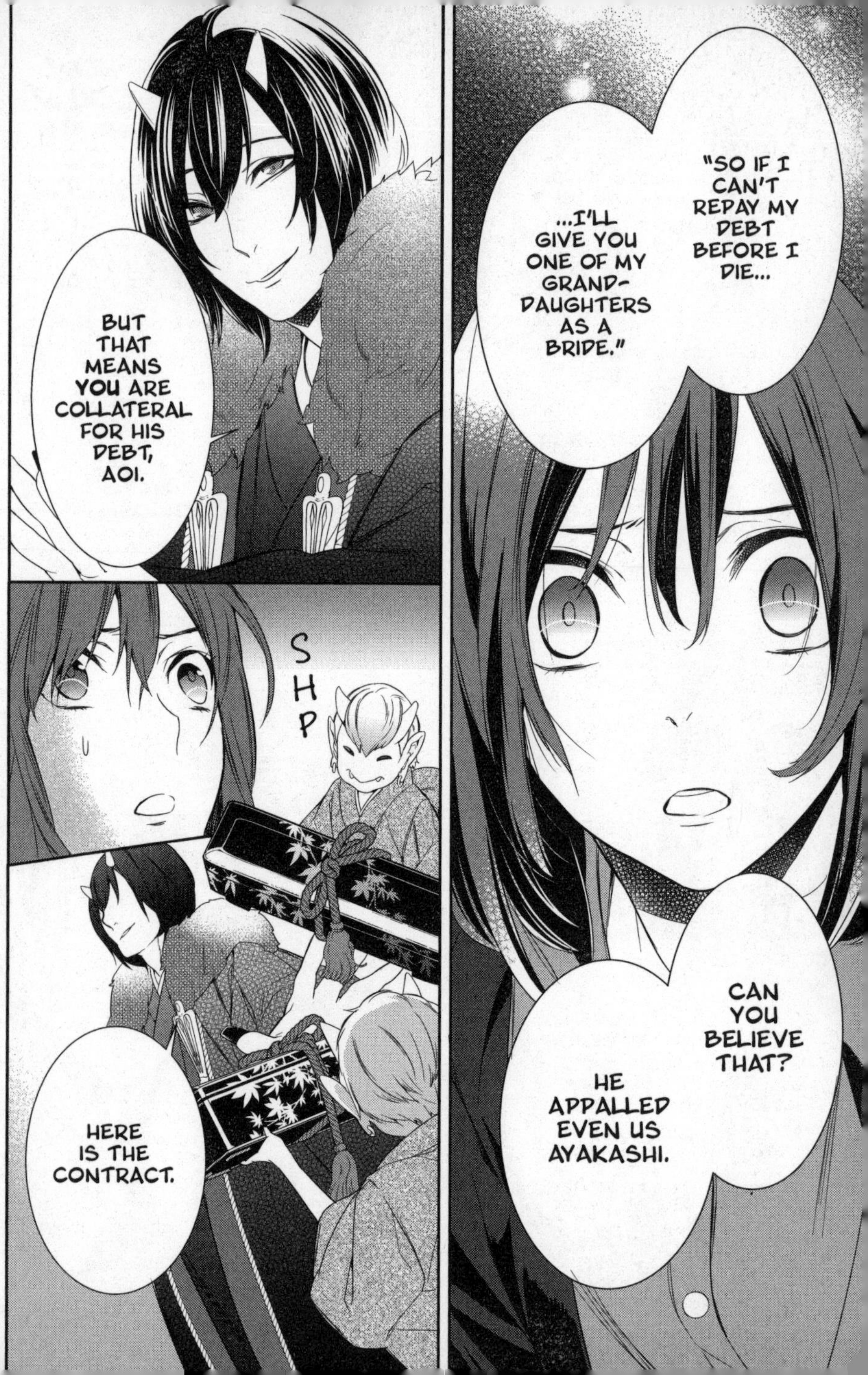
"SO IF I CAN'T REPAY MY DEBT BEFORE I DIE...
...I'LL GIVE YOU ONE OF MY GRAND-DAUGHTERS AS A BRIDE."
CAN YOU BELIEVE THAT?
HE APPALLED EVEN US AYAKASHI.
BUT THAT MEANS YOU ARE COLLATERAL FOR HIS DEBT, AOI.
SHP
HERE IS THE CONTRACT.

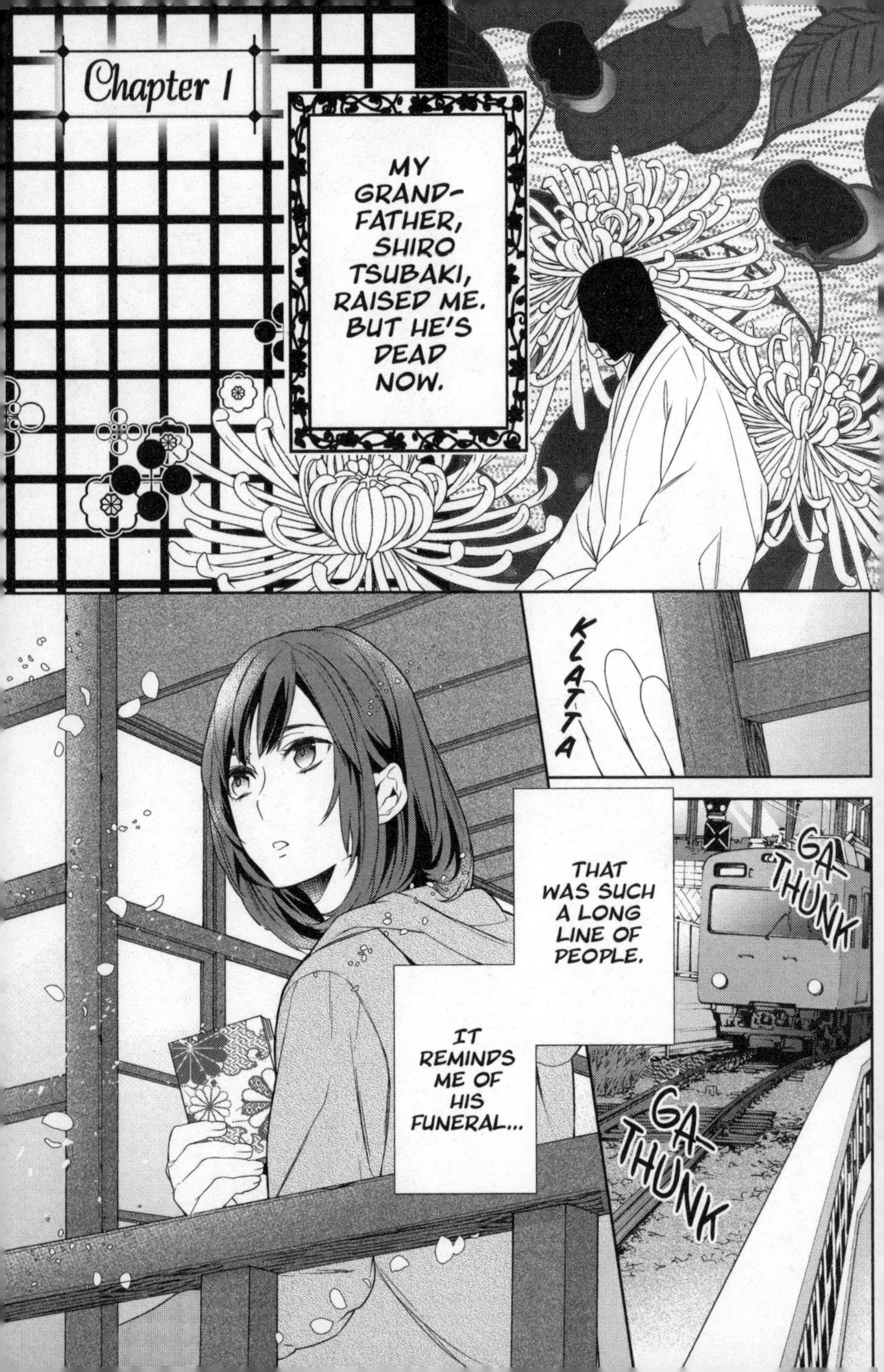
Chapter 1
MY GRAND-FATHER, SHIRO TSUBAKI, RAISED ME. BUT HE'S DEAD NOW.
KLATTA
GA THUNK
THAT WAS SUCH A LONG LINE OF PEOPLE.
IT REMINDS ME OF HIS FUNERAL...
GA THUNK

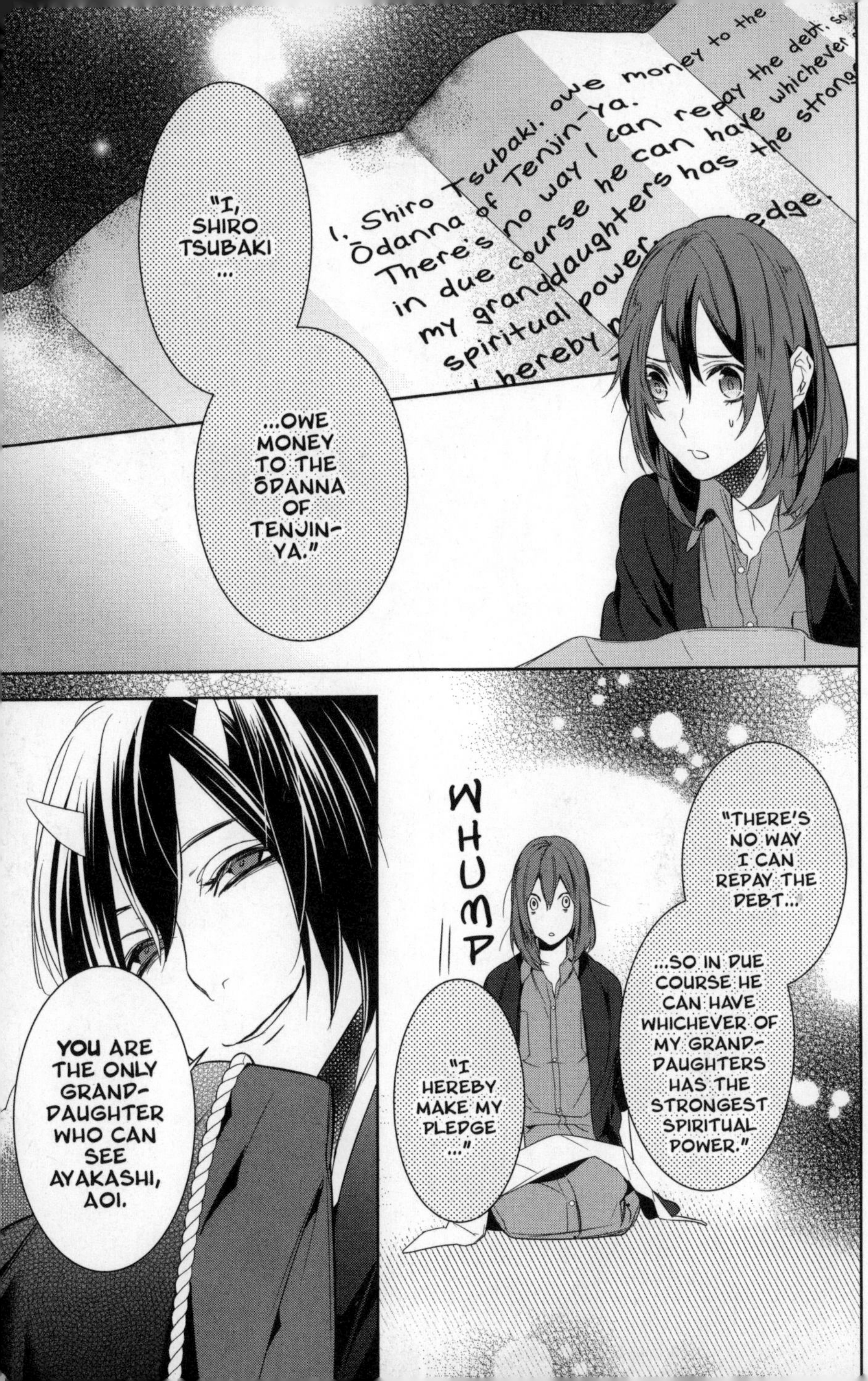
I, Shiro Tsubaki, owe money to the
Ōdanna of Tenjin-Ya.
There's no way I can repay the debt, so
in due course he can have whichever
my granddaughters has the strong
spiritual power.
I hereby
"I, SHIRO TSUBAKI ...
...OWE MONEY TO THE ŌDANNA OF TENJIN-YA."
"THERE'S NO WAY I CAN REPAY THE DEBT...
...SO IN DUE COURSE HE CAN HAVE WHICHEVER OF MY GRAND-DAUGHTERS HAS THE STRONGEST SPIRITUAL POWER."
WHUMP
"I HEREBY MAKE MY PLEDGE ..."
YOU ARE THE ONLY GRAND-DAUGHTER WHO CAN SEE AYAKASHI, AOI.

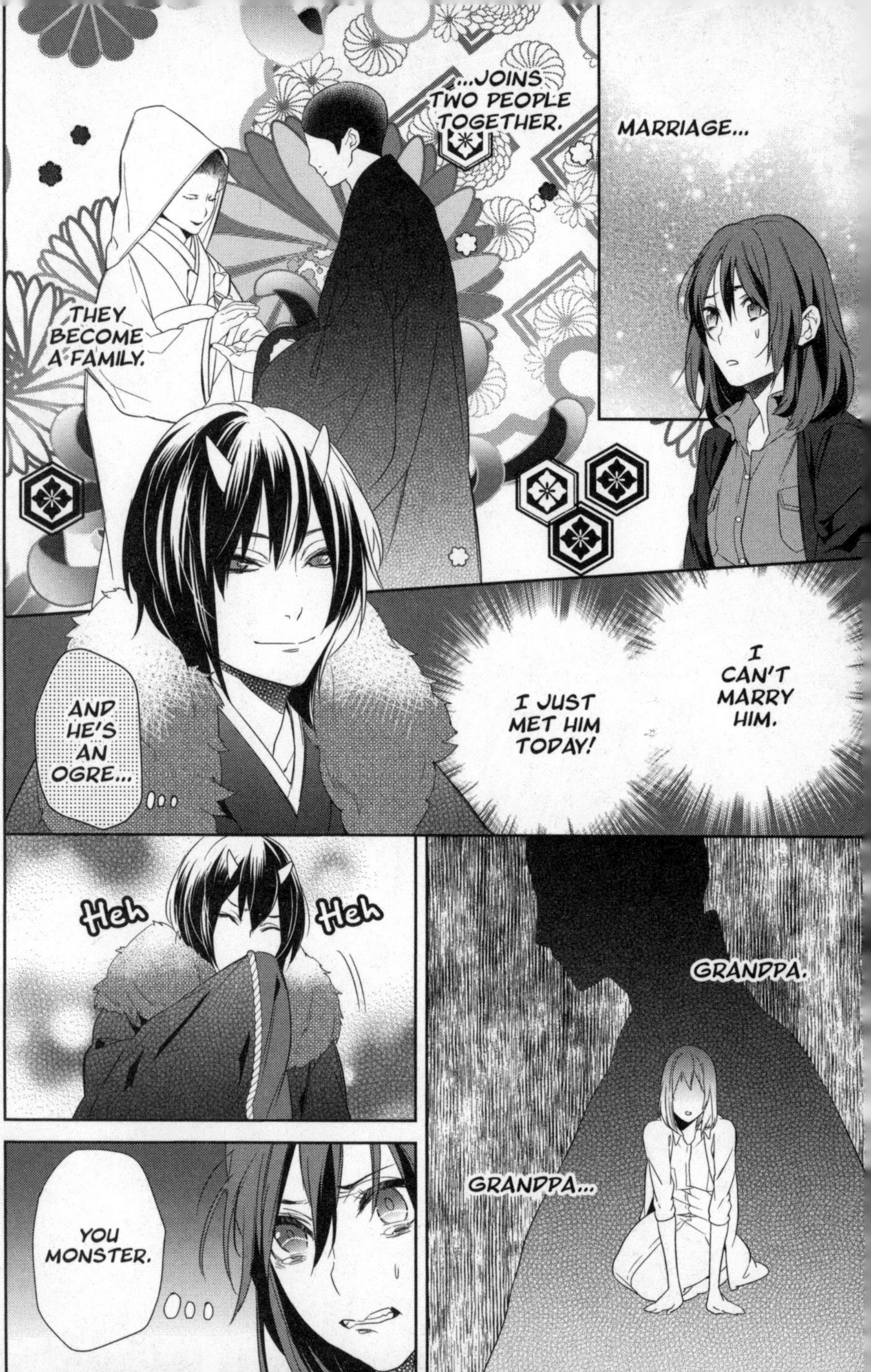
MARRIAGE...
...JOINS TWO PEOPLE TOGETHER.
THEY BECOME A FAMILY.
I CAN'T MARRY HIM.
I JUST MET HIM TODAY!
AND HE'S AN OGRE...
...
GRANDPA.
GRANDPA...
Heh Heh
YOU MONSTER.
...

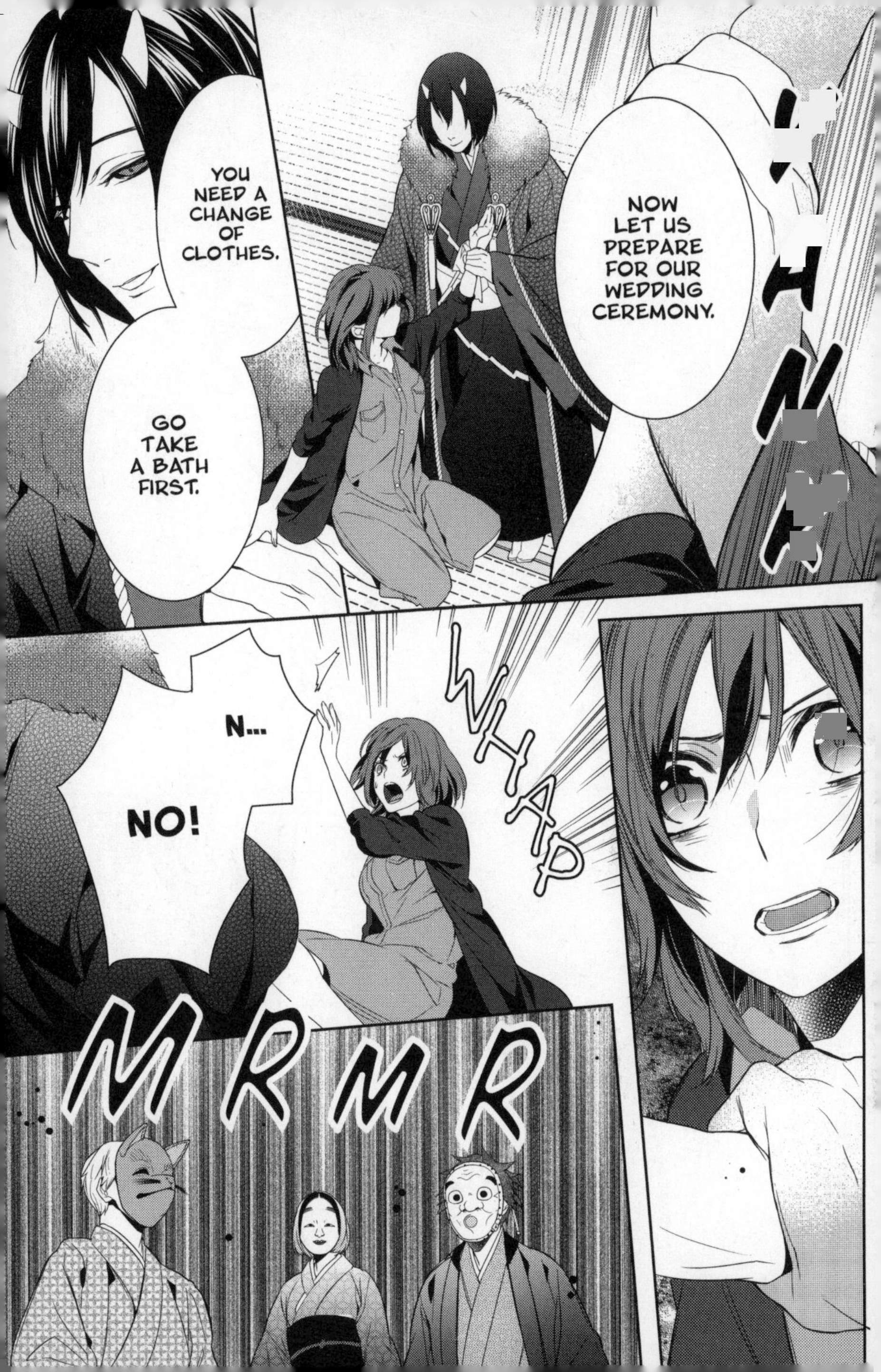
NOW LET US PREPARE FOR OUR WEDDING CEREMONY.
YOU NEED A CHANGE OF CLOTHES.
GO TAKE A BATH FIRST.
WHAP
N...
NO!
MRMR

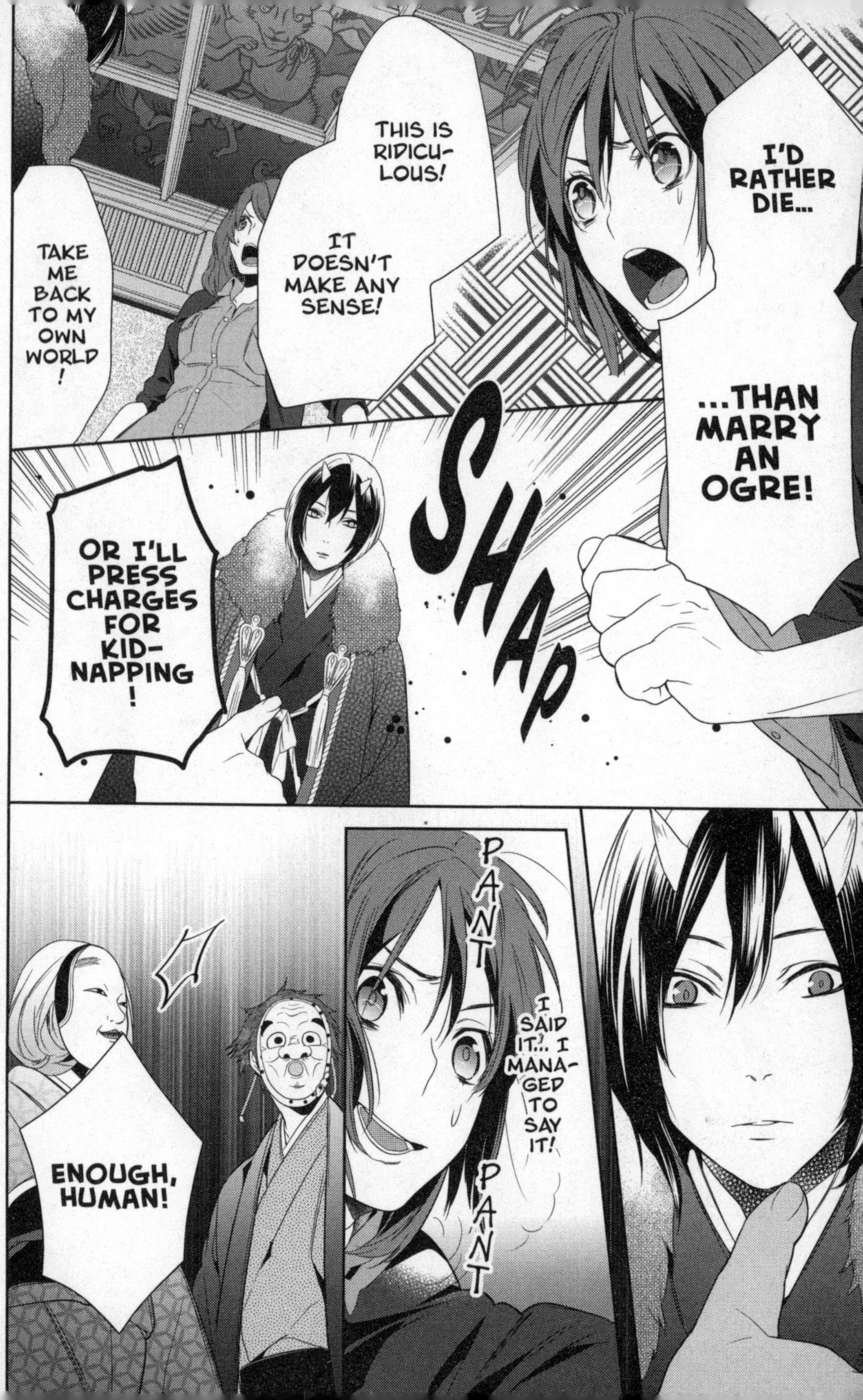
I'D RATHER DIE...
...THAN MARRY AN OGRE!
THIS IS RIDICULOUS!
IT DOESN'T MAKE ANY SENSE!
TAKE ME BACK TO MY OWN WORLD!
OR I'LL PRESS CHARGES FOR KIDNAPPING!
SHAP
PANT PANT
I SAID IT... I MANAGED TO SAY IT!
ENOUGH, HUMAN!

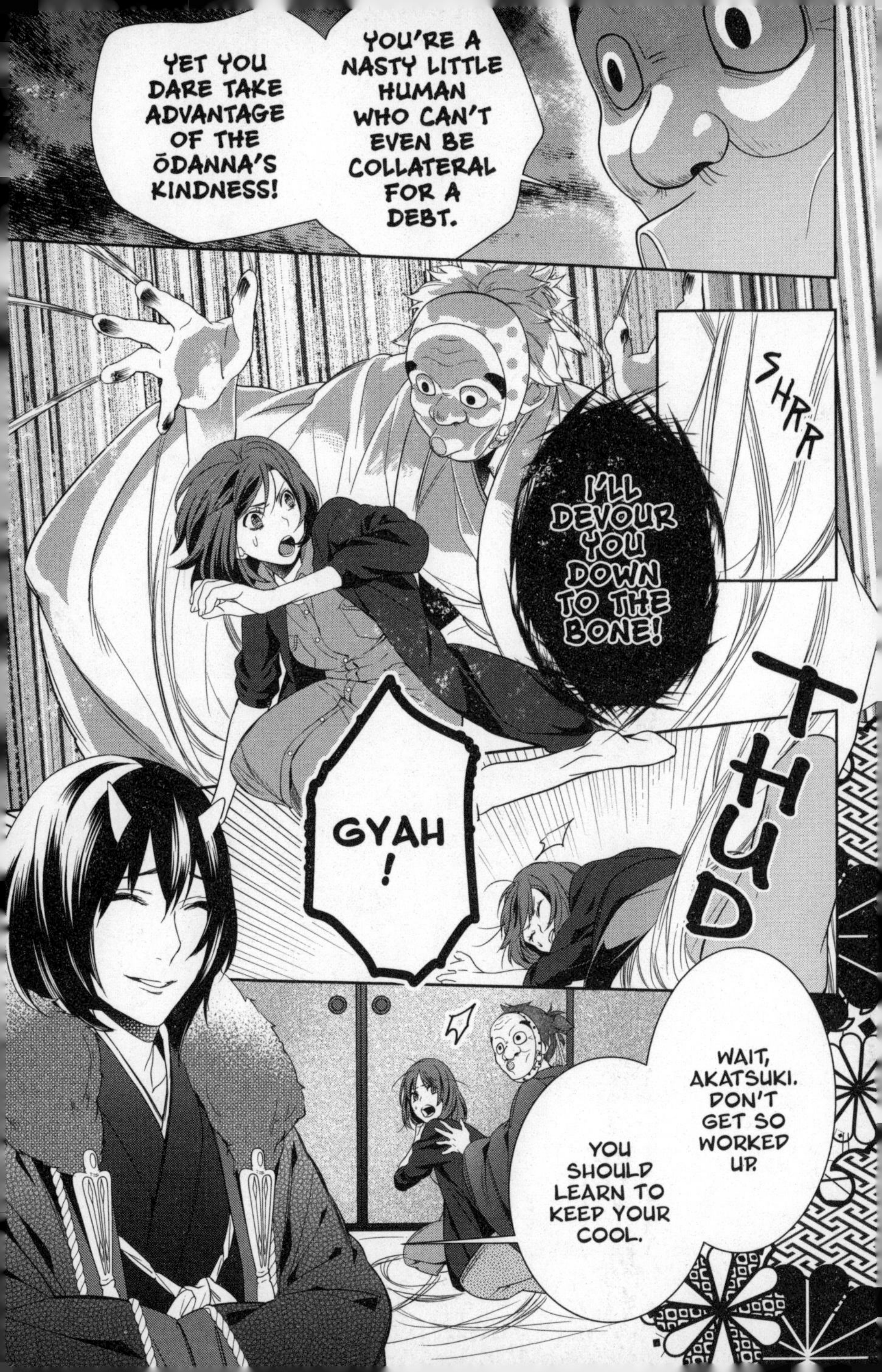
YOU'RE A NASTY LITTLE HUMAN WHO CAN'T EVEN BE COLLATERAL FOR A DEBT.
YET YOU DARE TAKE ADVANTAGE OF THE ŌDANNA'S KINDNESS!
SHRR
I'LL DEVOUR YOU DOWN TO THE BONE!
THUD
GYAH!
WAIT, AKATSUKI. DON'T GET SO WORKED UP.
YOU SHOULD LEARN TO KEEP YOUR COOL.

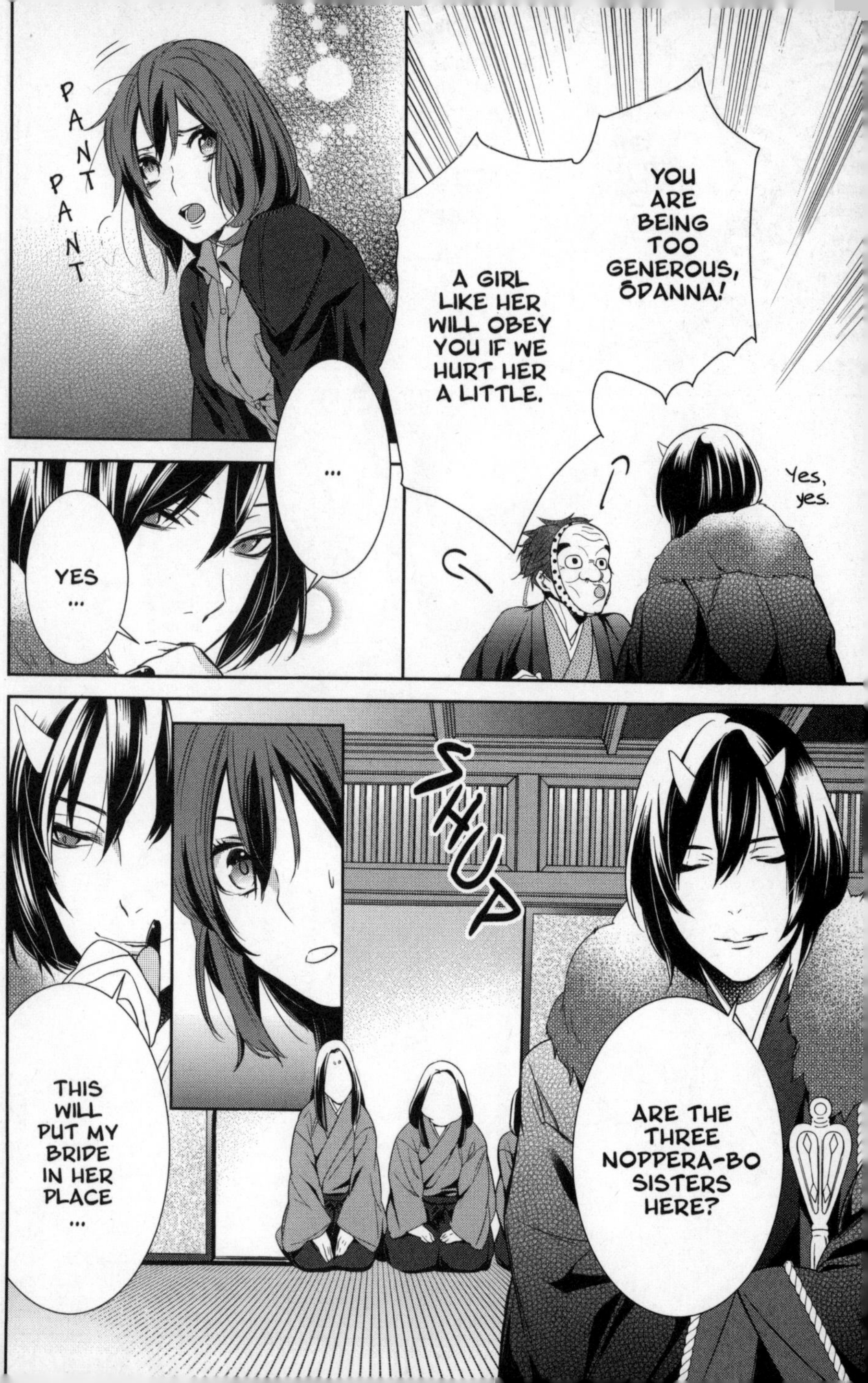
YOU ARE BEING TOO GENEROUS, ŌDANNA!
A GIRL LIKE HER WILL OBEY YOU IF WE HURT HER A LITTLE.
Yes, yes.
PANT PANT
...
YES ...
ARE THE THREE NOPPERA-BO SISTERS HERE?
SHUP
THIS WILL PUT MY BRIDE IN HER PLACE ...

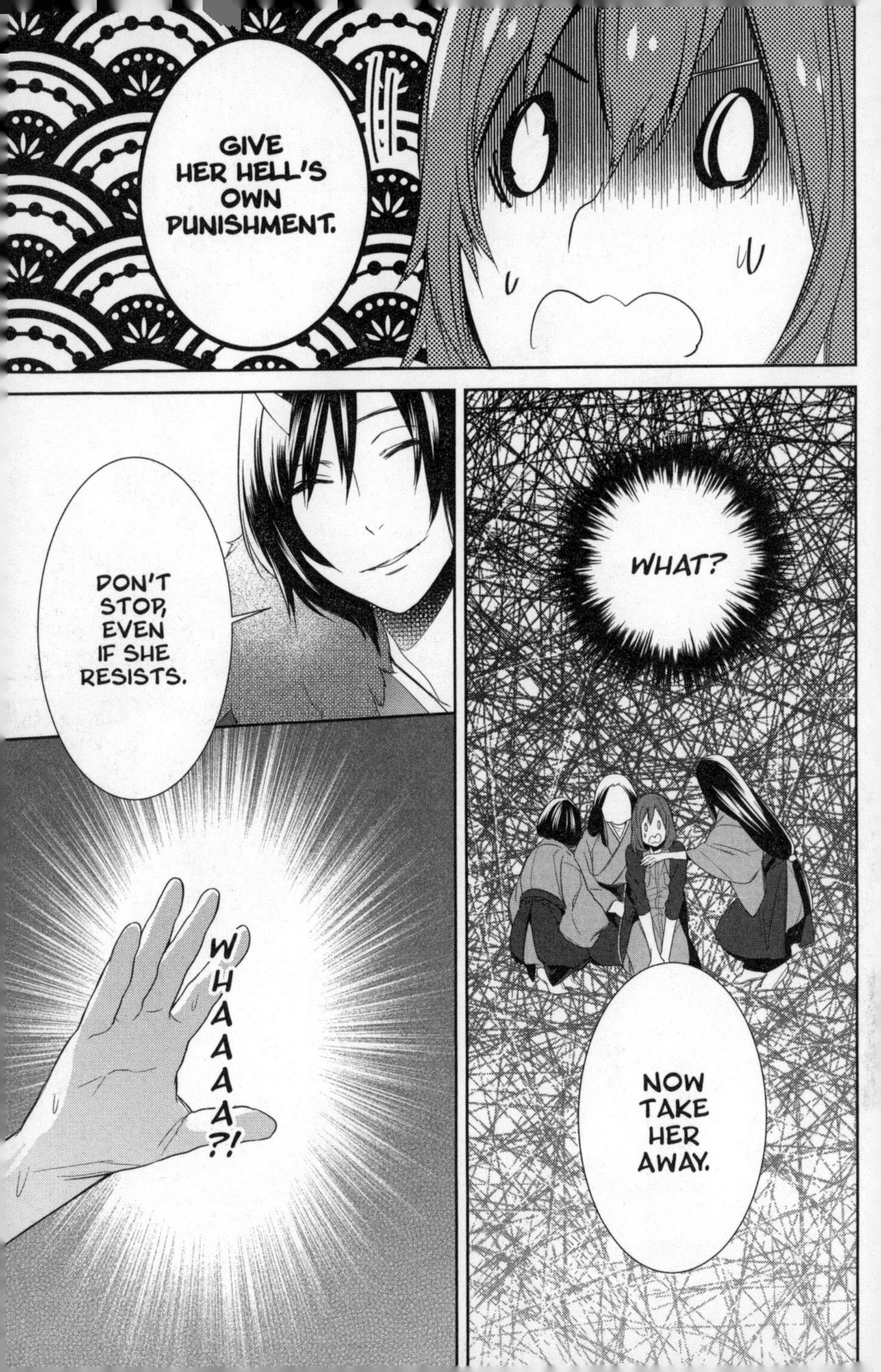
GIVE HER HELL'S OWN PUNISHMENT.
WHAT?
NOW TAKE HER AWAY.
DON'T STOP, EVEN IF SHE RESISTS.
WHAAAAA?!

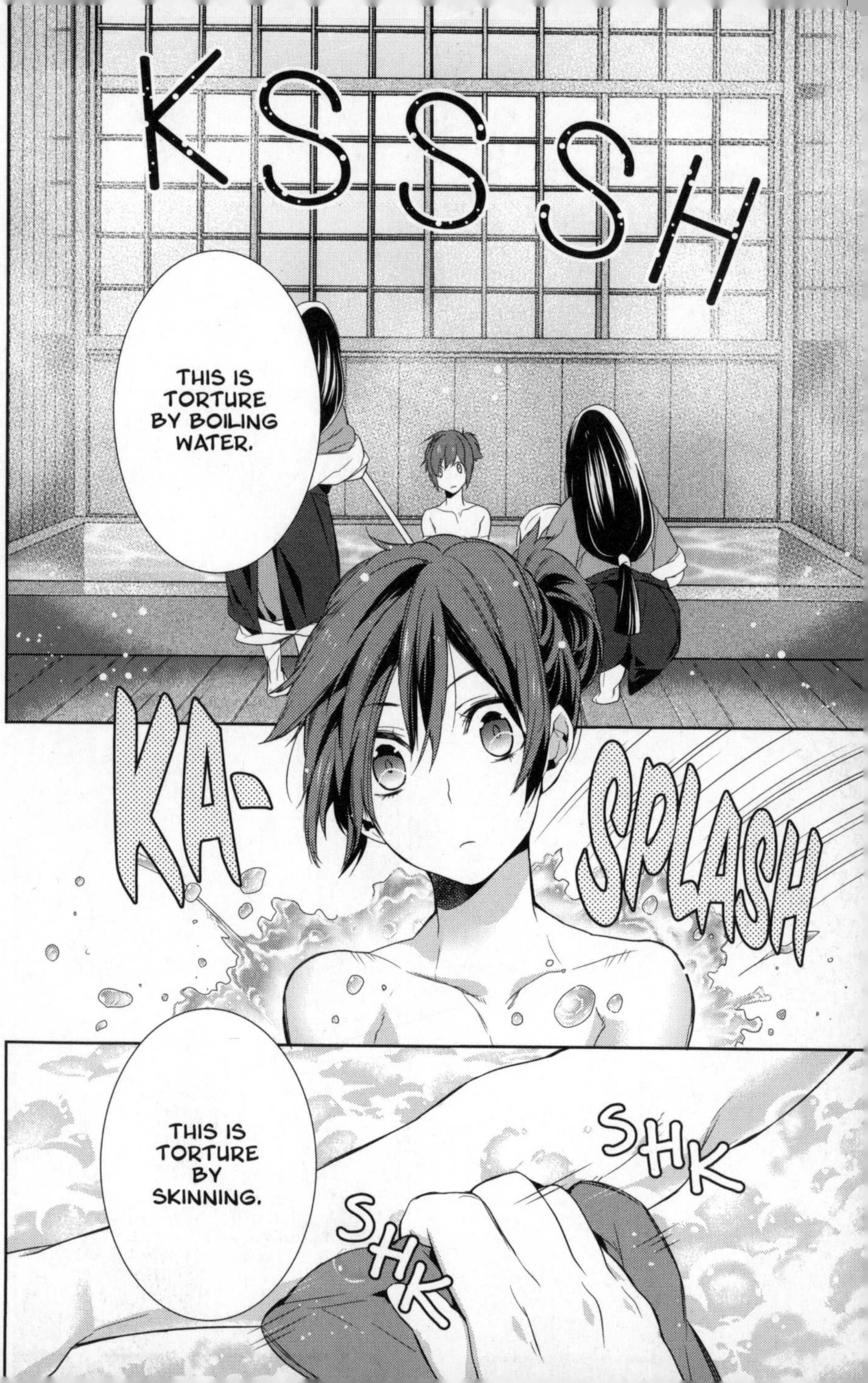
KSSSH
THIS IS TORTURE BY BOILING WATER.
KA-SPLASH
THIS IS TORTURE BY SKINNING.
SHK
SHK

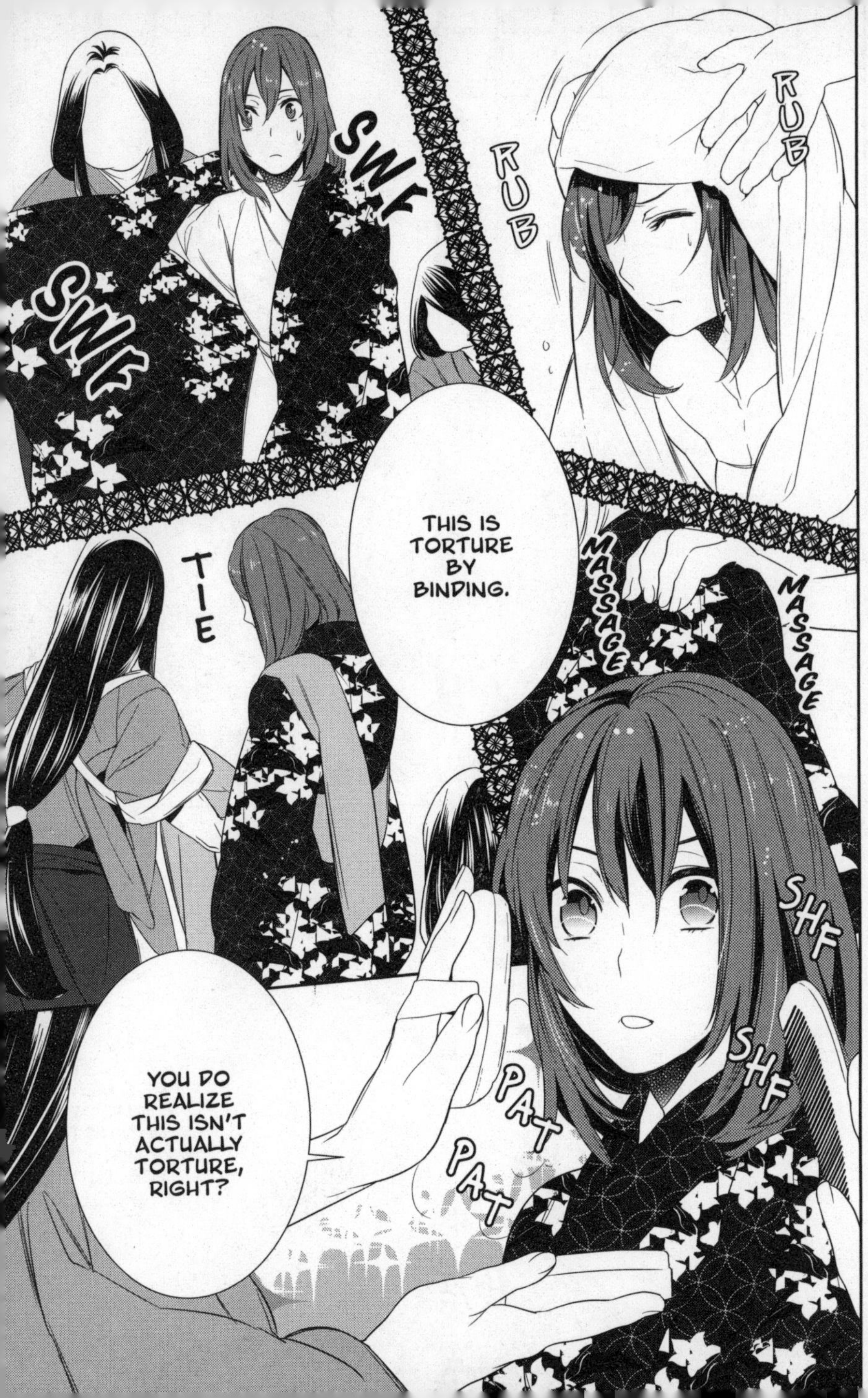

RUB
RUB
SWK
SWK
MASSAGE
MASSAGE
THIS IS TORTURE BY BINDING.
TIE
SHF
SHF
PAT
PAT
YOU DO REALIZE THIS ISN'T ACTUALLY TORTURE, RIGHT?

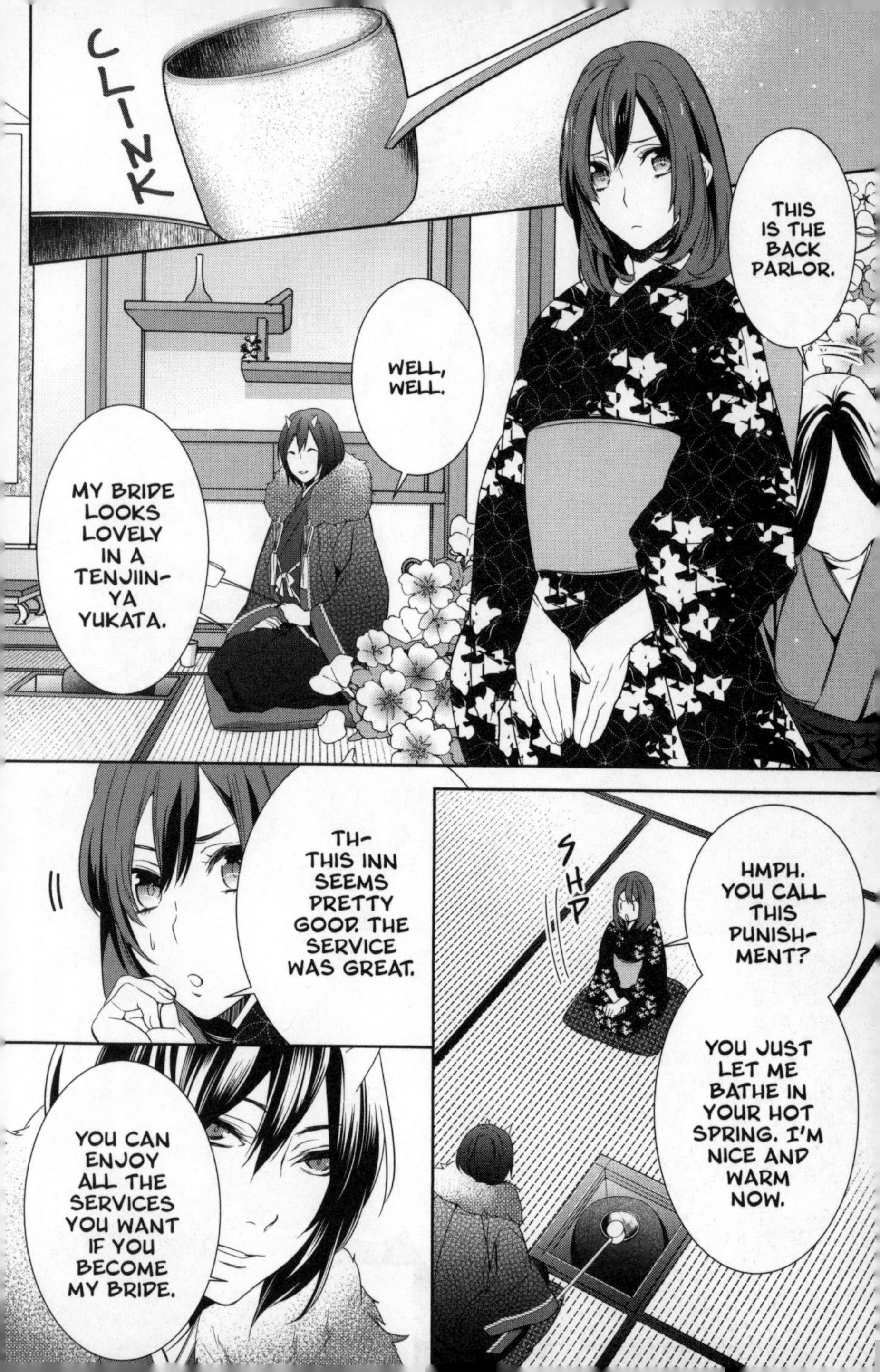

THIS IS THE BACK PARLOR.
CLINK
WELL, WELL.
MY BRIDE LOOKS LOVELY IN A TENJIIN-YA YUKATA.
SHP
HMPH. YOU CALL THIS PUNISH-MENT?
YOU JUST LET ME BATHE IN YOUR HOT SPRING. I'M NICE AND WARM NOW.
TH- THIS INN SEEMS PRETTY GOOD. THE SERVICE WAS GREAT.
YOU CAN ENJOY ALL THE SERVICES YOU WANT IF YOU BECOME MY BRIDE.

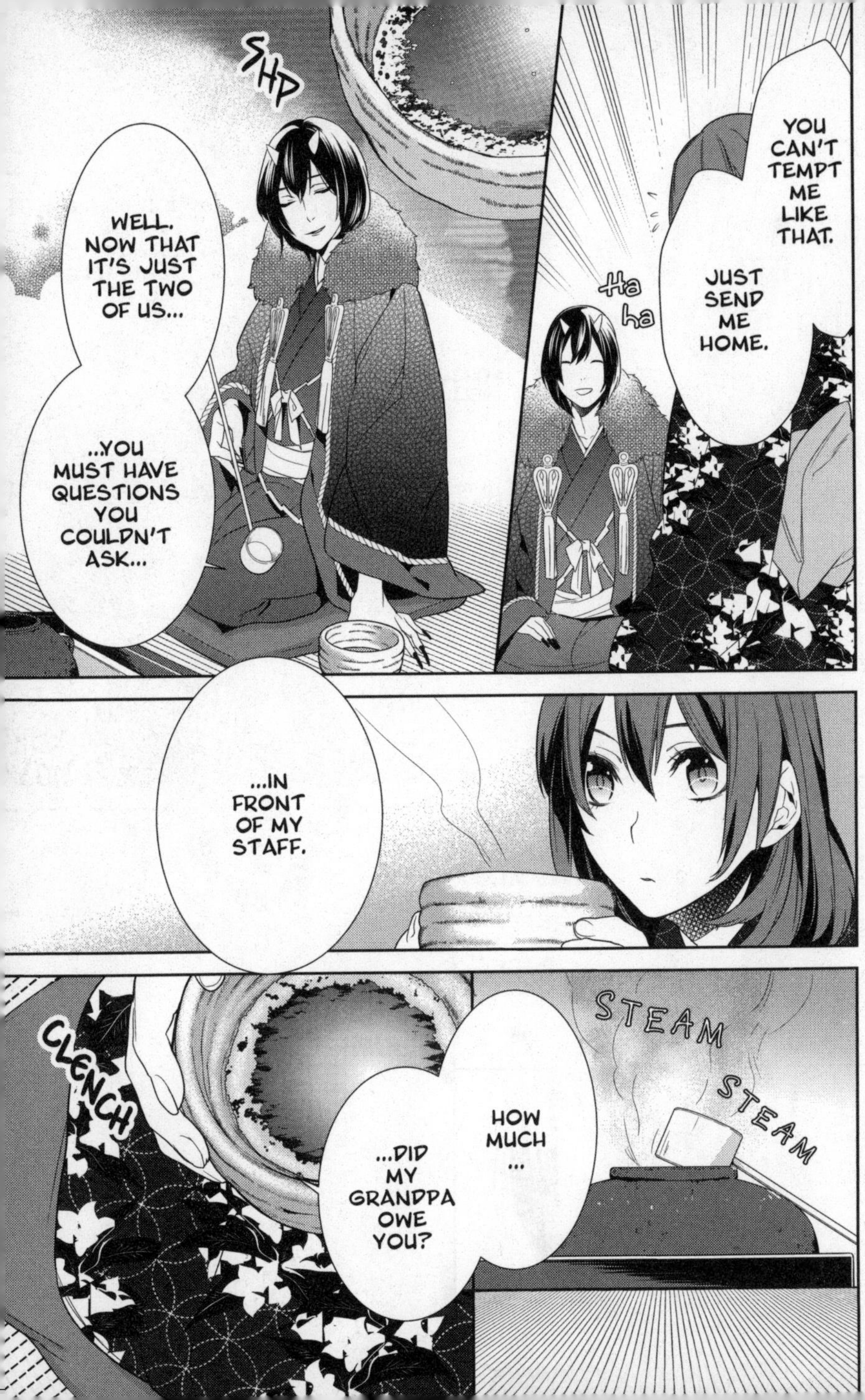
YOU CAN'T TEMPT ME LIKE THAT.
JUST SEND ME HOME.
Ha ha
SHP
WELL. NOW THAT IT'S JUST THE TWO OF US...
...YOU MUST HAVE QUESTIONS YOU COULDN'T ASK...
...IN FRONT OF MY STAFF.
STEAM
STEAM
HOW MUCH ...
...DID MY GRANDPA OWE YOU?
CLENCH

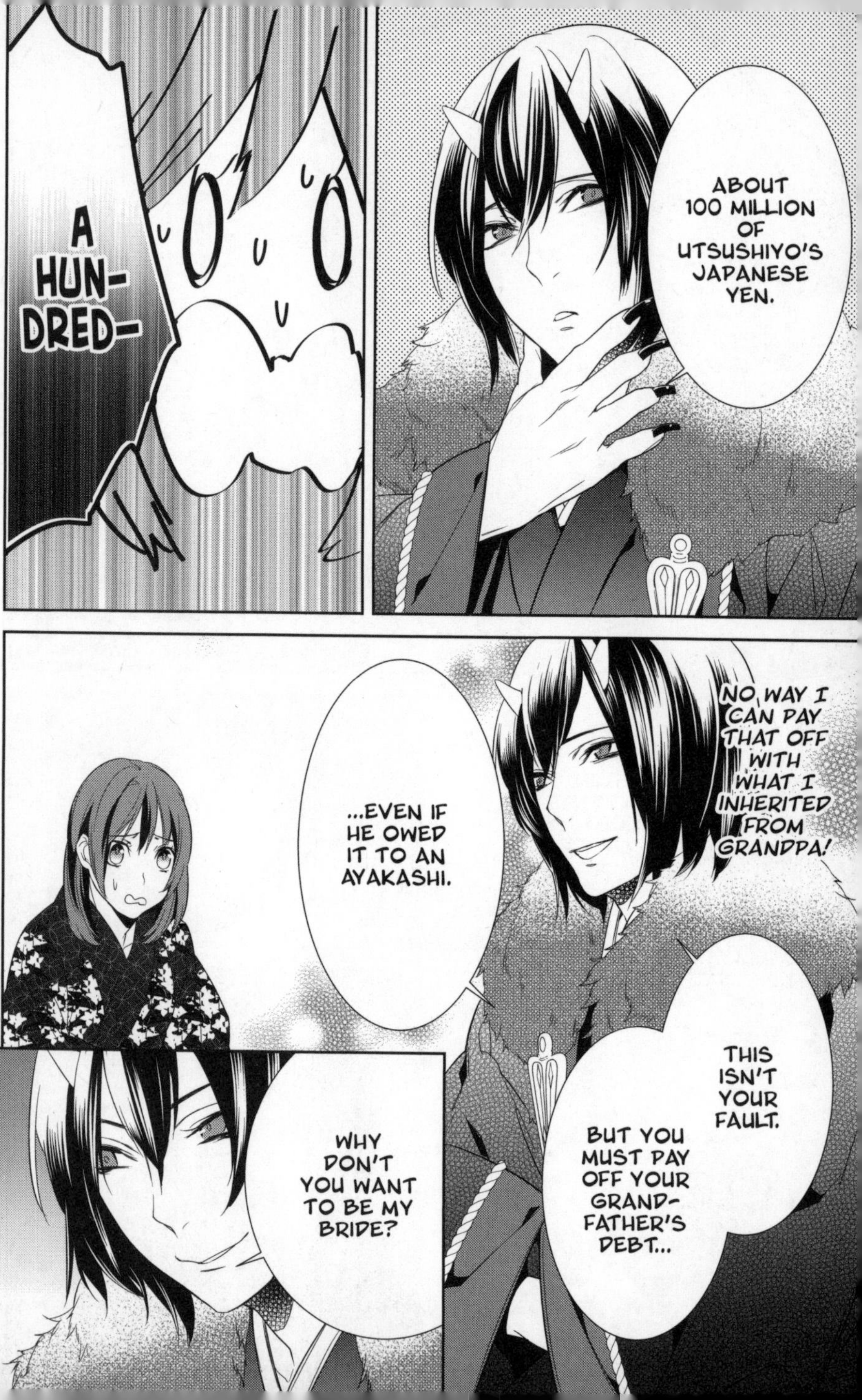
ABOUT 100 MILLION OF UTSUSHIYO'S JAPANESE YEN.
A HUN-DRED-
NO WAY I CAN PAY THAT OFF WITH WHAT I INHERITED FROM GRANDPA!
...EVEN IF HE OWED IT TO AN AYAKASHI.
THIS ISN'T YOUR FAULT.
BUT YOU MUST PAY OFF YOUR GRAND-FATHER'S DEBT...
WHY DON'T YOU WANT TO BE MY BRIDE?

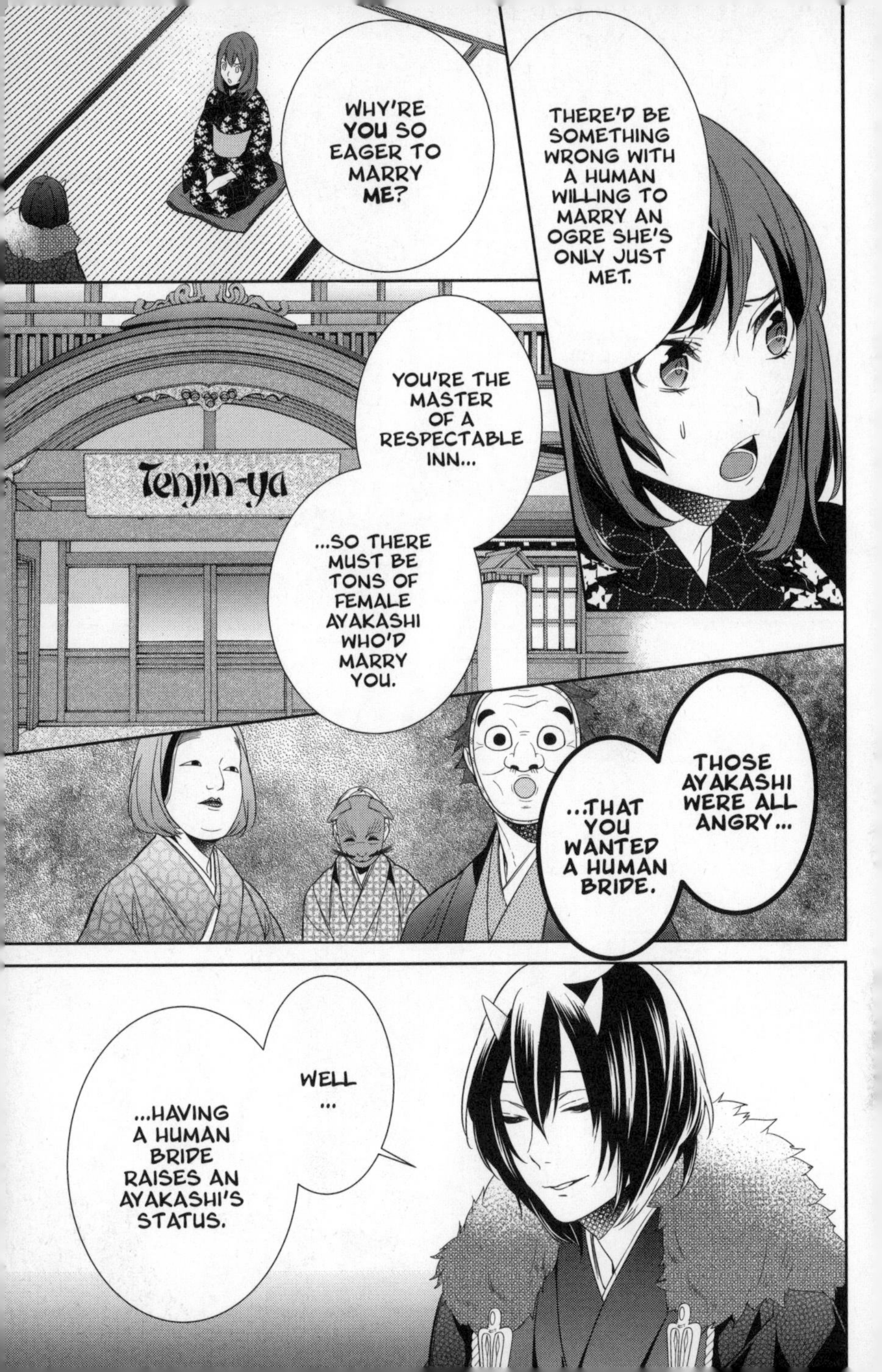
THERE'D BE SOMETHING WRONG WITH A HUMAN WILLING TO MARRY AN OGRE SHE'S ONLY JUST MET.
WHY'RE YOU SO EAGER TO MARRY ME?
YOU'RE THE MASTER OF A RESPECTABLE INN...
...SO THERE MUST BE TONS OF FEMALE AYAKASHI WHO'D MARRY YOU.
Tenjin-ya
THOSE AYAKASHI WERE ALL ANGRY...
...THAT YOU WANTED A HUMAN BRIDE.
WELL ...
...HAVING A HUMAN BRIDE RAISES AN AYAKASHI'S STATUS.

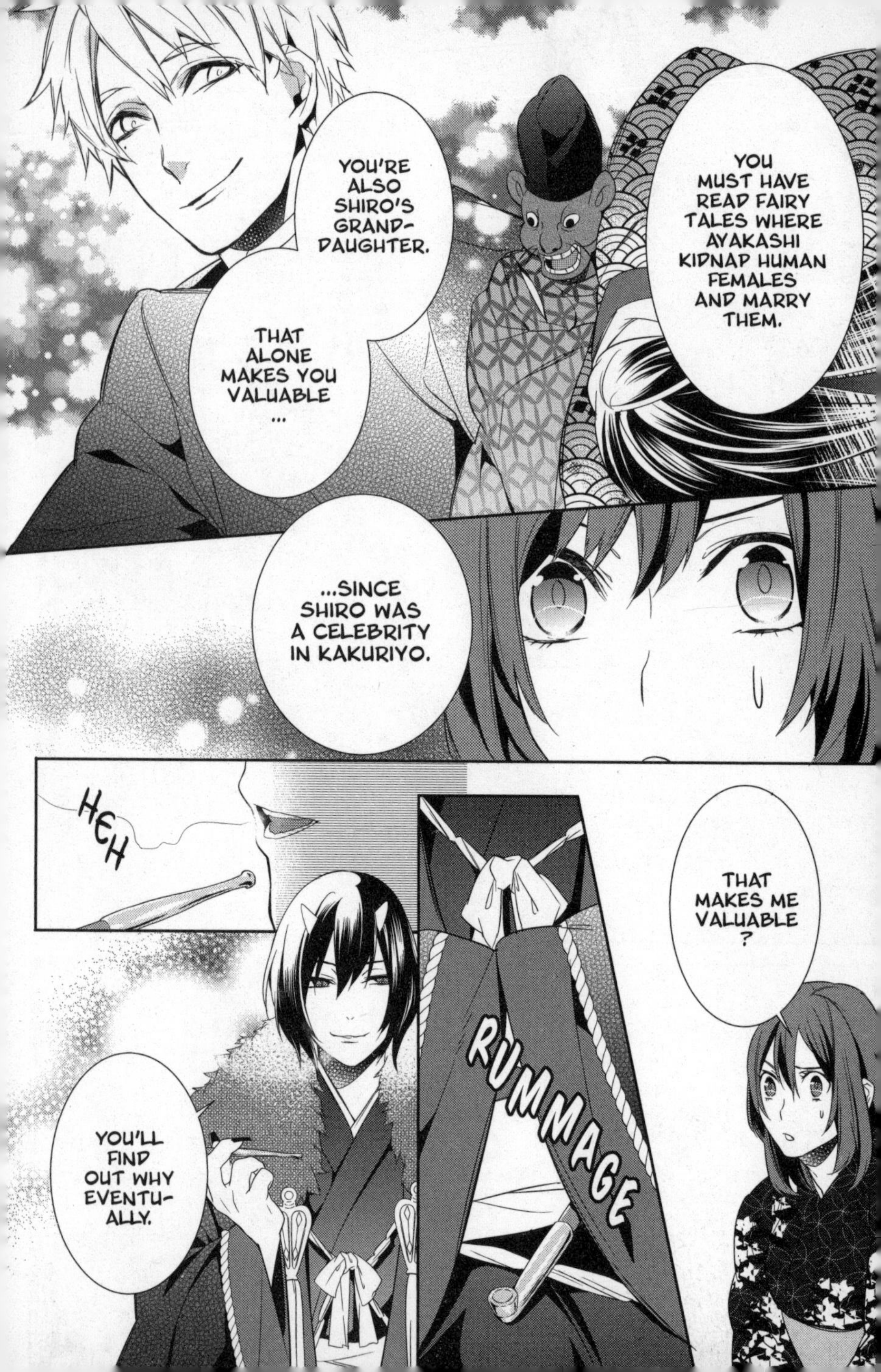
YOU MUST HAVE READ FAIRY TALES WHERE AYAKASHI KIDNAP HUMAN FEMALES AND MARRY THEM.
YOU'RE ALSO SHIRO'S GRAND-DAUGHTER.
THAT ALONE MAKES YOU VALUABLE ...
...SINCE SHIRO WAS A CELEBRITY IN KAKURIYO.
THAT MAKES ME VALUABLE?
RUMMAGE
HEH
YOU'LL FIND OUT WHY EVENTU-ALLY.

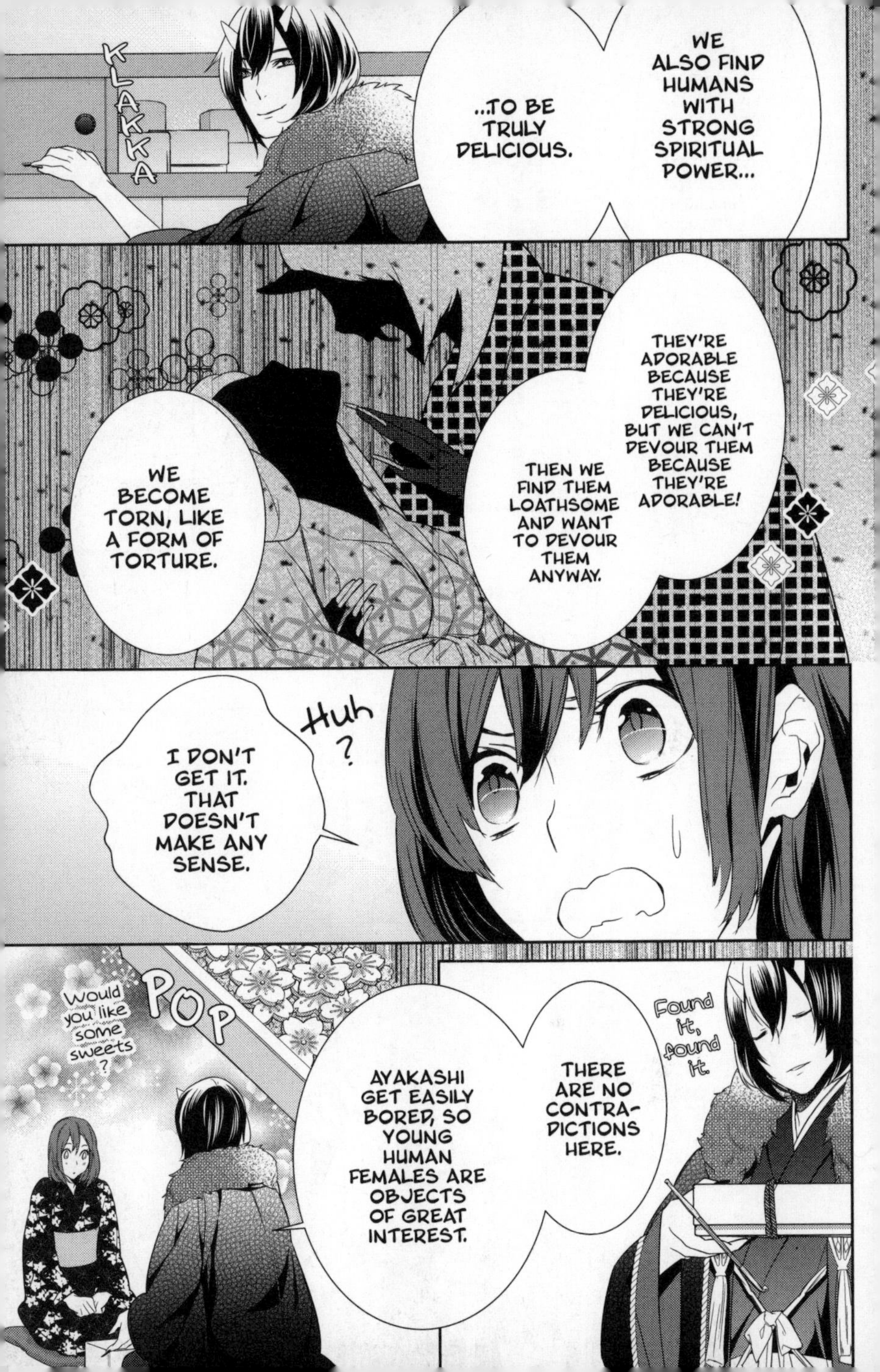
WE ALSO FIND HUMANS WITH STRONG SPIRITUAL POWER...
...TO BE TRULY DELICIOUS.
KLAKKA
THEY'RE ADORABLE BECAUSE THEY'RE DELICIOUS, BUT WE CAN'T DEVOUR THEM BECAUSE THEY'RE ADORABLE!
THEN WE FIND THEM LOATHSOME AND WANT TO DEVOUR THEM ANYWAY.
WE BECOME TORN, LIKE A FORM OF TORTURE.
Huh?
I DON'T GET IT. THAT DOESN'T MAKE ANY SENSE.
Found it, found it.
THERE ARE NO CONTRA-DICTIONS HERE.
AYAKASHI GET EASILY BORED, SO YOUNG HUMAN FEMALES ARE OBJECTS OF GREAT INTEREST.
POP
Would you like some sweets?

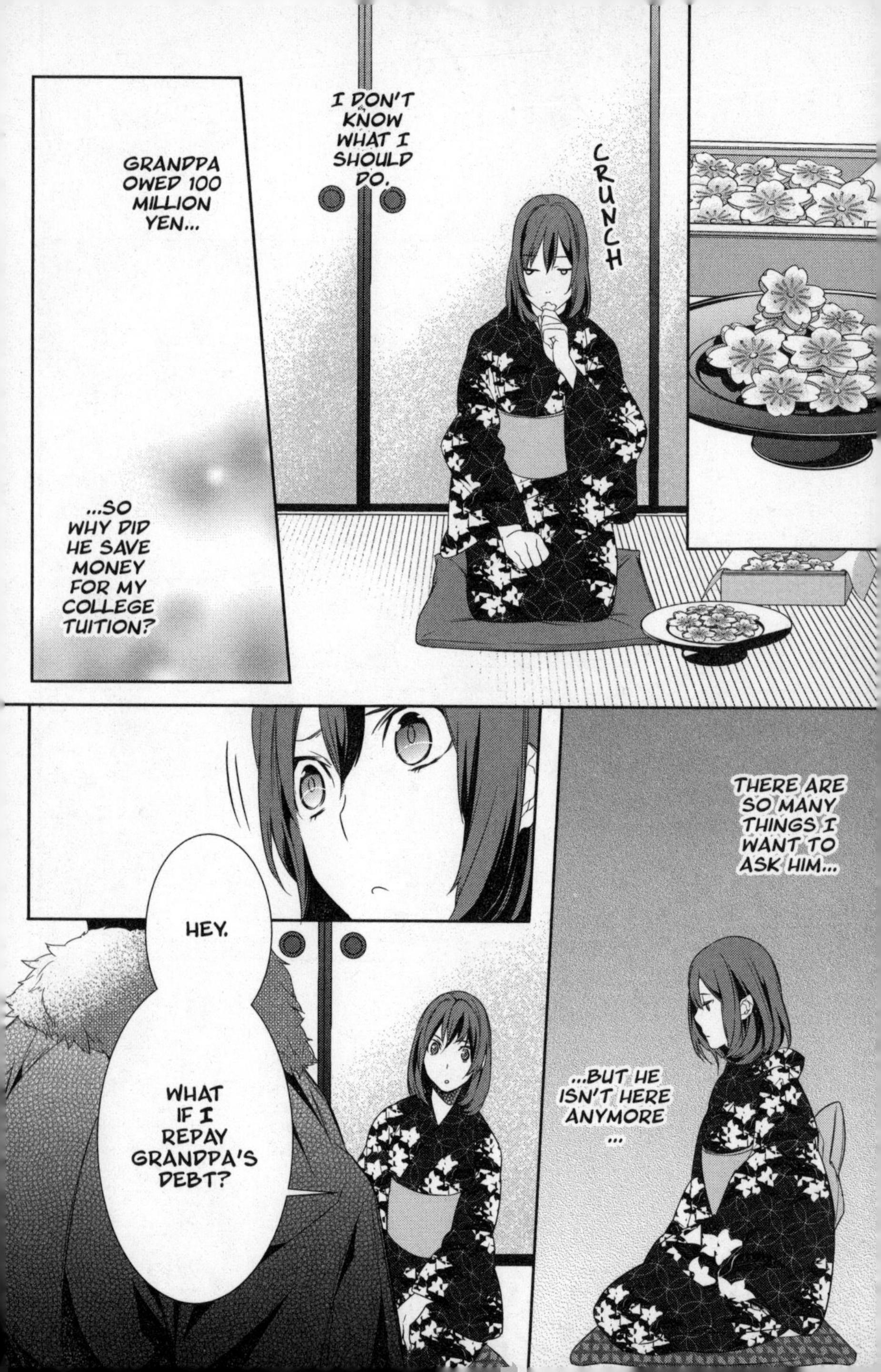
I DON'T KNOW WHAT I SHOULD DO.
CRUNCH
GRANDPA OWED 100 MILLION YEN...
...SO WHY DID HE SAVE MONEY FOR MY COLLEGE TUITION?
THERE ARE SO MANY THINGS I WANT TO ASK HIM...
...BUT HE ISN'T HERE ANYMORE ...
HEY.
WHAT IF I REPAY GRANDPA'S DEBT?

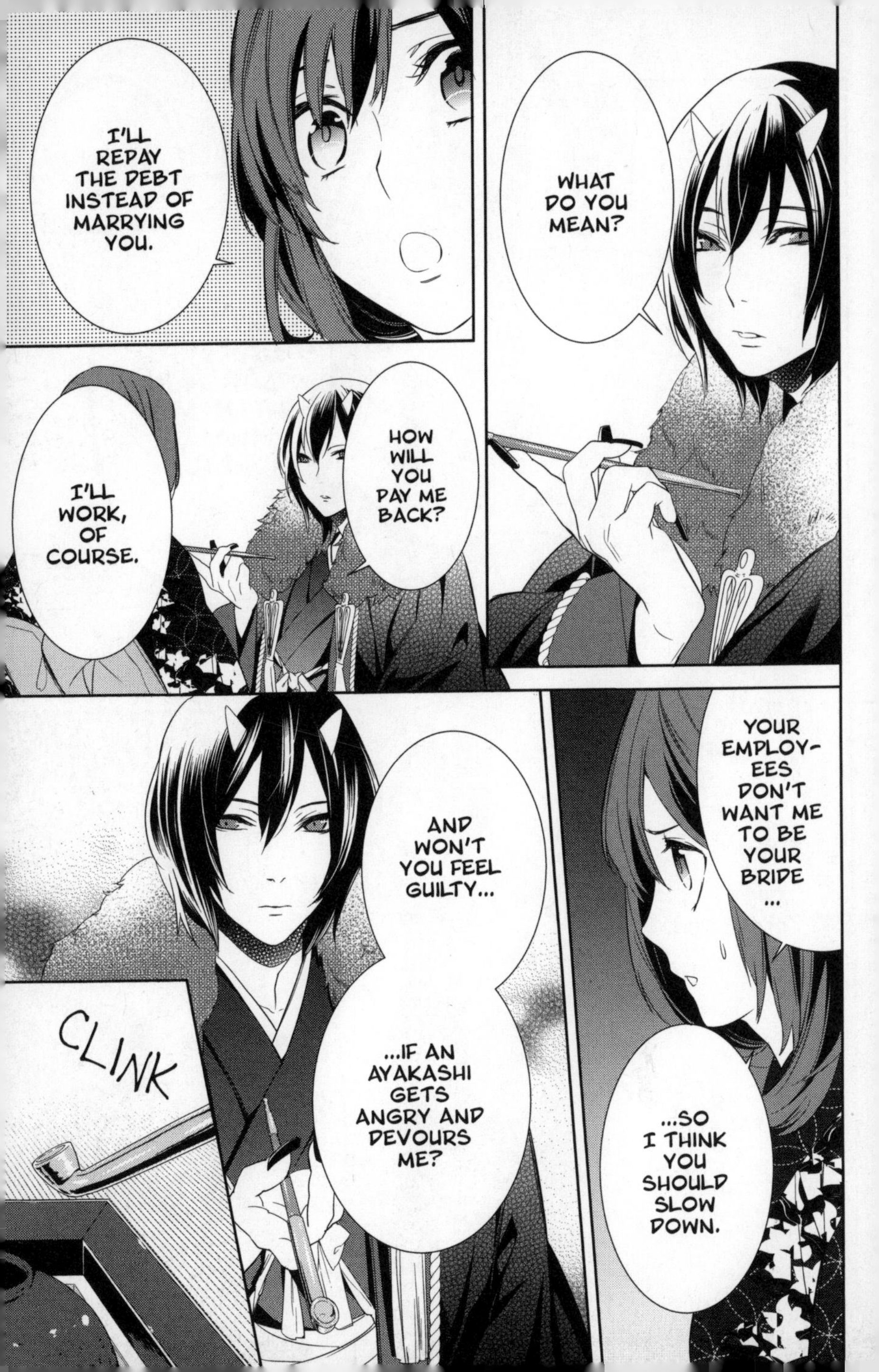
WHAT DO YOU MEAN?
I'LL REPAY THE DEBT INSTEAD OF MARRYING YOU.
HOW WILL YOU PAY ME BACK?
I'LL WORK, OF COURSE.
YOUR EMPLOY-EES DON'T WANT ME TO BE YOUR BRIDE...
...SO I THINK YOU SHOULD SLOW DOWN.
AND WON'T YOU FEEL GUILTY...
...IF AN AYAKASHI GETS ANGRY AND DEVOURS ME?
CLINK

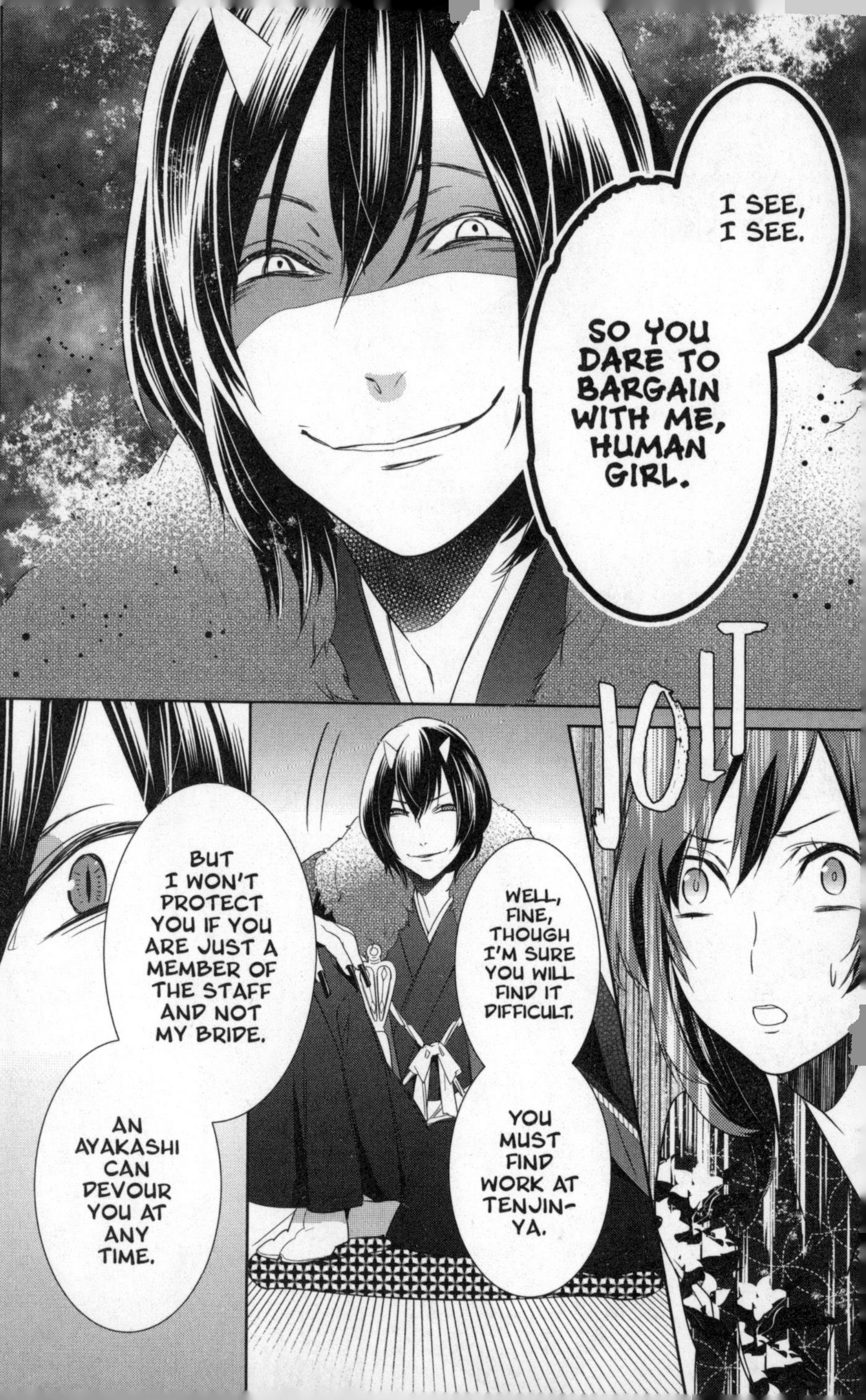
I SEE, I SEE.
SO YOU DARE TO BARGAIN WITH ME, HUMAN GIRL.
JOLT
WELL, FINE, THOUGH I'M SURE YOU WILL FIND IT DIFFICULT.
YOU MUST FIND WORK AT TENJIN-YA.
BUT I WON'T PROTECT YOU IF YOU ARE JUST A MEMBER OF THE STAFF AND NOT MY BRIDE.
AN AYAKASHI CAN DEVOUR YOU AT ANY TIME.

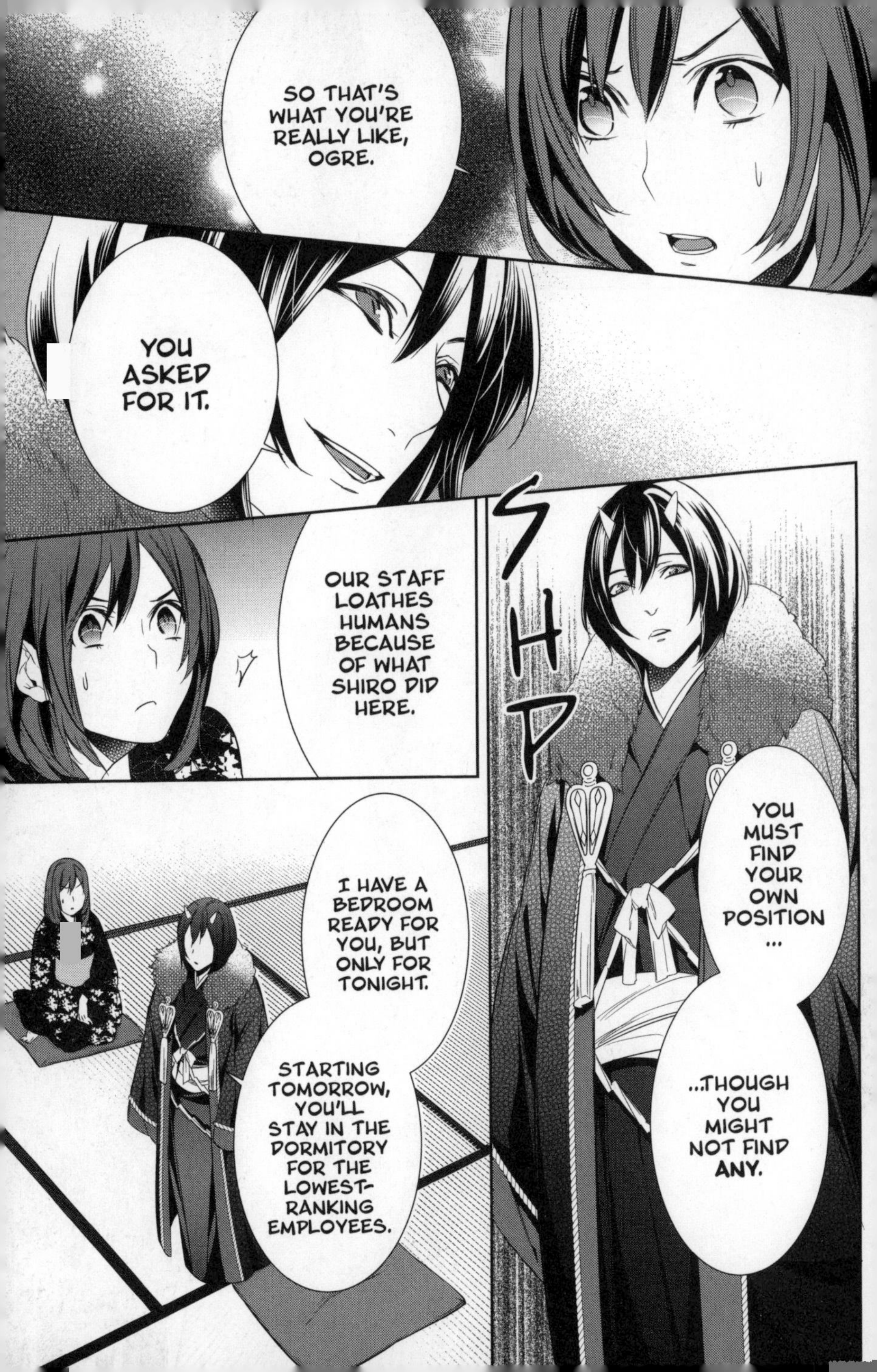
SO THAT'S WHAT YOU'RE REALLY LIKE, OGRE.
YOU ASKED FOR IT.
SHP
YOU MUST FIND YOUR OWN POSITION...
...THOUGH YOU MIGHT NOT FIND ANY.
OUR STAFF LOATHES HUMANS BECAUSE OF WHAT SHIRO DID HERE.
I HAVE A BEDROOM READY FOR YOU, BUT ONLY FOR TONIGHT.
STARTING TOMORROW, YOU'LL STAY IN THE DORMITORY FOR THE LOWEST-RANKING EMPLOYEES.

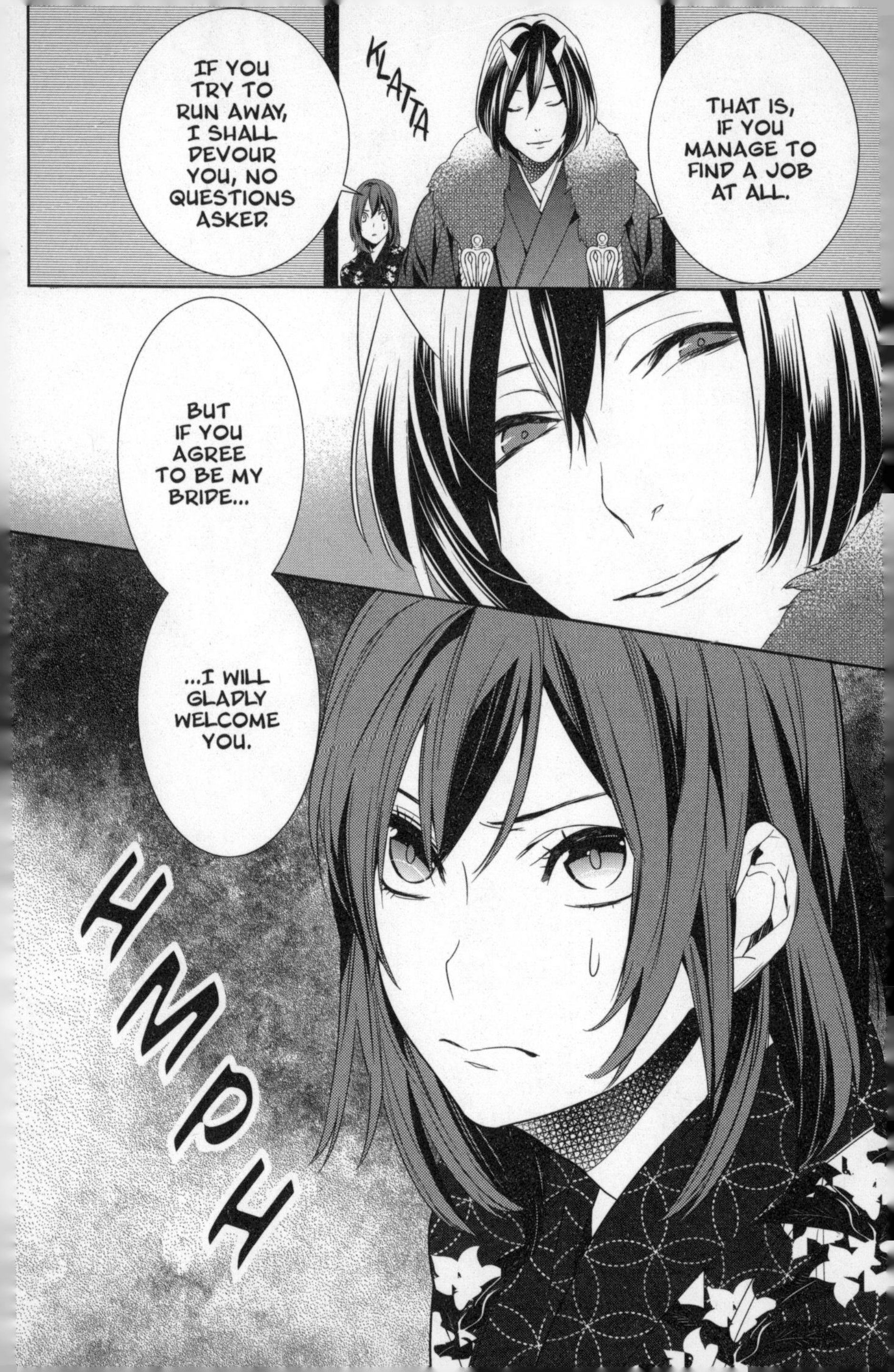
THAT IS, IF YOU MANAGE TO FIND A JOB AT ALL.
KLATTA
IF YOU TRY TO RUN AWAY, I SHALL DEVOUR YOU, NO QUESTIONS ASKED.
BUT IF YOU AGREE TO BE MY BRIDE...
...I WILL GLADLY WELCOME YOU.
HMPH

Kakuriyo

Bed & Breakfast for Spirits

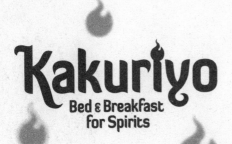

Kakuriyo
Bed & Breakfast
for Spirits

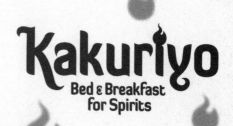

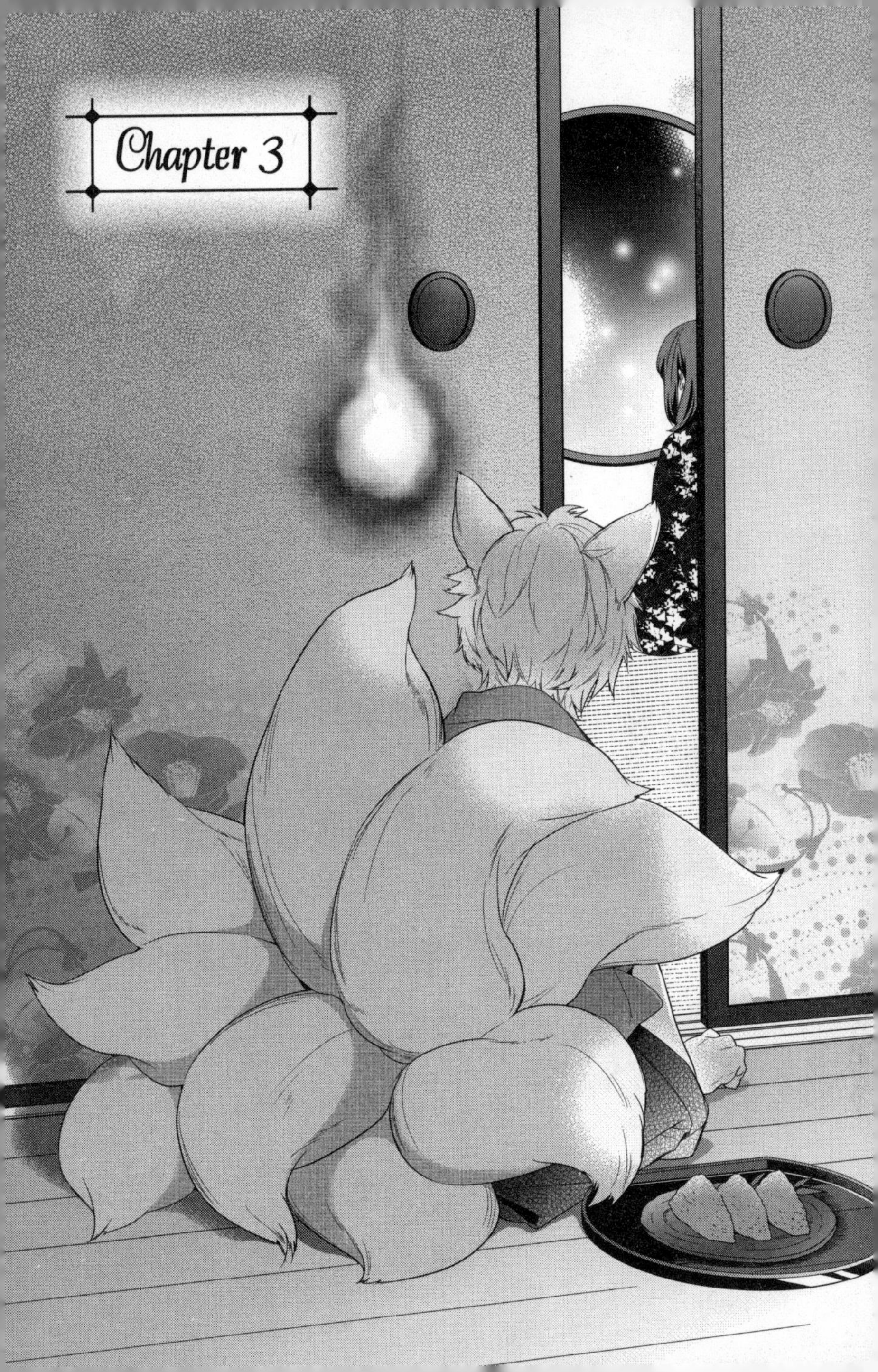
Chapter 3

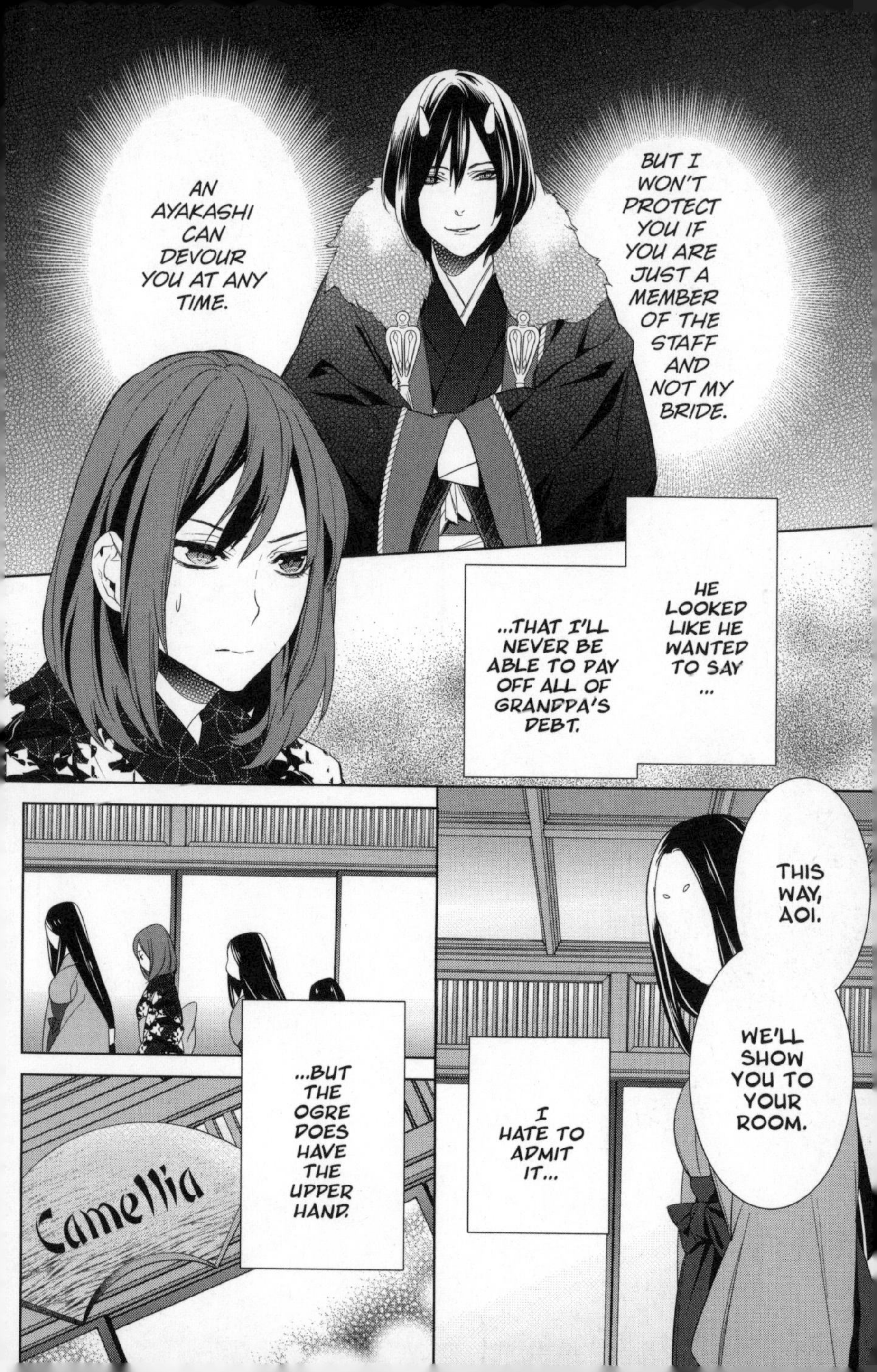
BUT I WON'T PROTECT YOU IF YOU ARE JUST A MEMBER OF THE STAFF AND NOT MY BRIDE.
AN AYAKASHI CAN DEVOUR YOU AT ANY TIME.
HE LOOKED LIKE HE WANTED TO SAY ...
...THAT I'LL NEVER BE ABLE TO PAY OFF ALL OF GRANDPA'S DEBT.
THIS WAY, AOI.
WE'LL SHOW YOU TO YOUR ROOM.
I HATE TO ADMIT IT...
...BUT THE OGRE DOES HAVE THE UPPER HAND.
Camellia

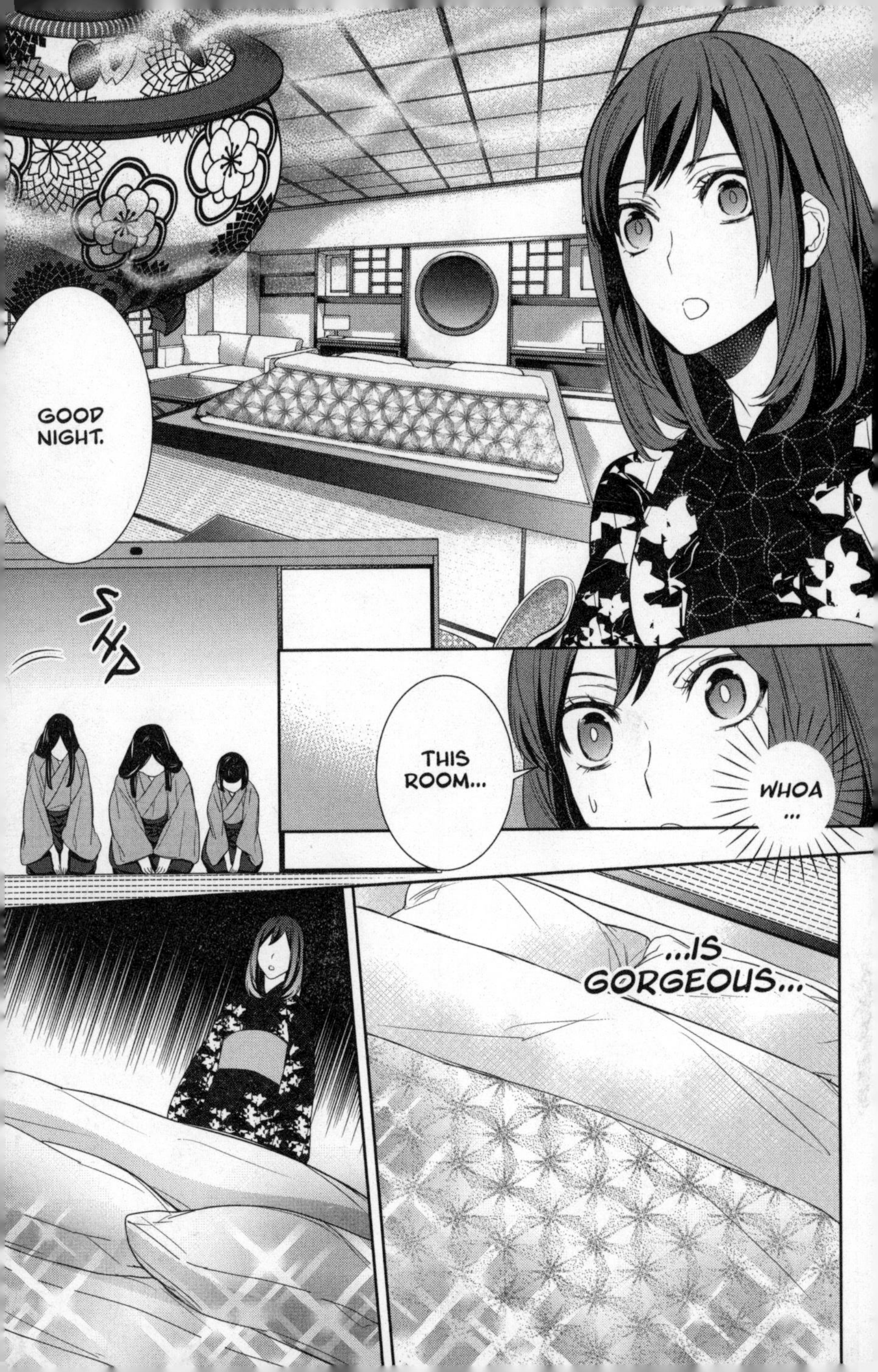
GOOD NIGHT.
WHOA ...
THIS ROOM...
SHP
...IS GORGEOUS...

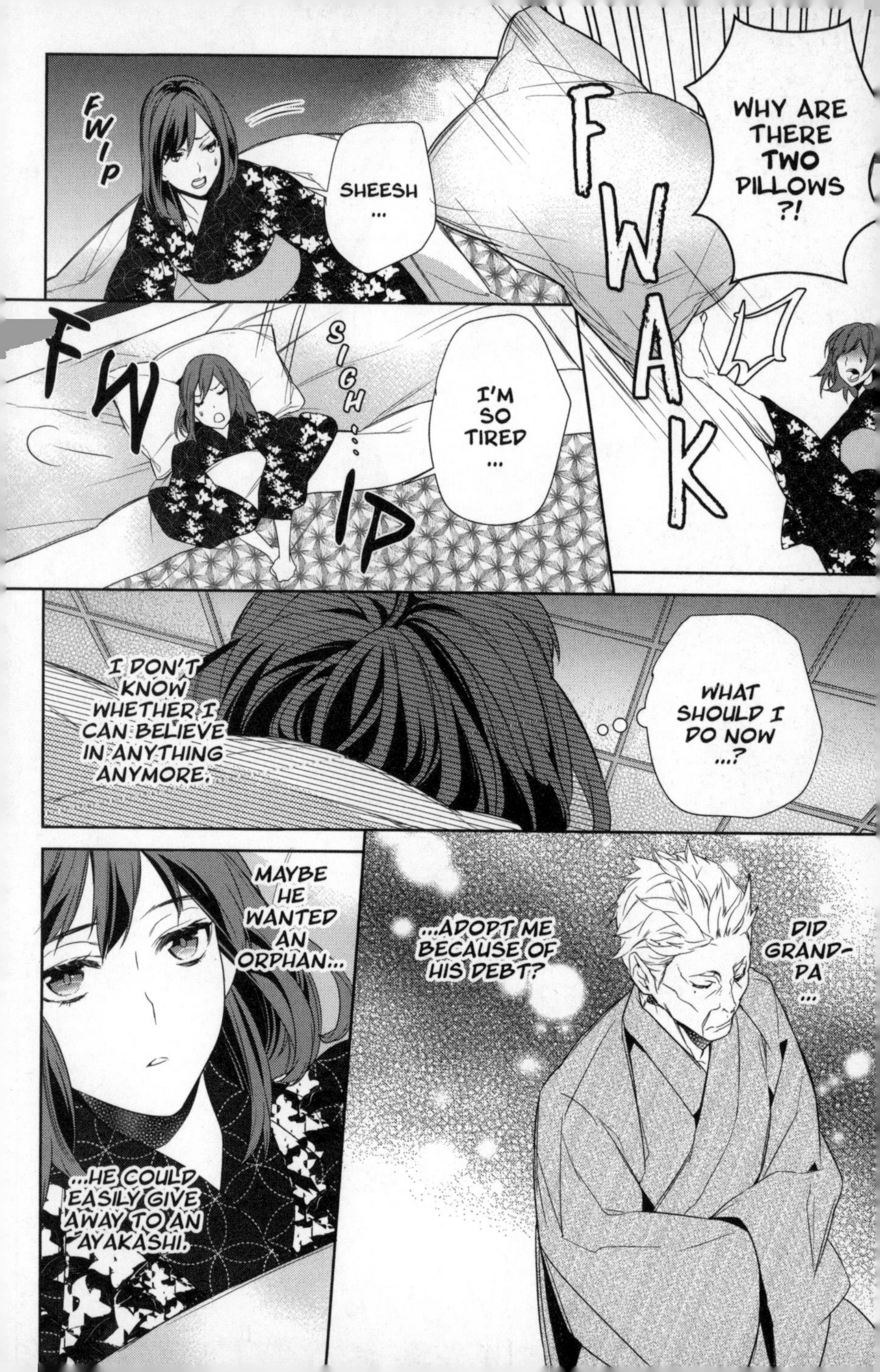
WHY ARE THERE TWO PILLOWS?!
FWAK
SHEESH...
FWIP
I'M SO TIRED...
SIGH...
FWIP
WHAT SHOULD I DO NOW...?
I DON'T KNOW WHETHER I CAN BELIEVE IN ANYTHING ANYMORE.
DID GRANDPA...
...ADOPT ME BECAUSE OF HIS DEBT?
MAYBE HE WANTED AN ORPHAN...
...HE COULD EASILY GIVE AWAY TO AN AYAKASHI.

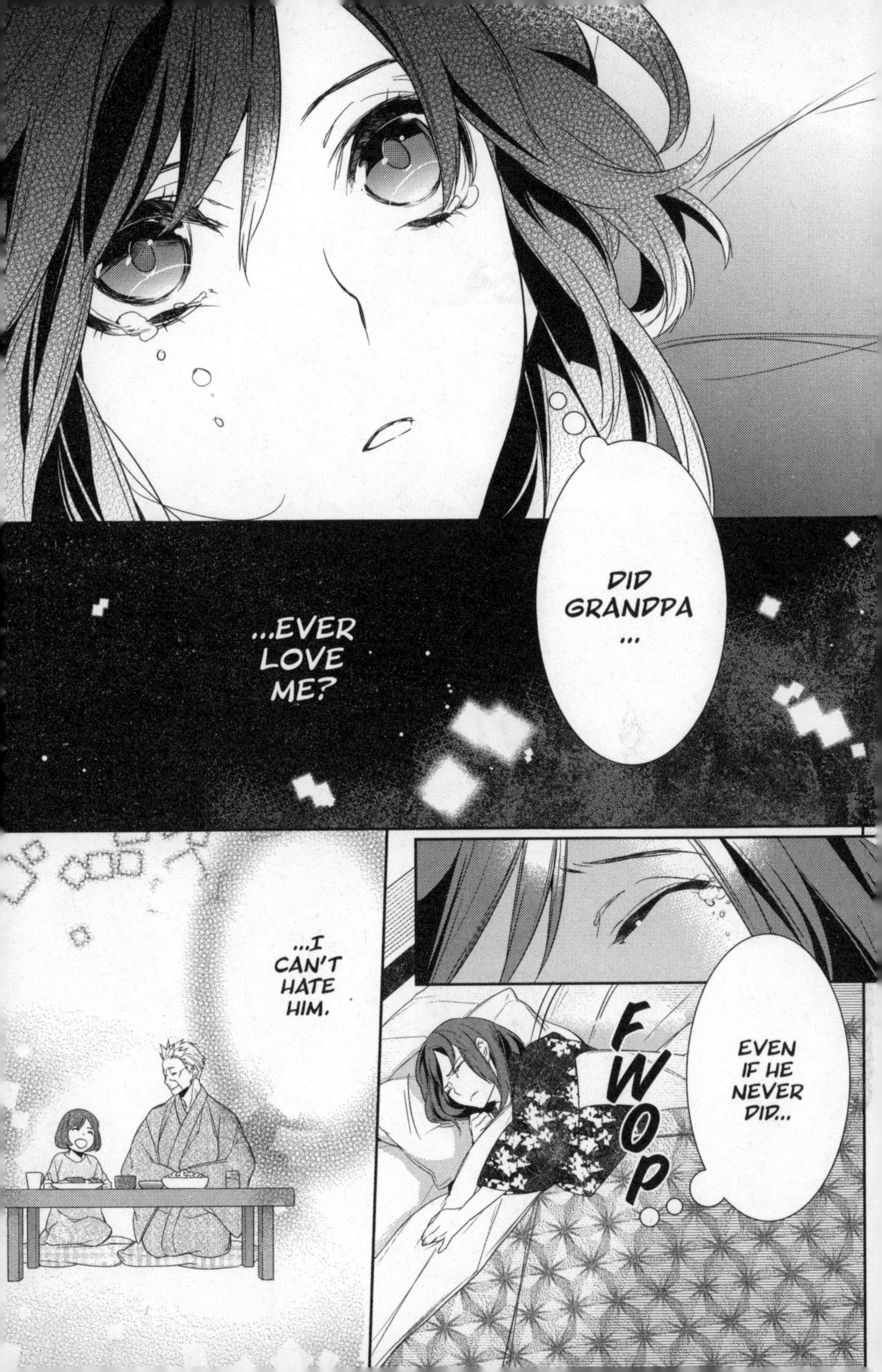
DID GRANDPA ...
...EVER LOVE ME?
EVEN IF HE NEVER DID...
FWOP
...I CAN'T HATE HIM.

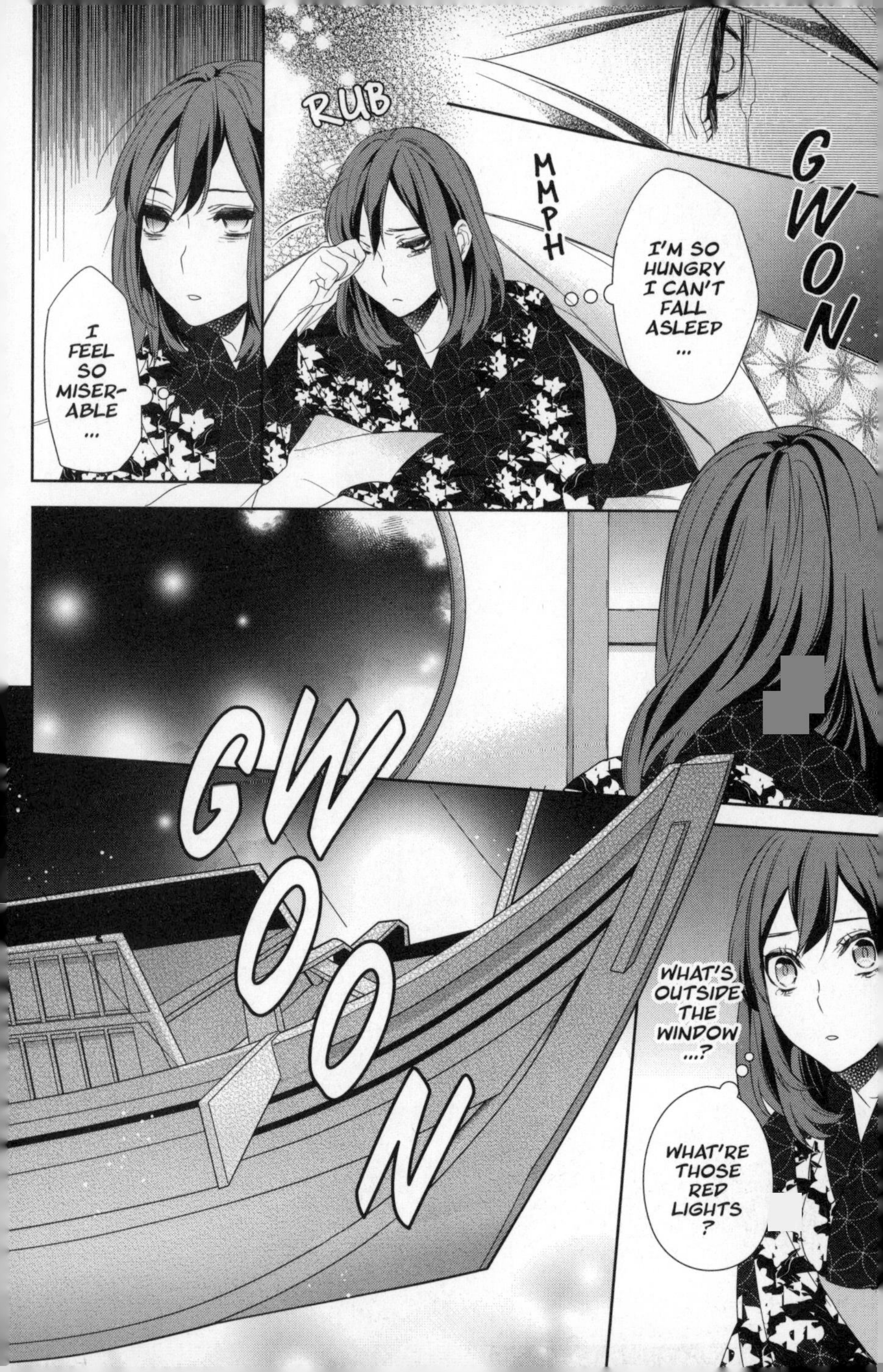
GWON
I'M SO HUNGRY I CAN'T FALL ASLEEP ...
MMPH
RUB
I FEEL SO MISER-ABLE ...
WHAT'S OUTSIDE THE WINDOW ...?
WHAT'RE THOSE RED LIGHTS ?
GWOOON

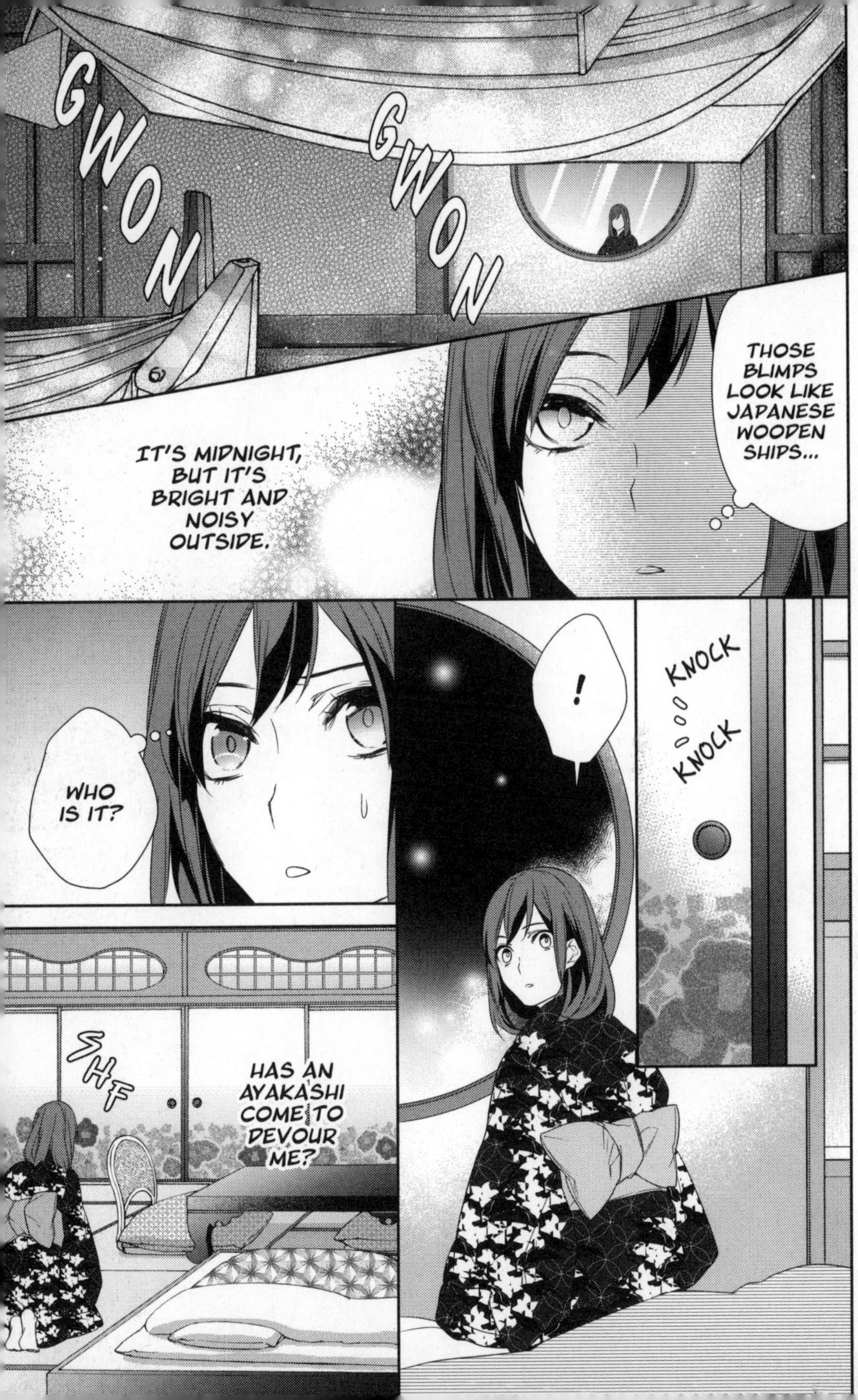
GWON
GWON
THOSE BLIMPS LOOK LIKE JAPANESE WOODEN SHIPS...
IT'S MIDNIGHT, BUT IT'S BRIGHT AND NOISY OUTSIDE.
KNOCK KNOCK
!
WHO IS IT?
SHF
HAS AN AYAKASHI COME TO DEVOUR ME?

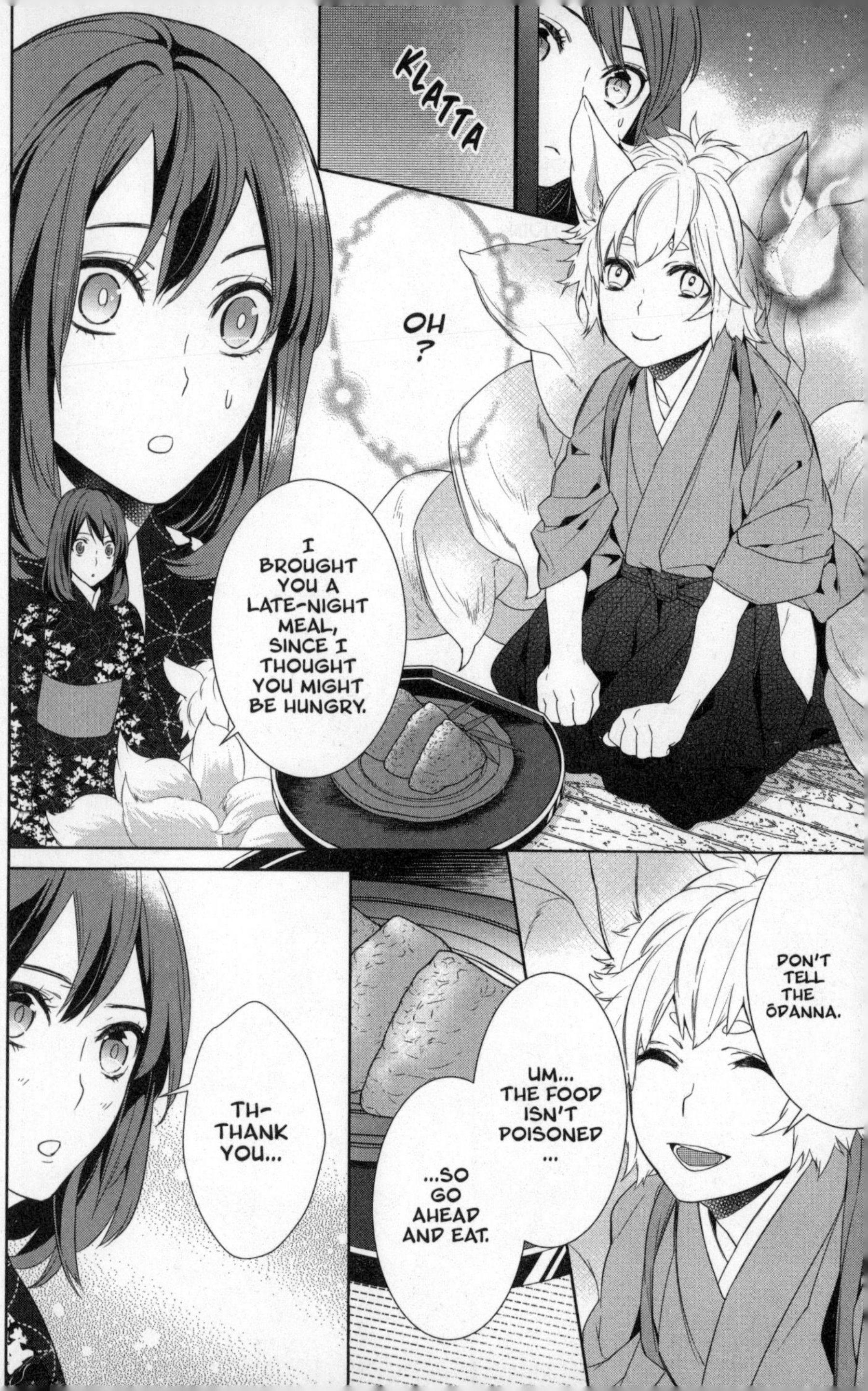
KLATTA
OH?
I BROUGHT YOU A LATE-NIGHT MEAL, SINCE I THOUGHT YOU MIGHT BE HUNGRY.
DON'T TELL THE ŌDANNA.
UM... THE FOOD ISN'T POISONED...
...SO GO AHEAD AND EAT.
TH-THANK YOU...

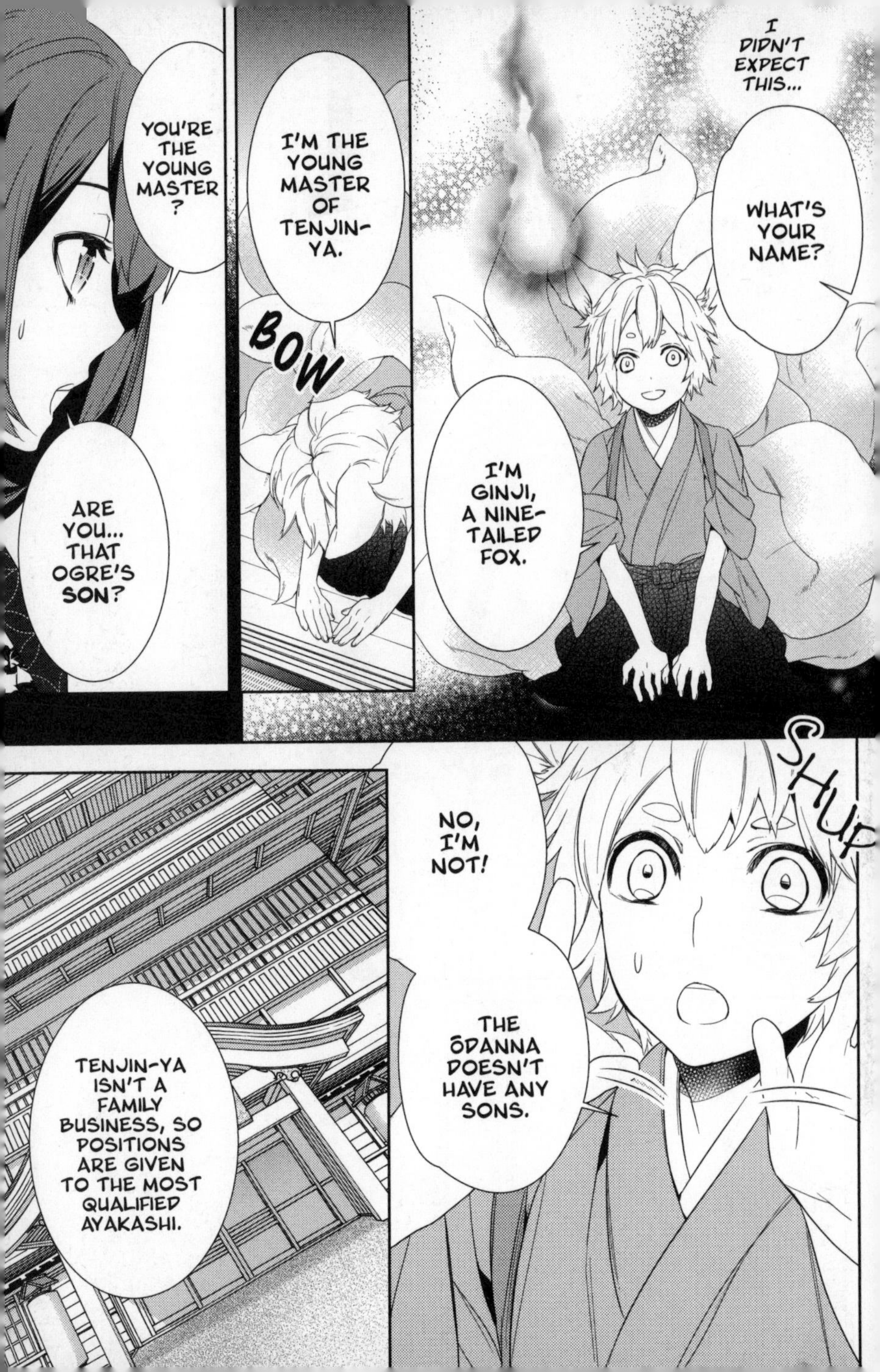
I DIDN'T EXPECT THIS...
WHAT'S YOUR NAME?
I'M GINJI, A NINE-TAILED FOX.
I'M THE YOUNG MASTER OF TENJIN-YA.
BOW
YOU'RE THE YOUNG MASTER?
ARE YOU... THAT OGRE'S SON?
SHUP
NO, I'M NOT!
THE ŌDANNA DOESN'T HAVE ANY SONS.
TENJIN-YA ISN'T A FAMILY BUSINESS, SO POSITIONS ARE GIVEN TO THE MOST QUALIFIED AYAKASHI.

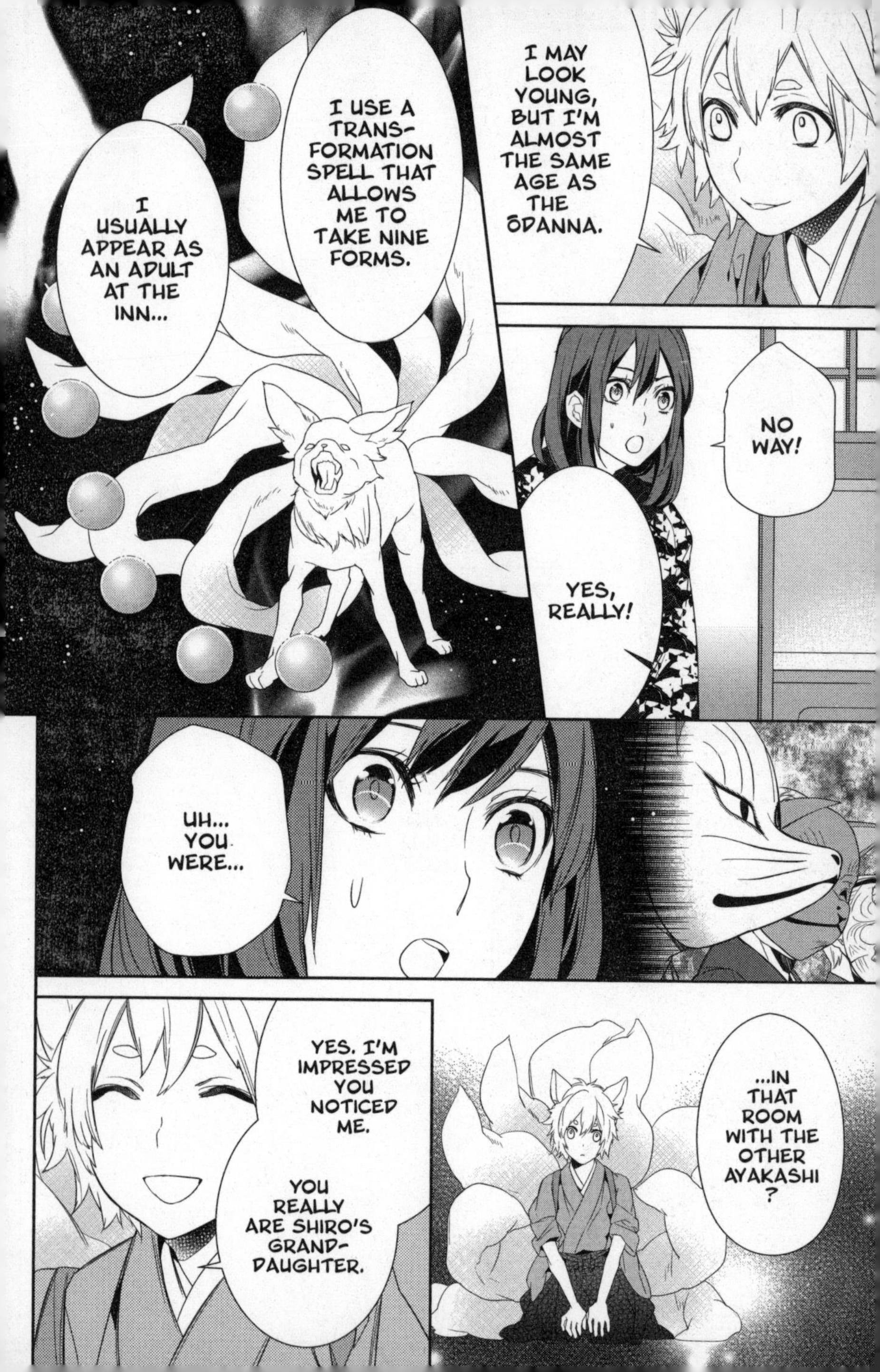
I MAY LOOK YOUNG, BUT I'M ALMOST THE SAME AGE AS THE ŌDANNA.
NO WAY!
YES, REALLY!
I USE A TRANSFORMATION SPELL THAT ALLOWS ME TO TAKE NINE FORMS.
I USUALLY APPEAR AS AN ADULT AT THE INN...
UH... YOU WERE...
...IN THAT ROOM WITH THE OTHER AYAKASHI?
YES. I'M IMPRESSED YOU NOTICED ME.
YOU REALLY ARE SHIRO'S GRANDDAUGHTER.

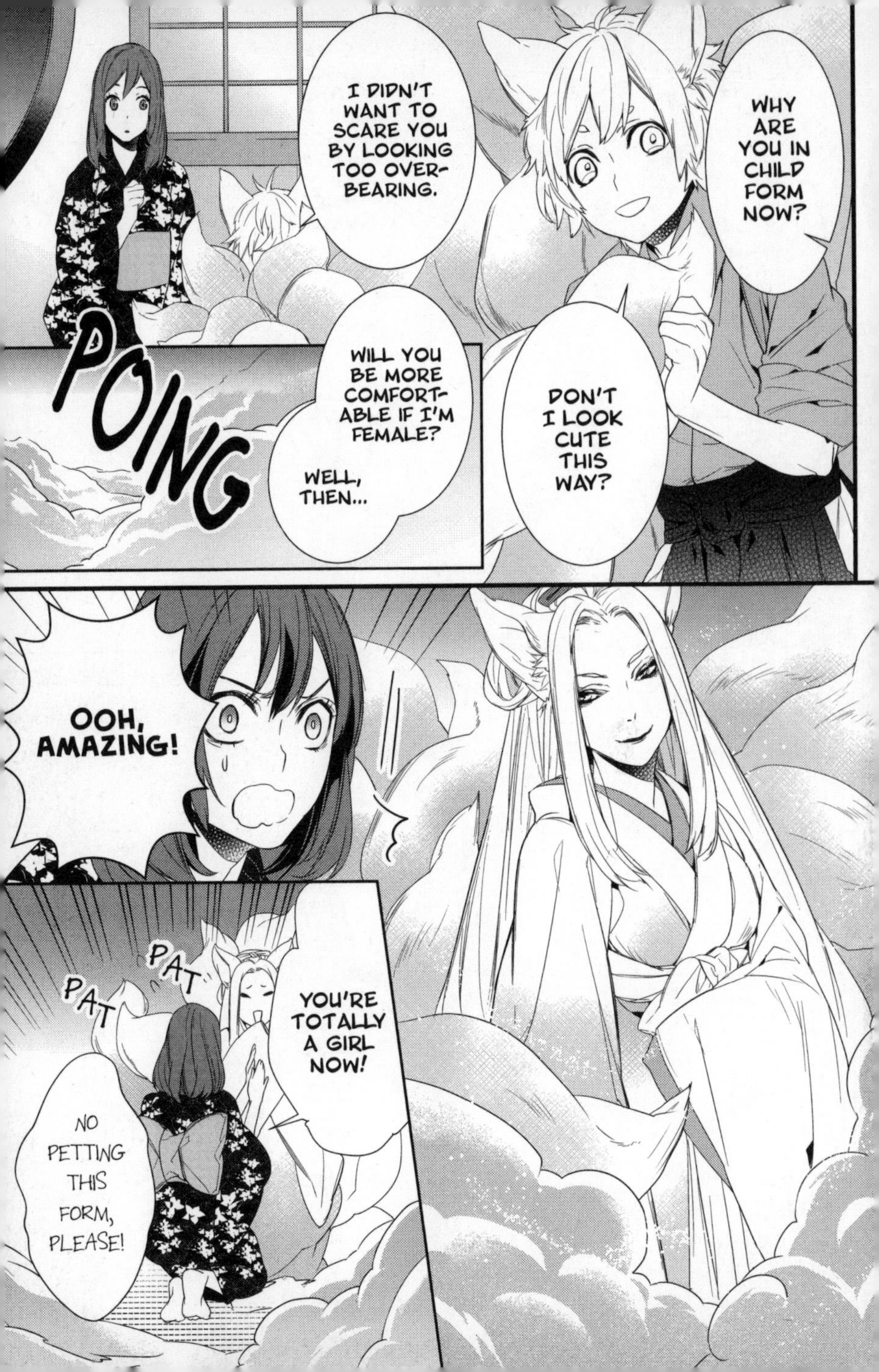
WHY ARE YOU IN CHILD FORM NOW?
I DIDN'T WANT TO SCARE YOU BY LOOKING TOO OVER-BEARING.
DON'T I LOOK CUTE THIS WAY?
WILL YOU BE MORE COMFORT-ABLE IF I'M FEMALE?
WELL, THEN...
POING
OOH, AMAZING!
YOU'RE TOTALLY A GIRL NOW!
PAT PAT
NO PETTING THIS FORM, PLEASE!

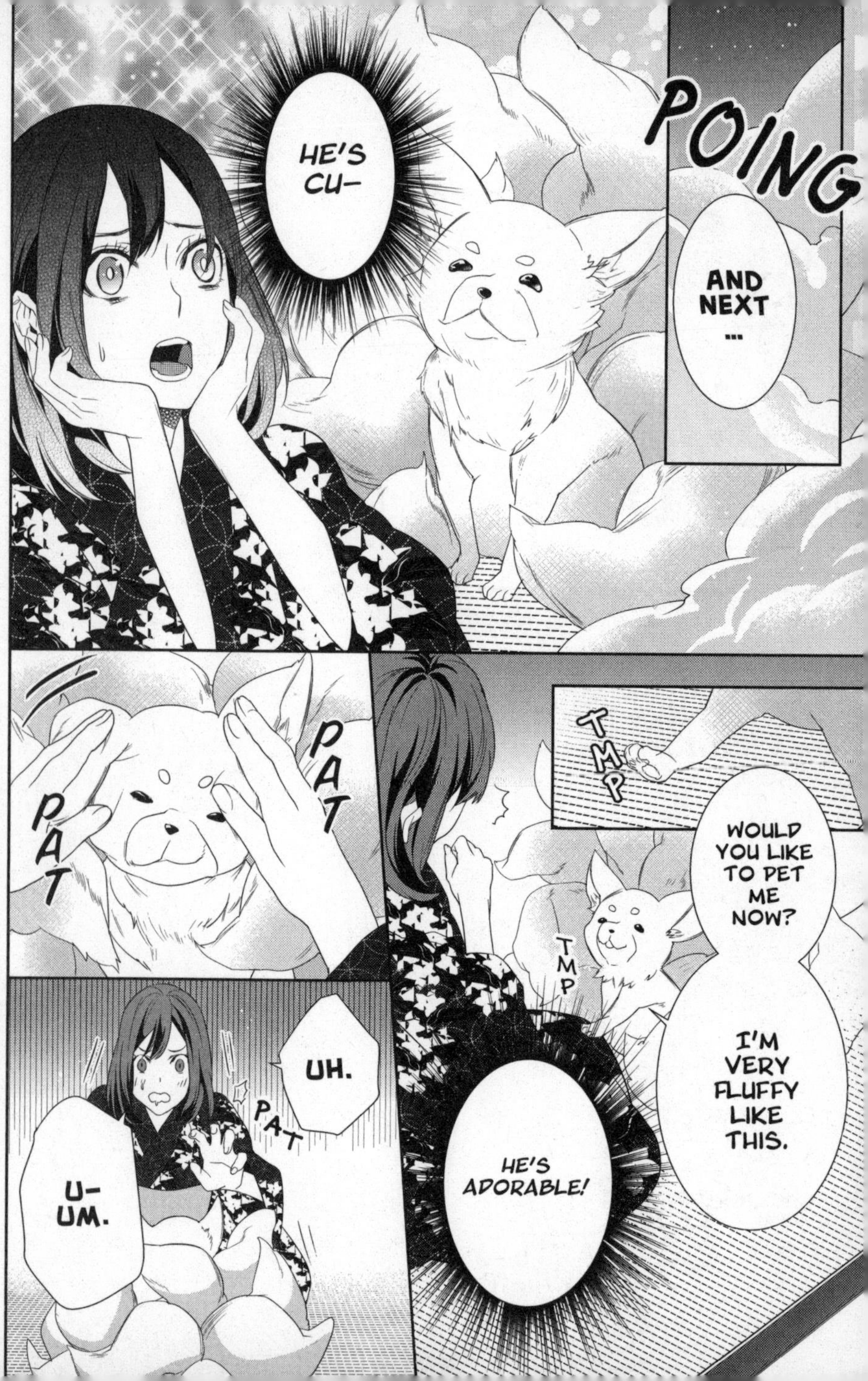
POING
AND NEXT ...
HE'S CU-
TMP
WOULD YOU LIKE TO PET ME NOW?
I'M VERY FLUFFY LIKE THIS.
TMP
HE'S ADORABLE!
PAT PAT
PAT PAT
UH.
PAT
U-UM.

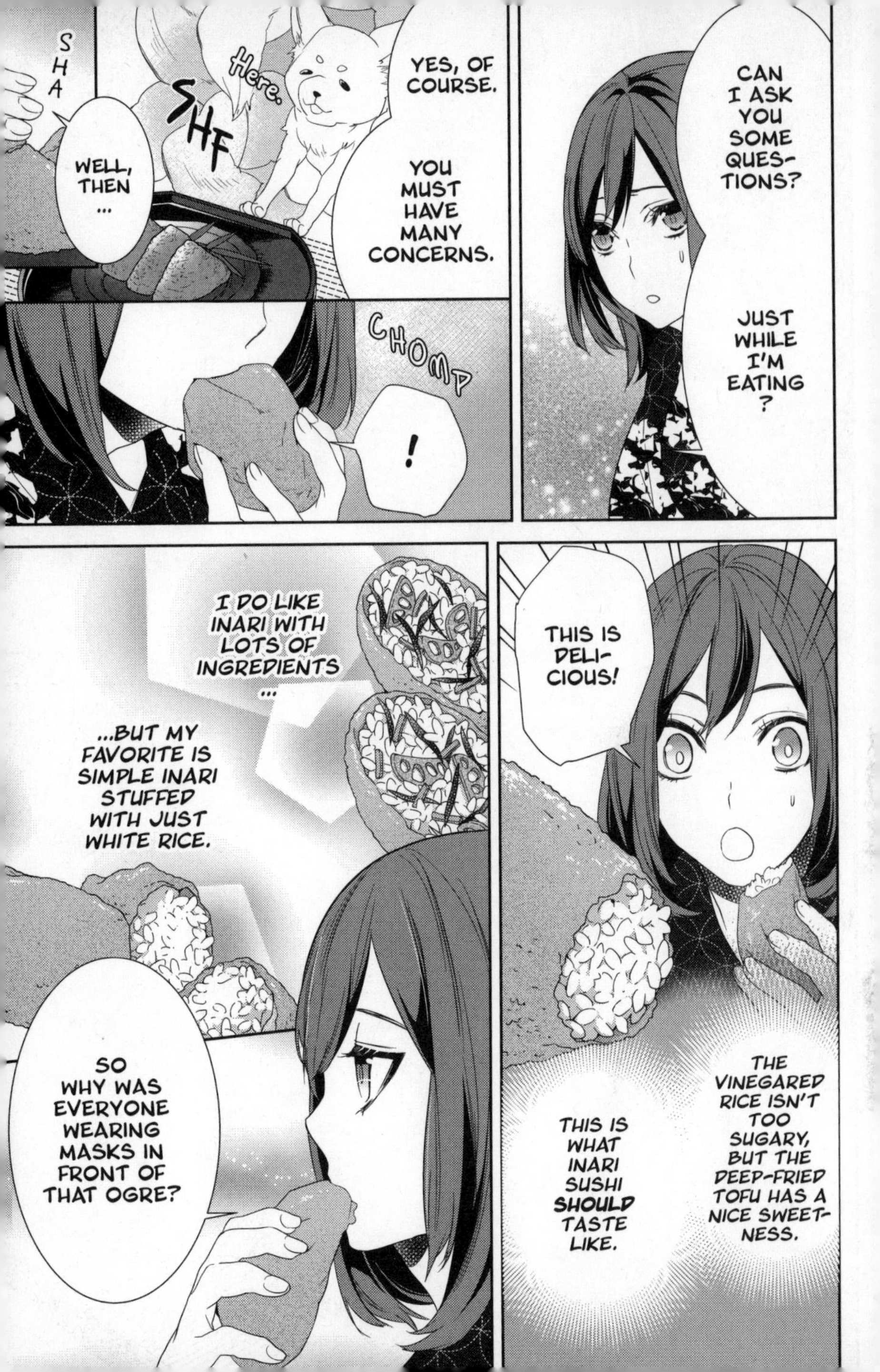
CAN I ASK YOU SOME QUESTIONS?
JUST WHILE I'M EATING?
YES, OF COURSE.
YOU MUST HAVE MANY CONCERNS.
Here.
SHF
SHA
WELL, THEN ...
CHOMP
!
THIS IS DELICIOUS!
THE VINEGARED RICE ISN'T TOO SUGARY, BUT THE DEEP-FRIED TOFU HAS A NICE SWEETNESS.
THIS IS WHAT INARI SUSHI **SHOULD** TASTE LIKE.
I DO LIKE INARI WITH LOTS OF INGREDIENTS ...
...BUT MY FAVORITE IS SIMPLE INARI STUFFED WITH JUST WHITE RICE.
SO WHY WAS EVERYONE WEARING MASKS IN FRONT OF THAT OGRE?

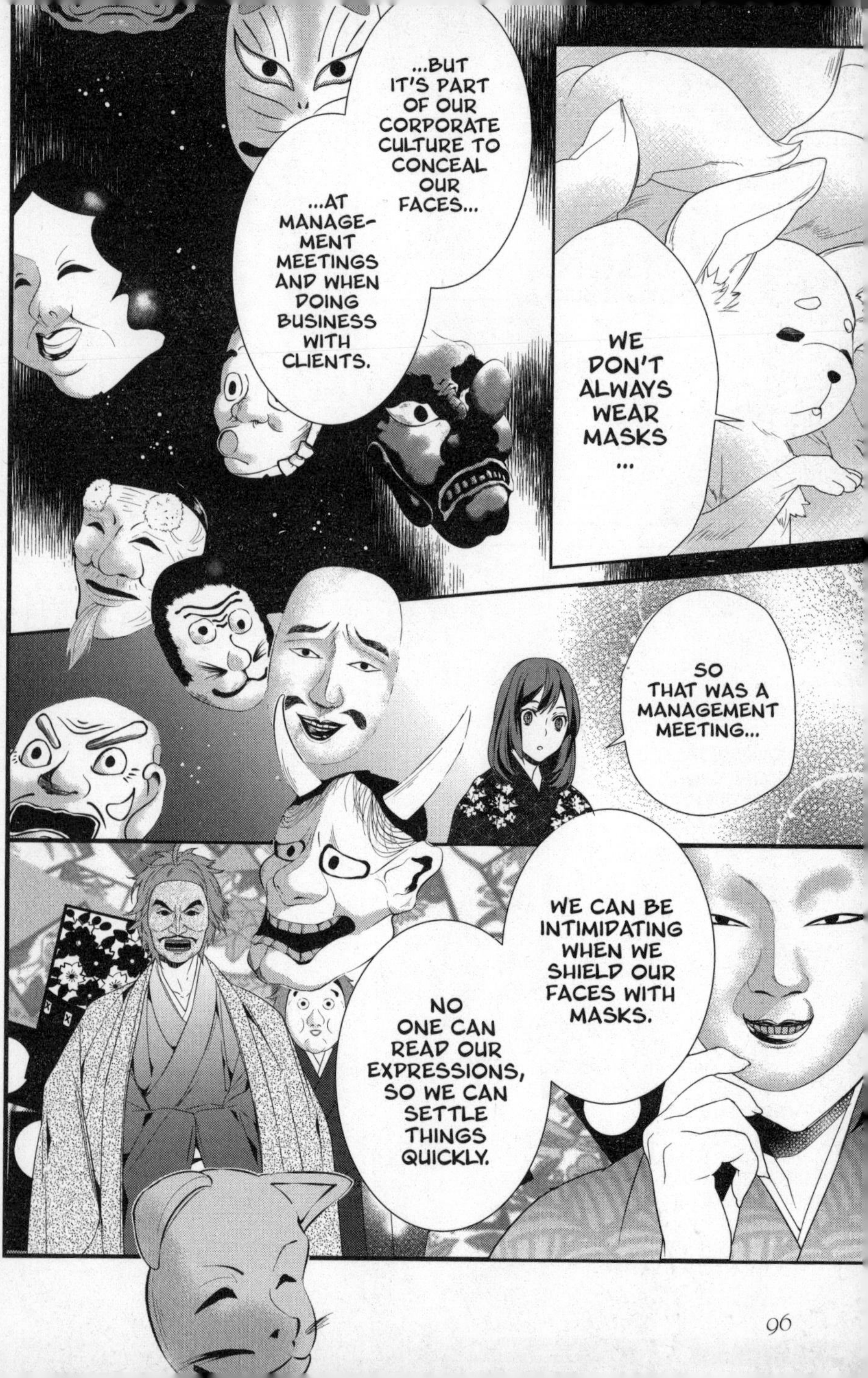
WE DON'T ALWAYS WEAR MASKS...
...BUT IT'S PART OF OUR CORPORATE CULTURE TO CONCEAL OUR FACES...
...AT MANAGEMENT MEETINGS AND WHEN DOING BUSINESS WITH CLIENTS.
SO THAT WAS A MANAGEMENT MEETING...
WE CAN BE INTIMIDATING WHEN WE SHIELD OUR FACES WITH MASKS.
NO ONE CAN READ OUR EXPRESSIONS, SO WE CAN SETTLE THINGS QUICKLY.

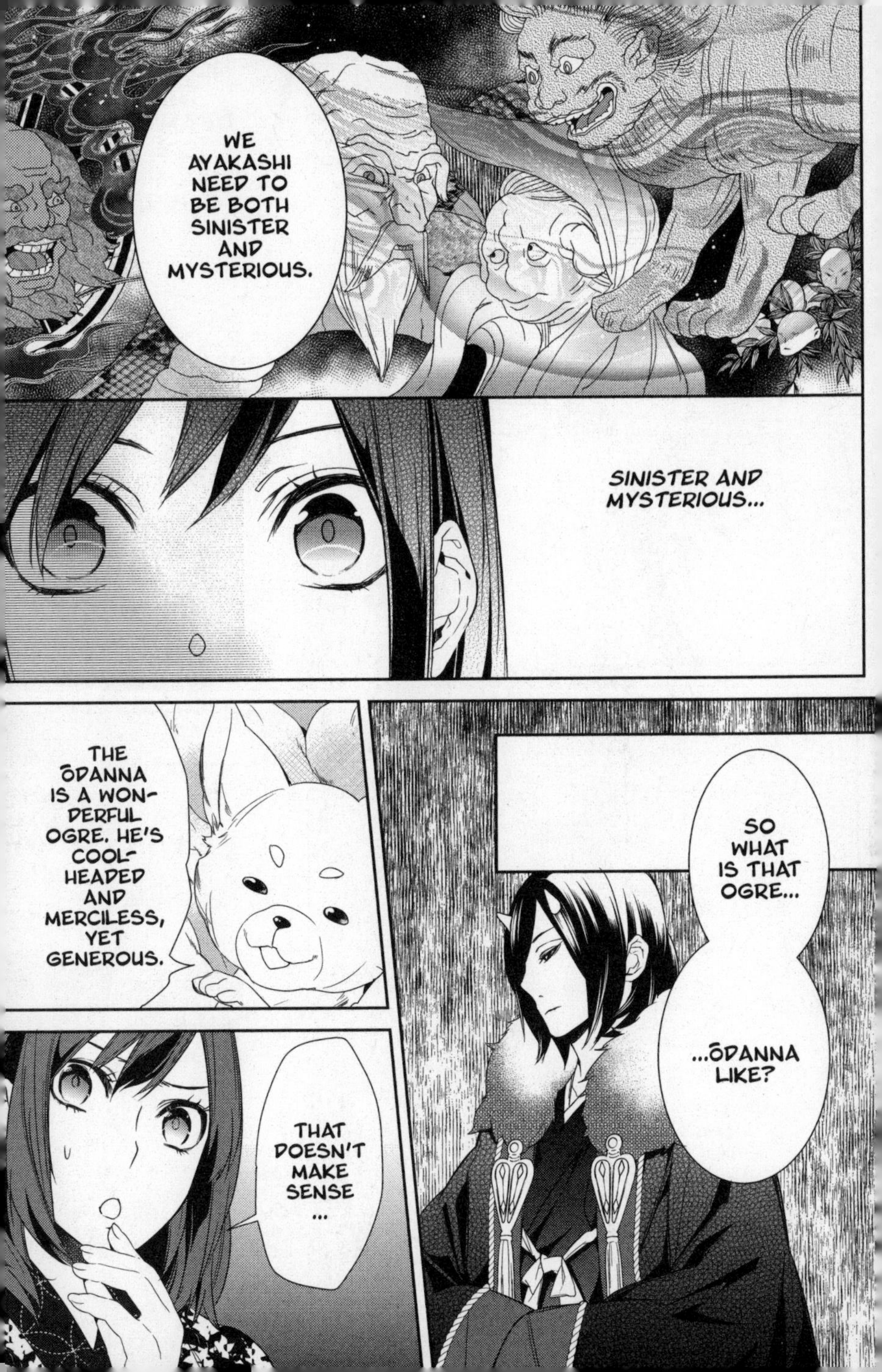
WE AYAKASHI NEED TO BE BOTH SINISTER AND MYSTERIOUS.
SINISTER AND MYSTERIOUS...
SO WHAT IS THAT OGRE...
...ŌDANNA LIKE?
THE ŌDANNA IS A WON-DERFUL OGRE. HE'S COOL-HEADED AND MERCILESS, YET GENEROUS.
THAT DOESN'T MAKE SENSE...

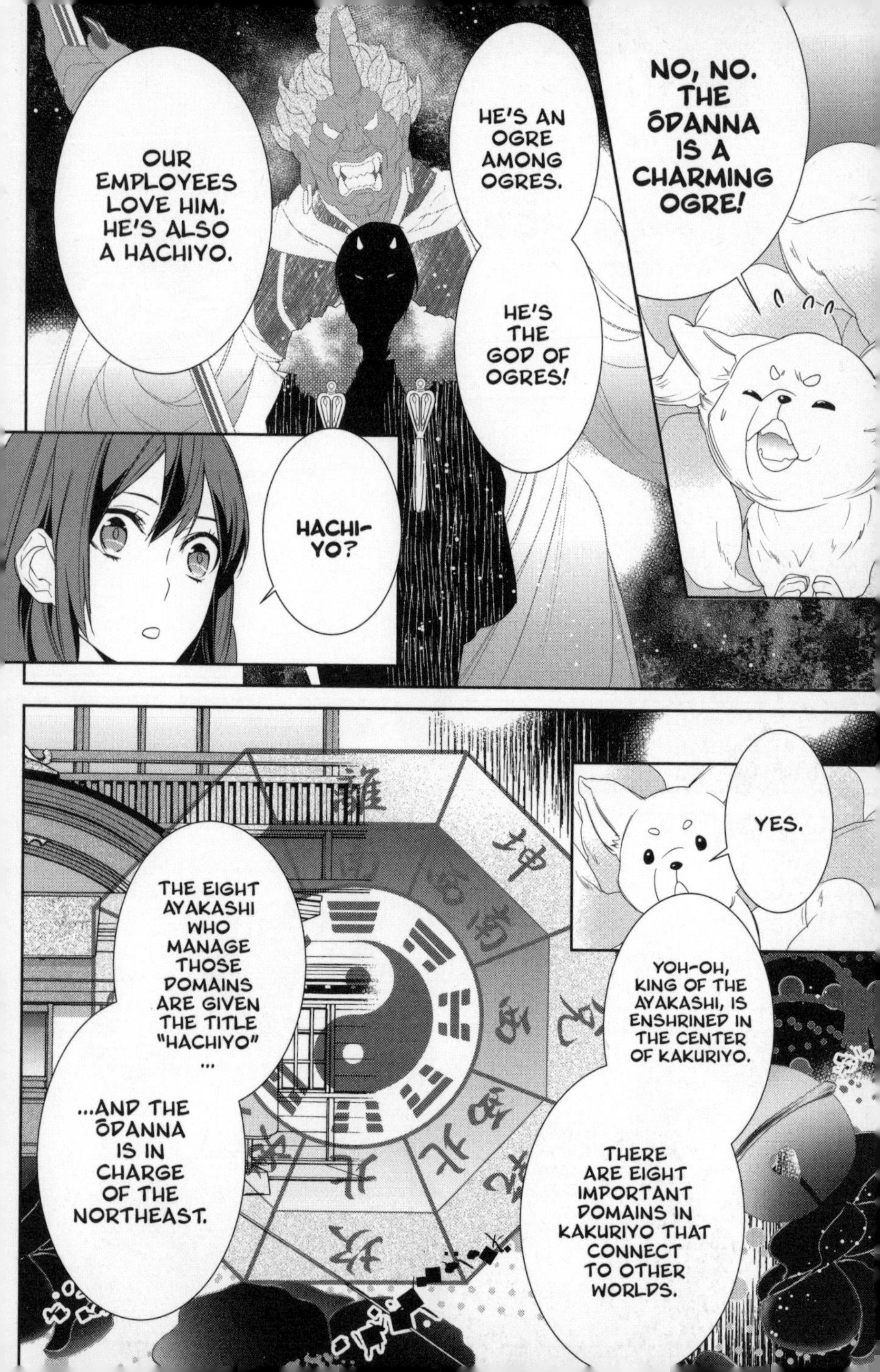
NO, NO. THE ŌDANNA IS A CHARMING OGRE!
HE'S AN OGRE AMONG OGRES.
HE'S THE GOD OF OGRES!
OUR EMPLOYEES LOVE HIM. HE'S ALSO A HACHIYO.
HACHI-YO?
YES.
YOH-OH, KING OF THE AYAKASHI, IS ENSHRINED IN THE CENTER OF KAKURIYO.
THERE ARE EIGHT IMPORTANT DOMAINS IN KAKURIYO THAT CONNECT TO OTHER WORLDS.
THE EIGHT AYAKASHI WHO MANAGE THOSE DOMAINS ARE GIVEN THE TITLE "HACHIYO" ...
...AND THE ŌDANNA IS IN CHARGE OF THE NORTHEAST.

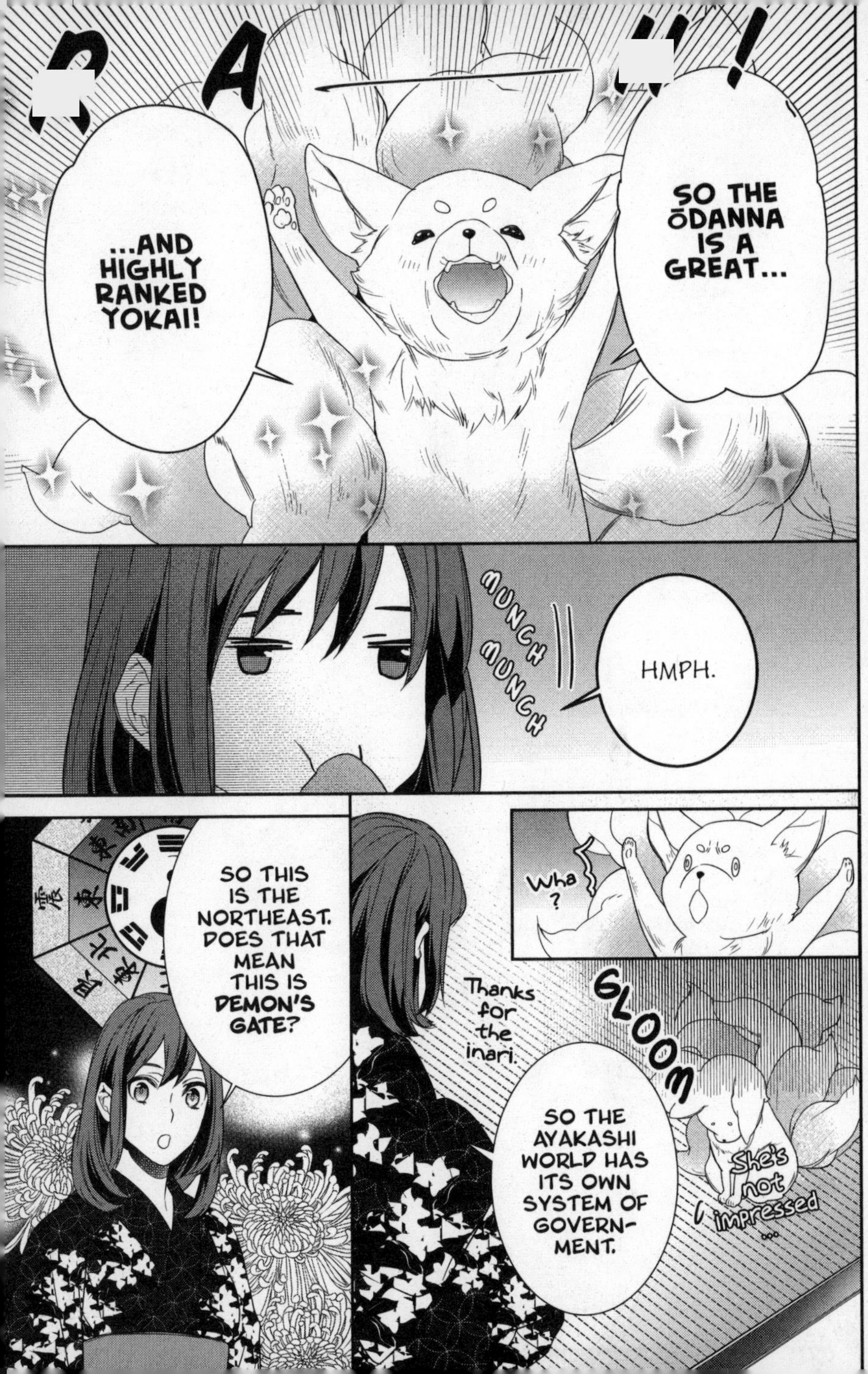
SO THE ŌDANNA IS A GREAT...
...AND HIGHLY RANKED YOKAI!
MUNCH MUNCH
HMPH.
Wha?
GLOOM
Thanks for the inari.
She's not impressed...
SO THE AYAKASHI WORLD HAS ITS OWN SYSTEM OF GOVERNMENT.
SO THIS IS THE NORTHEAST. DOES THAT MEAN THIS IS DEMON'S GATE?

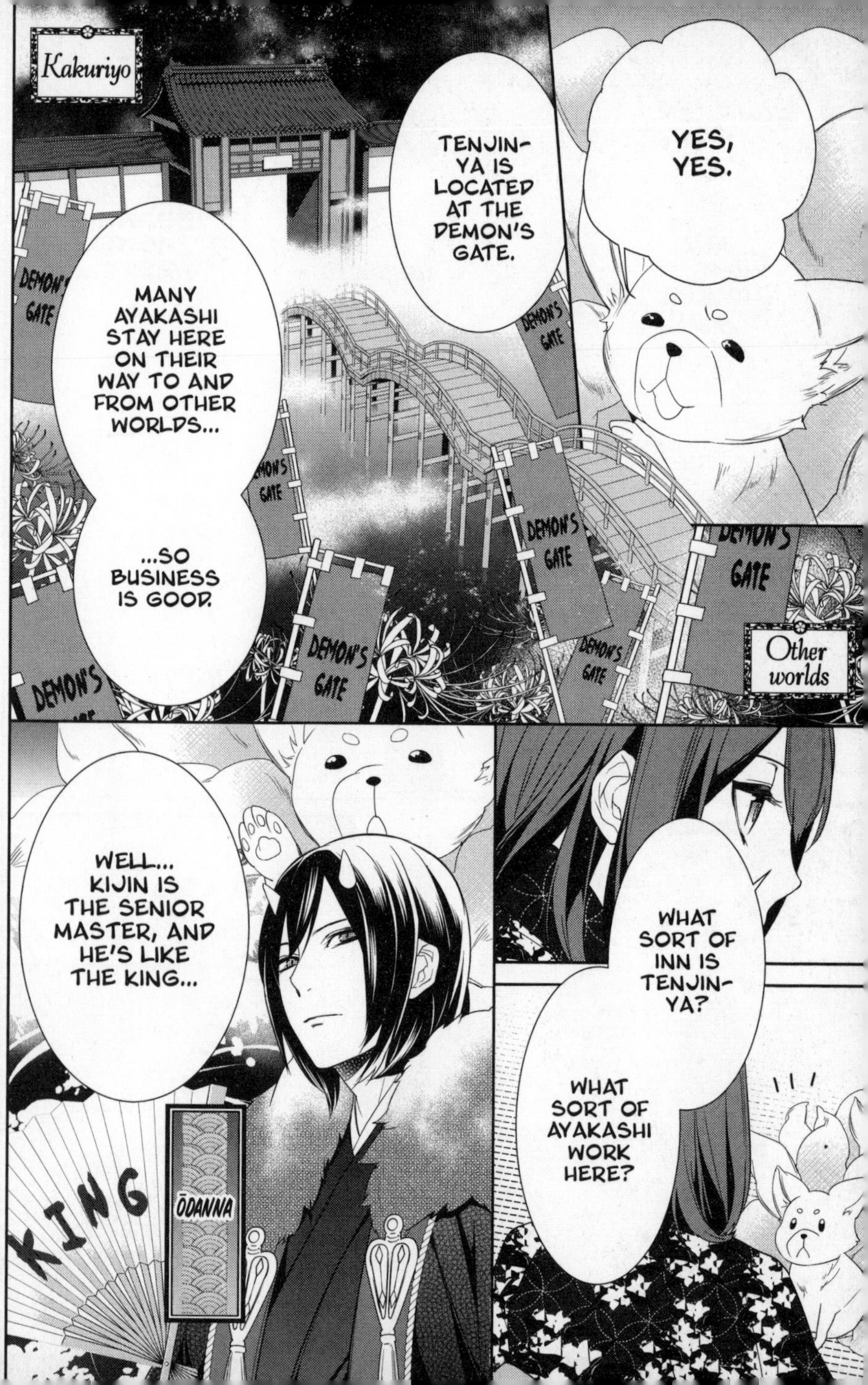
TENJIN-YA IS LOCATED AT THE DEMON'S GATE.
YES, YES.
Kakuriyo
MANY AYAKASHI STAY HERE ON THEIR WAY TO AND FROM OTHER WORLDS...
...SO BUSINESS IS GOOD.
DEMON'S GATE
Other worlds
WHAT SORT OF INN IS TENJIN-YA?
WHAT SORT OF AYAKASHI WORK HERE?
WELL... KIJIN IS THE SENIOR MASTER, AND HE'S LIKE THE KING...
KING
ŌDANNA

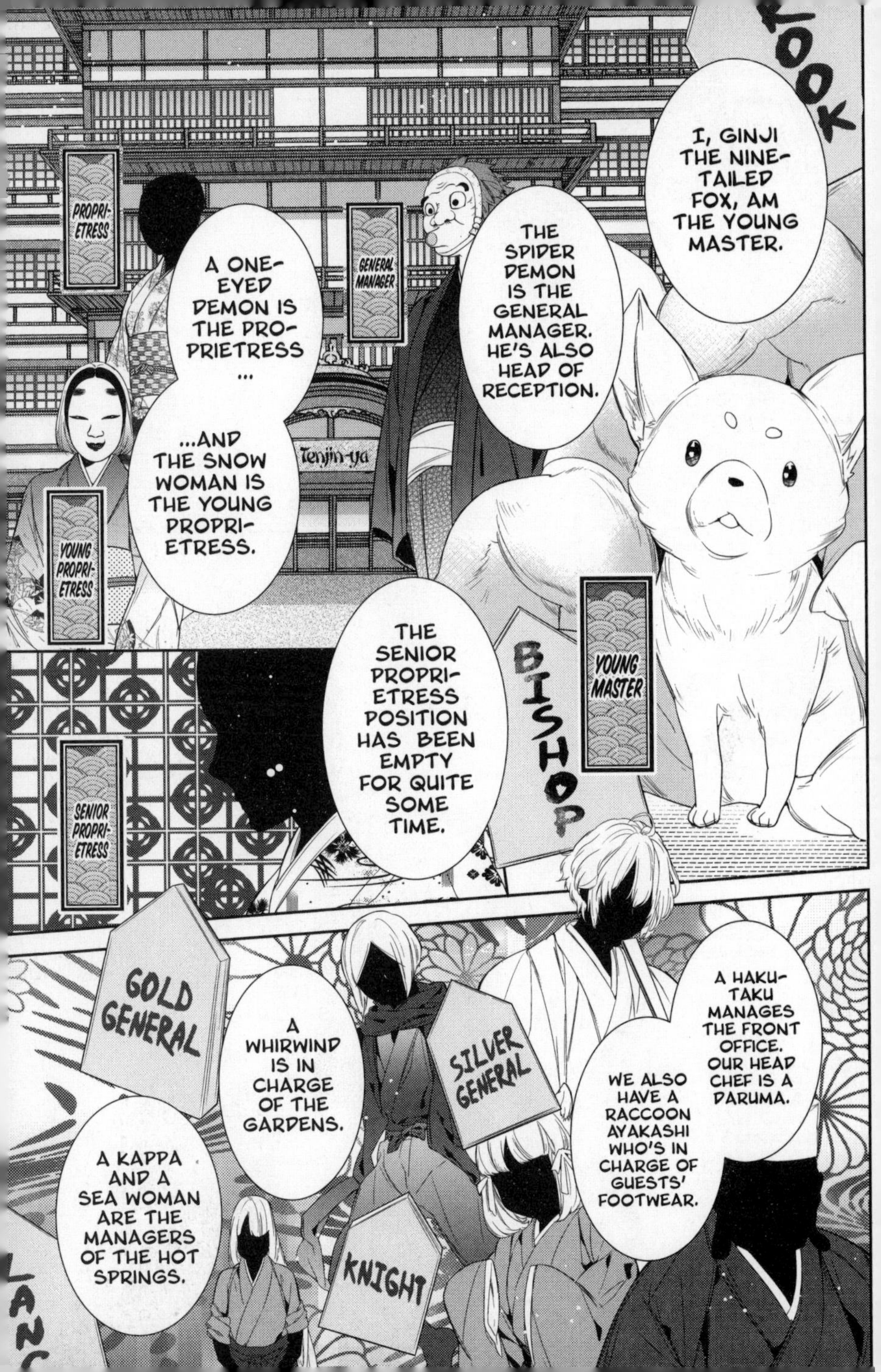
OOK
I, GINJI THE NINE-TAILED FOX, AM THE YOUNG MASTER.
YOUNG MASTER
THE SPIDER DEMON IS THE GENERAL MANAGER. HE'S ALSO HEAD OF RECEPTION.
GENERAL MANAGER
A ONE-EYED DEMON IS THE PROPRIETRESS...
PROPRIETRESS
...AND THE SNOW WOMAN IS THE YOUNG PROPRIETRESS.
YOUNG PROPRIETRESS
Tenjin-ya
BISHOP
THE SENIOR PROPRIETRESS POSITION HAS BEEN EMPTY FOR QUITE SOME TIME.
SENIOR PROPRIETRESS
A HAKU-TAKU MANAGES THE FRONT OFFICE. OUR HEAD CHEF IS A DARUMA.
WE ALSO HAVE A RACCOON AYAKASHI WHO'S IN CHARGE OF GUESTS' FOOTWEAR.
SILVER GENERAL
A WHIRWIND IS IN CHARGE OF THE GARDENS.
GOLD GENERAL
A KAPPA AND A SEA WOMAN ARE THE MANAGERS OF THE HOT SPRINGS.
KNIGHT
LANC

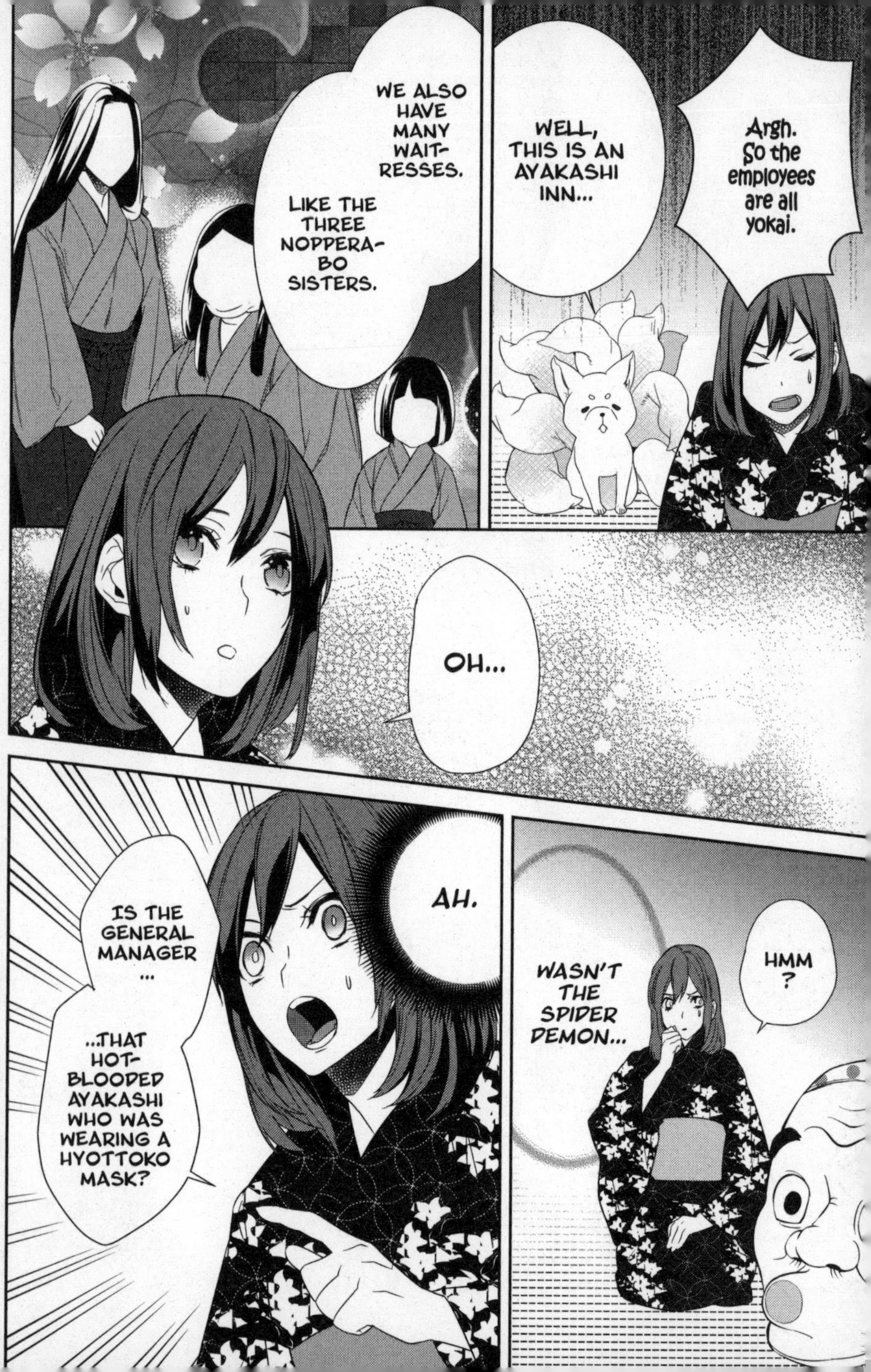
Argh. So the employees are all yokai.
WELL, THIS IS AN AYAKASHI INN...
WE ALSO HAVE MANY WAIT-RESSES.
LIKE THE THREE NOPPERA-BO SISTERS.
OH...
HMM?
WASN'T THE SPIDER DEMON...
AH.
IS THE GENERAL MANAGER ...
...THAT HOT-BLOODED AYAKASHI WHO WAS WEARING A HYOTTOKO MASK?

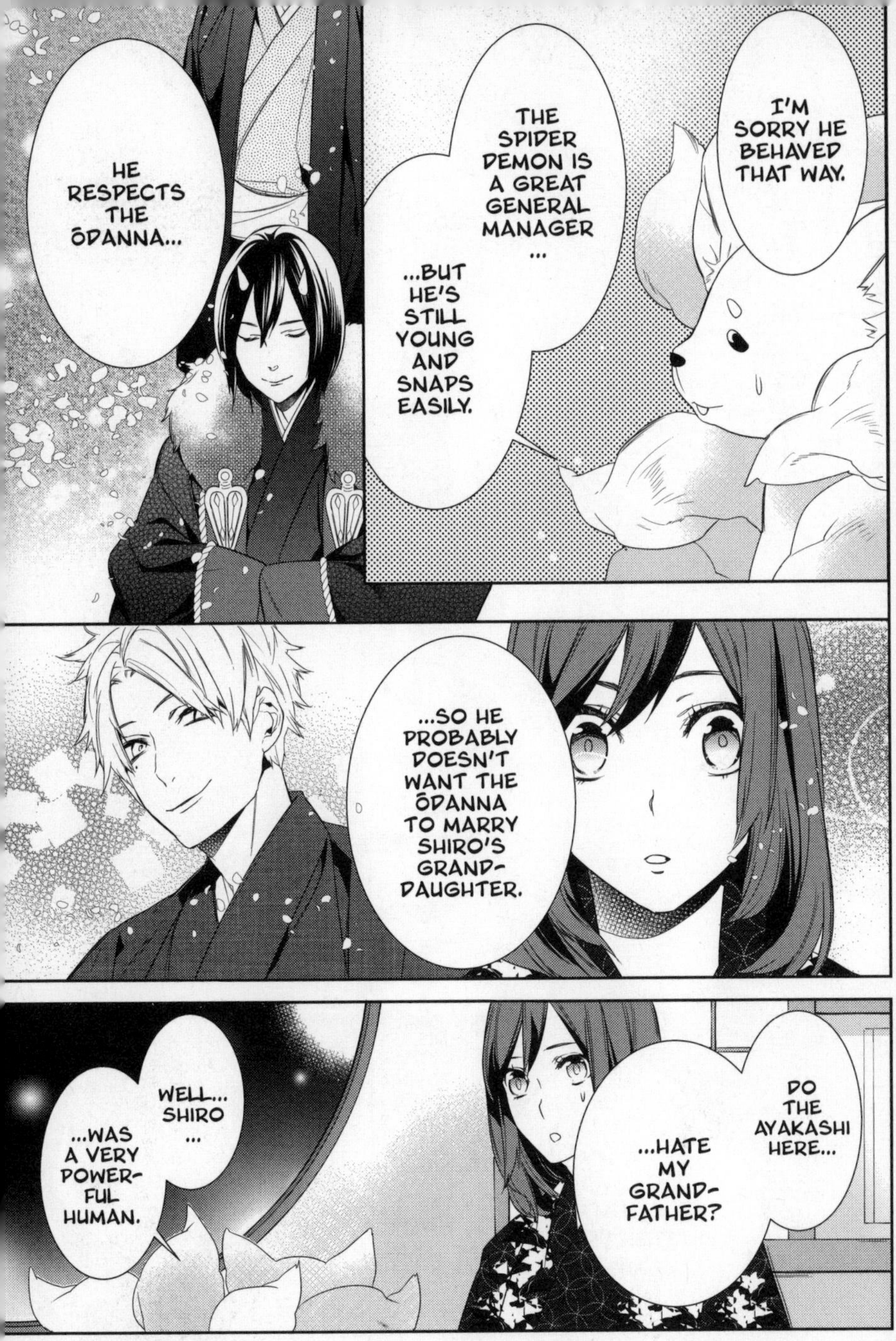
I'M SORRY HE BEHAVED THAT WAY.
THE SPIDER DEMON IS A GREAT GENERAL MANAGER ...
...BUT HE'S STILL YOUNG AND SNAPS EASILY.
HE RESPECTS THE ŌDANNA...
...SO HE PROBABLY DOESN'T WANT THE ŌDANNA TO MARRY SHIRO'S GRAND-DAUGHTER.
DO THE AYAKASHI HERE...
...HATE MY GRAND-FATHER?
WELL... SHIRO ...
...WAS A VERY POWER-FUL HUMAN.

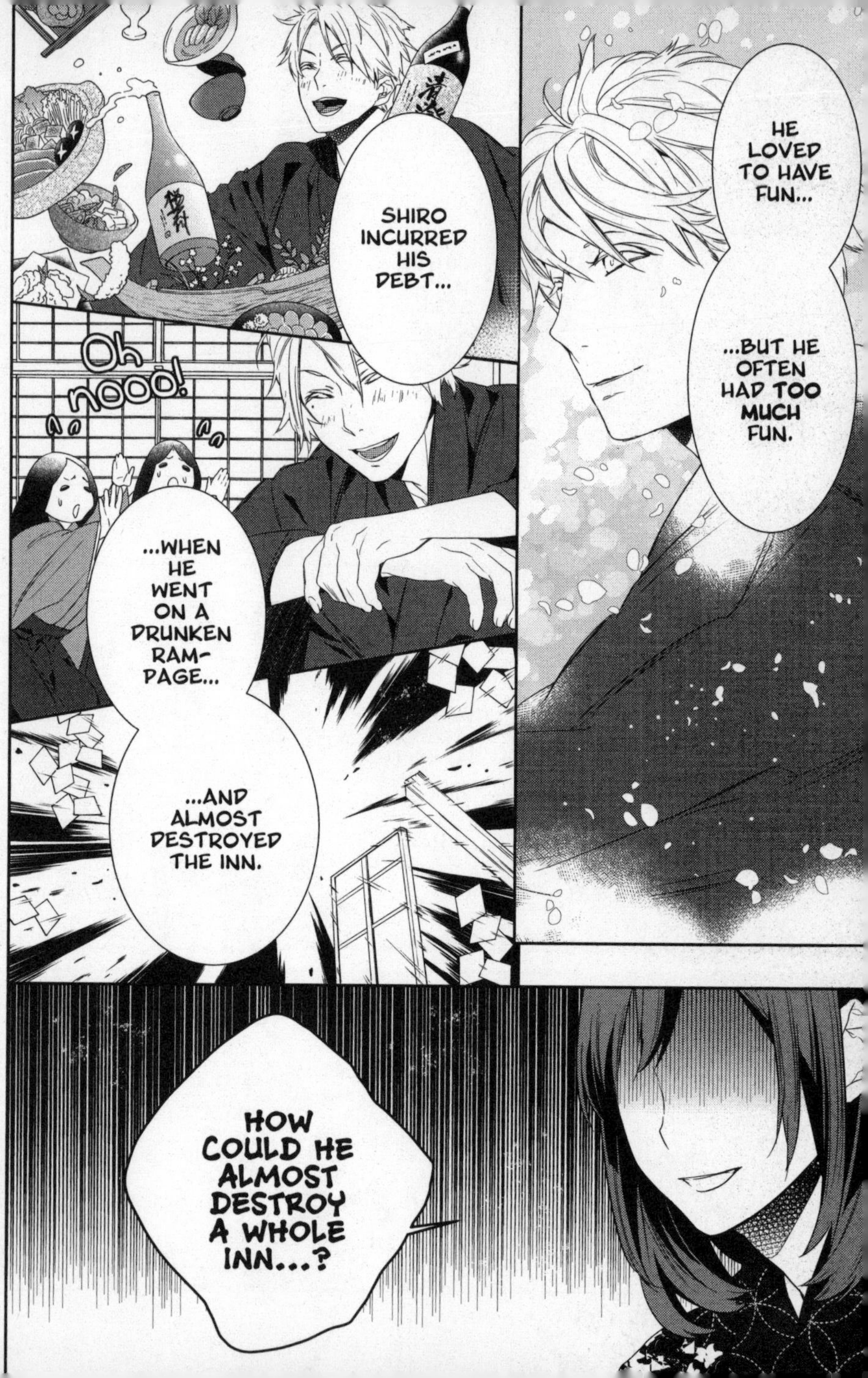
HE LOVED TO HAVE FUN...
...BUT HE OFTEN HAD TOO MUCH FUN.
SHIRO INCURRED HIS DEBT...
Oh nooo!
...WHEN HE WENT ON A DRUNKEN RAM-PAGE...
...AND ALMOST DESTROYED THE INN.
HOW COULD HE ALMOST DESTROY A WHOLE INN...?

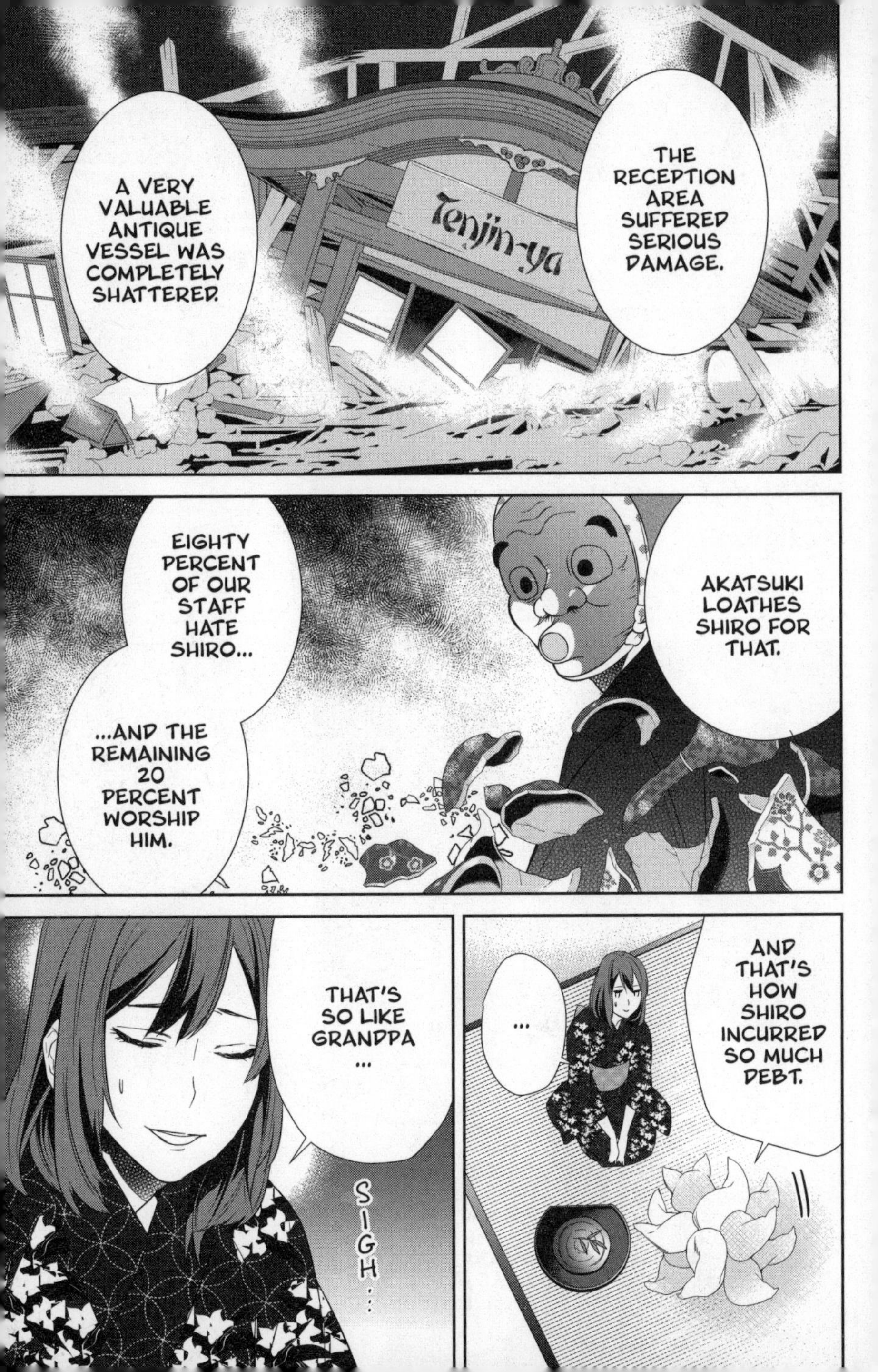
THE RECEPTION AREA SUFFERED SERIOUS DAMAGE.
Tenjin-ya
A VERY VALUABLE ANTIQUE VESSEL WAS COMPLETELY SHATTERED.
AKATSUKI LOATHES SHIRO FOR THAT.
EIGHTY PERCENT OF OUR STAFF HATE SHIRO...
...AND THE REMAINING 20 PERCENT WORSHIP HIM.
AND THAT'S HOW SHIRO INCURRED SO MUCH DEBT.
...
THAT'S SO LIKE GRANDPA ...
SIGH...

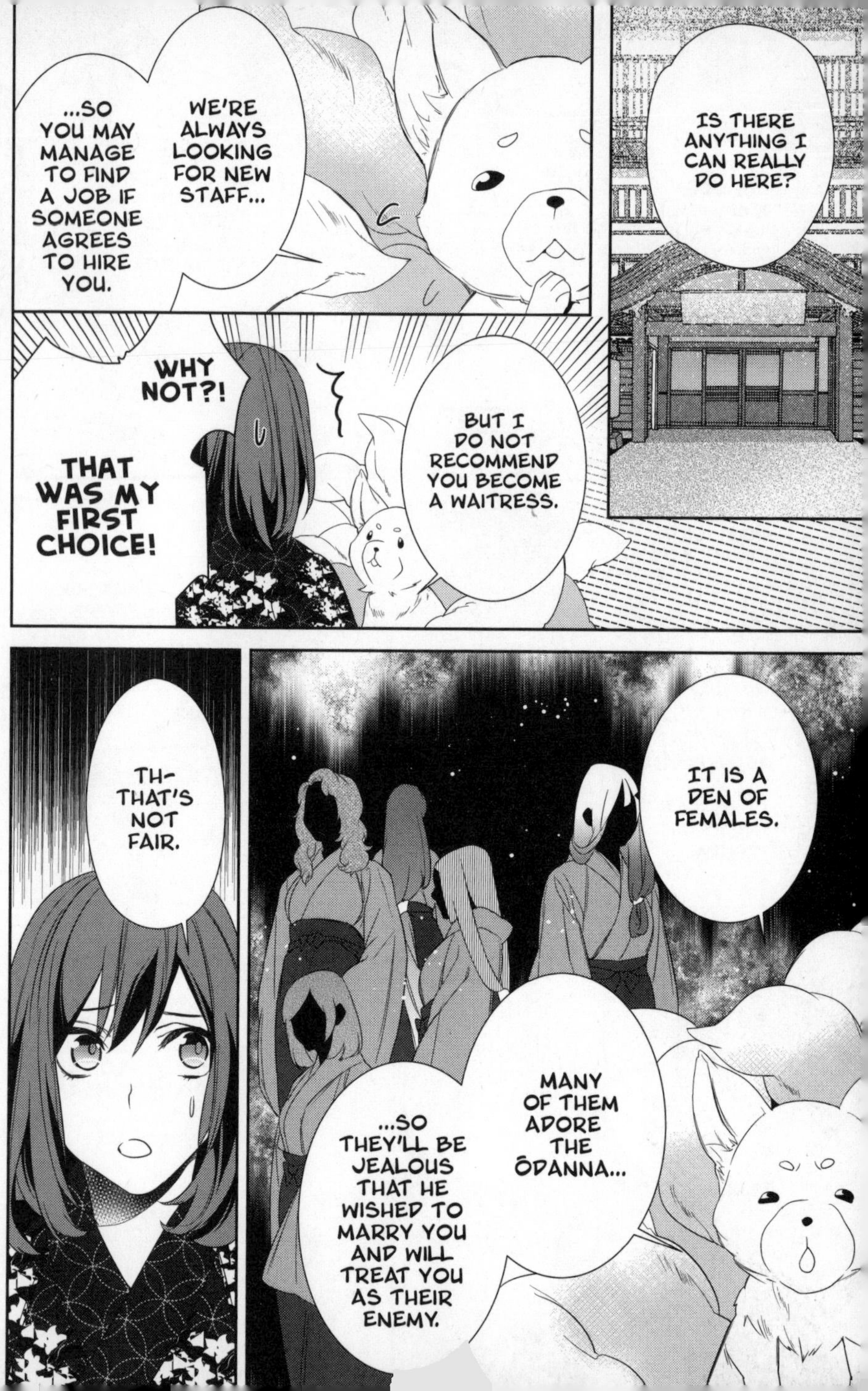
IS THERE ANYTHING I CAN REALLY DO HERE?
WE'RE ALWAYS LOOKING FOR NEW STAFF...
...SO YOU MAY MANAGE TO FIND A JOB IF SOMEONE AGREES TO HIRE YOU.
BUT I DO NOT RECOMMEND YOU BECOME A WAITRESS.
WHY NOT?!
THAT WAS MY FIRST CHOICE!
IT IS A DEN OF FEMALES.
MANY OF THEM ADORE THE ŌDANNA...
...SO THEY'LL BE JEALOUS THAT HE WISHED TO MARRY YOU AND WILL TREAT YOU AS THEIR ENEMY.
TH-THAT'S NOT FAIR.

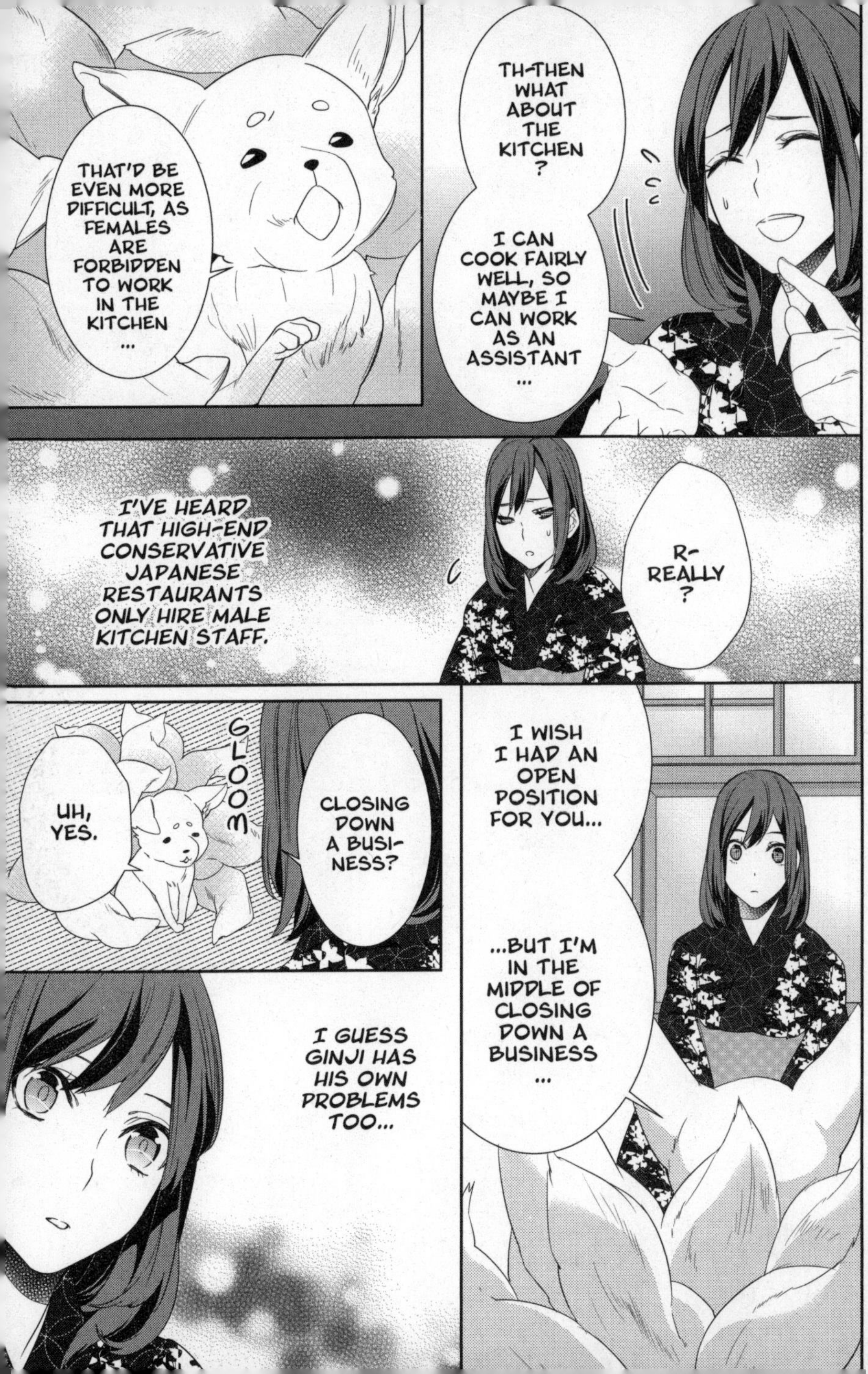
TH-THEN WHAT ABOUT THE KITCHEN?
I CAN COOK FAIRLY WELL, SO MAYBE I CAN WORK AS AN ASSISTANT...
THAT'D BE EVEN MORE DIFFICULT, AS FEMALES ARE FORBIDDEN TO WORK IN THE KITCHEN...
R-REALLY?
I'VE HEARD THAT HIGH-END CONSERVATIVE JAPANESE RESTAURANTS ONLY HIRE MALE KITCHEN STAFF.
I WISH I HAD AN OPEN POSITION FOR YOU...
...BUT I'M IN THE MIDDLE OF CLOSING DOWN A BUSINESS...
CLOSING DOWN A BUSI-NESS?
UH, YES.
GLOOM
I GUESS GINJI HAS HIS OWN PROBLEMS TOO...

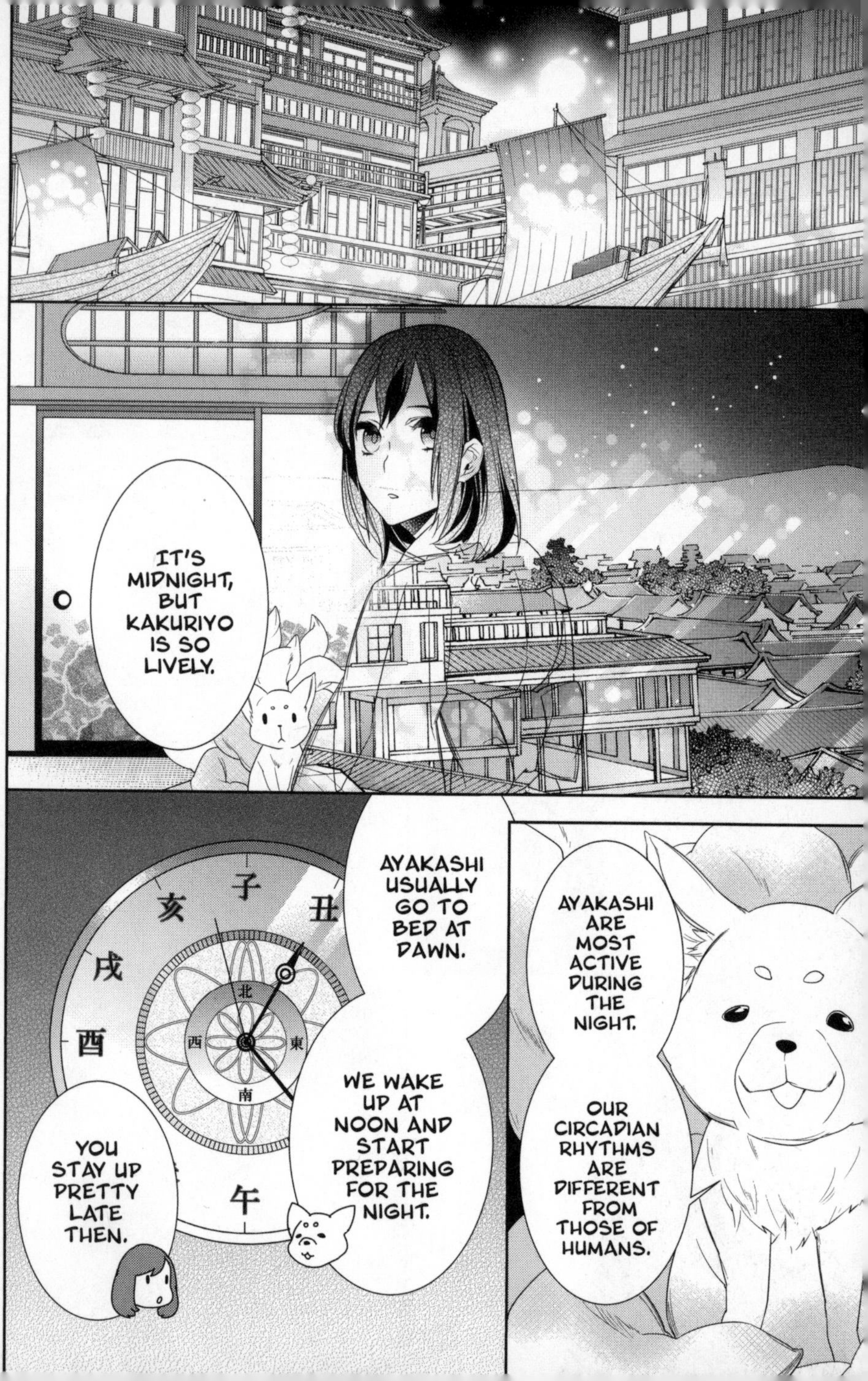
IT'S MIDNIGHT, BUT KAKURIYO IS SO LIVELY.
AYAKASHI ARE MOST ACTIVE DURING THE NIGHT.
OUR CIRCADIAN RHYTHMS ARE DIFFERENT FROM THOSE OF HUMANS.
AYAKASHI USUALLY GO TO BED AT DAWN.
WE WAKE UP AT NOON AND START PREPARING FOR THE NIGHT.
YOU STAY UP PRETTY LATE THEN.

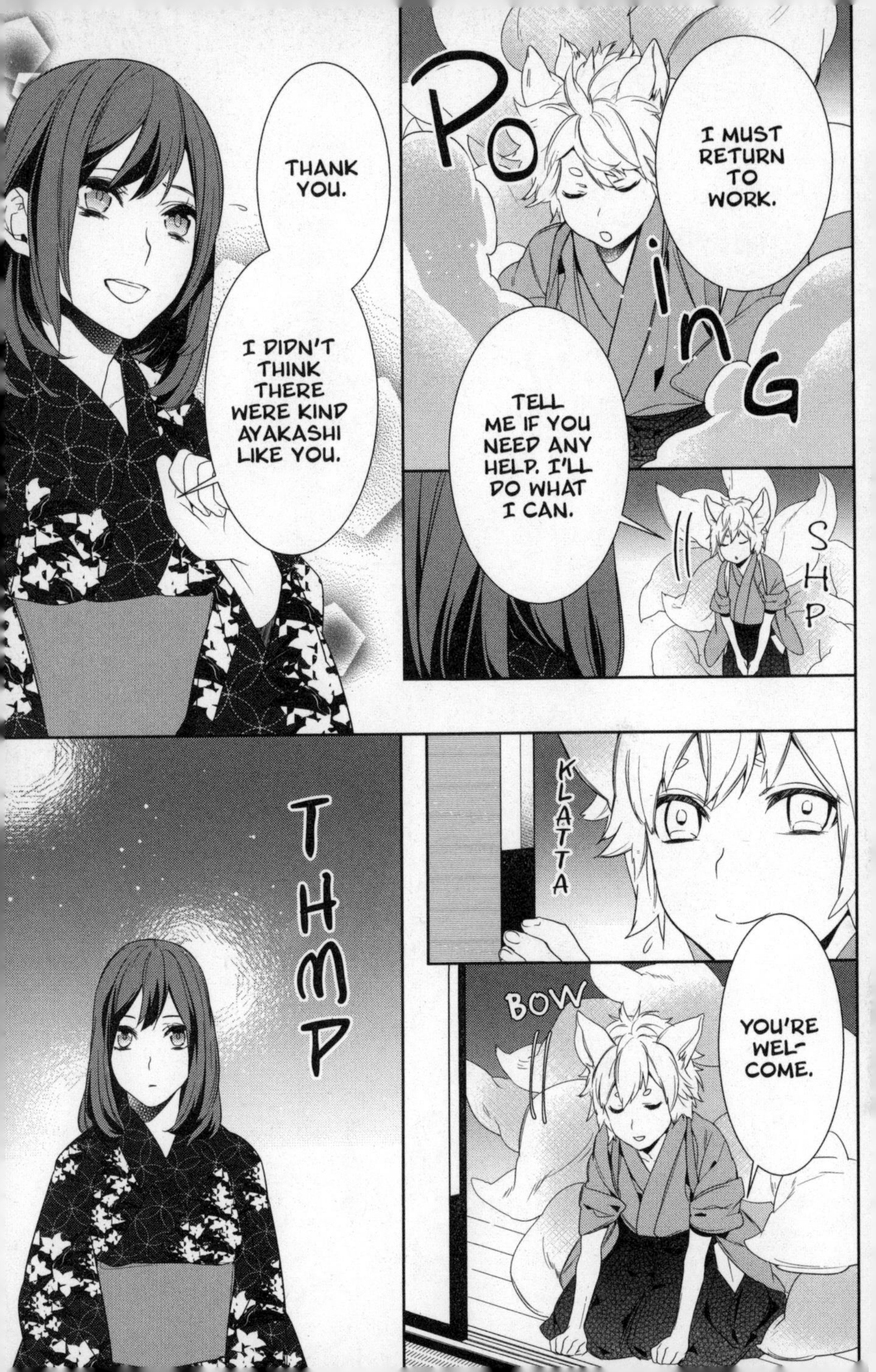
POING
I MUST RETURN TO WORK.
TELL ME IF YOU NEED ANY HELP. I'LL DO WHAT I CAN.
SHP
THANK YOU.
I DIDN'T THINK THERE WERE KIND AYAKASHI LIKE YOU.
KLATTA
BOW
YOU'RE WEL-COME.
THMP

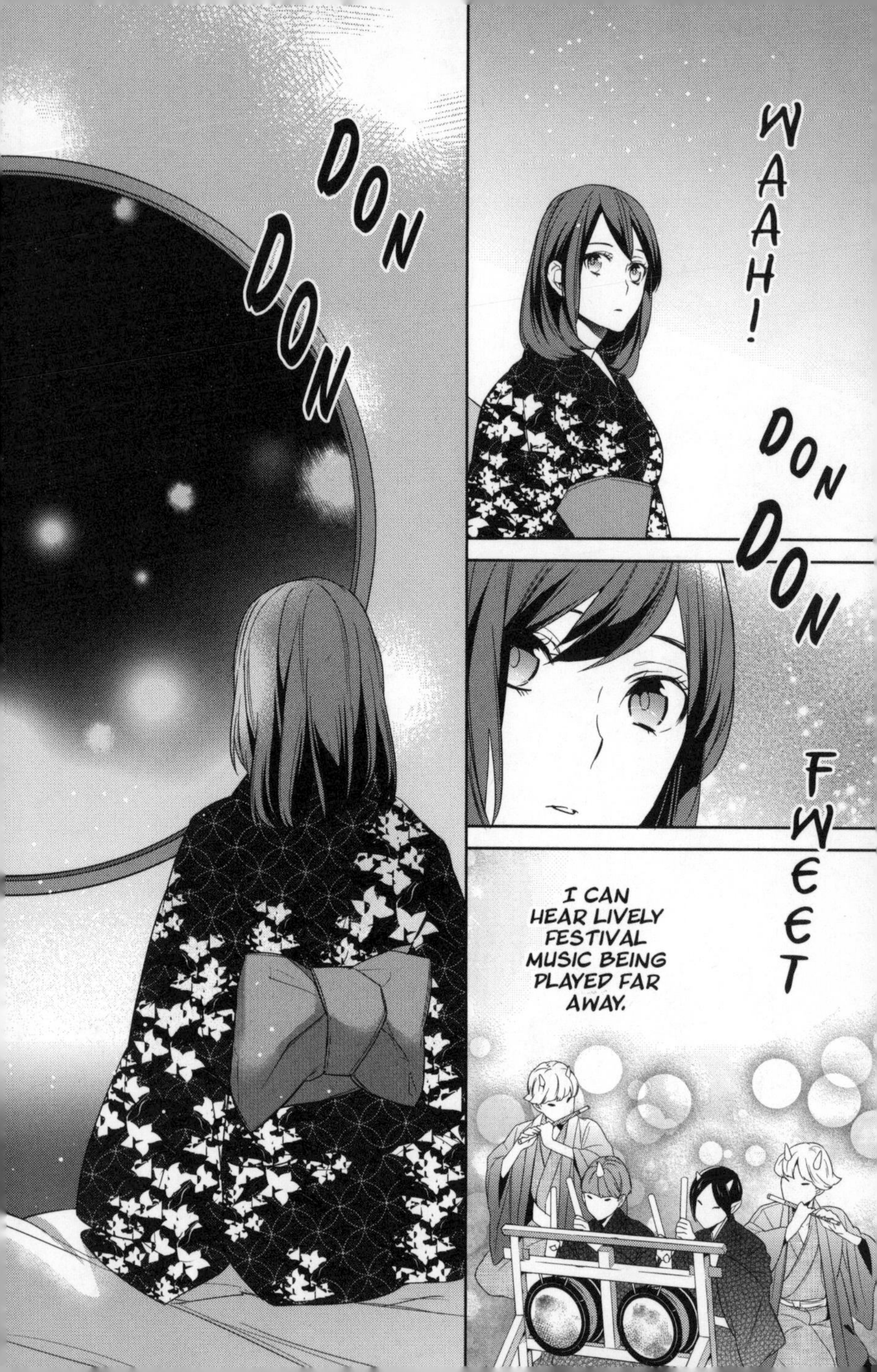
WAAAH!
DON DON DON
FWEET
I CAN HEAR LIVELY FESTIVAL MUSIC BEING PLAYED FAR AWAY.
DON DON DON

Kakuriyo
Bed & Breakfast
for Spirits

Kakuriyo
Bed & Breakfast for Spirits

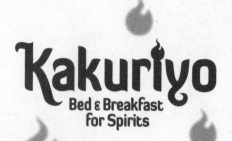

Chapter 4

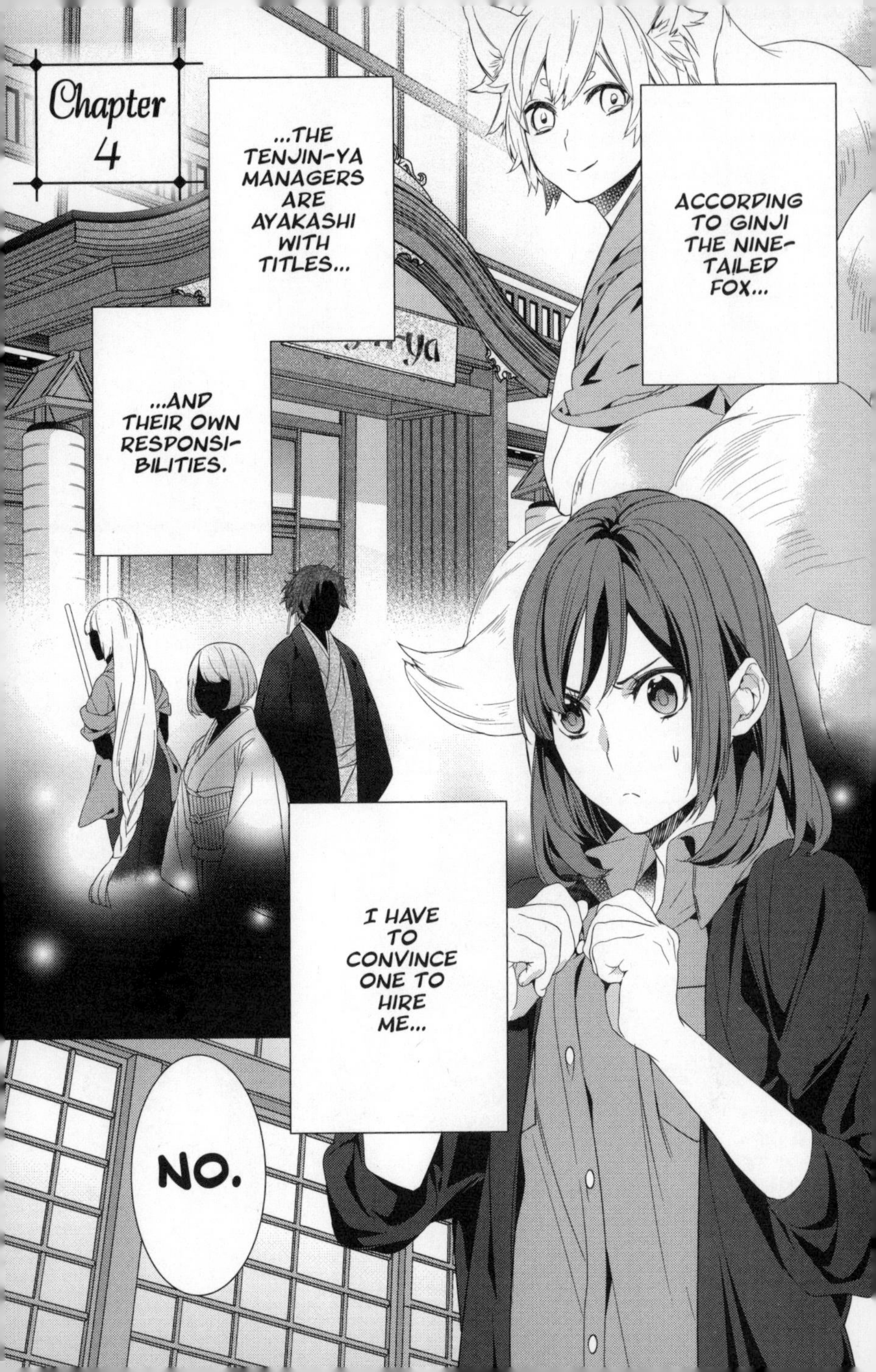
ACCORDING TO GINJI THE NINE-TAILED FOX...
...THE TENJIN-YA MANAGERS ARE AYAKASHI WITH TITLES...
...AND THEIR OWN RESPONSIBILITIES.
I HAVE TO CONVINCE ONE TO HIRE ME...
NO.

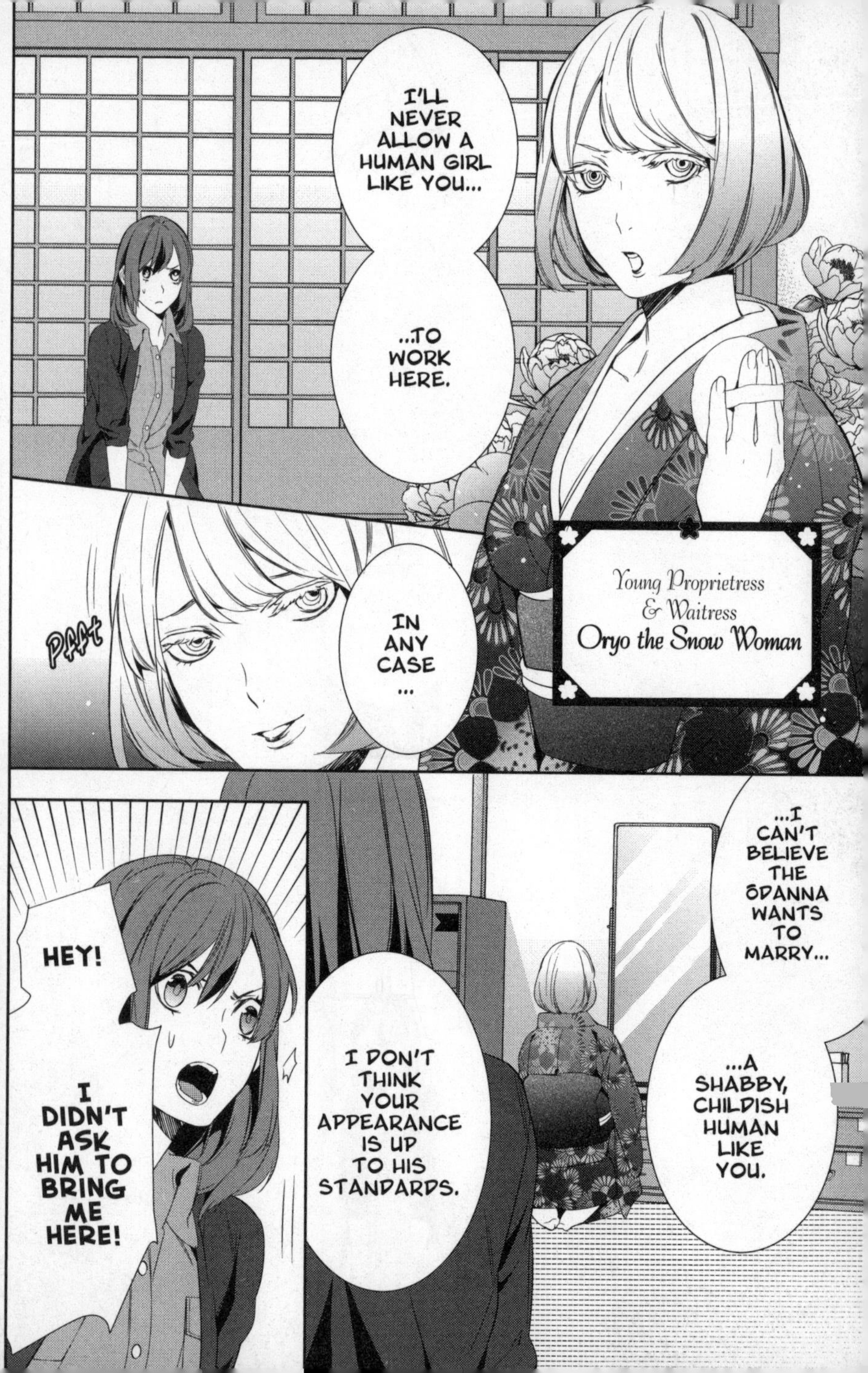

I'LL NEVER ALLOW A HUMAN GIRL LIKE YOU...
...TO WORK HERE.
Young Proprietress & Waitress
Oryo the Snow Woman
IN ANY CASE...
Pfft
...I CAN'T BELIEVE THE ŌDANNA WANTS TO MARRY...
...A SHABBY, CHILDISH HUMAN LIKE YOU.
I DON'T THINK YOUR APPEARANCE IS UP TO HIS STANDARDS.
HEY!
I DIDN'T ASK HIM TO BRING ME HERE!

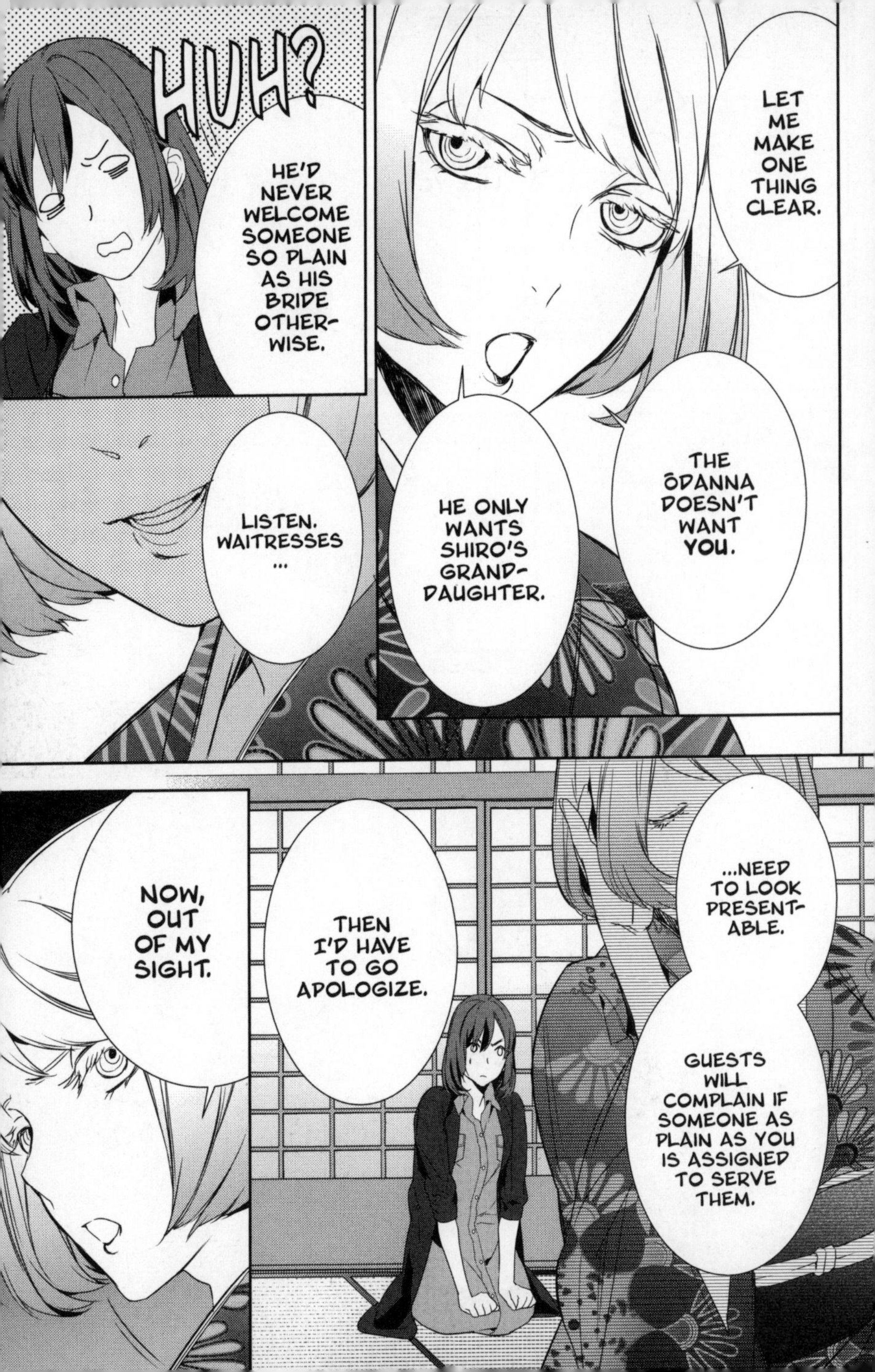
LET ME MAKE ONE THING CLEAR.
THE ŌDANNA DOESN'T WANT YOU.
HE ONLY WANTS SHIRO'S GRAND-DAUGHTER.
HUH?
HE'D NEVER WELCOME SOMEONE SO PLAIN AS HIS BRIDE OTHER-WISE.
LISTEN. WAITRESSES ...
...NEED TO LOOK PRESENT-ABLE.
GUESTS WILL COMPLAIN IF SOMEONE AS PLAIN AS YOU IS ASSIGNED TO SERVE THEM.
THEN I'D HAVE TO GO APOLOGIZE.
NOW, OUT OF MY SIGHT.

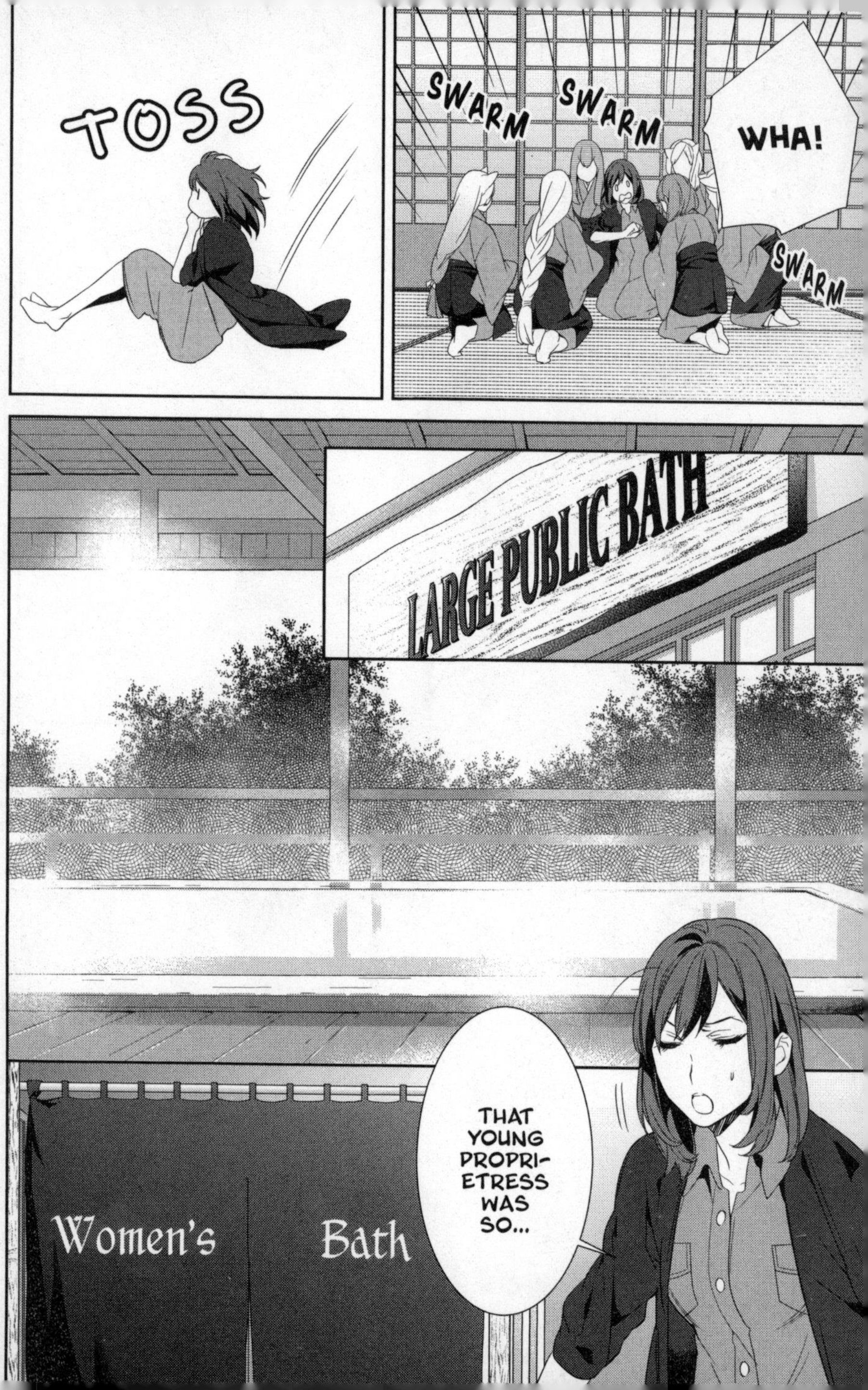
WHA!
SWARM
SWARM
SWARM
TOSS
LARGE PUBLIC BATH
Women's Bath
THAT YOUNG PROPRI-ETRESS WAS SO...

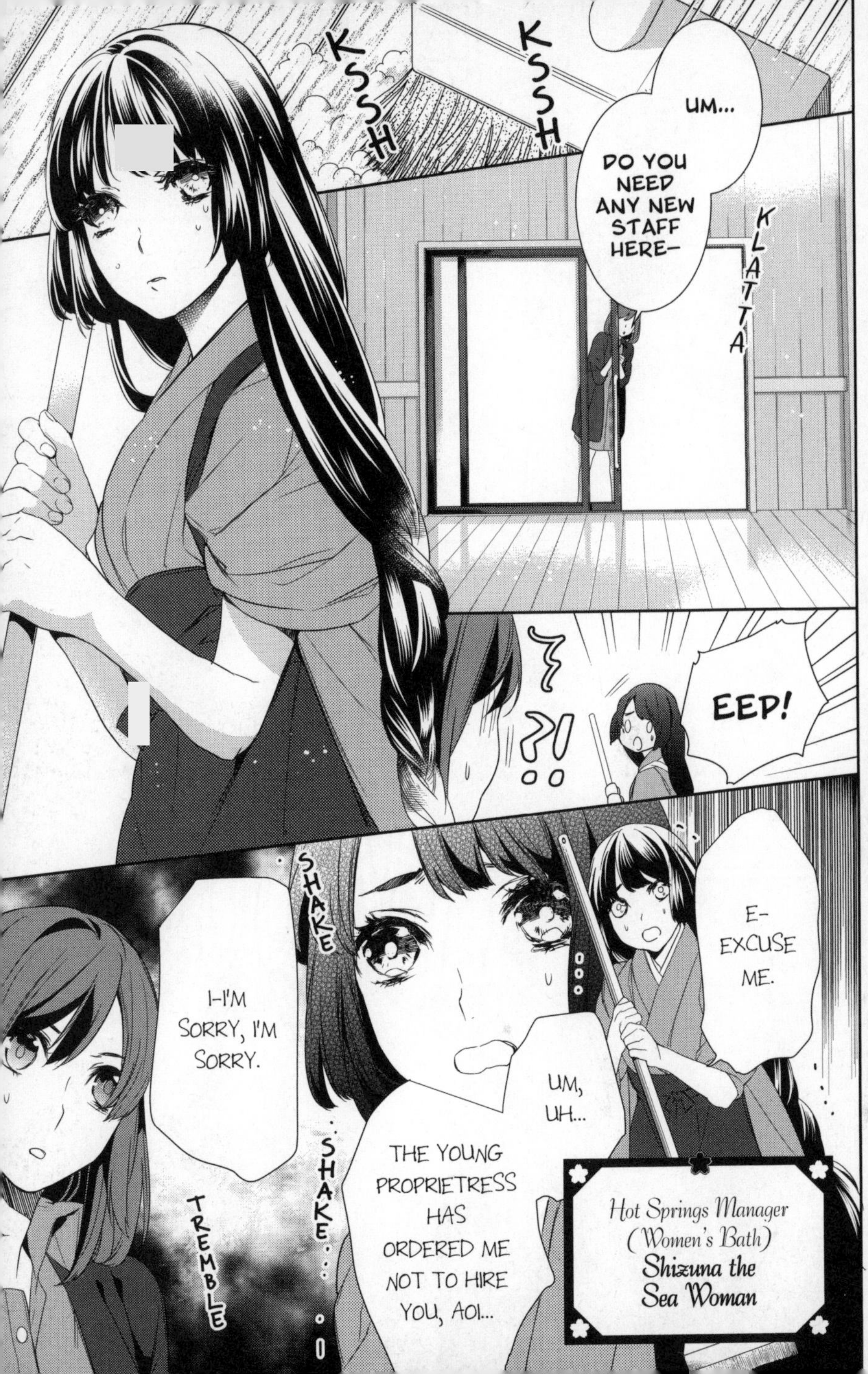
UM...
DO YOU NEED ANY NEW STAFF HERE—
KLATTA
KSSH
KSSH
EEP!
?!
E-EXCUSE ME.
UM, UH...
Hot Springs Manager (Women's Bath) Shizuna the Sea Woman
THE YOUNG PROPRIETRESS HAS ORDERED ME NOT TO HIRE YOU, AOI...
SHAKE
SHAKE...
I-I'M SORRY, I'M SORRY.
TREMBLE

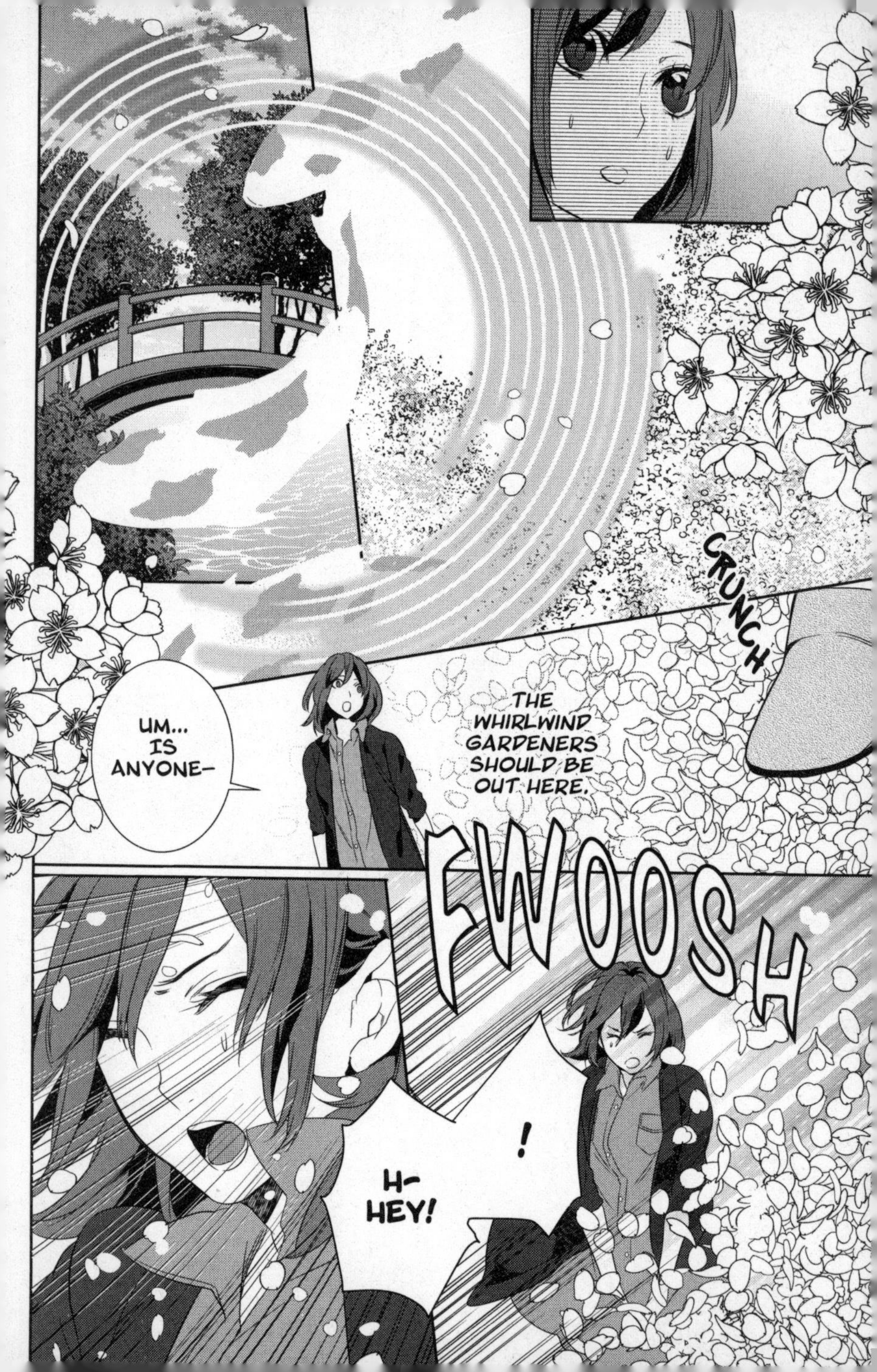
CRUNCH
THE WHIRLWIND GARDENERS SHOULD BE OUT HERE.
UM... IS ANYONE—
FWOOSH
!
H-HEY!

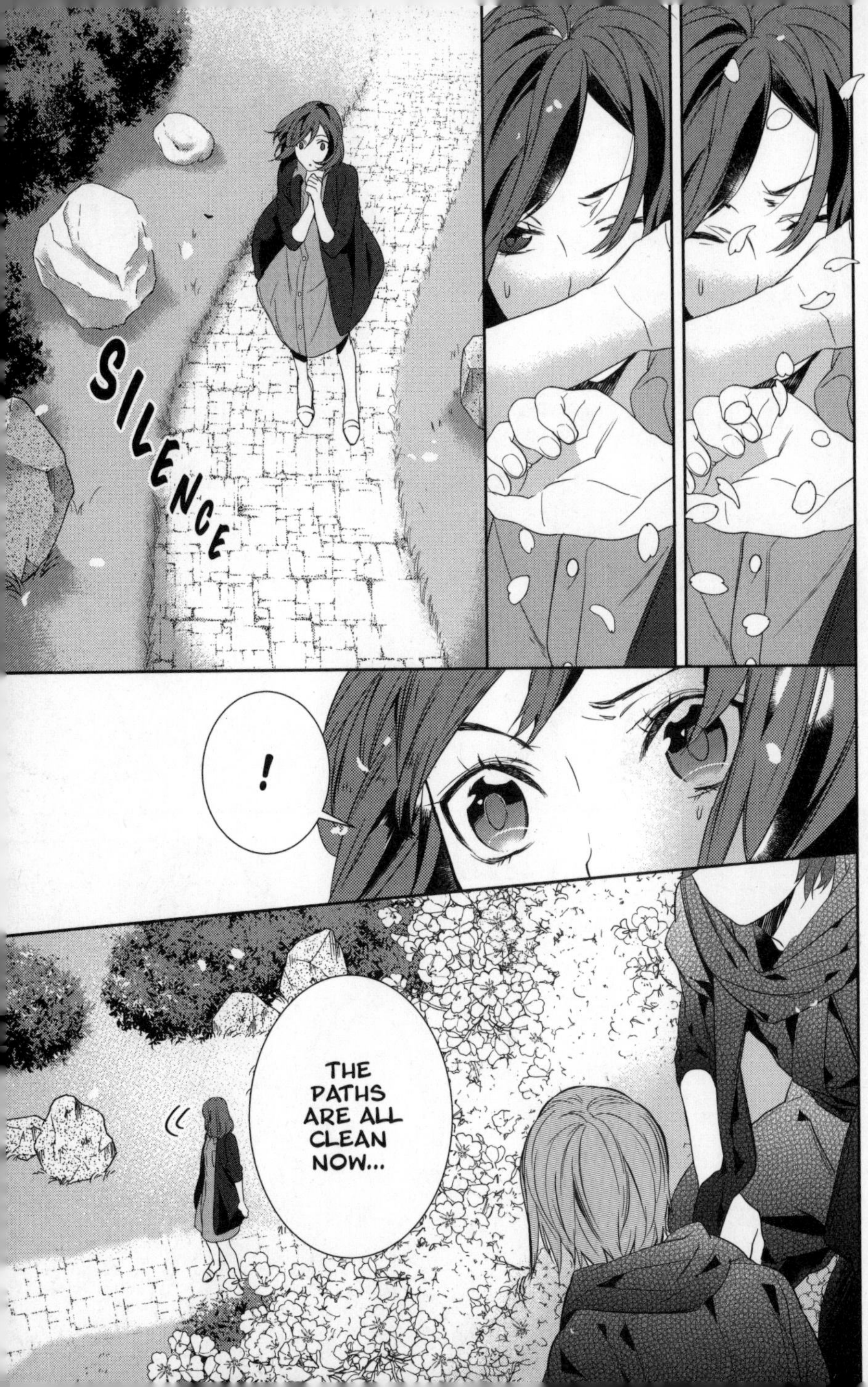
SILENCE
!
THE PATHS ARE ALL CLEAN NOW...

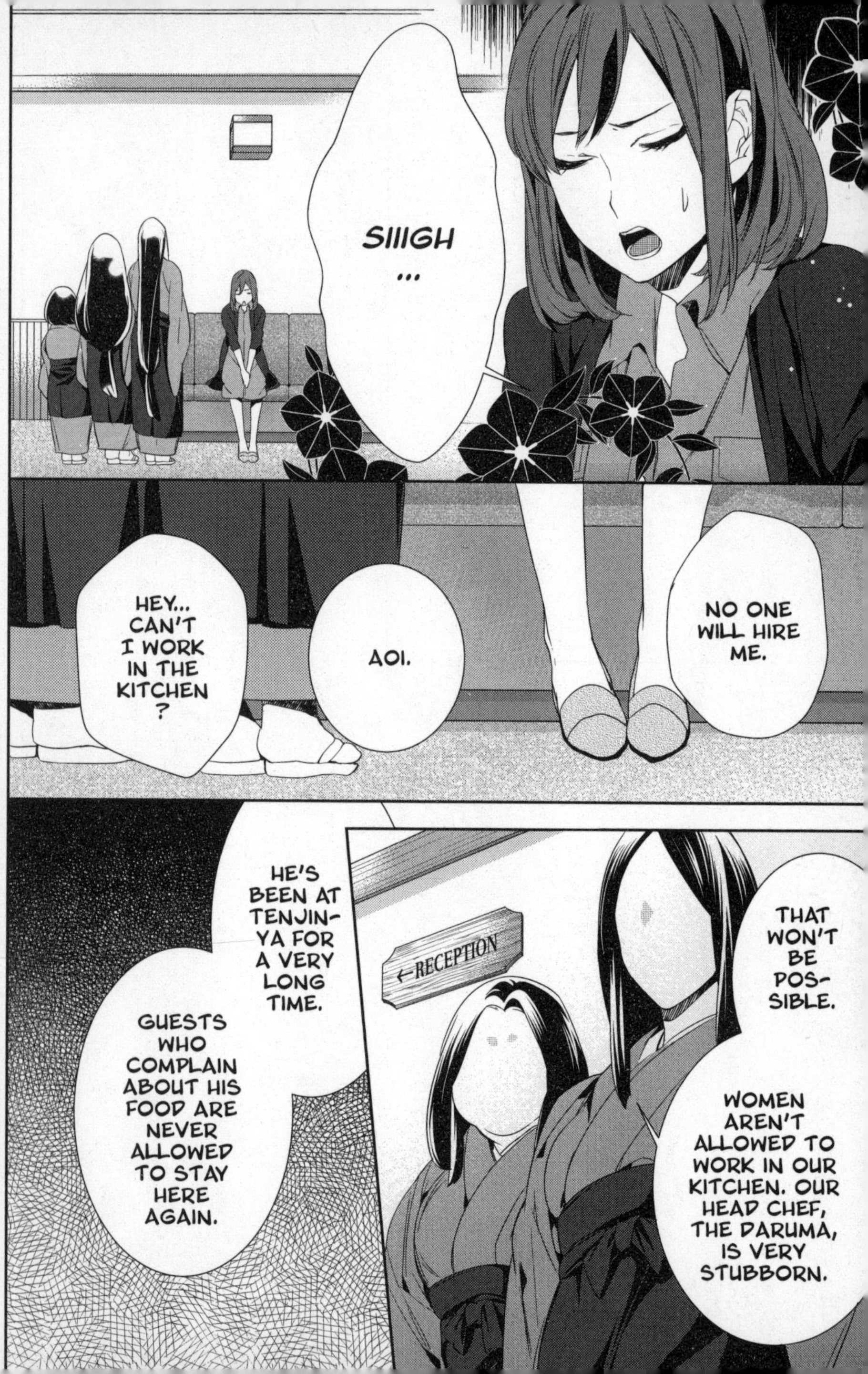
SIIGH ...
NO ONE WILL HIRE ME.
AOI.
HEY... CAN'T I WORK IN THE KITCHEN?
THAT WON'T BE POSSIBLE.
←RECEPTION
WOMEN AREN'T ALLOWED TO WORK IN OUR KITCHEN. OUR HEAD CHEF, THE DARUMA, IS VERY STUBBORN.
HE'S BEEN AT TENJIN-YA FOR A VERY LONG TIME.
GUESTS WHO COMPLAIN ABOUT HIS FOOD ARE NEVER ALLOWED TO STAY HERE AGAIN.

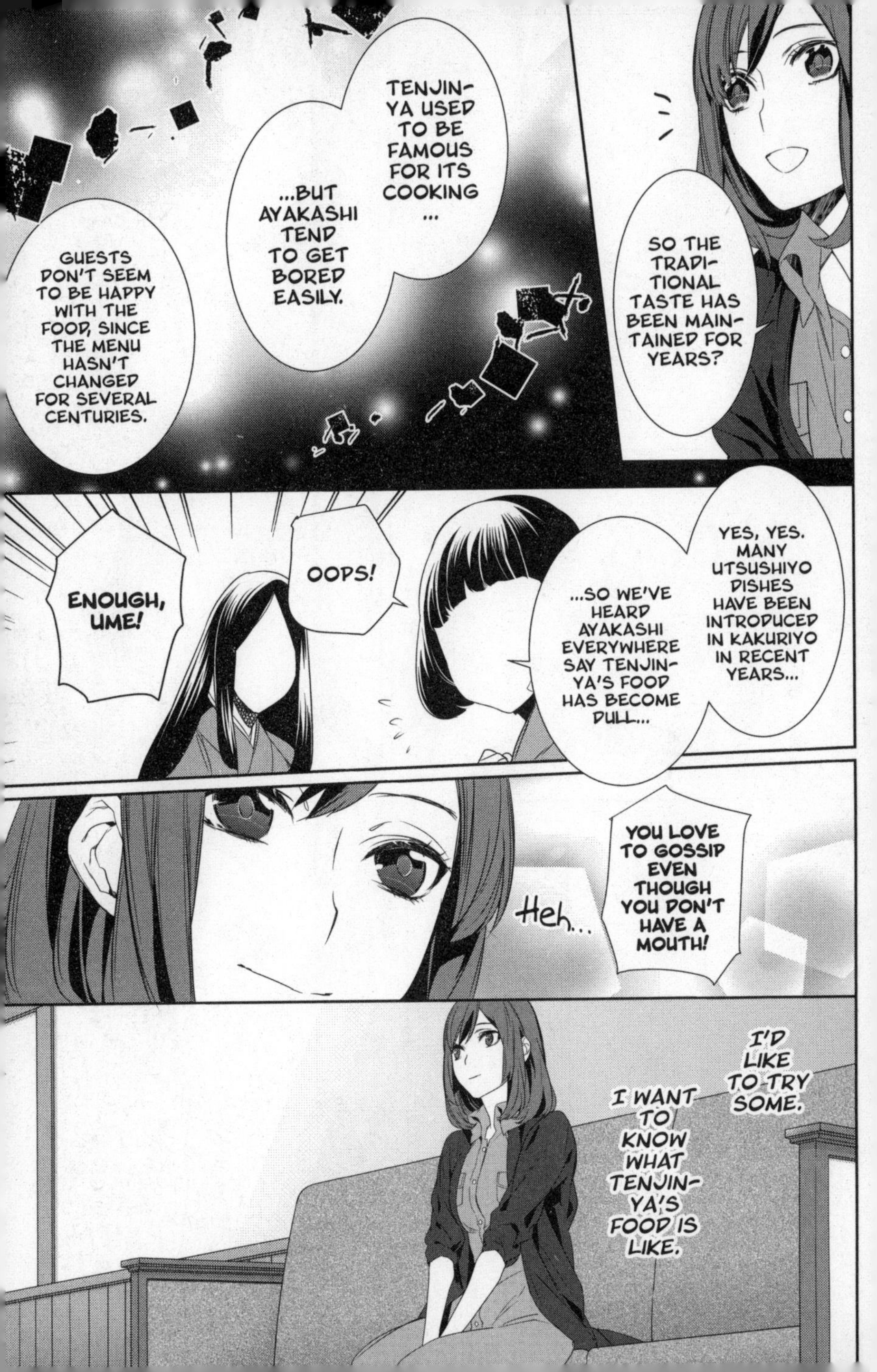
SO THE TRADITIONAL TASTE HAS BEEN MAINTAINED FOR YEARS?
TENJIN-YA USED TO BE FAMOUS FOR ITS COOKING...
...BUT AYAKASHI TEND TO GET BORED EASILY.
GUESTS DON'T SEEM TO BE HAPPY WITH THE FOOD, SINCE THE MENU HASN'T CHANGED FOR SEVERAL CENTURIES.
YES, YES. MANY UTSUSHIYO DISHES HAVE BEEN INTRODUCED IN KAKURIYO IN RECENT YEARS...
...SO WE'VE HEARD AYAKASHI EVERYWHERE SAY TENJIN-YA'S FOOD HAS BECOME DULL...
OOPS!
ENOUGH, UME!
YOU LOVE TO GOSSIP EVEN THOUGH YOU DON'T HAVE A MOUTH!
Heh...
I'D LIKE TO TRY SOME.
I WANT TO KNOW WHAT TENJIN-YA'S FOOD IS LIKE.

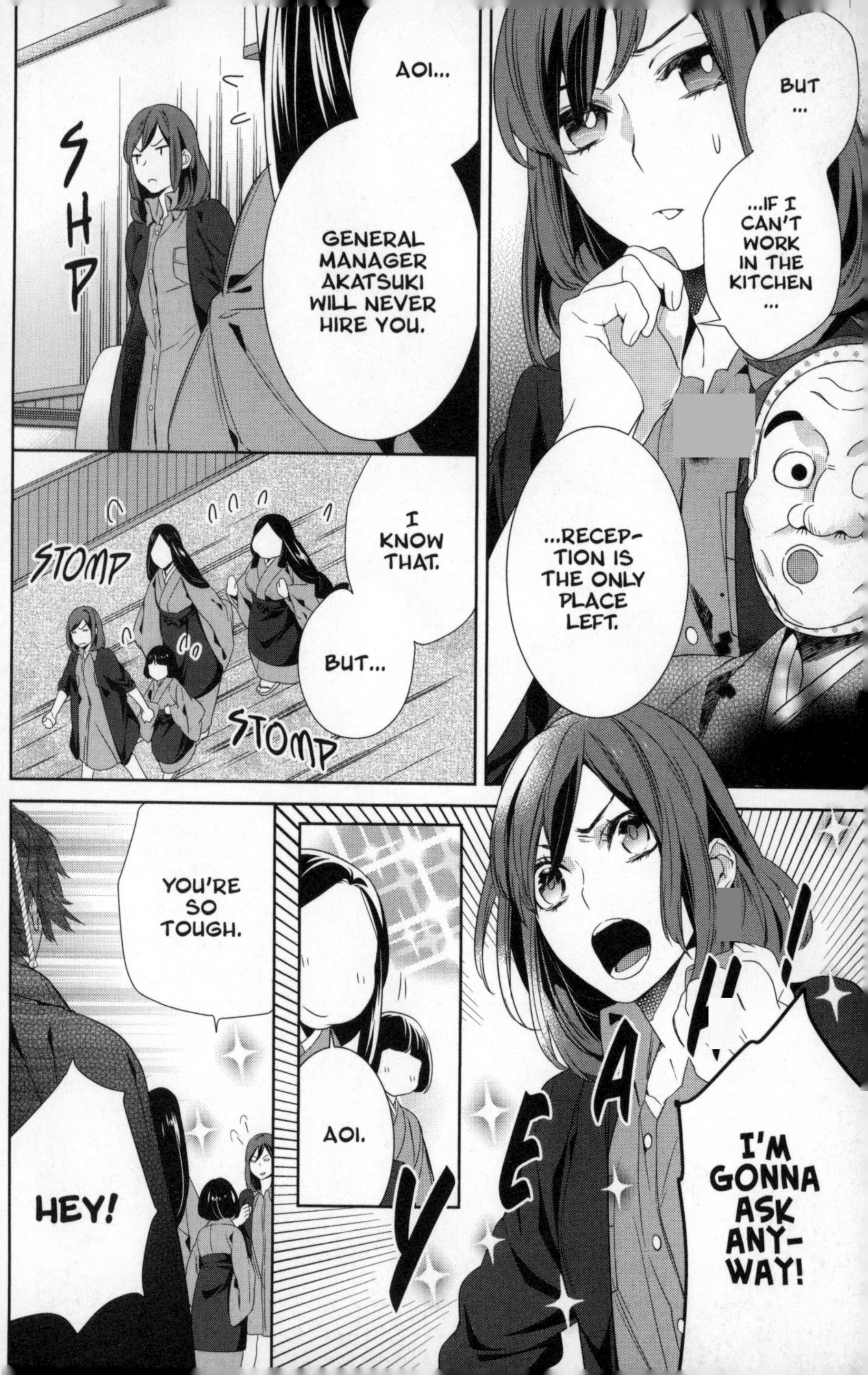

BUT...
...IF I CAN'T WORK IN THE KITCHEN...
...RECEPTION IS THE ONLY PLACE LEFT.
AOI...
GENERAL MANAGER AKATSUKI WILL NEVER HIRE YOU.
SHP
I KNOW THAT.
BUT...
STOMP
STOMP
YEAH!
I'M GONNA ASK ANYWAY!
AOI.
YOU'RE SO TOUGH.
HEY!

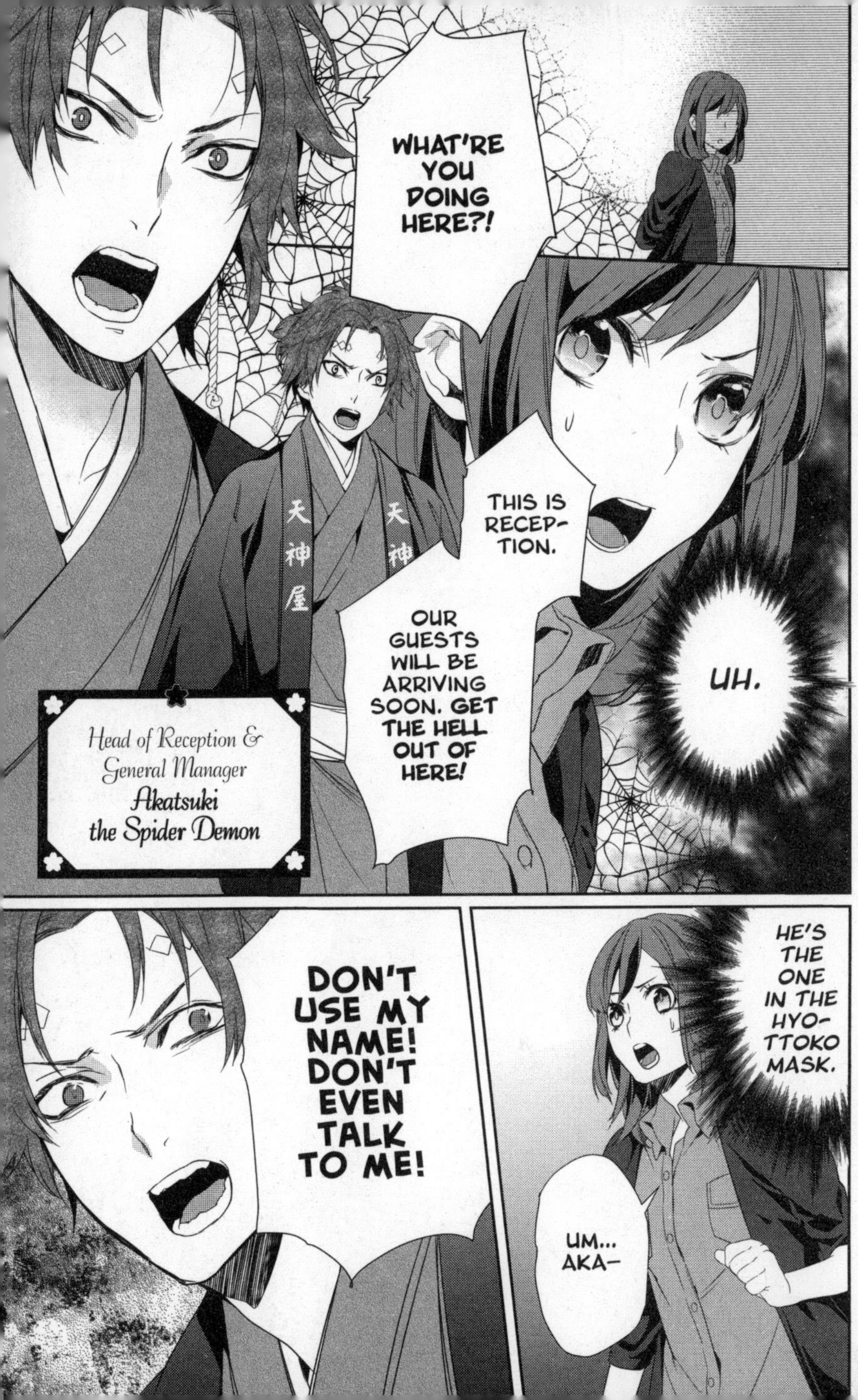
WHAT'RE YOU DOING HERE?!
UH.
THIS IS RECEPTION.
OUR GUESTS WILL BE ARRIVING SOON. GET THE HELL OUT OF HERE!
天神屋
天神
Head of Reception & General Manager
Akatsuki the Spider Demon
HE'S THE ONE IN THE HYO-TTOKO MASK.
UM... AKA-
DON'T USE MY NAME! DON'T EVEN TALK TO ME!

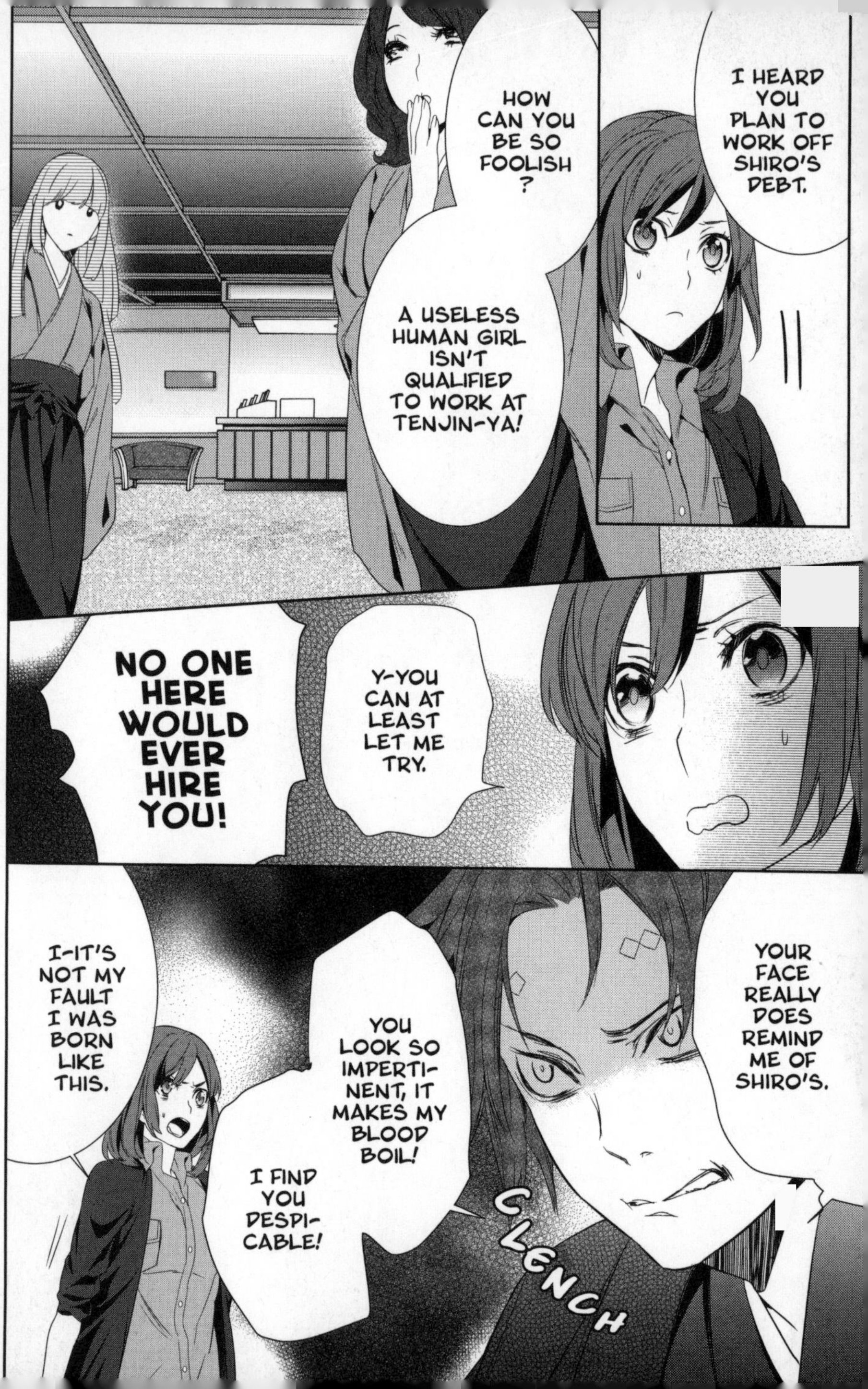
I HEARD YOU PLAN TO WORK OFF SHIRO'S DEBT.
HOW CAN YOU BE SO FOOLISH?
A USELESS HUMAN GIRL ISN'T QUALIFIED TO WORK AT TENJIN-YA!
Y-YOU CAN AT LEAST LET ME TRY.
NO ONE HERE WOULD EVER HIRE YOU!
YOUR FACE REALLY DOES REMIND ME OF SHIRO'S.
YOU LOOK SO IMPERTI-NENT, IT MAKES MY BLOOD BOIL!
CLENCH
I FIND YOU DESPI-CABLE!
I-IT'S NOT MY FAULT I WAS BORN LIKE THIS.

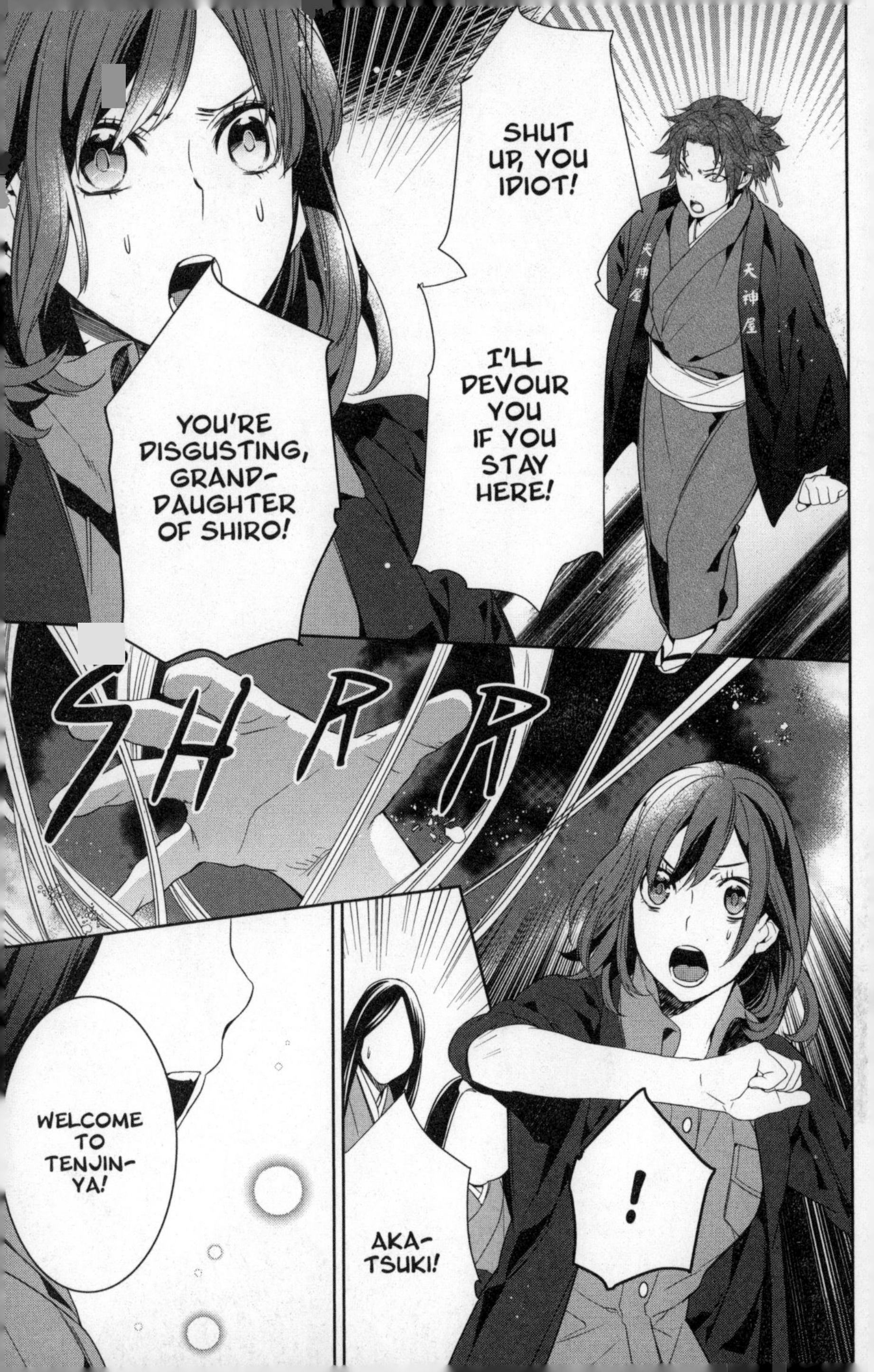
SHUT UP, YOU IDIOT!
I'LL DEVOUR YOU IF YOU STAY HERE!
天神屋
YOU'RE DISGUSTING, GRAND-DAUGHTER OF SHIRO!
SHRR
!
AKA-TSUKI!
WELCOME TO TENJIN-YA!

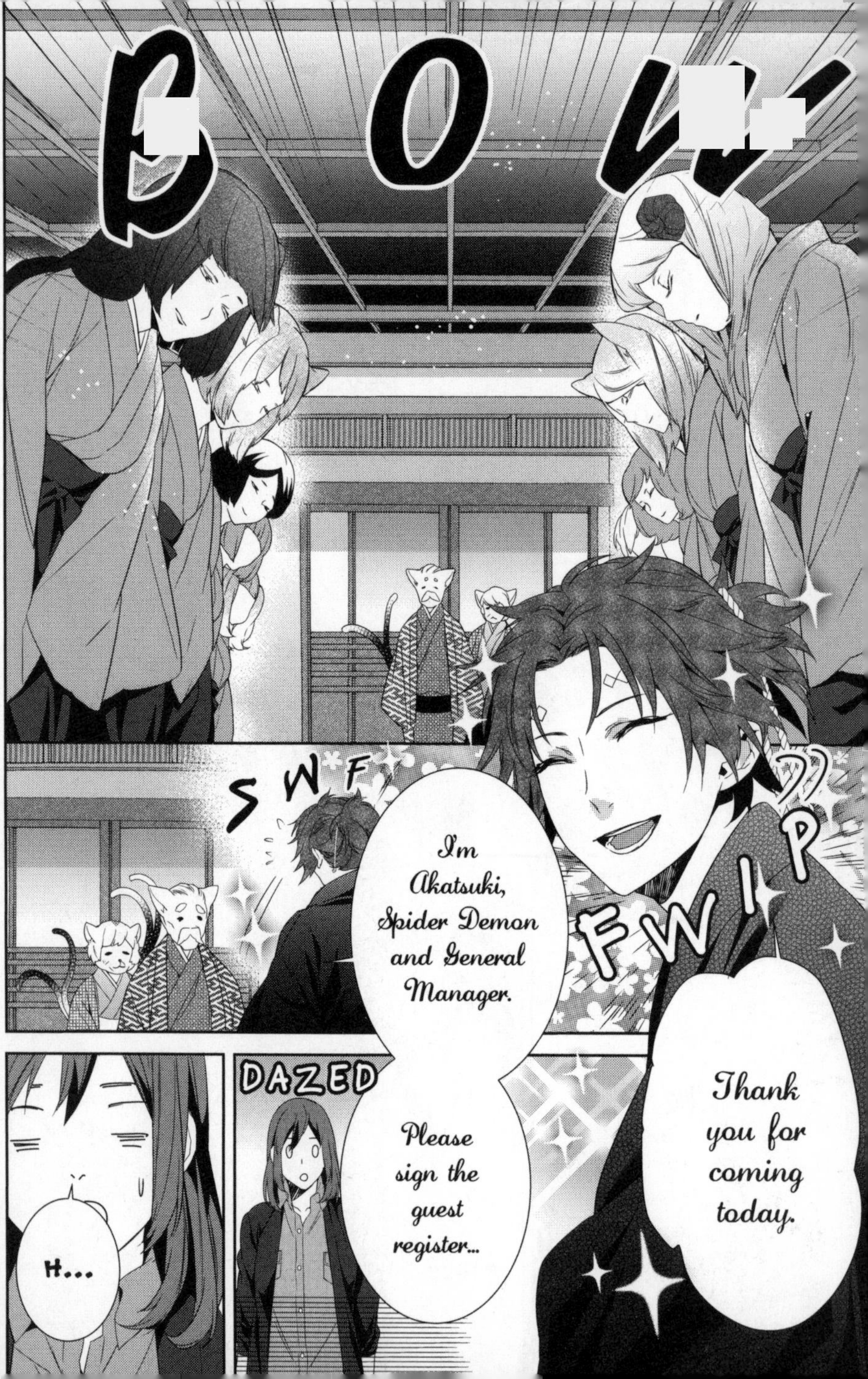
BOW
FWIP
SWF
Thank you for coming today.
I'm Akatsuki, Spider Demon and General Manager.
Please sign the guest register...
DAZED
H...

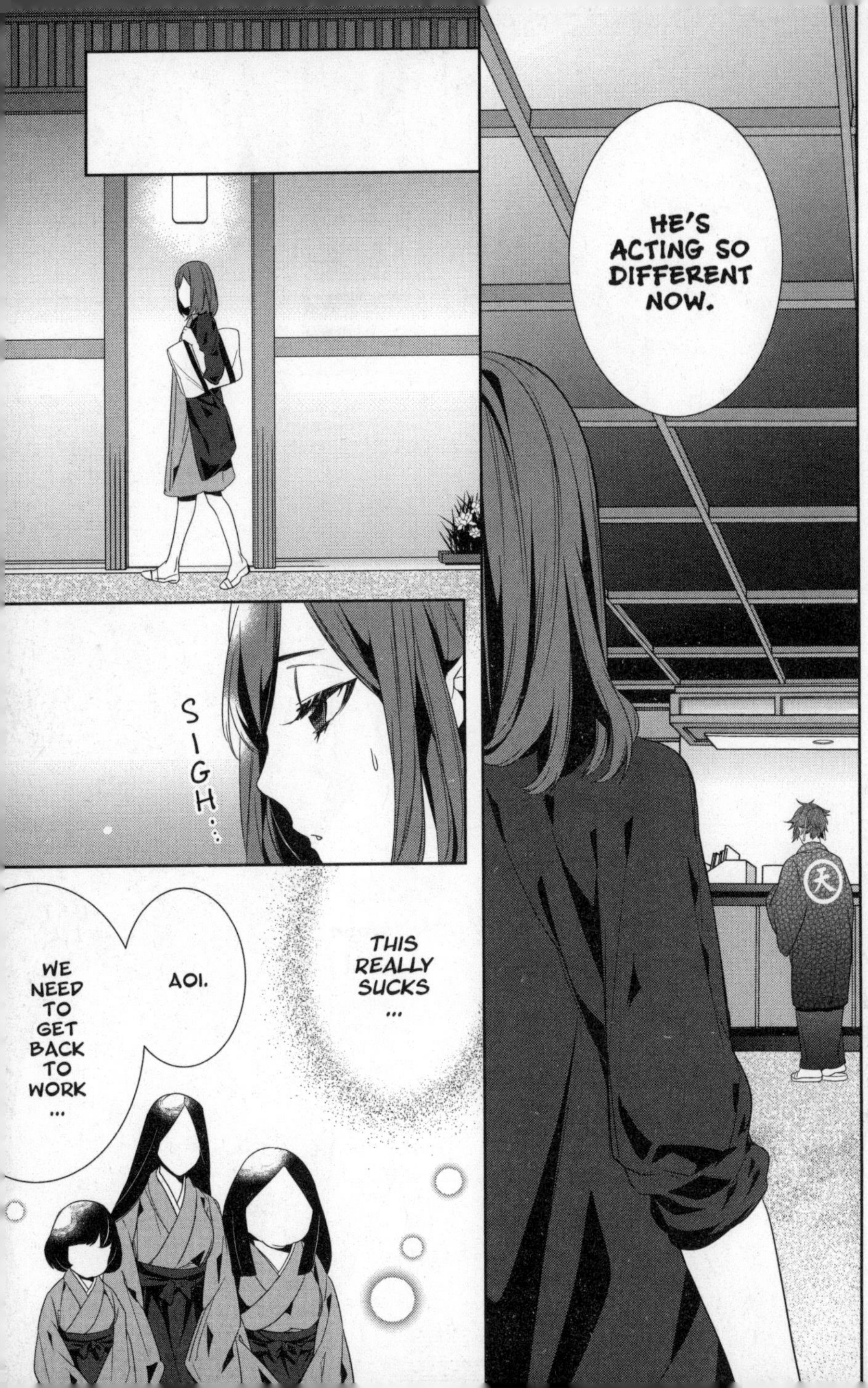
HE'S ACTING SO DIFFERENT NOW.
SIGH...
THIS REALLY SUCKS...
AOI. WE NEED TO GET BACK TO WORK...

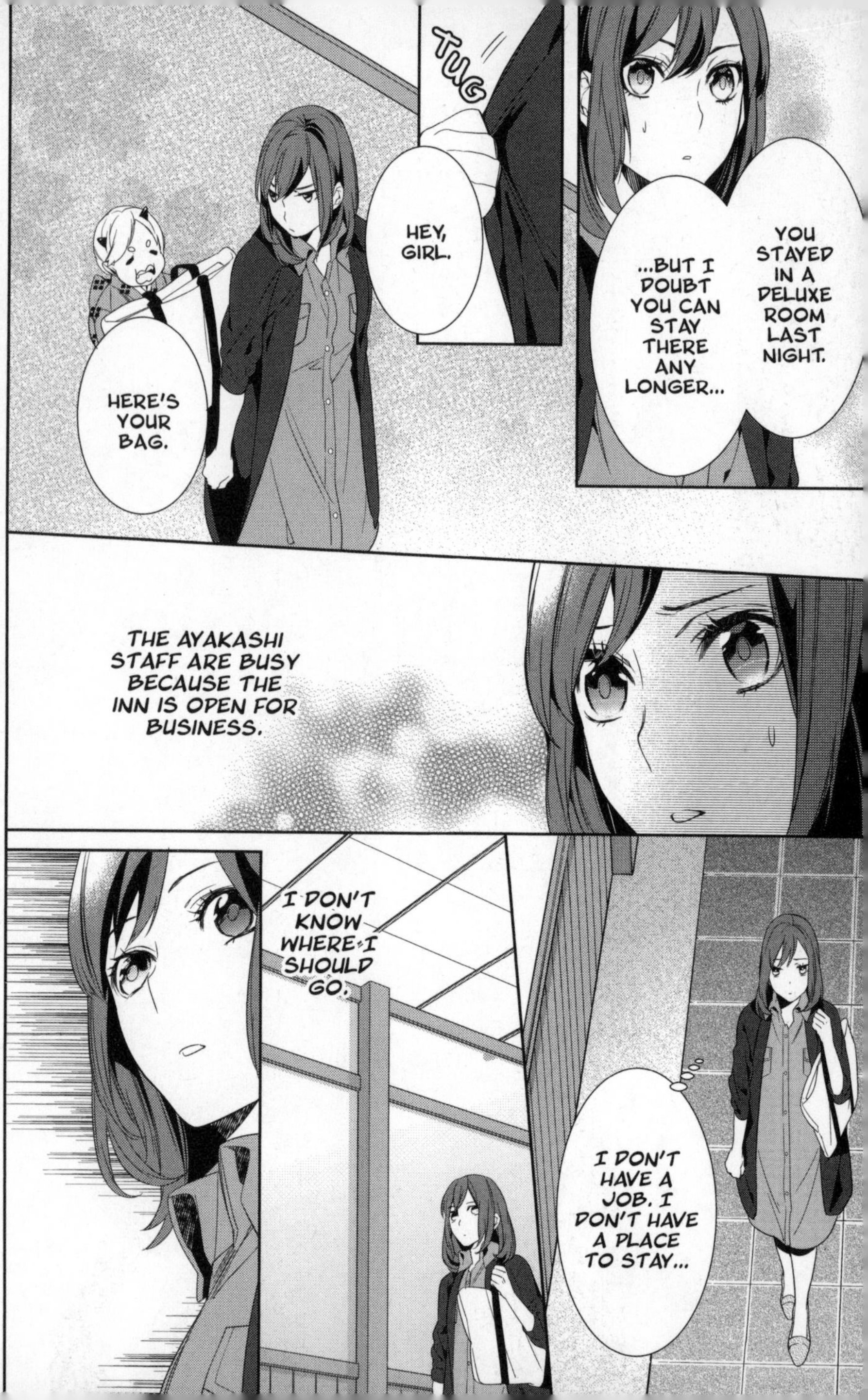
YOU STAYED IN A DELUXE ROOM LAST NIGHT.
...BUT I DOUBT YOU CAN STAY THERE ANY LONGER...
TUG
HEY, GIRL.
HERE'S YOUR BAG.
THE AYAKASHI STAFF ARE BUSY BECAUSE THE INN IS OPEN FOR BUSINESS.
I DON'T HAVE A JOB. I DON'T HAVE A PLACE TO STAY...
I DON'T KNOW WHERE I SHOULD GO.

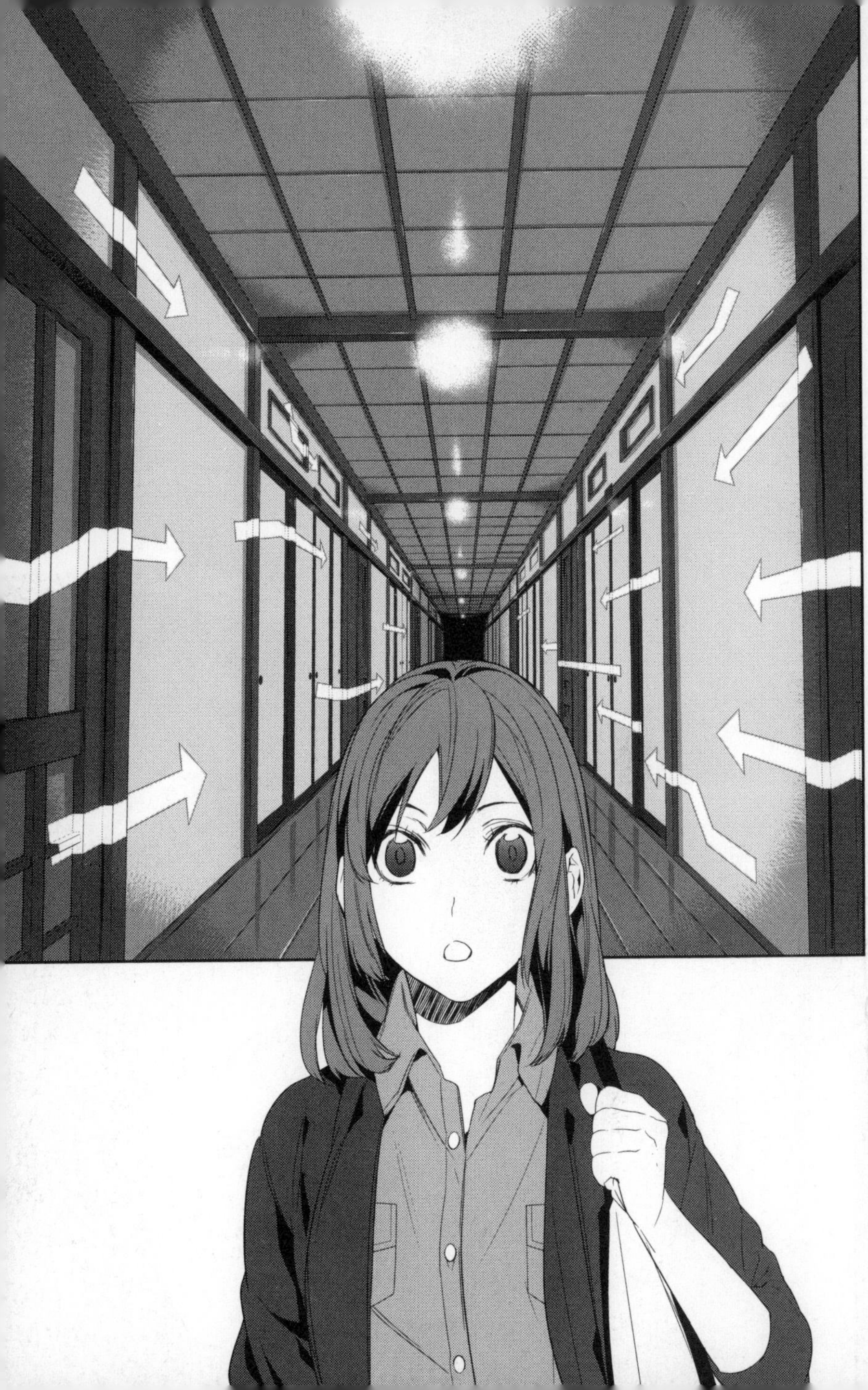

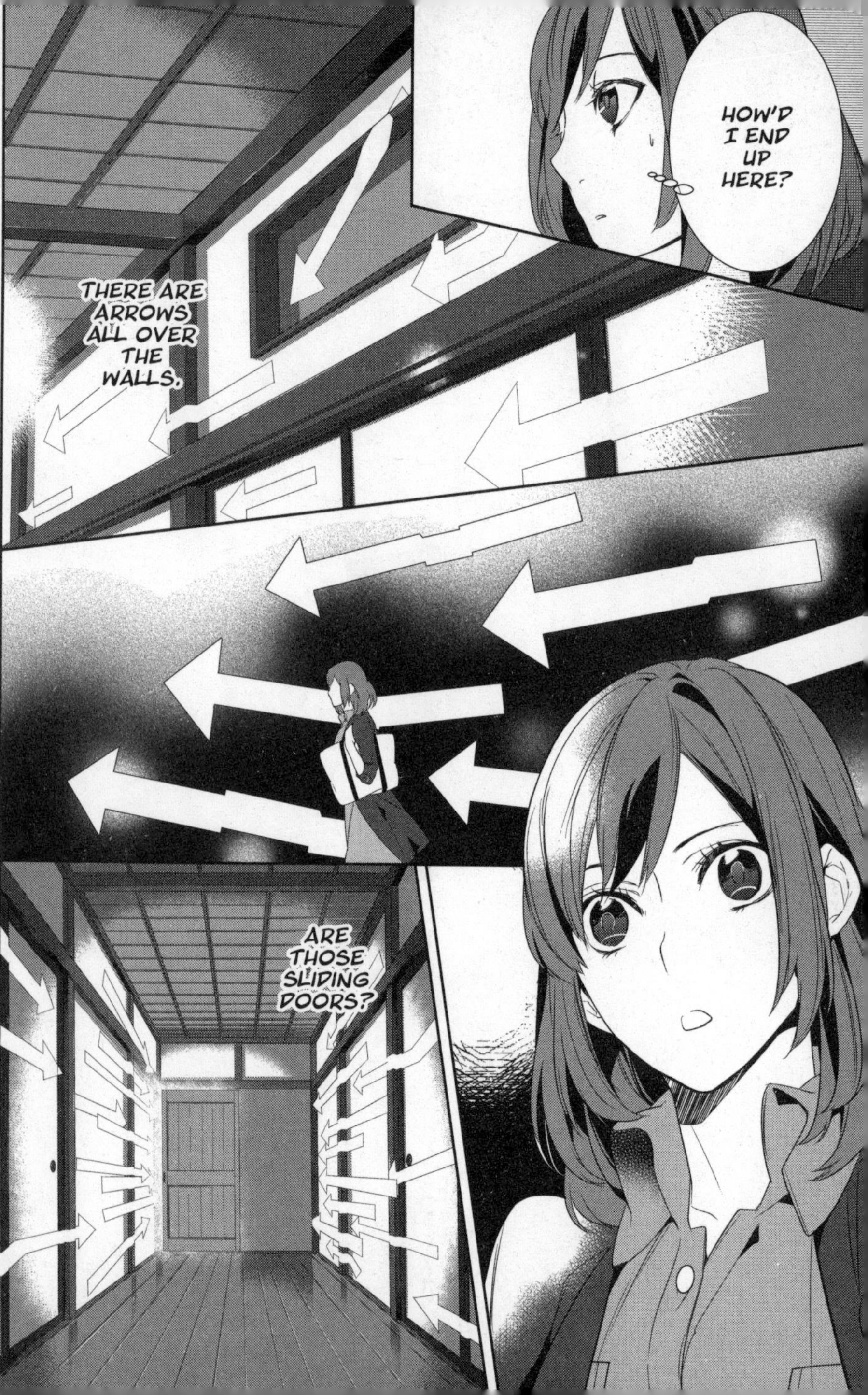
HOW'D I END UP HERE?
THERE ARE ARROWS ALL OVER THE WALLS.
ARE THOSE SLIDING DOORS?

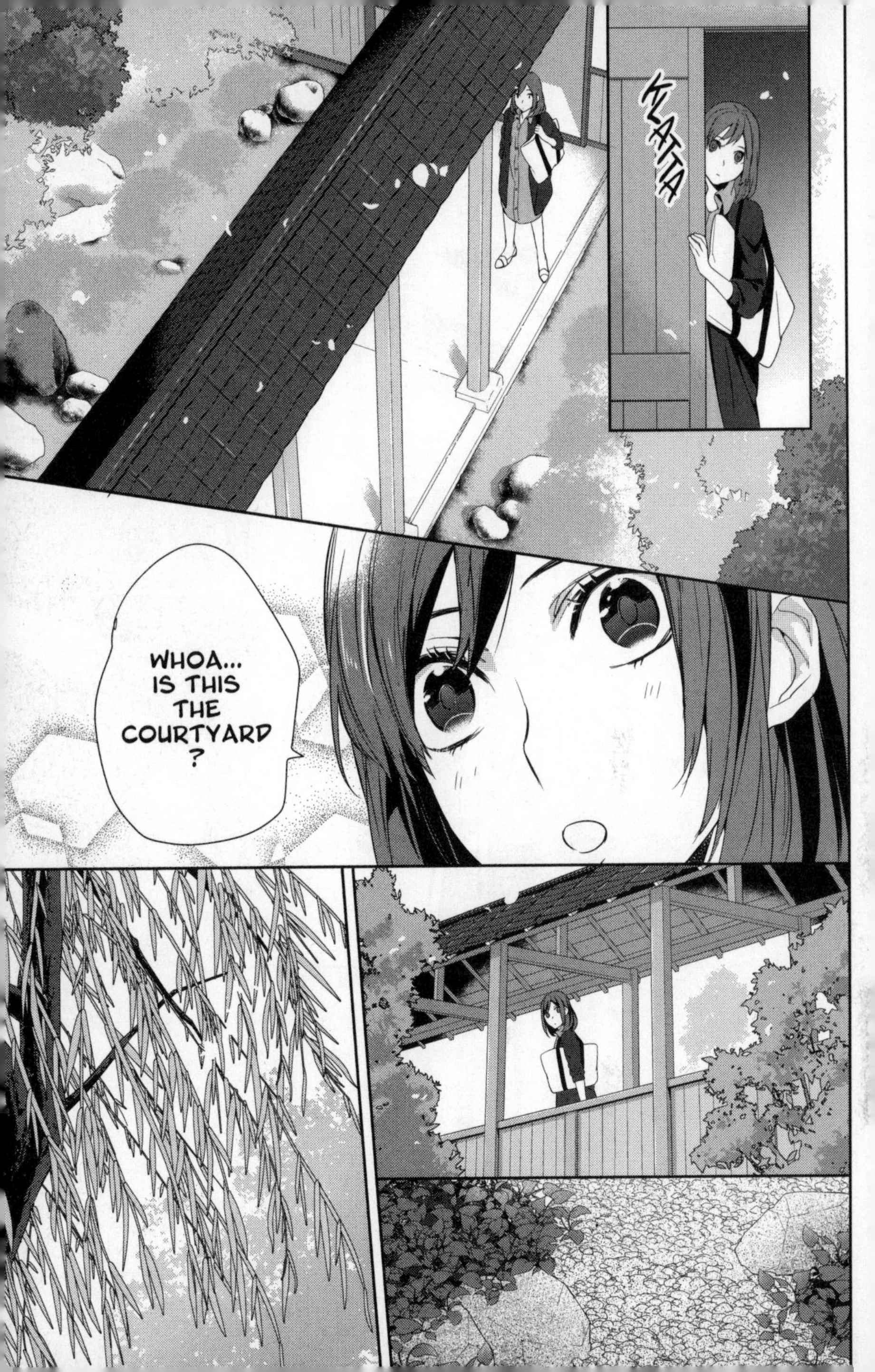
KLATTA
WHOA... IS THIS THE COURTYARD?

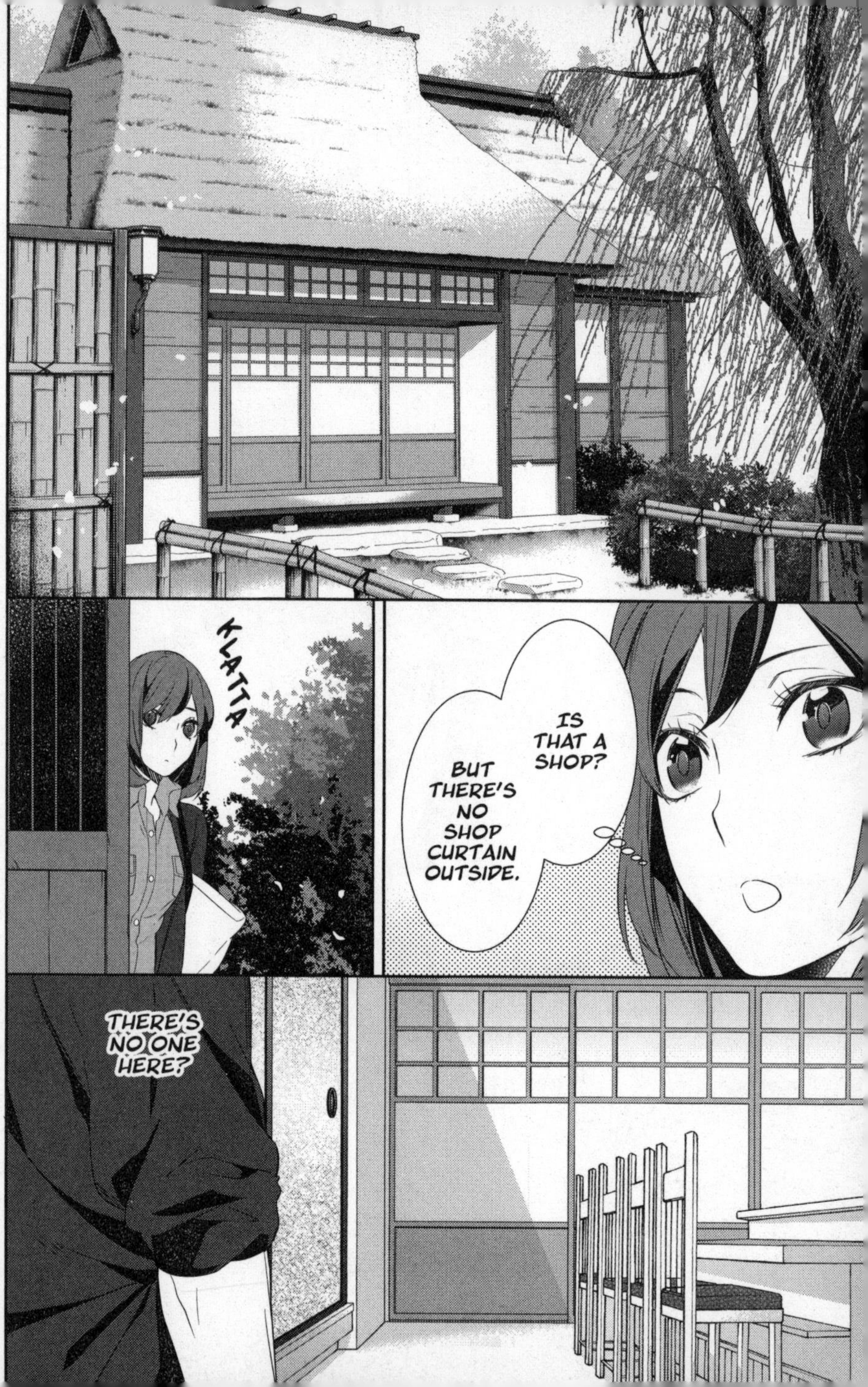
IS THAT A SHOP?
BUT THERE'S NO SHOP CURTAIN OUTSIDE.
KLATTA
THERE'S NO ONE HERE?

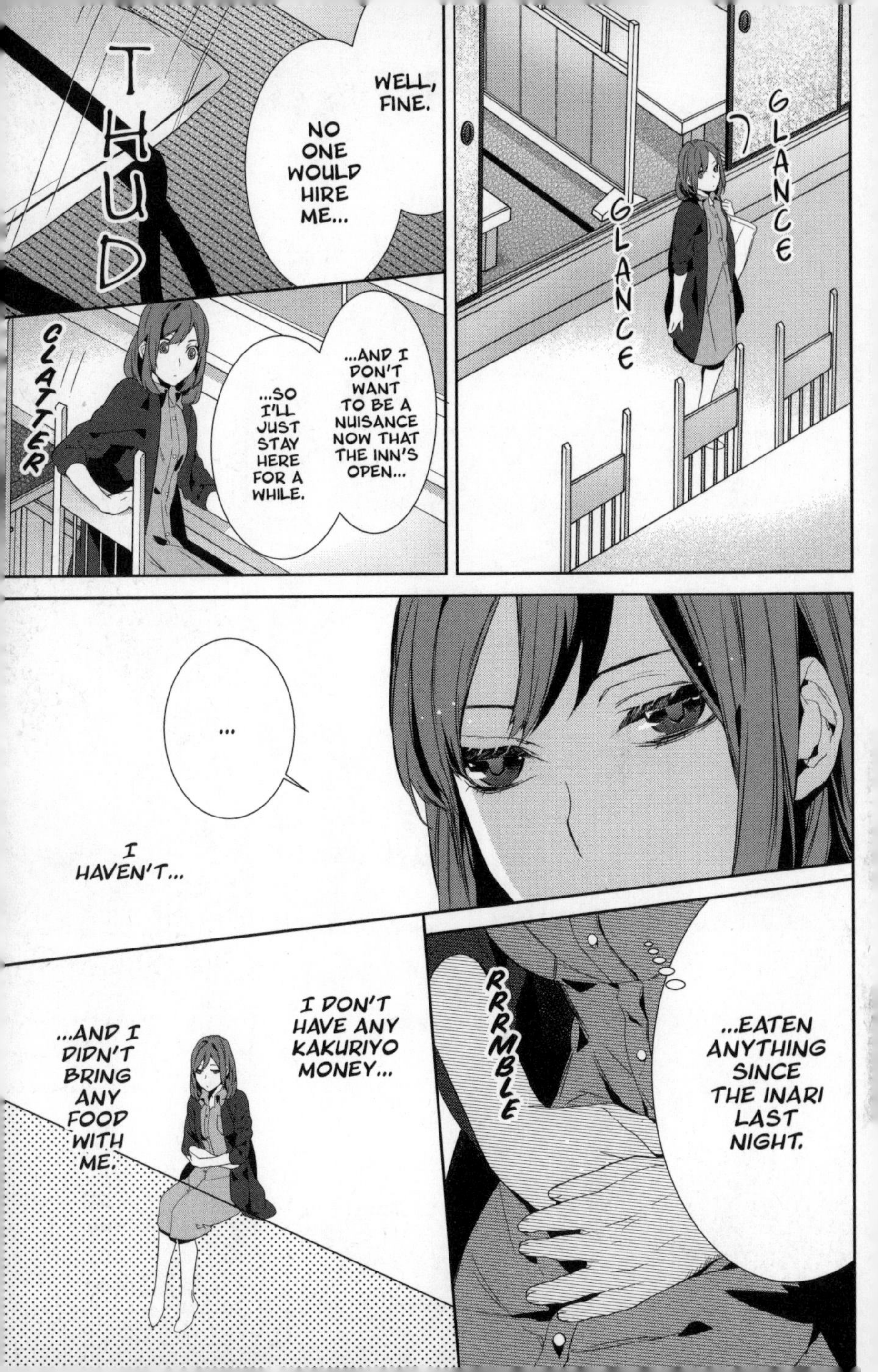
GLANCE
GLANCE
THUD
WELL, FINE.
NO ONE WOULD HIRE ME...
CLATTER
...AND I DON'T WANT TO BE A NUISANCE NOW THAT THE INN'S OPEN...
...SO I'LL JUST STAY HERE FOR A WHILE.
...
I HAVEN'T...
RRRMBLE
...EATEN ANYTHING SINCE THE INARI LAST NIGHT.
I DON'T HAVE ANY KAKURIYO MONEY...
...AND I DIDN'T BRING ANY FOOD WITH ME.

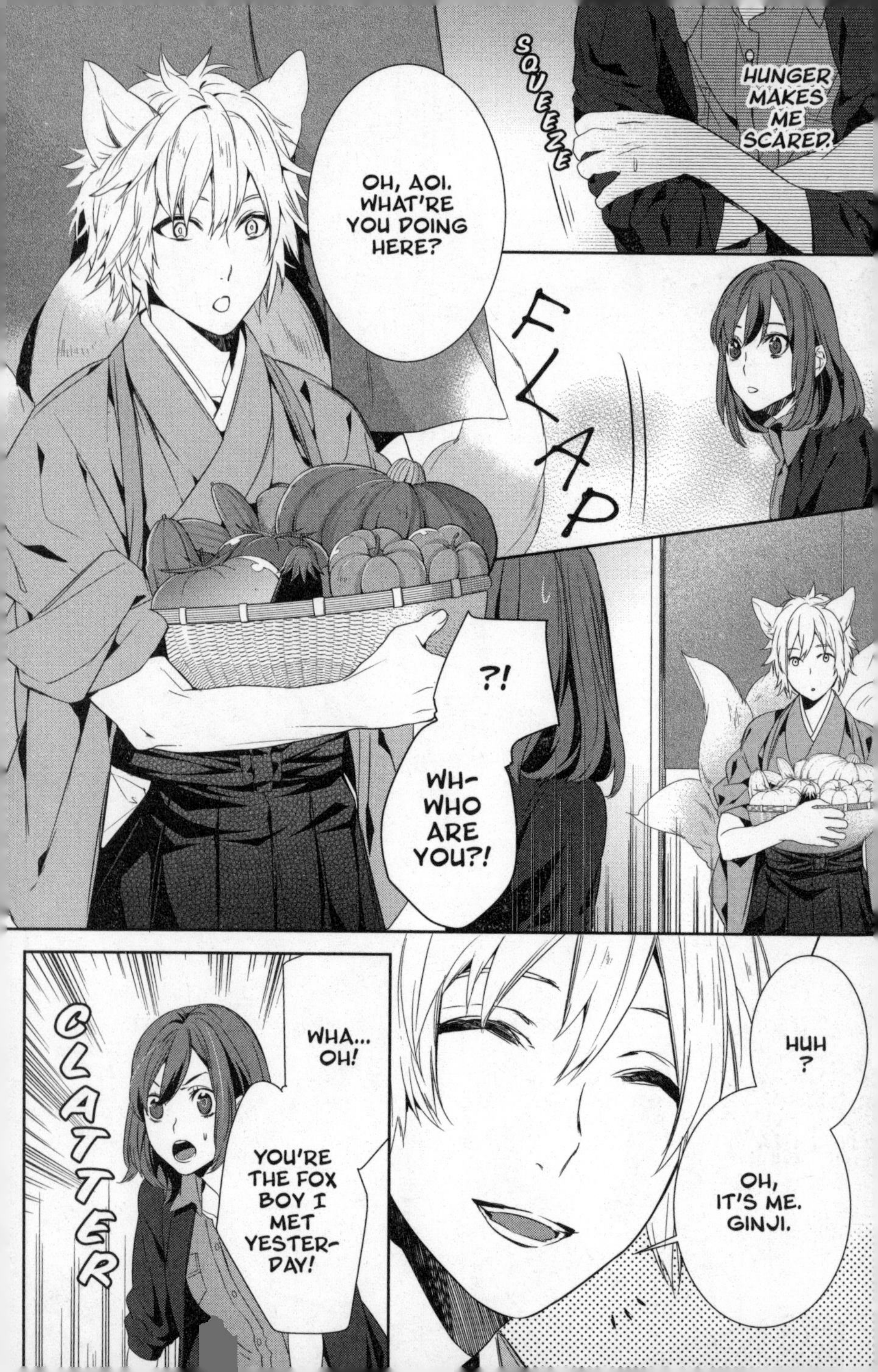
SQUEEZE
HUNGER MAKES ME SCARED.
FLAP
?!
WH-WHO ARE YOU?!
OH, AOI. WHAT'RE YOU DOING HERE?
HUH?
OH, IT'S ME. GINJI.
CLATTER
WHA... OH!
YOU'RE THE FOX BOY I MET YESTER-DAY!

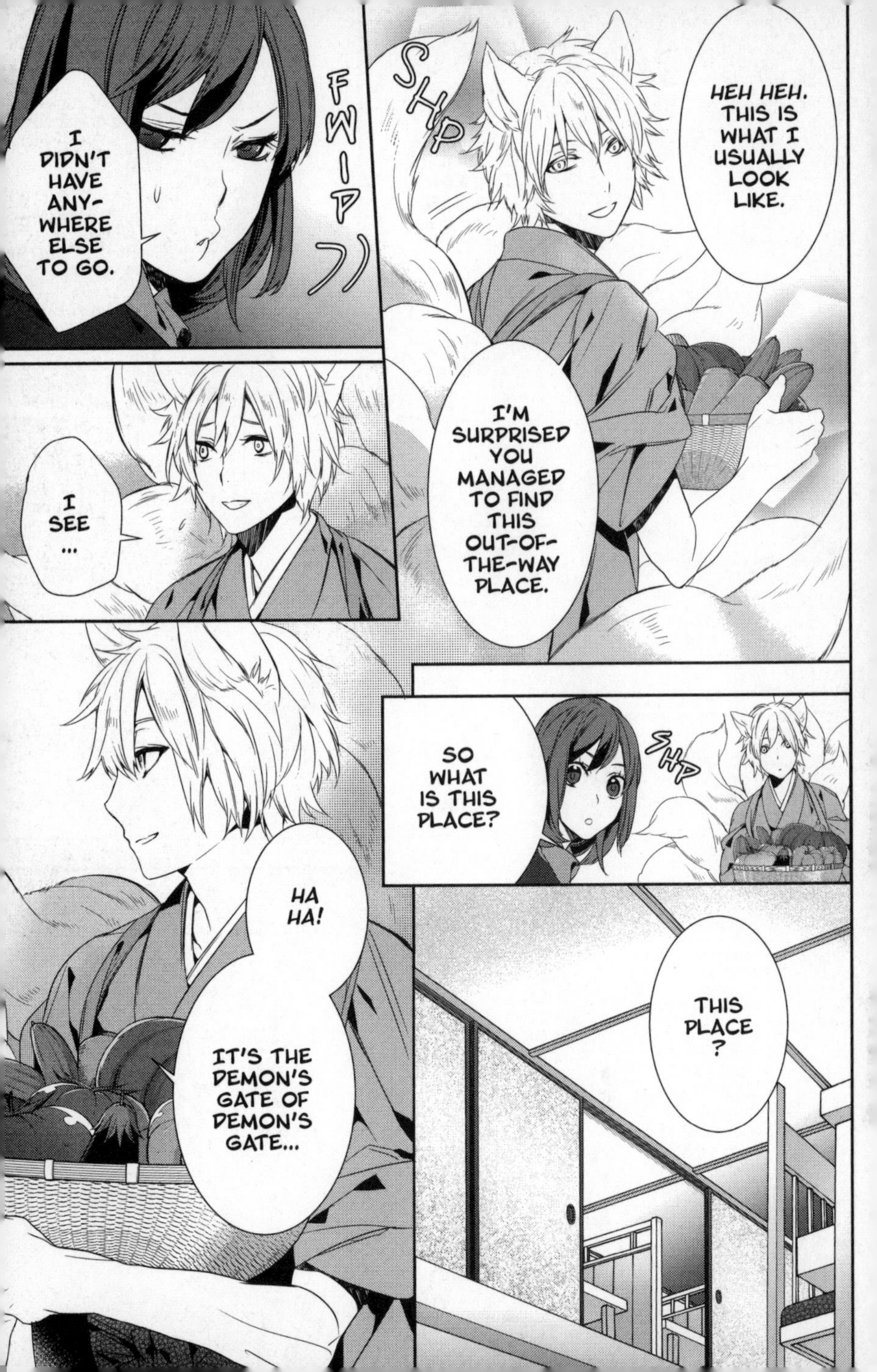

SHP
HEH HEH. THIS IS WHAT I USUALLY LOOK LIKE.
I'M SURPRISED YOU MANAGED TO FIND THIS OUT-OF-THE-WAY PLACE.
FWIP
I DIDN'T HAVE ANY-WHERE ELSE TO GO.
I SEE...
SHP
SO WHAT IS THIS PLACE?
THIS PLACE?
HA HA!
IT'S THE DEMON'S GATE OF DEMON'S GATE...

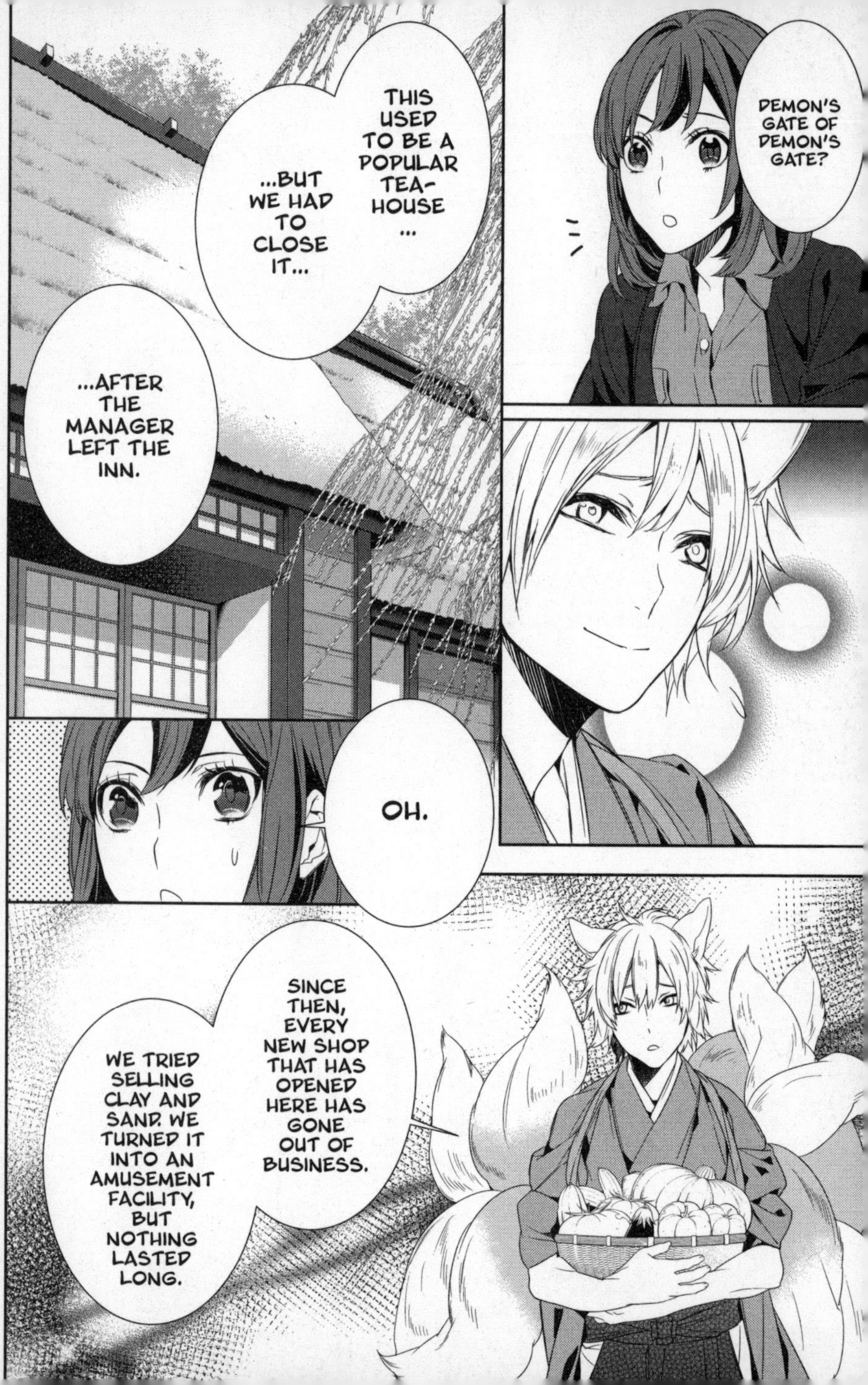
DEMON'S GATE OF DEMON'S GATE?
THIS USED TO BE A POPULAR TEA-HOUSE ...
...BUT WE HAD TO CLOSE IT...
...AFTER THE MANAGER LEFT THE INN.
OH.
SINCE THEN, EVERY NEW SHOP THAT HAS OPENED HERE HAS GONE OUT OF BUSINESS.
WE TRIED SELLING CLAY AND SAND. WE TURNED IT INTO AN AMUSEMENT FACILITY, BUT NOTHING LASTED LONG.

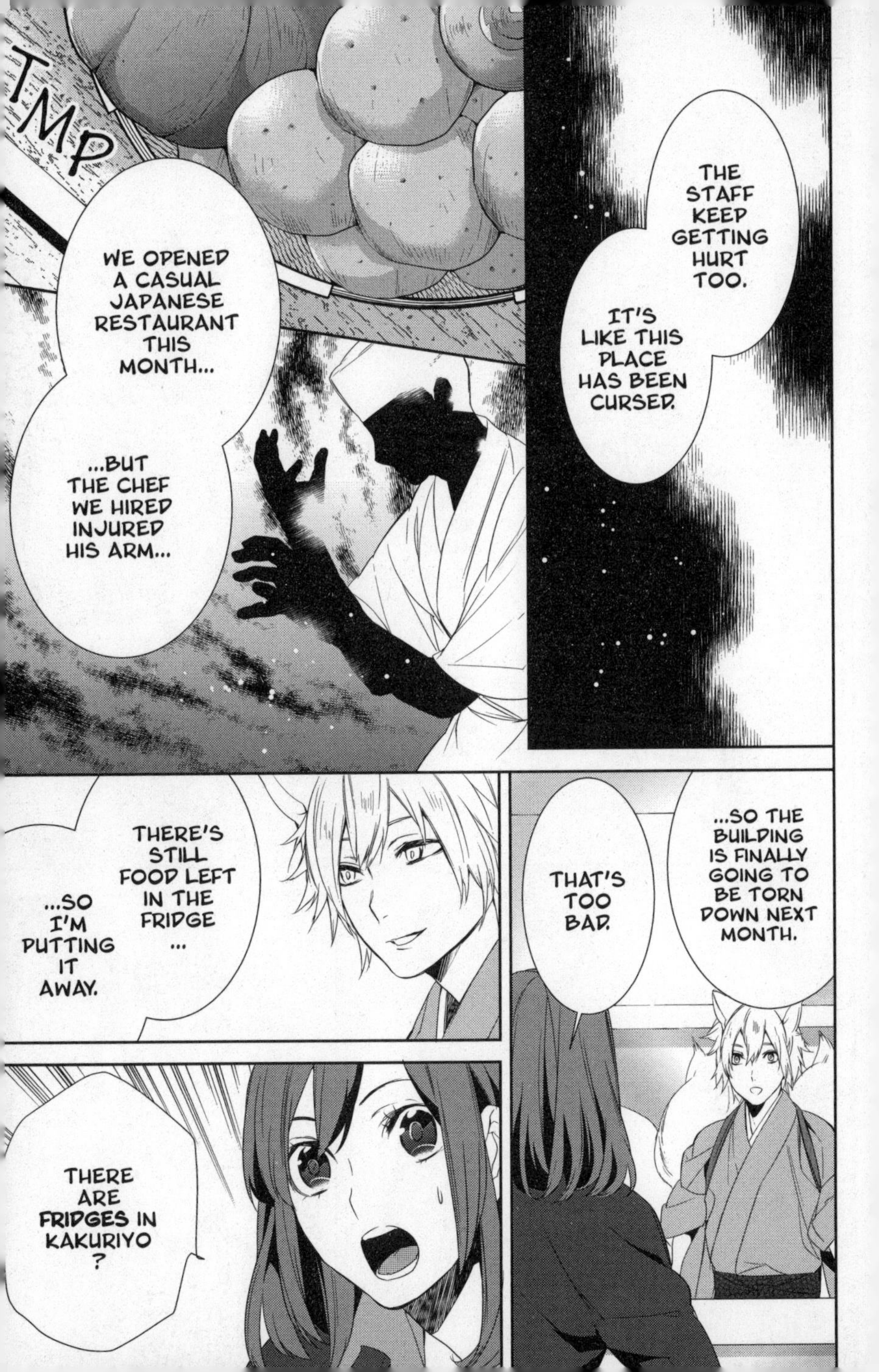
THE STAFF KEEP GETTING HURT TOO.
IT'S LIKE THIS PLACE HAS BEEN CURSED.
TMP
WE OPENED A CASUAL JAPANESE RESTAURANT THIS MONTH...
...BUT THE CHEF WE HIRED INJURED HIS ARM...
...SO THE BUILDING IS FINALLY GOING TO BE TORN DOWN NEXT MONTH.
THAT'S TOO BAD.
THERE'S STILL FOOD LEFT IN THE FRIDGE...
...SO I'M PUTTING IT AWAY.
THERE ARE FRIDGES IN KAKURIYO?

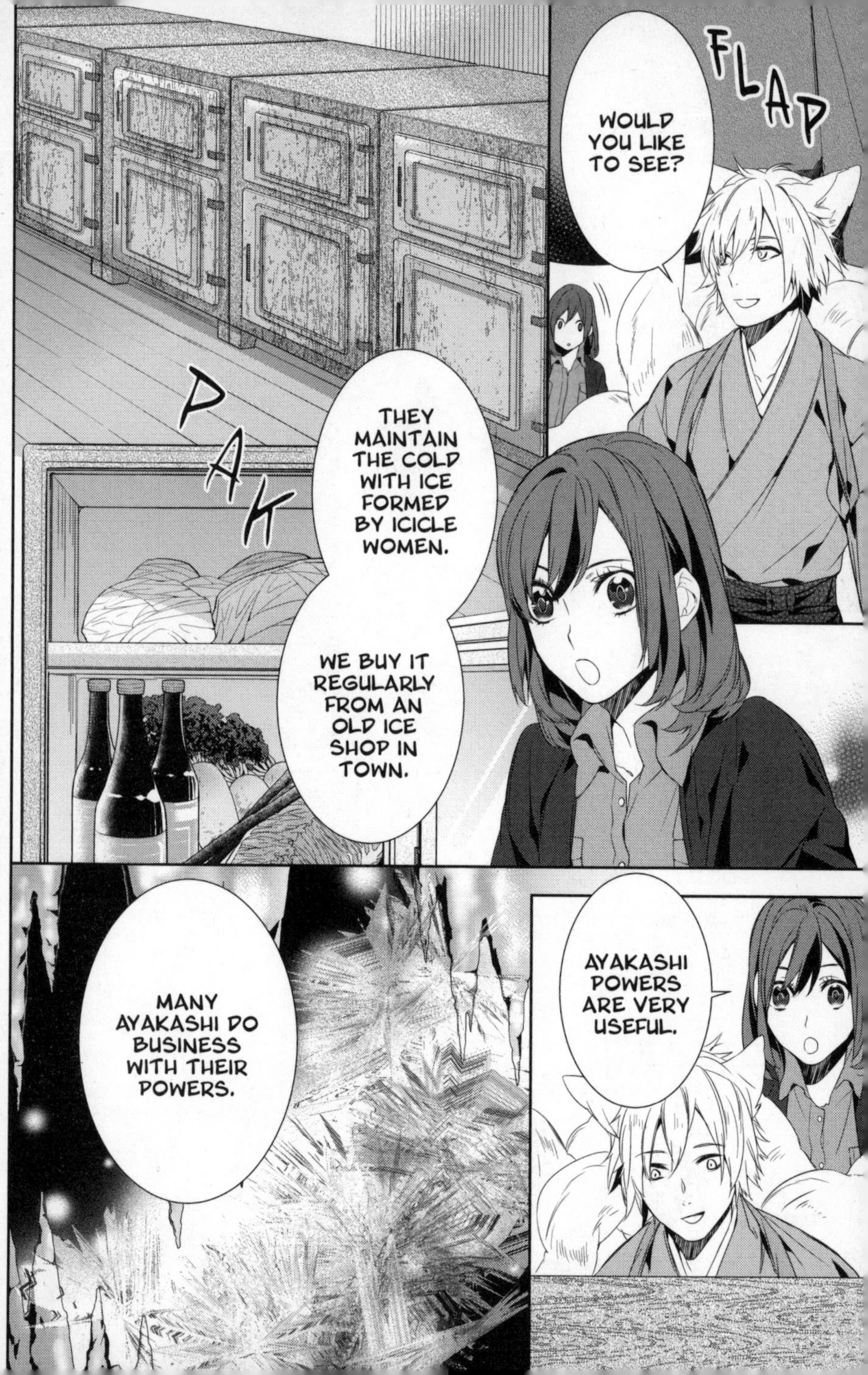
FLAP
WOULD YOU LIKE TO SEE?
PAK
THEY MAINTAIN THE COLD WITH ICE FORMED BY ICICLE WOMEN.
WE BUY IT REGULARLY FROM AN OLD ICE SHOP IN TOWN.
AYAKASHI POWERS ARE VERY USEFUL.
MANY AYAKASHI DO BUSINESS WITH THEIR POWERS.

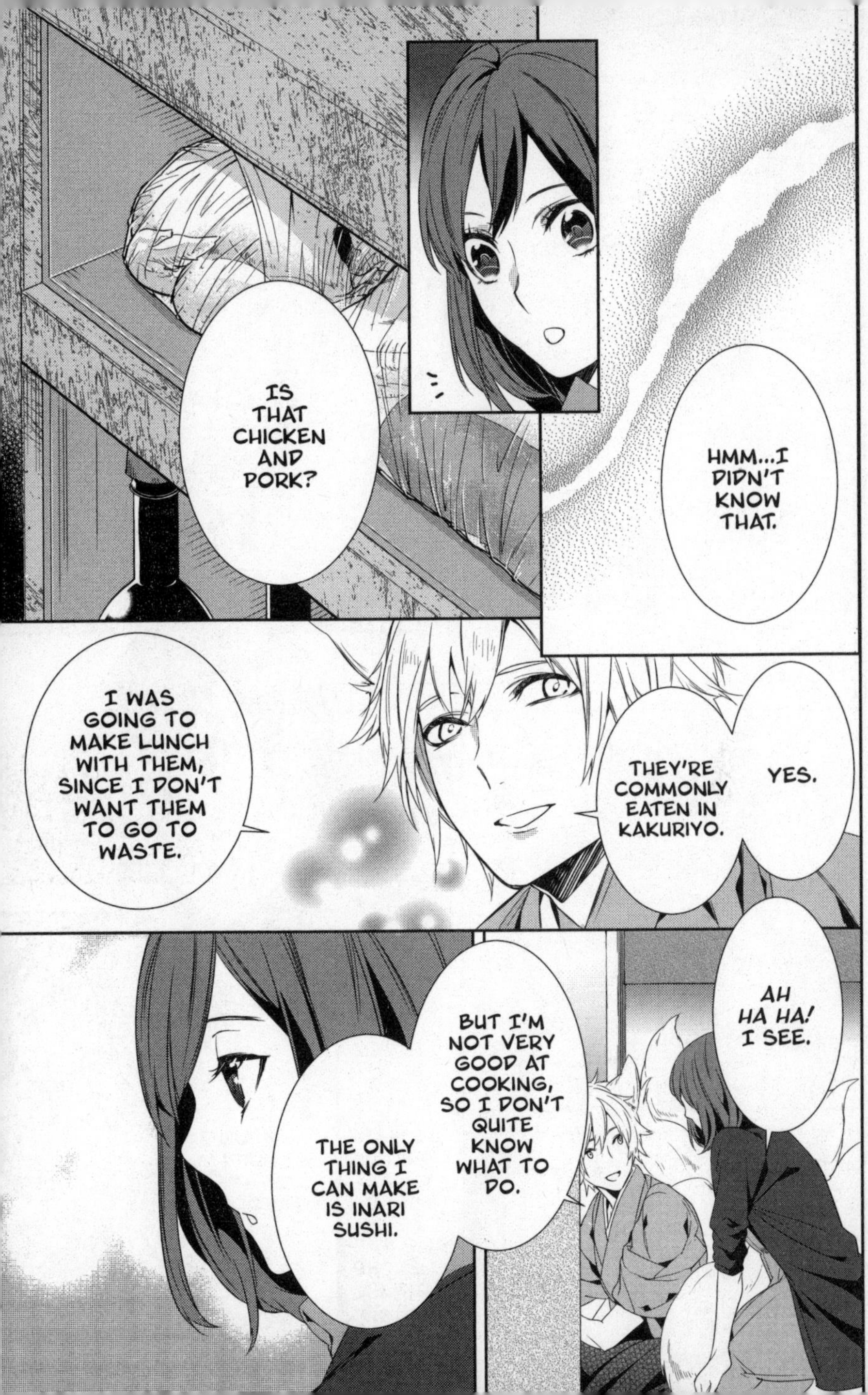
IS THAT CHICKEN AND PORK?
YES.
THEY'RE COMMONLY EATEN IN KAKURIYO.
HMM...I DIDN'T KNOW THAT.
I WAS GOING TO MAKE LUNCH WITH THEM, SINCE I DON'T WANT THEM TO GO TO WASTE.
AH HA HA! I SEE.
BUT I'M NOT VERY GOOD AT COOKING, SO I DON'T QUITE KNOW WHAT TO DO.
THE ONLY THING I CAN MAKE IS INARI SUSHI.

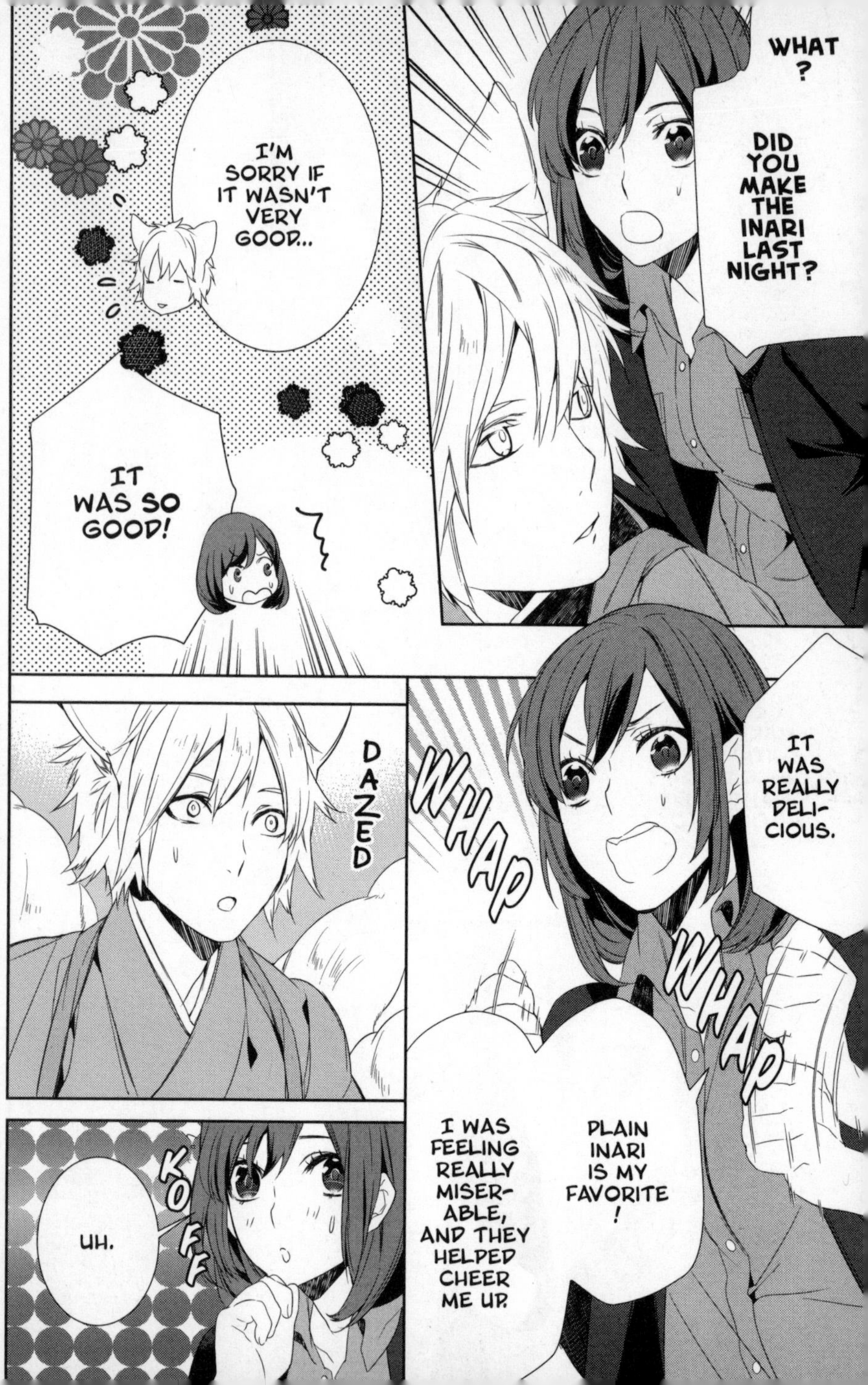
WHAT?
DID YOU MAKE THE INARI LAST NIGHT?
I'M SORRY IF IT WASN'T VERY GOOD...
IT WAS SO GOOD!
IT WAS REALLY DELI-CIOUS.
WHAP
WHAP
PLAIN INARI IS MY FAVORITE!
I WAS FEELING REALLY MISER-ABLE, AND THEY HELPED CHEER ME UP.
DAZED
KOFF
UH.

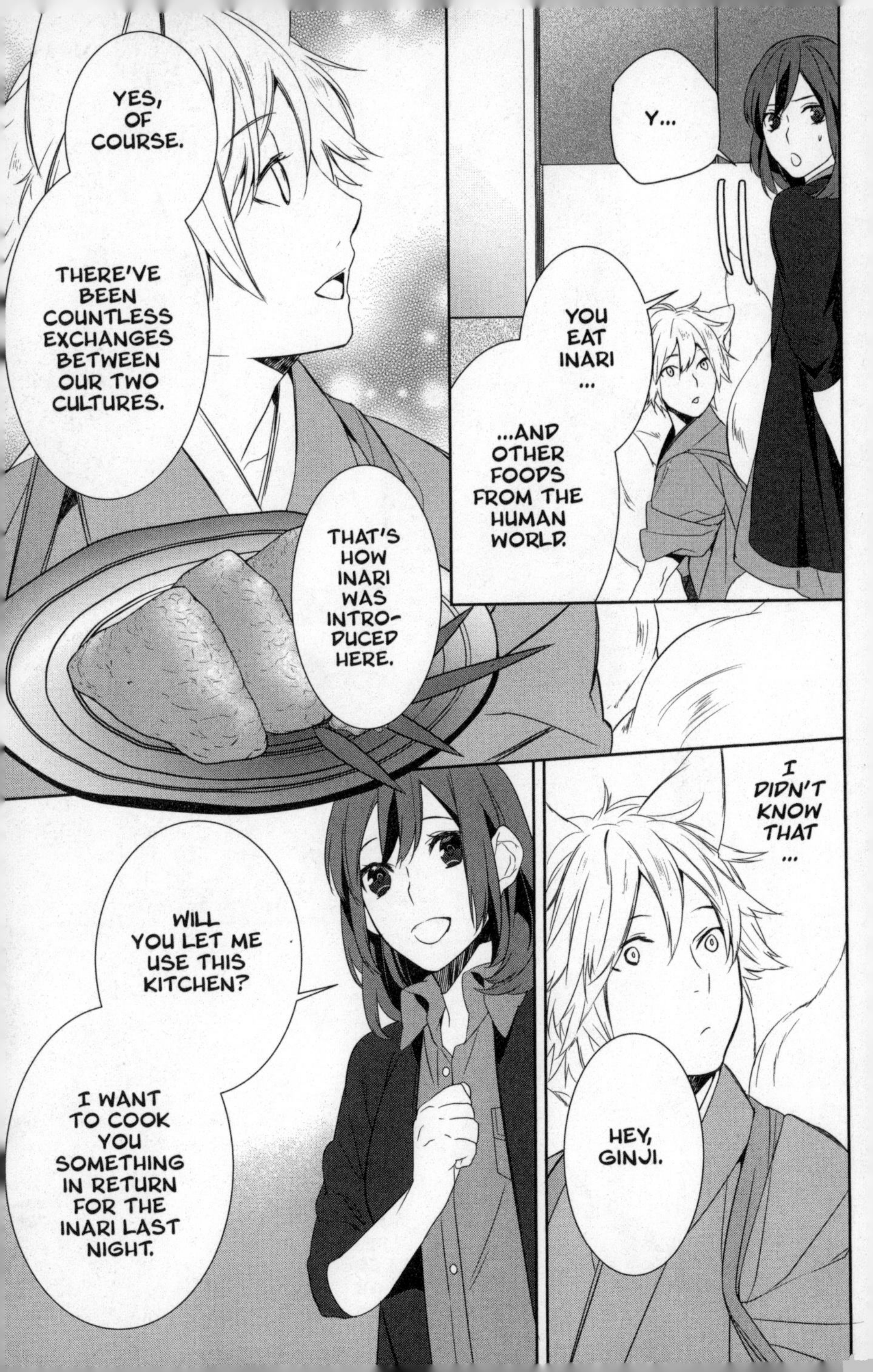
Y...
YOU EAT INARI ...
...AND OTHER FOODS FROM THE HUMAN WORLD.
YES, OF COURSE.
THERE'VE BEEN COUNTLESS EXCHANGES BETWEEN OUR TWO CULTURES.
THAT'S HOW INARI WAS INTRO-DUCED HERE.
I DIDN'T KNOW THAT ...
HEY, GINJI.
WILL YOU LET ME USE THIS KITCHEN?
I WANT TO COOK YOU SOMETHING IN RETURN FOR THE INARI LAST NIGHT.

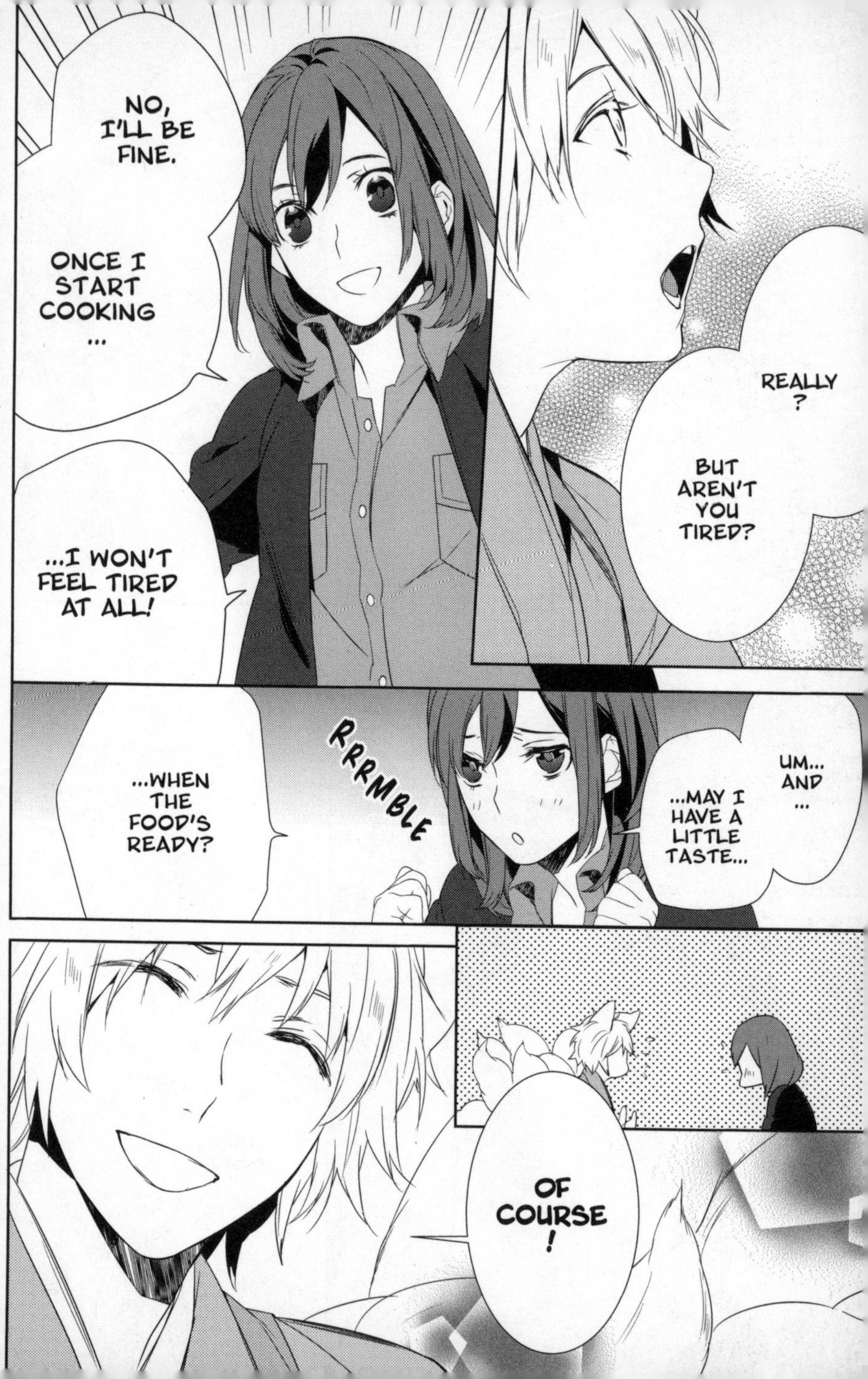
REALLY?
BUT AREN'T YOU TIRED?
NO, I'LL BE FINE.
ONCE I START COOKING...
...I WON'T FEEL TIRED AT ALL!
UM... AND...
...MAY I HAVE A LITTLE TASTE...
RRRMBLE
...WHEN THE FOOD'S READY?
OF COURSE!

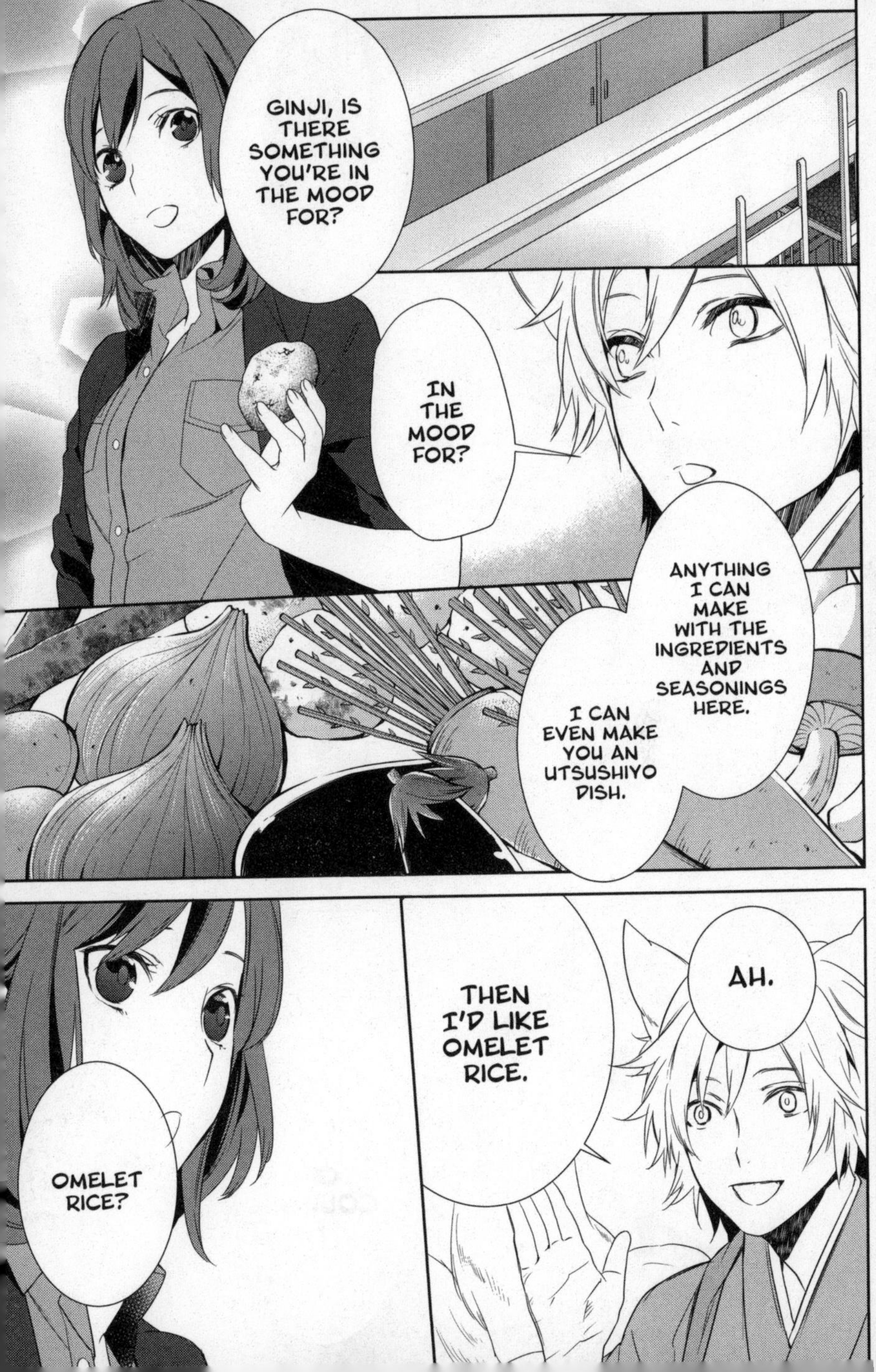
GINJI, IS THERE SOMETHING YOU'RE IN THE MOOD FOR?
IN THE MOOD FOR?
ANYTHING I CAN MAKE WITH THE INGREDIENTS AND SEASONINGS HERE.
I CAN EVEN MAKE YOU AN UTSUSHIYO DISH.
AH.
THEN I'D LIKE OMELET RICE.
OMELET RICE?

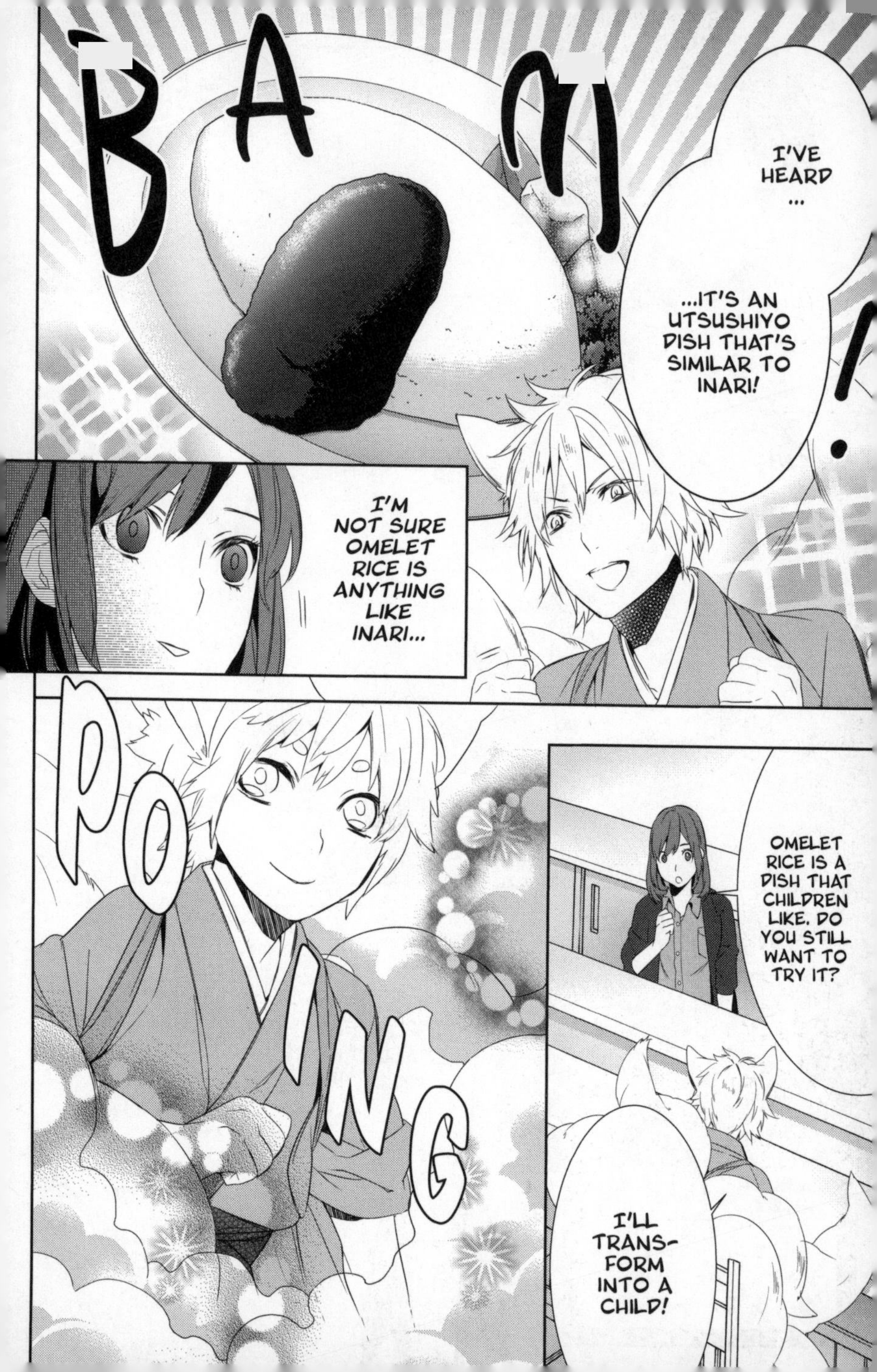
BAM
I'VE HEARD...
...IT'S AN UTSUSHIYO DISH THAT'S SIMILAR TO INARI!
I'M NOT SURE OMELET RICE IS ANYTHING LIKE INARI...
OMELET RICE IS A DISH THAT CHILDREN LIKE. DO YOU STILL WANT TO TRY IT?
I'LL TRANS-FORM INTO A CHILD!
POING

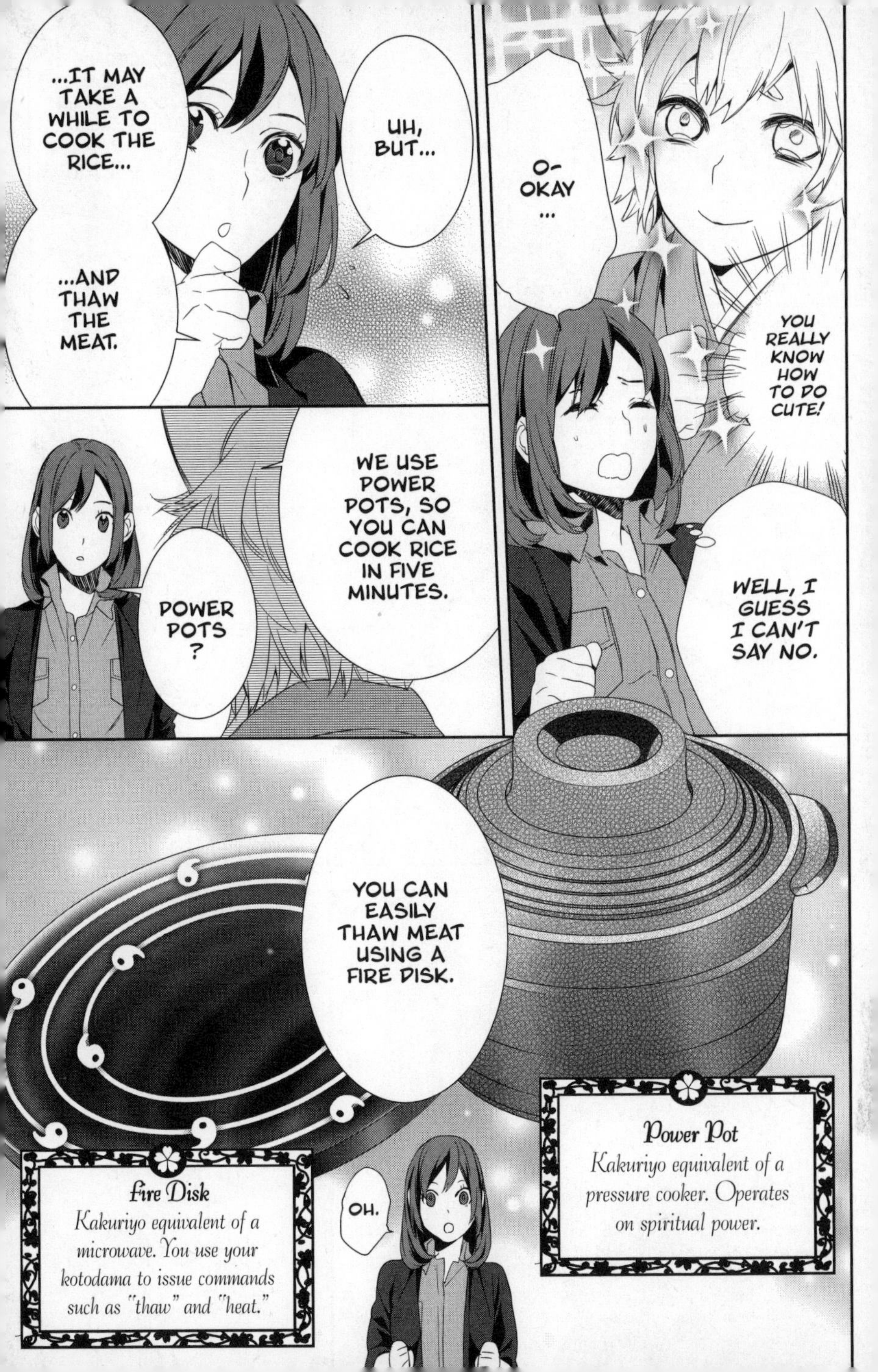
O-OKAY...
YOU REALLY KNOW HOW TO DO CUTE!
WELL, I GUESS I CAN'T SAY NO.
UH, BUT...
...IT MAY TAKE A WHILE TO COOK THE RICE...
...AND THAW THE MEAT.
WE USE POWER POTS, SO YOU CAN COOK RICE IN FIVE MINUTES.
POWER POTS?
YOU CAN EASILY THAW MEAT USING A FIRE DISK.
Power Pot
Kakuriyo equivalent of a pressure cooker. Operates on spiritual power.
OH.
Fire Disk
Kakuriyo equivalent of a microwave. You use your kotodama to issue commands such as "thaw" and "heat."

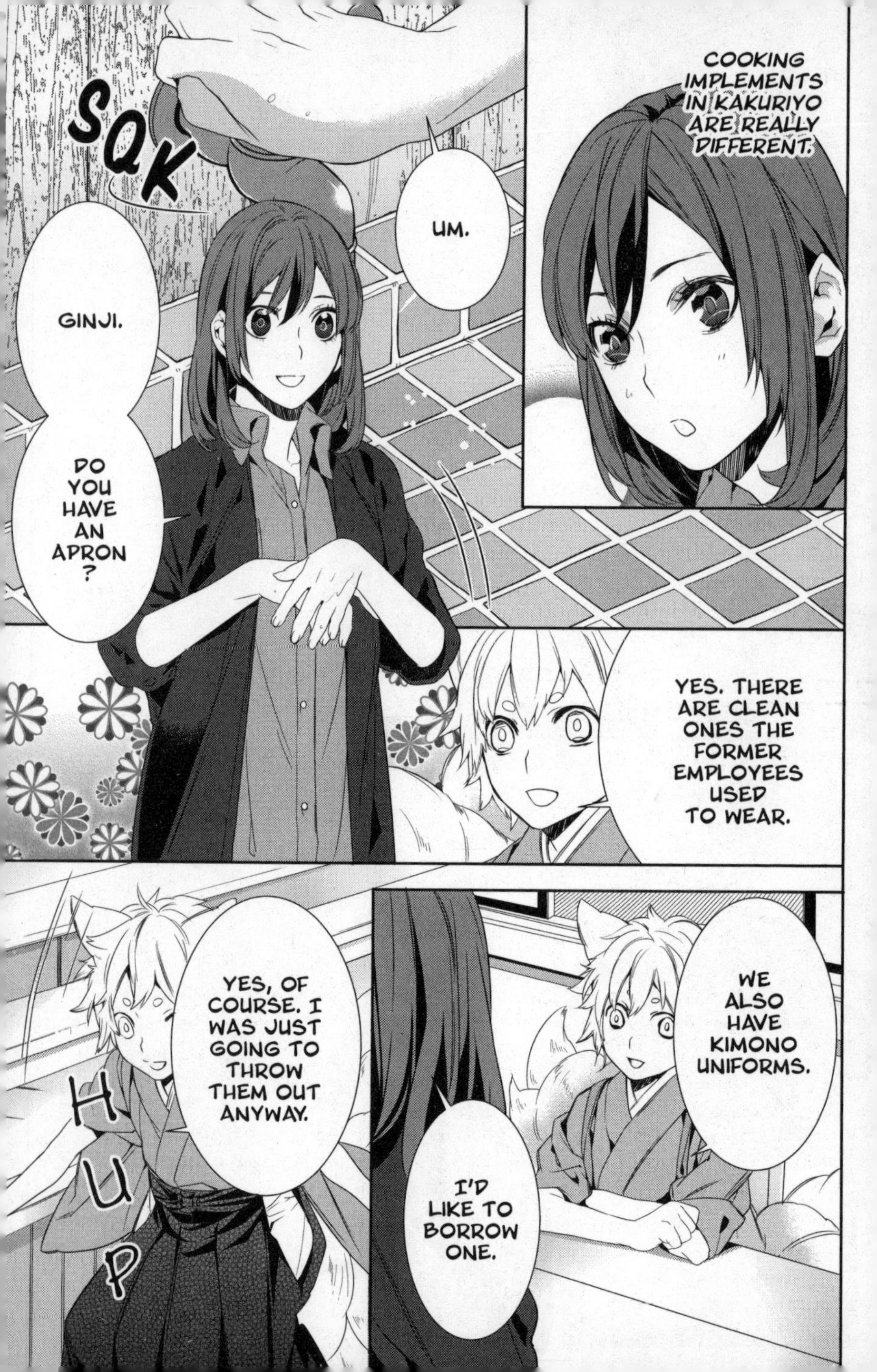
COOKING IMPLEMENTS IN KAKURIYO ARE REALLY DIFFERENT.
SQK
UM.
GINJI.
DO YOU HAVE AN APRON?
YES. THERE ARE CLEAN ONES THE FORMER EMPLOYEES USED TO WEAR.
WE ALSO HAVE KIMONO UNIFORMS.
I'D LIKE TO BORROW ONE.
YES, OF COURSE. I WAS JUST GOING TO THROW THEM OUT ANYWAY.
HUP

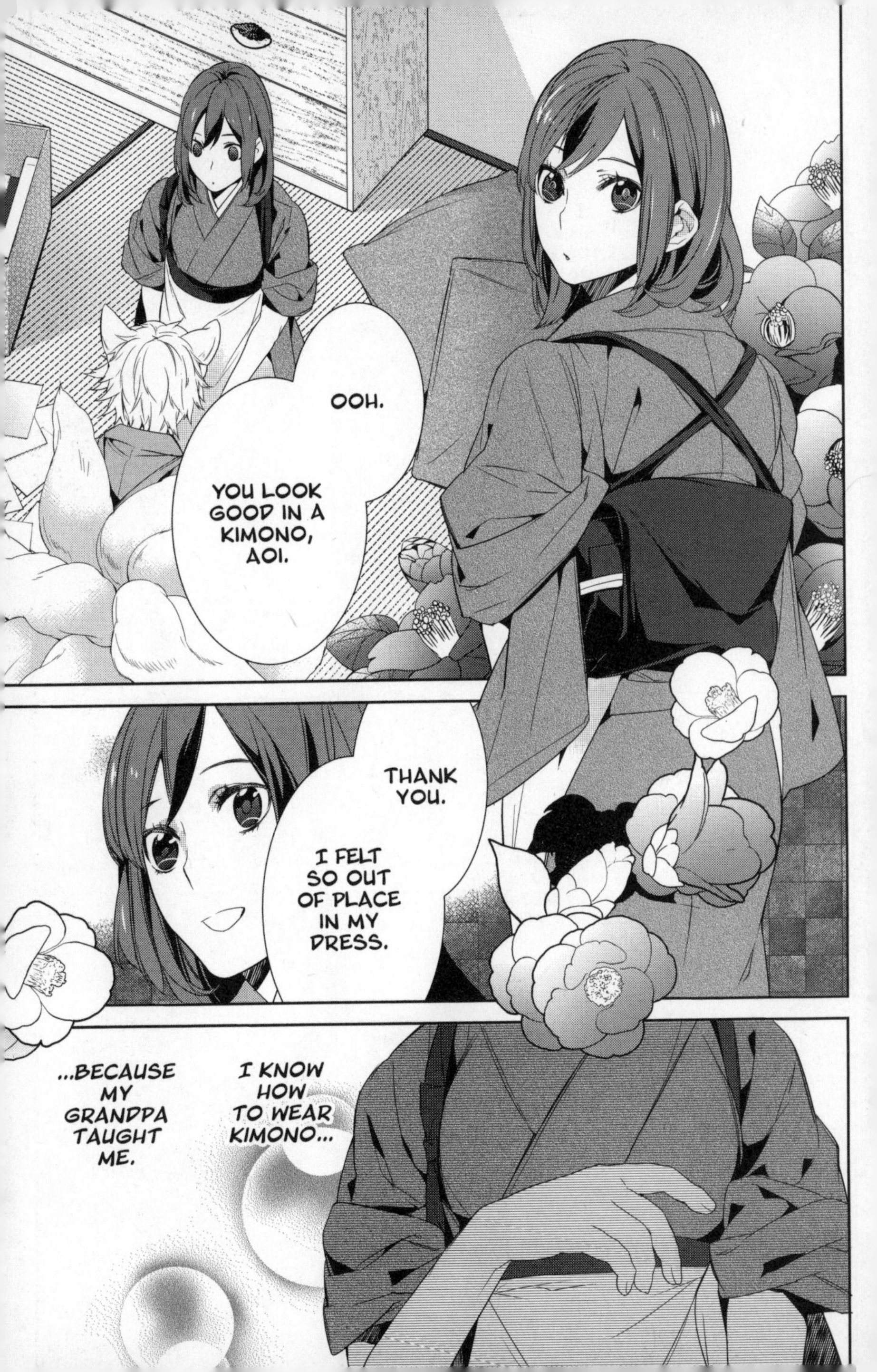
OOH.
YOU LOOK GOOD IN A KIMONO, AOI.
THANK YOU.
I FELT SO OUT OF PLACE IN MY DRESS.
I KNOW HOW TO WEAR KIMONO...
...BECAUSE MY GRANDPA TAUGHT ME.

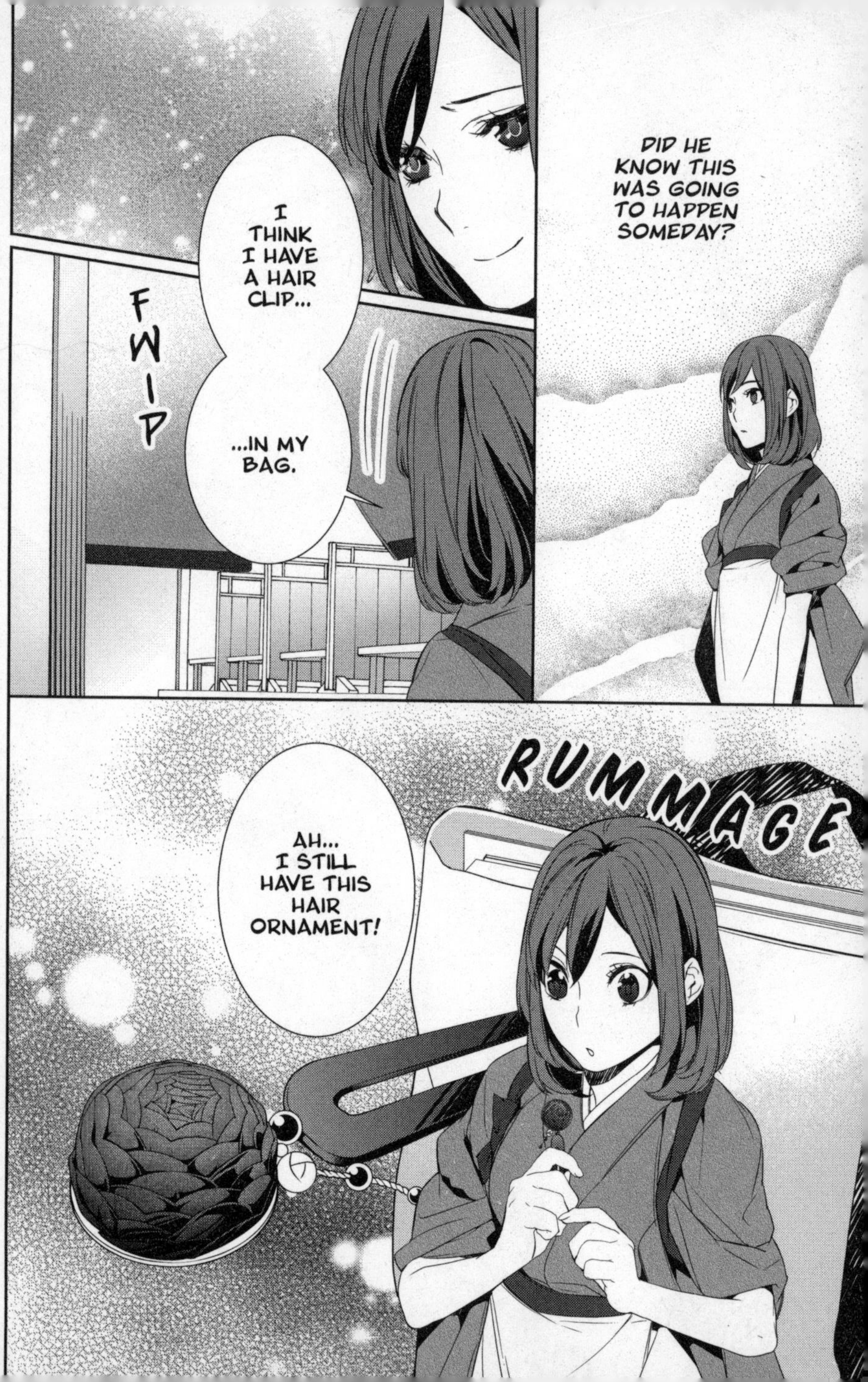
DID HE KNOW THIS WAS GOING TO HAPPEN SOMEDAY?
I THINK I HAVE A HAIR CLIP...
FWIP
...IN MY BAG.
RUMMAGE
AH... I STILL HAVE THIS HAIR ORNAMENT!

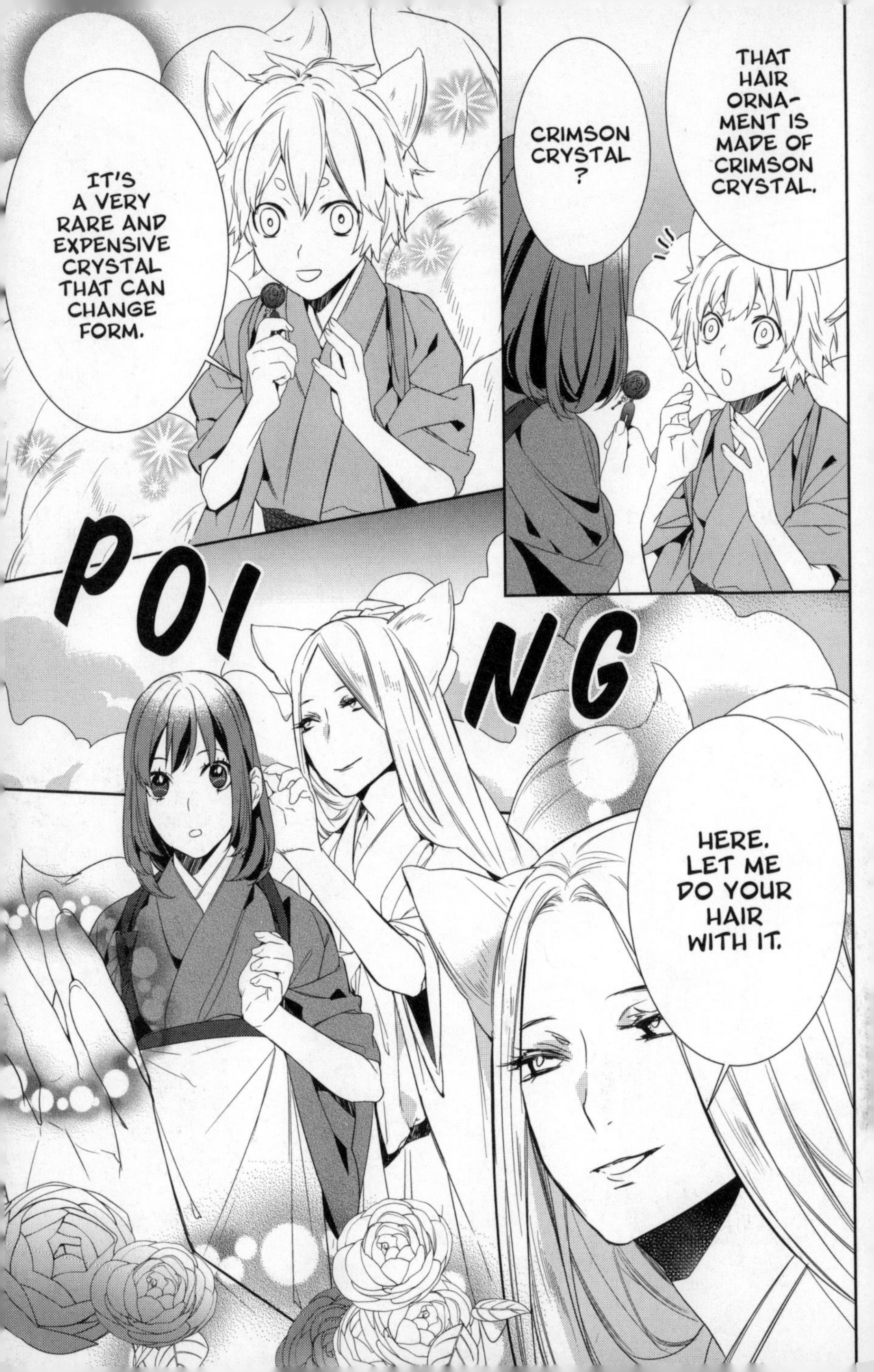
THAT HAIR ORNA-MENT IS MADE OF CRIMSON CRYSTAL.
CRIMSON CRYSTAL?
IT'S A VERY RARE AND EXPENSIVE CRYSTAL THAT CAN CHANGE FORM.
POING
HERE. LET ME DO YOUR HAIR WITH IT.

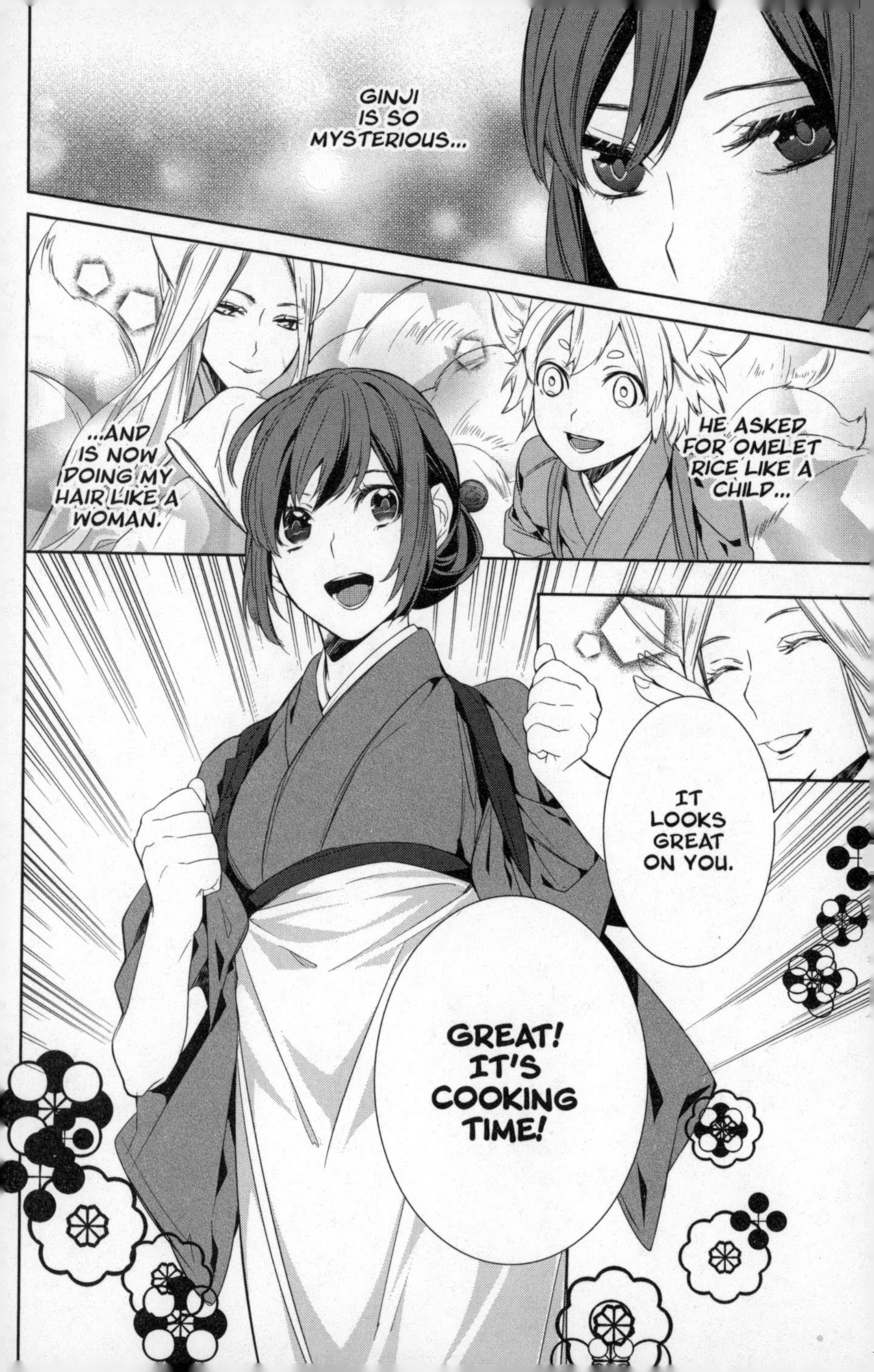
GINJI IS SO MYSTERIOUS...
HE ASKED FOR OMELET RICE LIKE A CHILD...
...AND IS NOW DOING MY HAIR LIKE A WOMAN.
IT LOOKS GREAT ON YOU.
GREAT! IT'S COOKING TIME!

Kakuriyo

Bed & Breakfast for Spirits

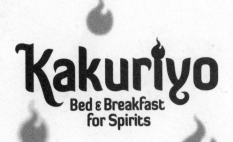

Kakuriyo
Bed & Breakfast
for Spirits

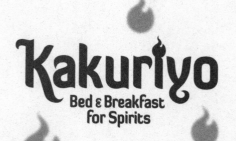

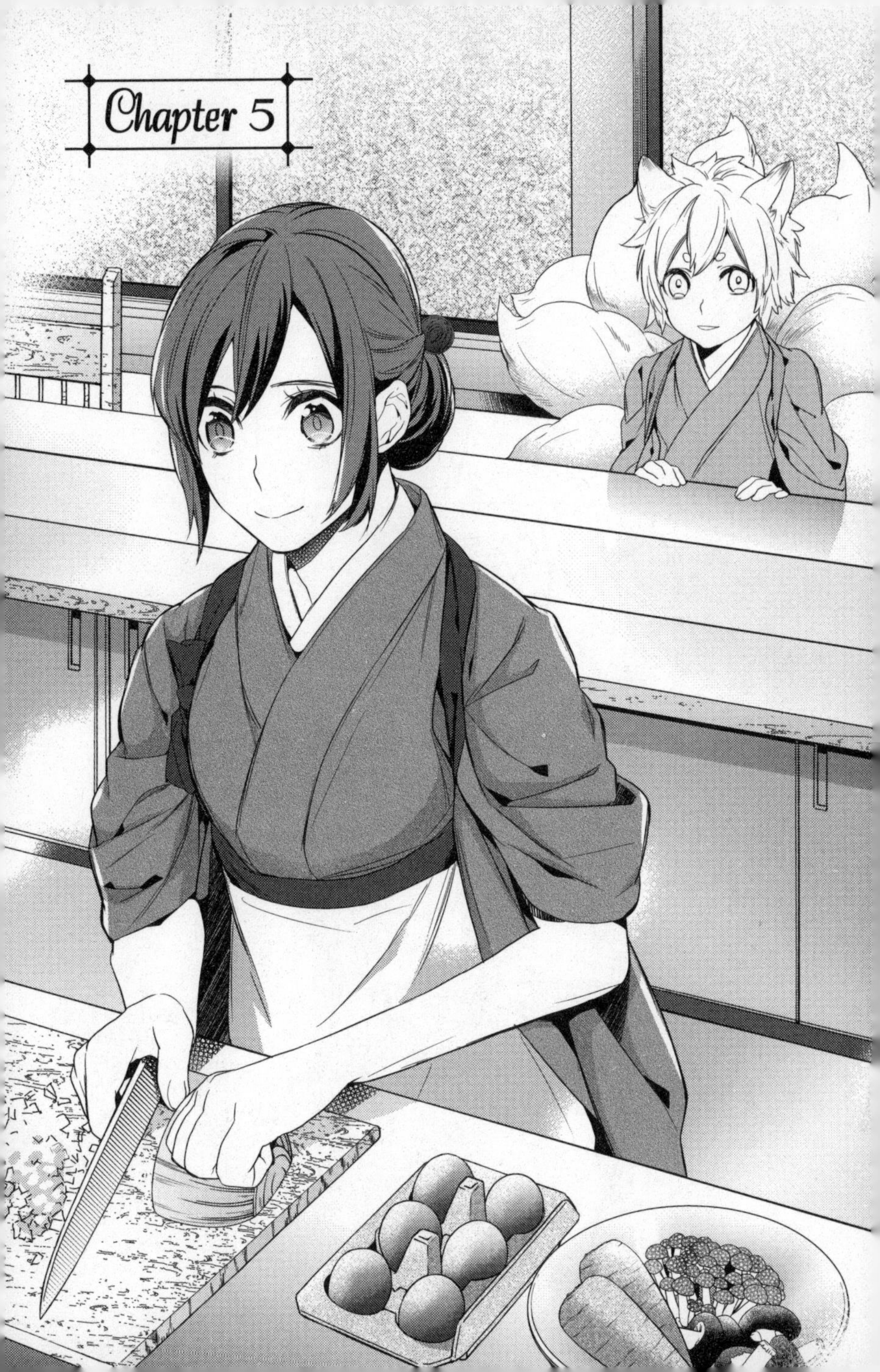
Chapter 5

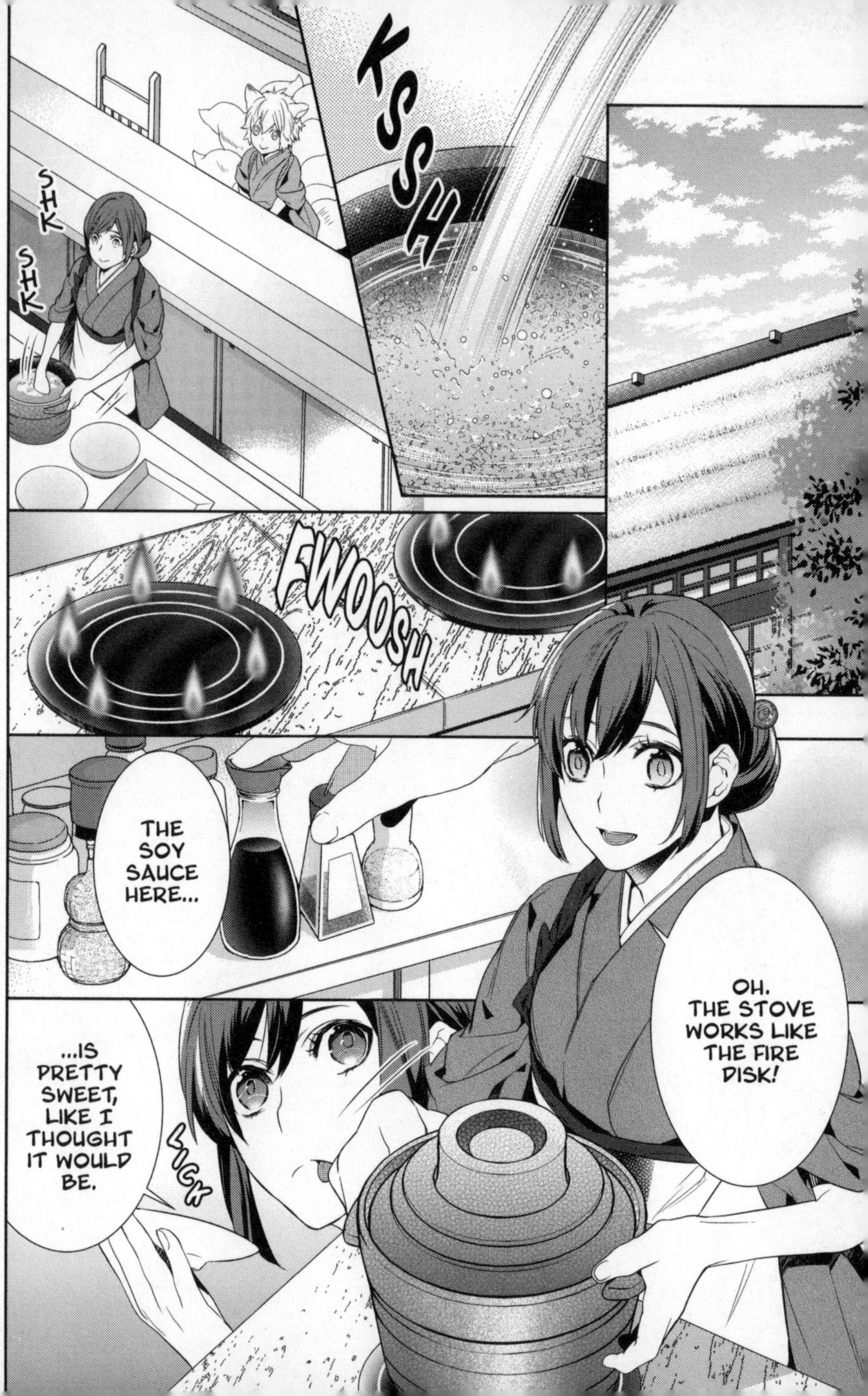
KSSH
SHK SHK
OH. THE STOVE WORKS LIKE THE FIRE DISK!
FWOOSH
THE SOY SAUCE HERE...
...IS PRETTY SWEET, LIKE I THOUGHT IT WOULD BE.
LICK

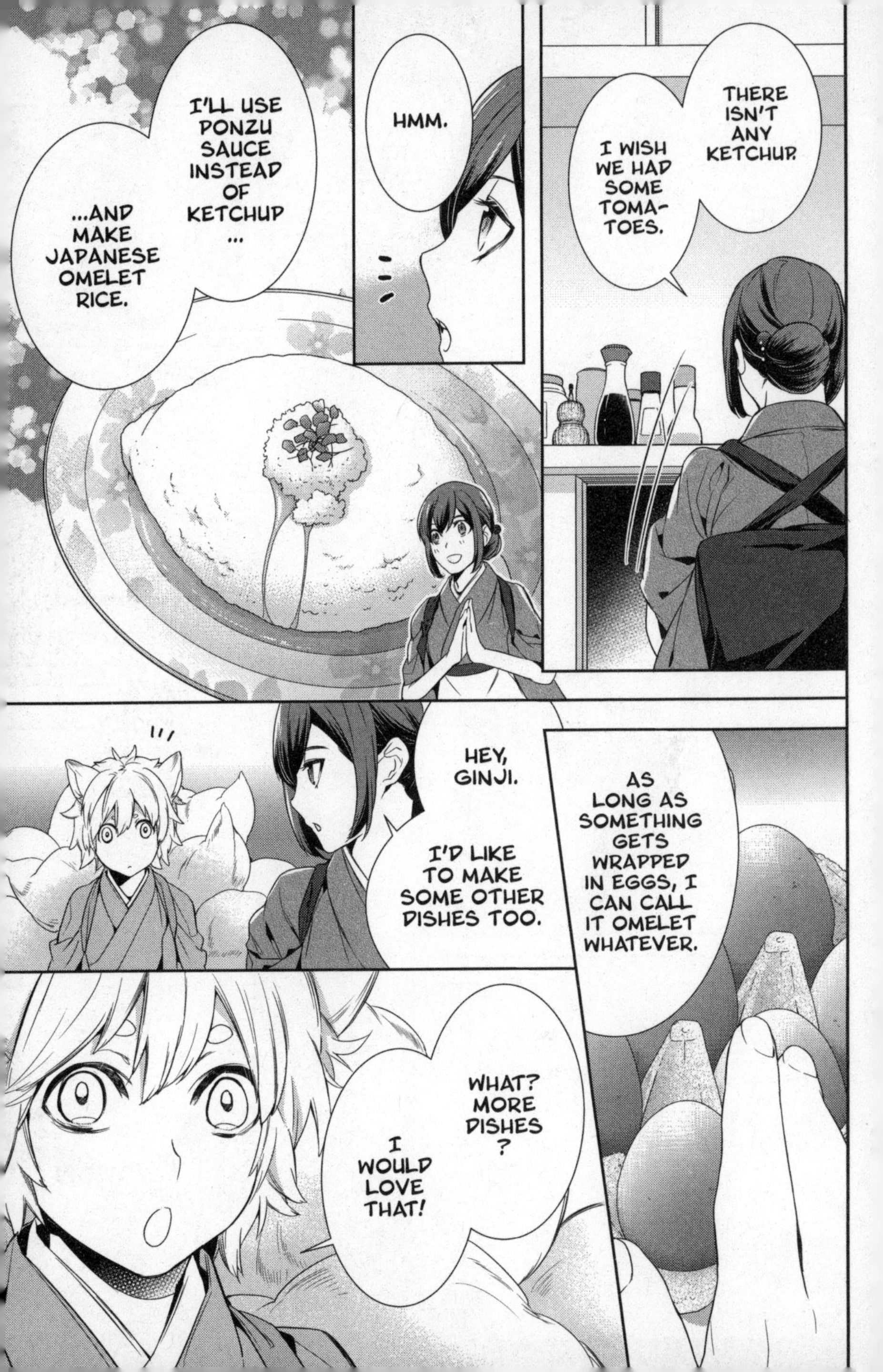
THERE ISN'T ANY KETCHUP.
I WISH WE HAD SOME TOMATOES.
HMM.
...
I'LL USE PONZU SAUCE INSTEAD OF KETCHUP...
...AND MAKE JAPANESE OMELET RICE.
AS LONG AS SOMETHING GETS WRAPPED IN EGGS, I CAN CALL IT OMELET WHATEVER.
HEY, GINJI.
I'D LIKE TO MAKE SOME OTHER DISHES TOO.
WHAT? MORE DISHES?
I WOULD LOVE THAT!

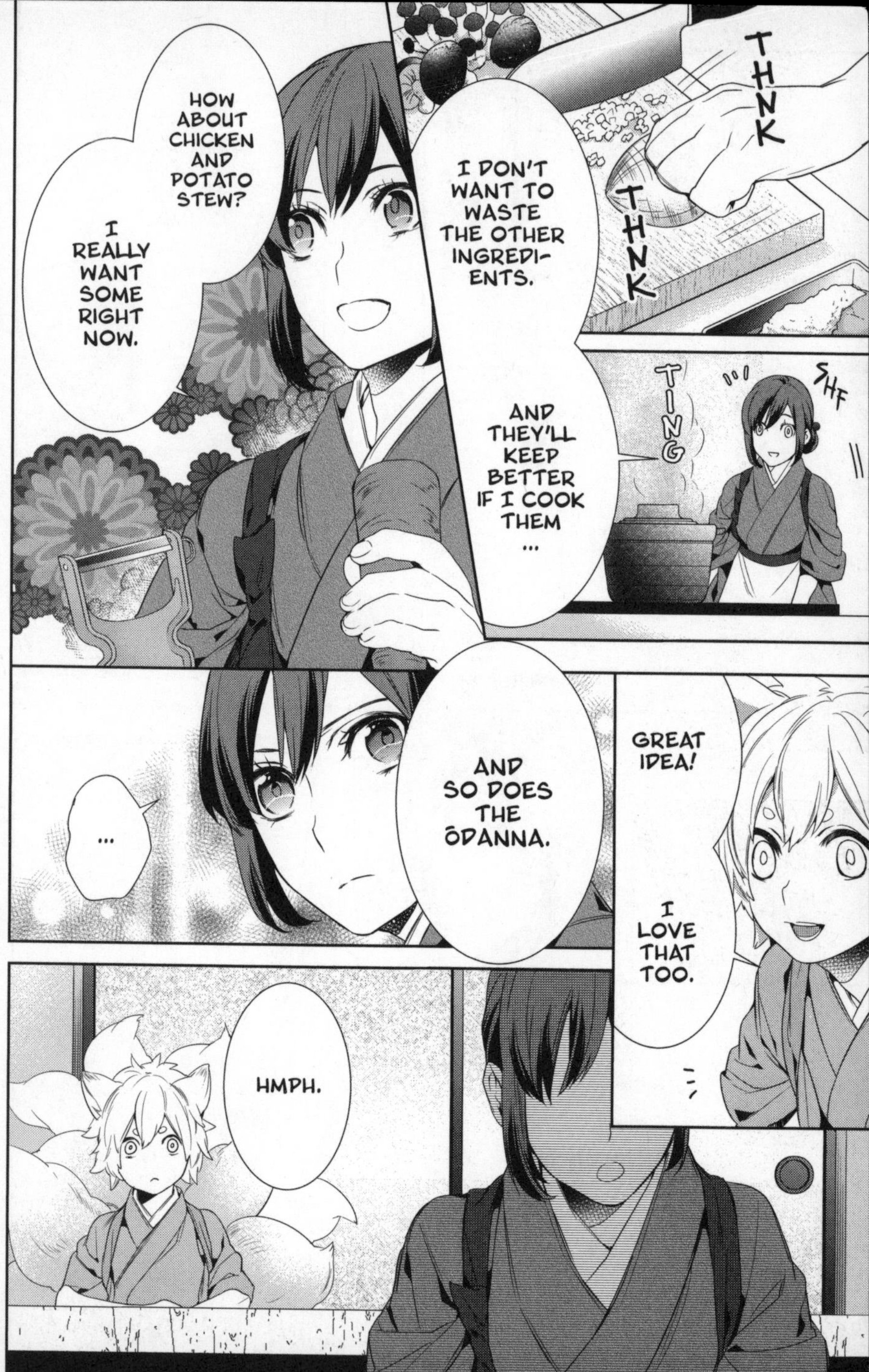
THNK
THNK
I DON'T WANT TO WASTE THE OTHER INGREDI-ENTS.
TING
SHF
AND THEY'LL KEEP BETTER IF I COOK THEM ...
HOW ABOUT CHICKEN AND POTATO STEW?
I REALLY WANT SOME RIGHT NOW.
GREAT IDEA!
I LOVE THAT TOO.
AND SO DOES THE ŌDANNA.
...
HMPH.

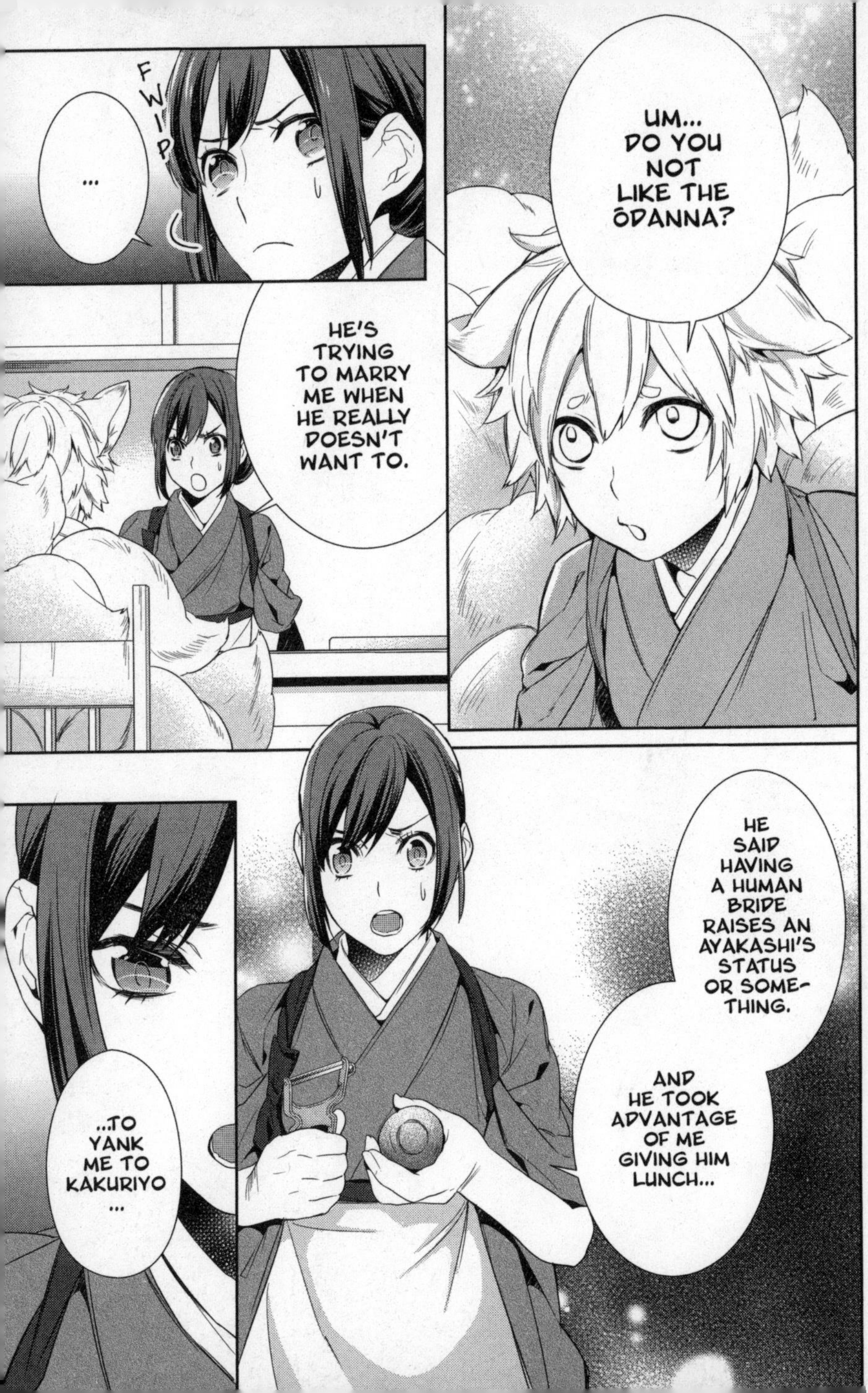
UM... DO YOU NOT LIKE THE ŌDANNA?
FWIP
...
HE'S TRYING TO MARRY ME WHEN HE REALLY DOESN'T WANT TO.
HE SAID HAVING A HUMAN BRIDE RAISES AN AYAKASHI'S STATUS OR SOME-THING.
AND HE TOOK ADVANTAGE OF ME GIVING HIM LUNCH...
...TO YANK ME TO KAKURIYO ...

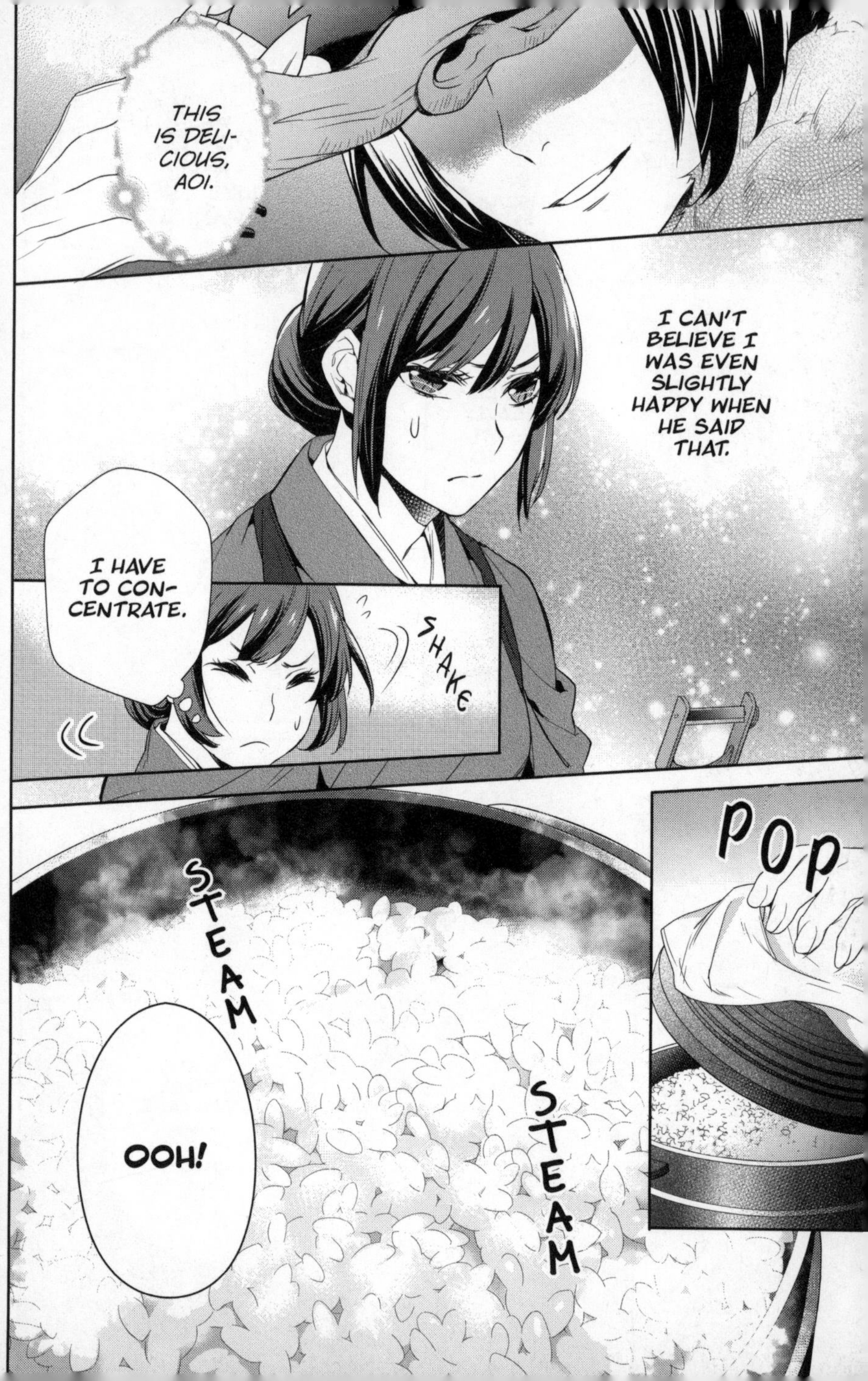
THIS IS DELICIOUS, AOI.
I CAN'T BELIEVE I WAS EVEN SLIGHTLY HAPPY WHEN HE SAID THAT.
SHAKE
I HAVE TO CONCENTRATE.
POP
STEAM
STEAM
OOH!

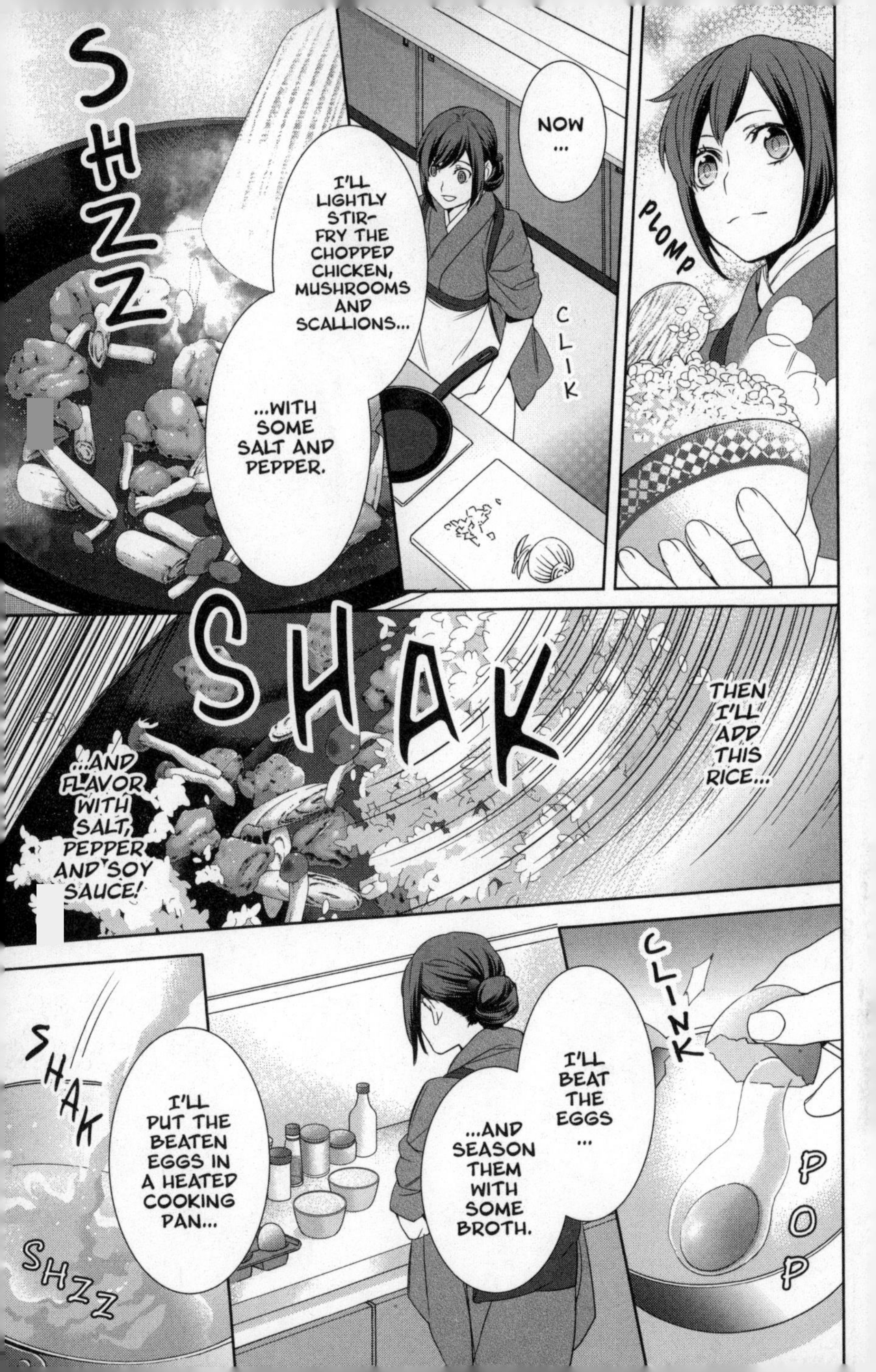
PLOMP
NOW...
I'LL LIGHTLY STIR-FRY THE CHOPPED CHICKEN, MUSHROOMS AND SCALLIONS...
CLIK
...WITH SOME SALT AND PEPPER.
SHZZ
THEN I'LL ADD THIS RICE...
SHAK
...AND FLAVOR WITH SALT, PEPPER AND SOY SAUCE!
CLINK
I'LL BEAT THE EGGS...
...AND SEASON THEM WITH SOME BROTH.
POP
I'LL PUT THE BEATEN EGGS IN A HEATED COOKING PAN...
SHAK
SHZZ

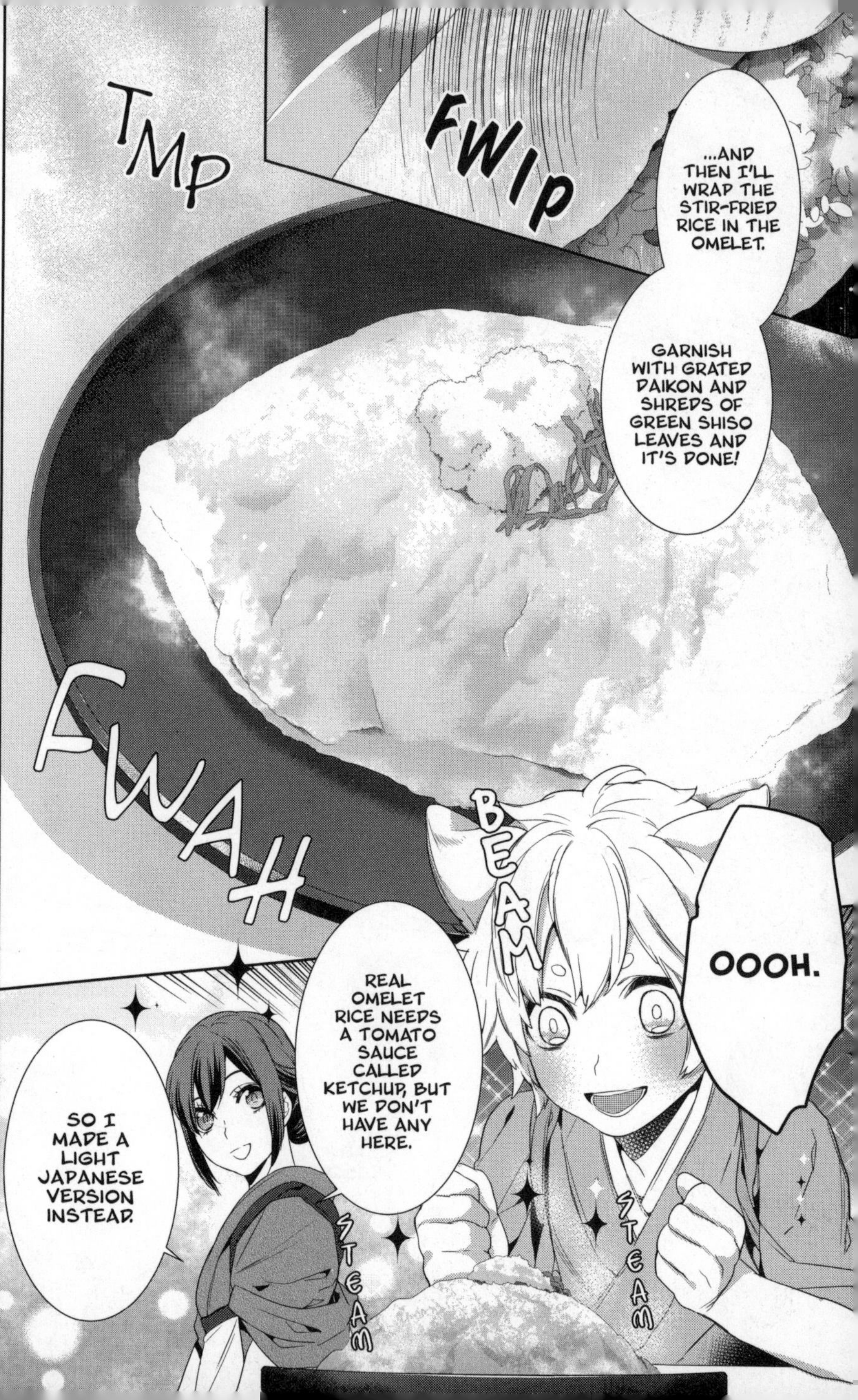
FWIP
...AND THEN I'LL WRAP THE STIR-FRIED RICE IN THE OMELET.
TMP
GARNISH WITH GRATED DAIKON AND SHREDS OF GREEN SHISO LEAVES AND IT'S DONE!
FWAH
OOOH.
BEAM
REAL OMELET RICE NEEDS A TOMATO SAUCE CALLED KETCHUP, BUT WE DON'T HAVE ANY HERE.
SO I MADE A LIGHT JAPANESE VERSION INSTEAD.
STEAM
STEAM

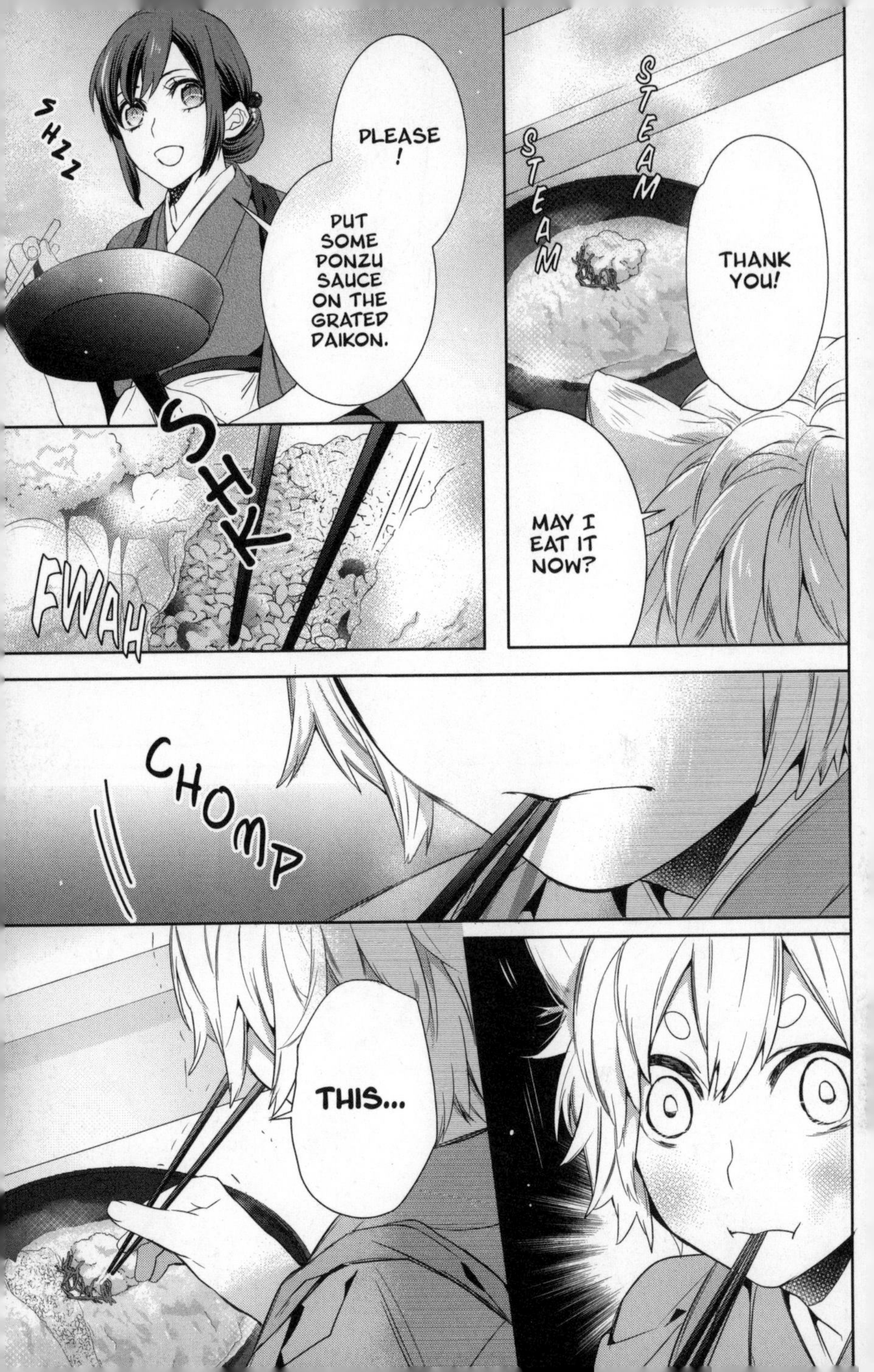
STEAM
STEAM
THANK YOU!
MAY I EAT IT NOW?
SHZZ
PLEASE!
PUT SOME PONZU SAUCE ON THE GRATED DAIKON.
SHK
FWAH
CHOMP
THIS...

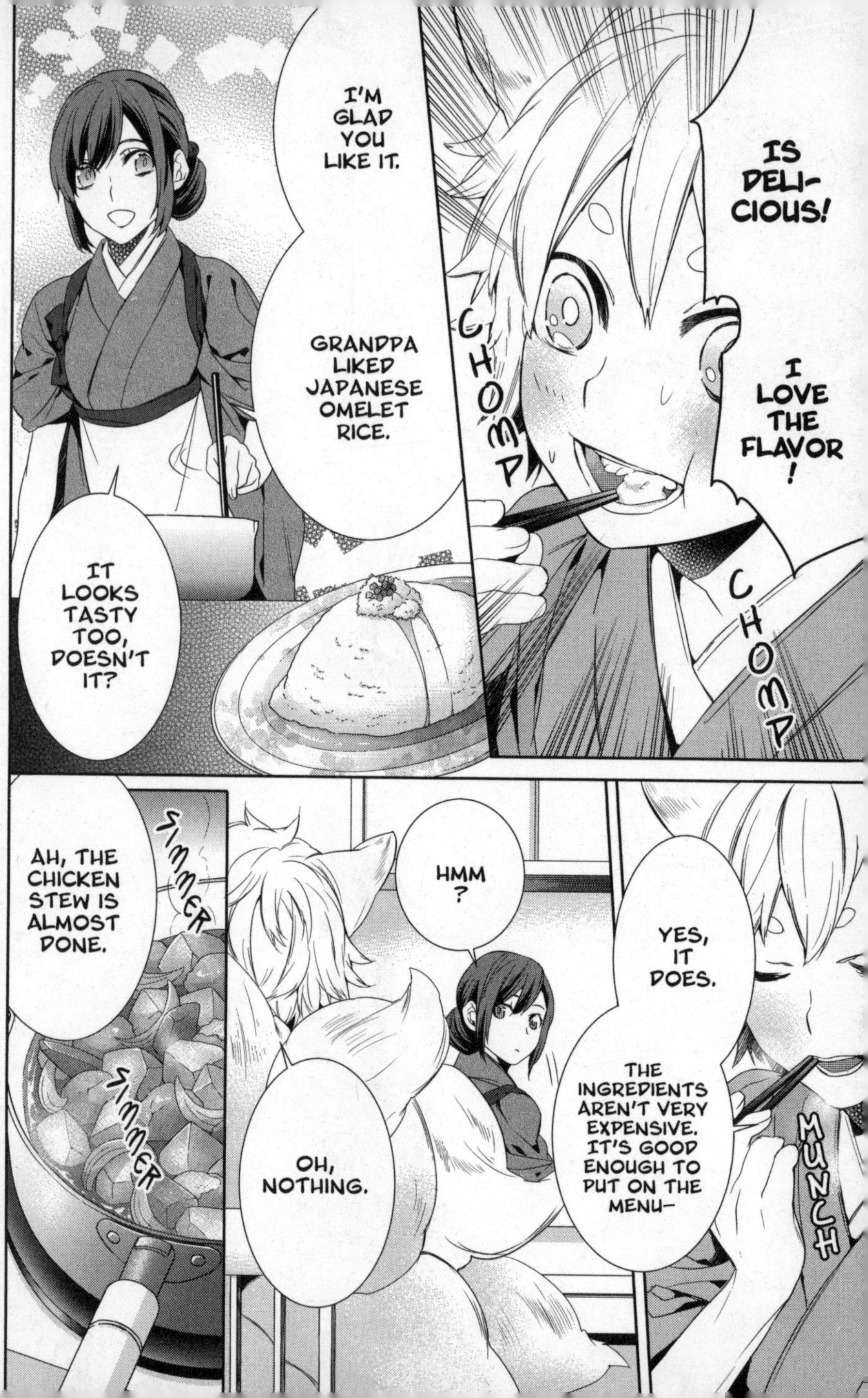
IS DELI-CIOUS!
I LOVE THE FLAVOR!
CHOMP
CHOMP
I'M GLAD YOU LIKE IT.
GRANDPA LIKED JAPANESE OMELET RICE.
IT LOOKS TASTY TOO, DOESN'T IT?
YES, IT DOES.
THE INGREDIENTS AREN'T VERY EXPENSIVE. IT'S GOOD ENOUGH TO PUT ON THE MENU–
MUNCH
HMM?
OH, NOTHING.
AH, THE CHICKEN STEW IS ALMOST DONE.
SIMMER
SIMMER

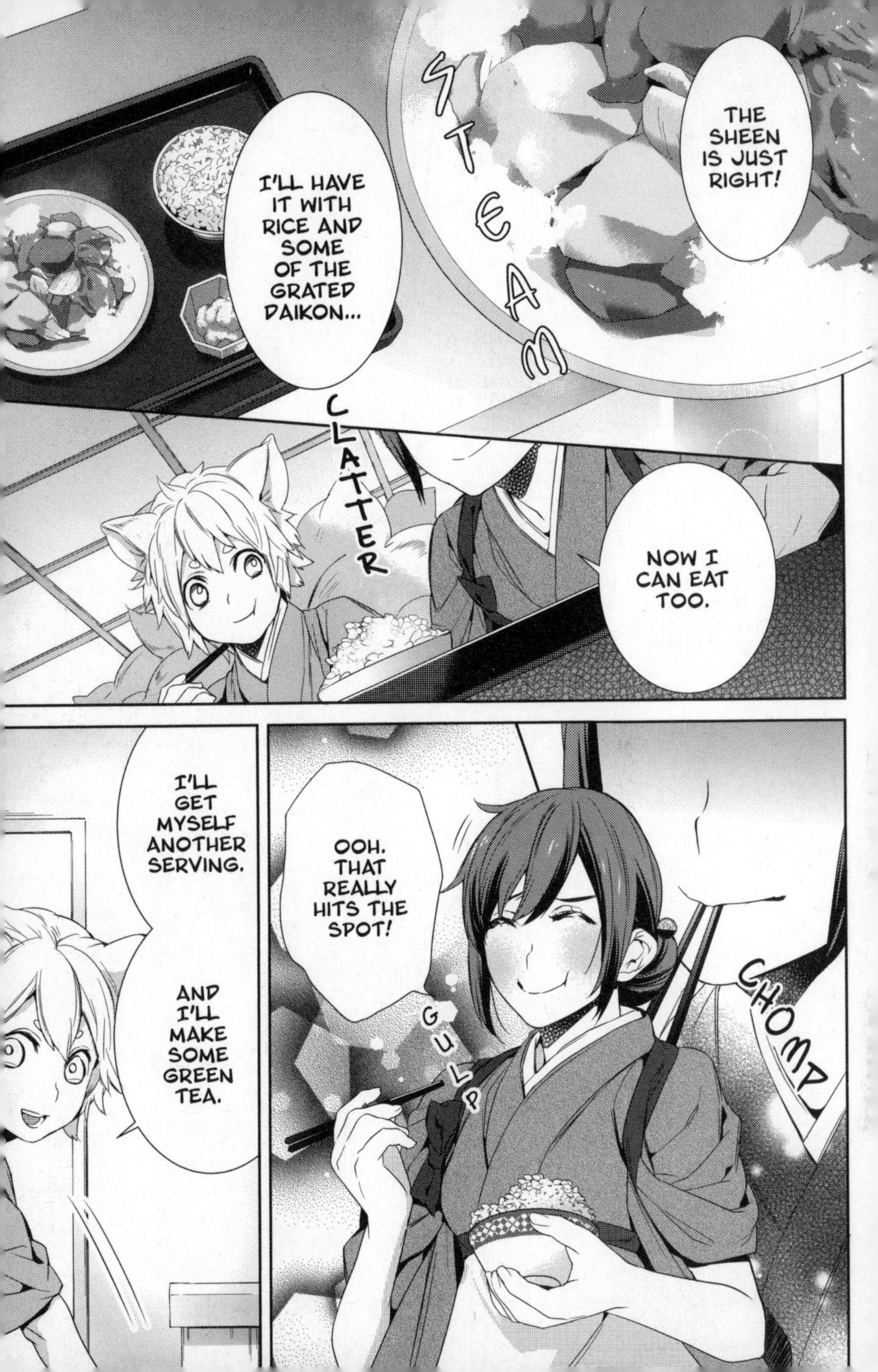
THE SHEEN IS JUST RIGHT!
STEAM
I'LL HAVE IT WITH RICE AND SOME OF THE GRATED DAIKON...
NOW I CAN EAT TOO.
CLATTER
CHOMP
OOH. THAT REALLY HITS THE SPOT!
GULP
I'LL GET MYSELF ANOTHER SERVING.
AND I'LL MAKE SOME GREEN TEA.

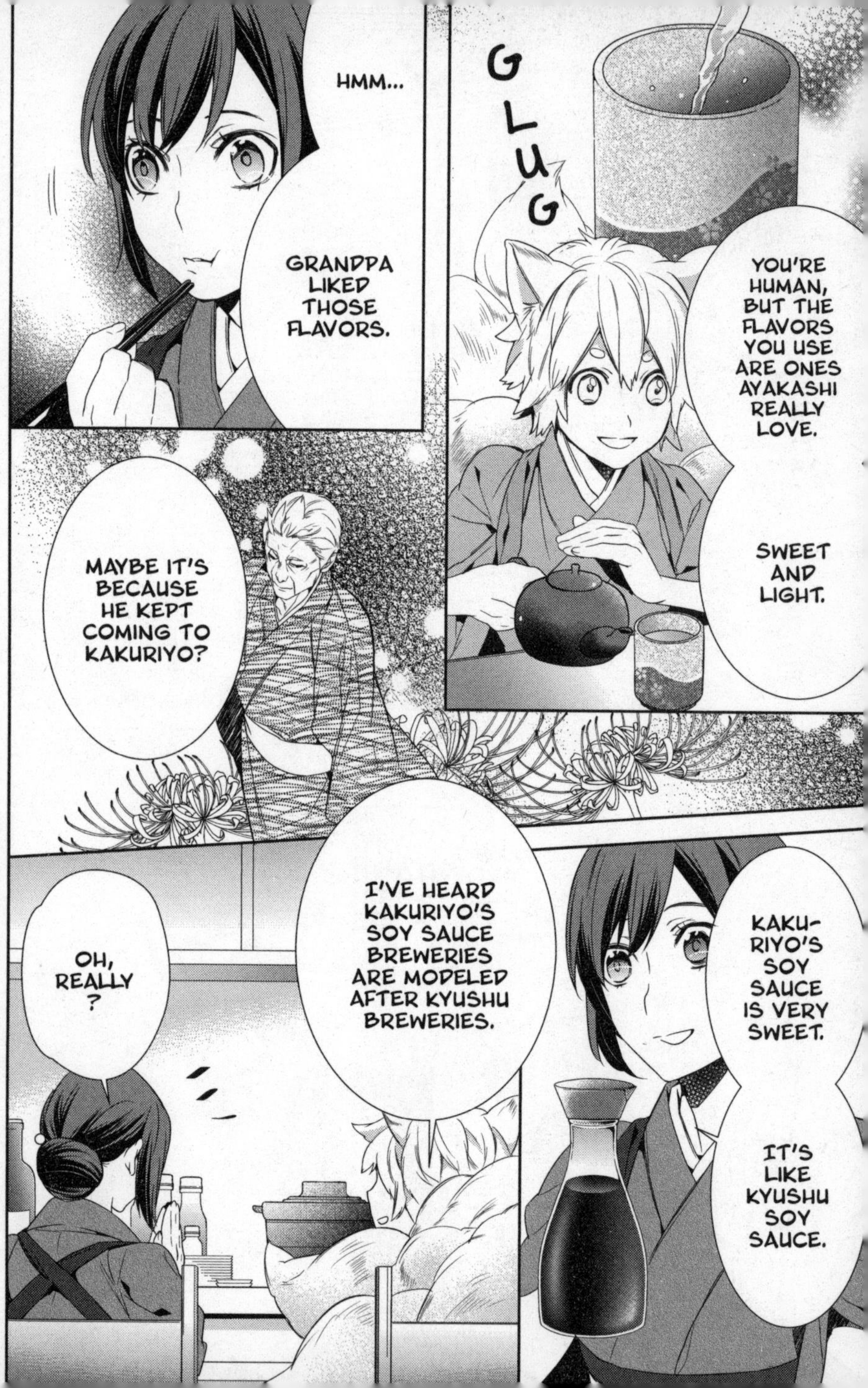
GLUG
YOU'RE HUMAN, BUT THE FLAVORS YOU USE ARE ONES AYAKASHI REALLY LOVE.
SWEET AND LIGHT.
HMM...
GRANDPA LIKED THOSE FLAVORS.
MAYBE IT'S BECAUSE HE KEPT COMING TO KAKURIYO?
KAKU-RIYO'S SOY SAUCE IS VERY SWEET.
IT'S LIKE KYUSHU SOY SAUCE.
I'VE HEARD KAKURIYO'S SOY SAUCE BREWERIES ARE MODELED AFTER KYUSHU BREWERIES.
OH, REALLY?

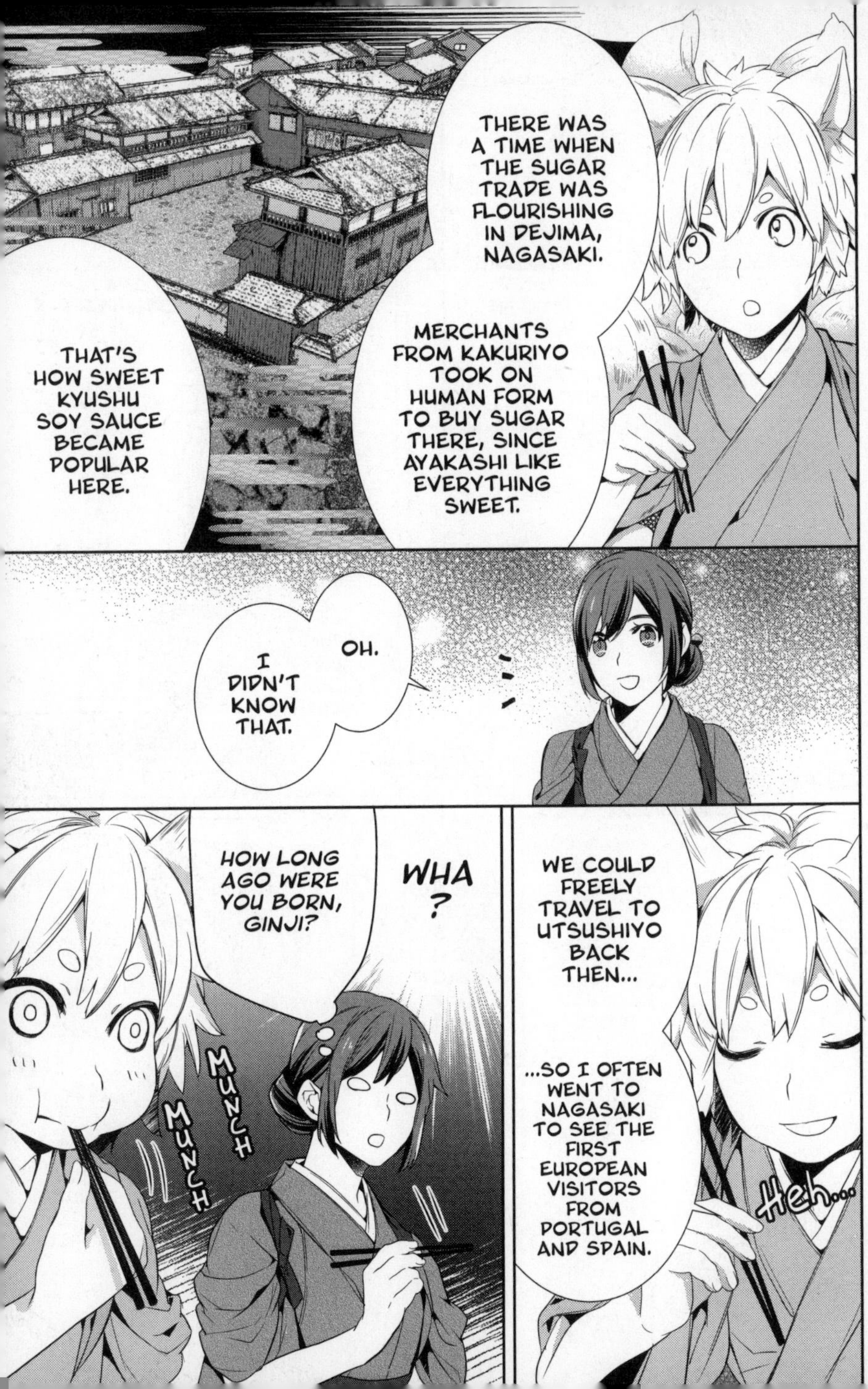
THERE WAS A TIME WHEN THE SUGAR TRADE WAS FLOURISHING IN DEJIMA, NAGASAKI.
MERCHANTS FROM KAKURIYO TOOK ON HUMAN FORM TO BUY SUGAR THERE, SINCE AYAKASHI LIKE EVERYTHING SWEET.
THAT'S HOW SWEET KYUSHU SOY SAUCE BECAME POPULAR HERE.
OH.
I DIDN'T KNOW THAT.
WE COULD FREELY TRAVEL TO UTSUSHIYO BACK THEN...
...SO I OFTEN WENT TO NAGASAKI TO SEE THE FIRST EUROPEAN VISITORS FROM PORTUGAL AND SPAIN.
Heh...
WHA ?
HOW LONG AGO WERE YOU BORN, GINJI?
MUNCH
MUNCH

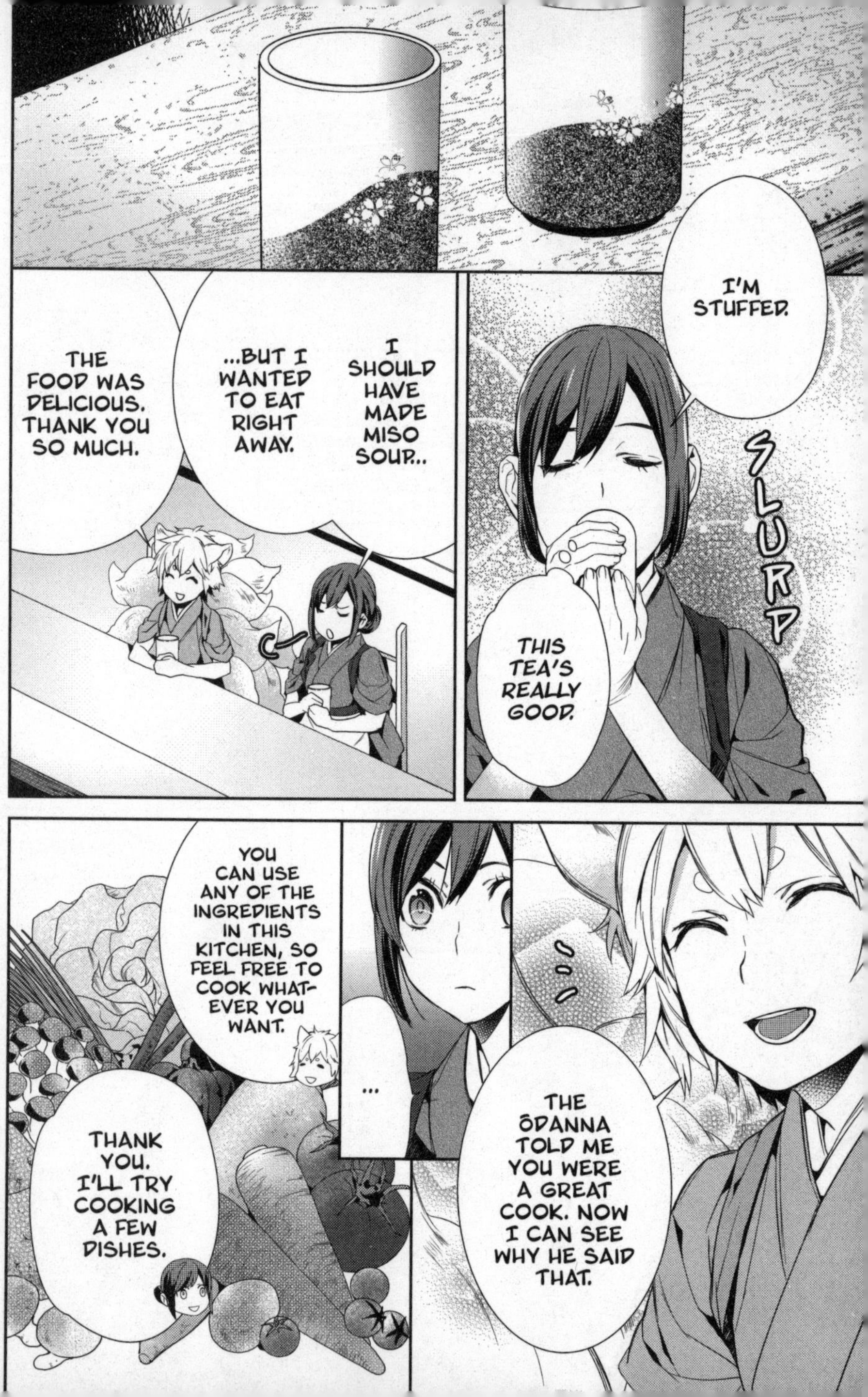
I'M STUFFED.
SLURP
THIS TEA'S REALLY GOOD.
I SHOULD HAVE MADE MISO SOUP...
...BUT I WANTED TO EAT RIGHT AWAY.
THE FOOD WAS DELICIOUS. THANK YOU SO MUCH.
...
THE ŌDANNA TOLD ME YOU WERE A GREAT COOK. NOW I CAN SEE WHY HE SAID THAT.
...
YOU CAN USE ANY OF THE INGREDIENTS IN THIS KITCHEN, SO FEEL FREE TO COOK WHATEVER YOU WANT.
THANK YOU. I'LL TRY COOKING A FEW DISHES.

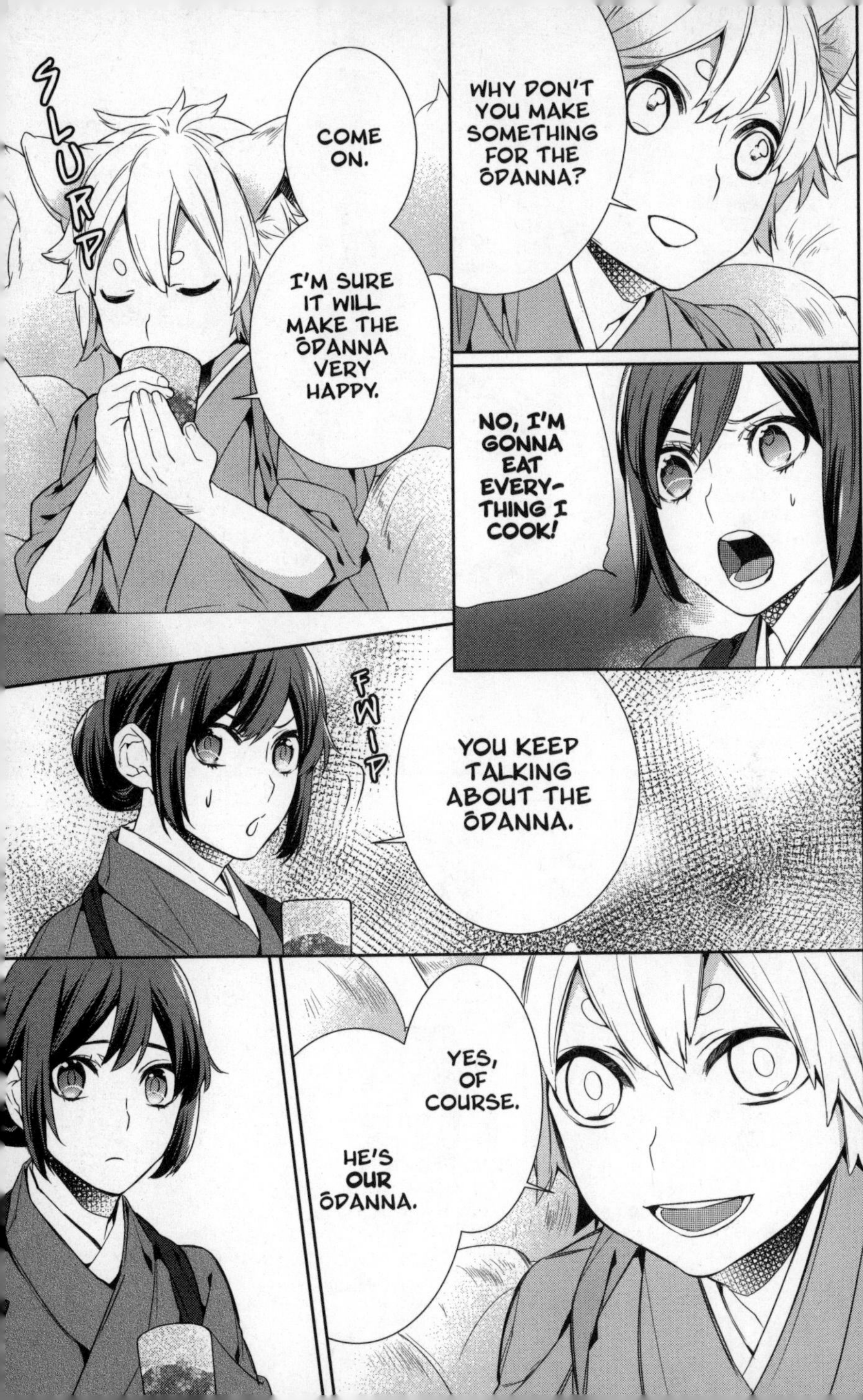
WHY DON'T YOU MAKE SOMETHING FOR THE ŌDANNA?
NO, I'M GONNA EAT EVERY-THING I COOK!
COME ON.
I'M SURE IT WILL MAKE THE ŌDANNA VERY HAPPY.
SLURP
YOU KEEP TALKING ABOUT THE ŌDANNA.
FWIP
YES, OF COURSE.
HE'S OUR ŌDANNA.

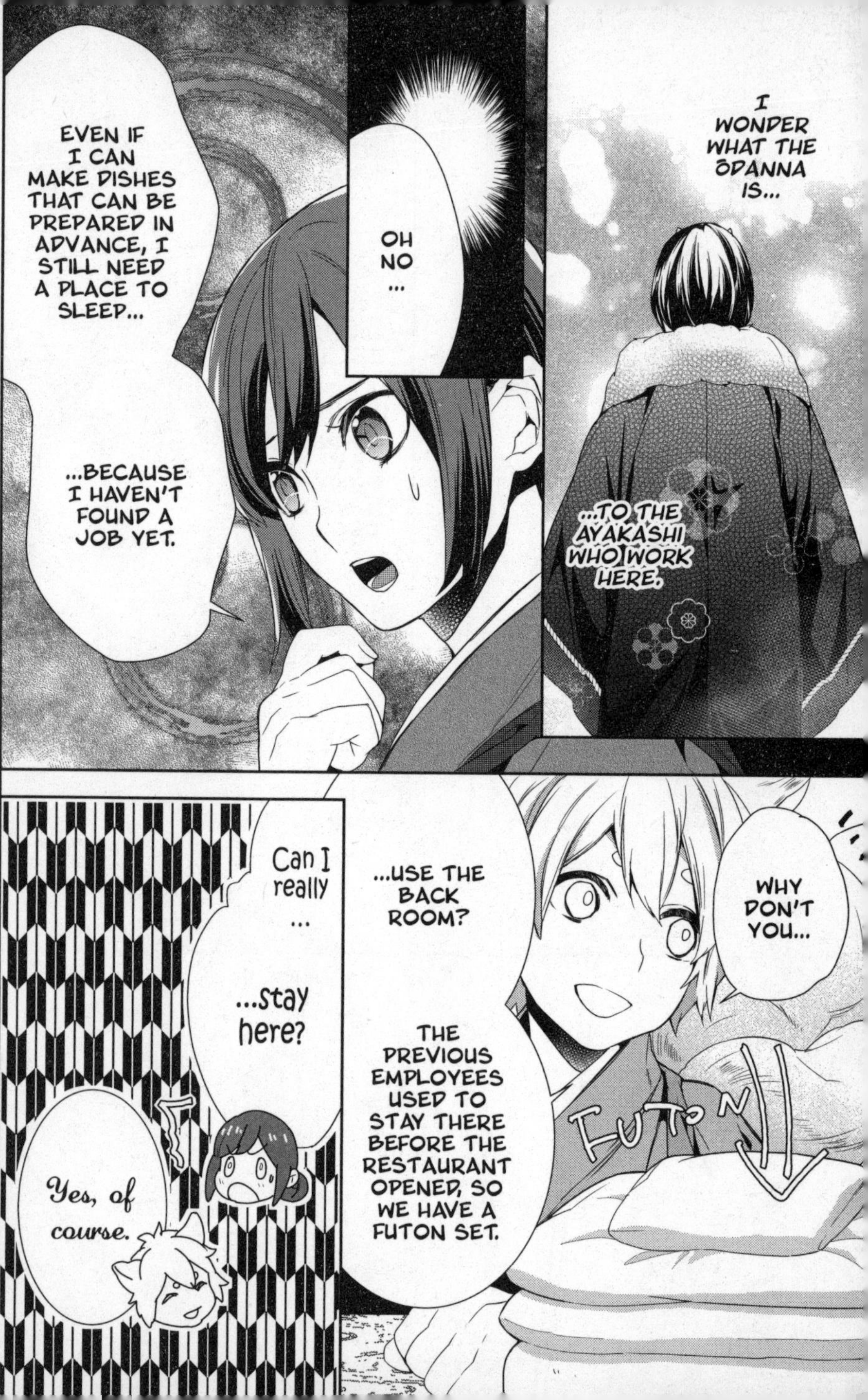
I WONDER WHAT THE ŌDANNA IS...
...TO THE AYAKASHI WHO WORK HERE.
OH NO...
EVEN IF I CAN MAKE DISHES THAT CAN BE PREPARED IN ADVANCE, I STILL NEED A PLACE TO SLEEP...
...BECAUSE I HAVEN'T FOUND A JOB YET.
WHY DON'T YOU...
...USE THE BACK ROOM?
THE PREVIOUS EMPLOYEES USED TO STAY THERE BEFORE THE RESTAURANT OPENED, SO WE HAVE A FUTON SET.
FUTON
Can I really...
...stay here?
Yes, of course.

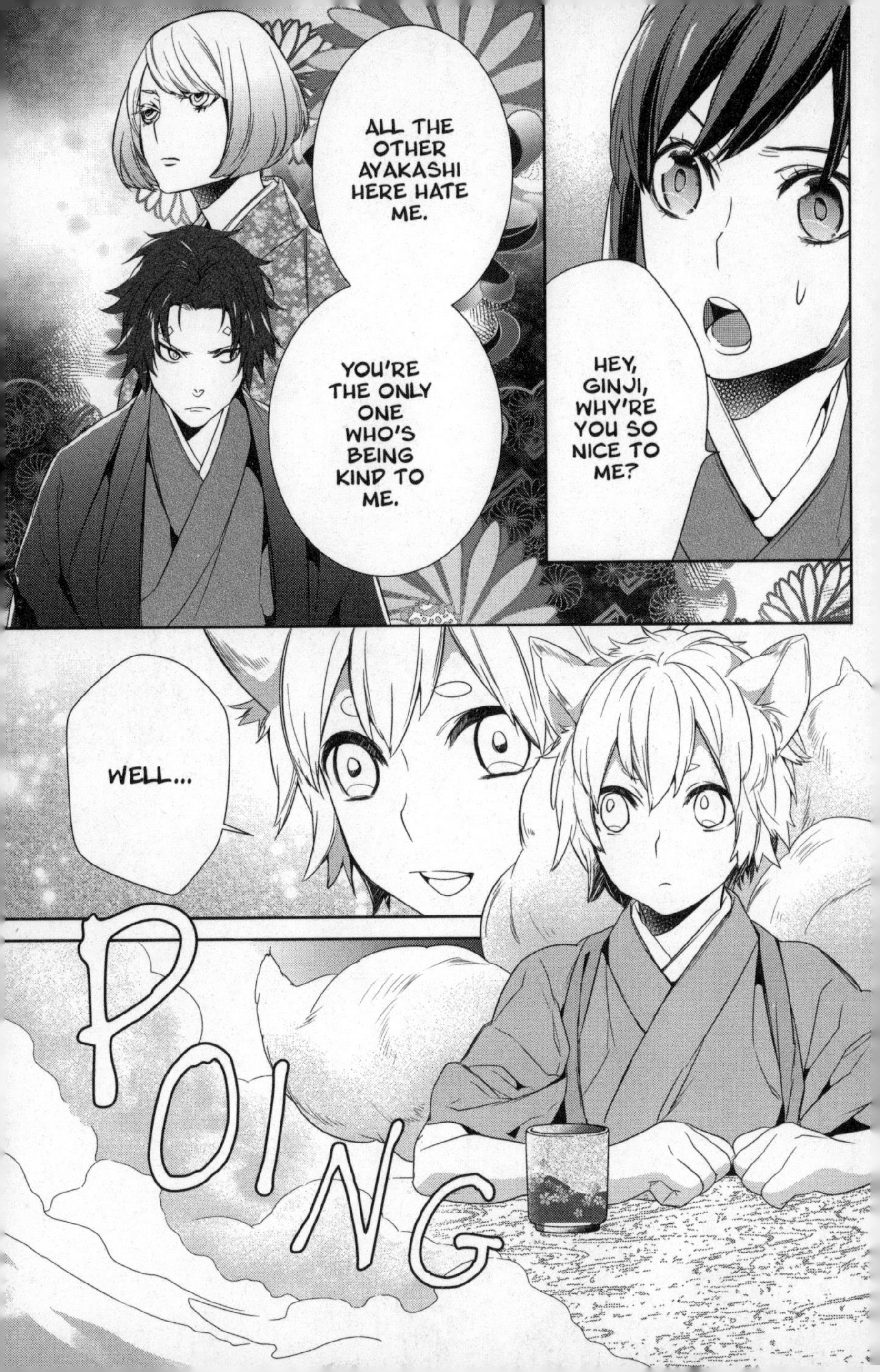
HEY, GINJI, WHY'RE YOU SO NICE TO ME?
ALL THE OTHER AYAKASHI HERE HATE ME.
YOU'RE THE ONLY ONE WHO'S BEING KIND TO ME.
WELL...
POING

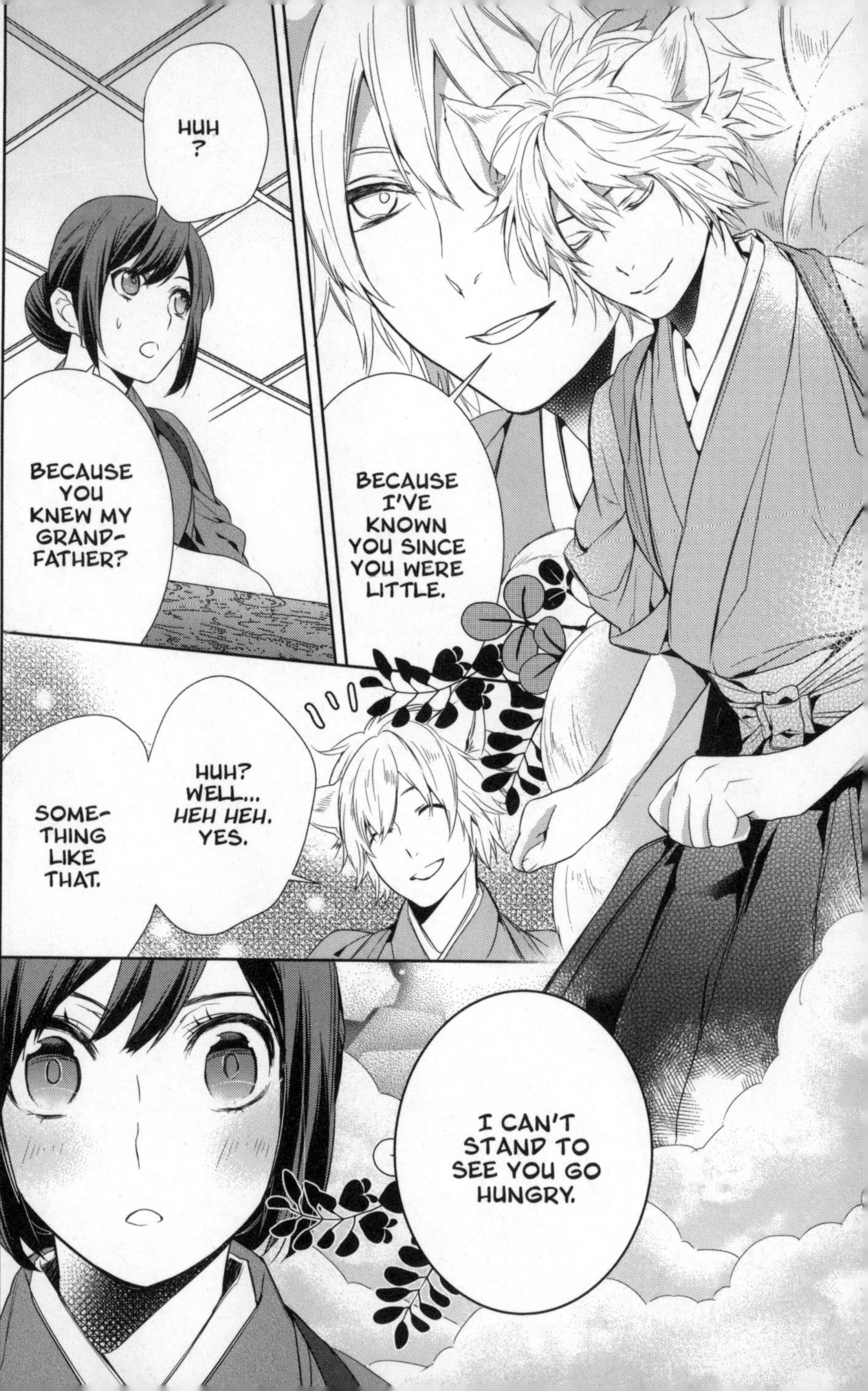
BECAUSE I'VE KNOWN YOU SINCE YOU WERE LITTLE.
HUH?
BECAUSE YOU KNEW MY GRAND-FATHER?
HUH? WELL... HEH HEH. YES.
SOME-THING LIKE THAT.
I CAN'T STAND TO SEE YOU GO HUNGRY.

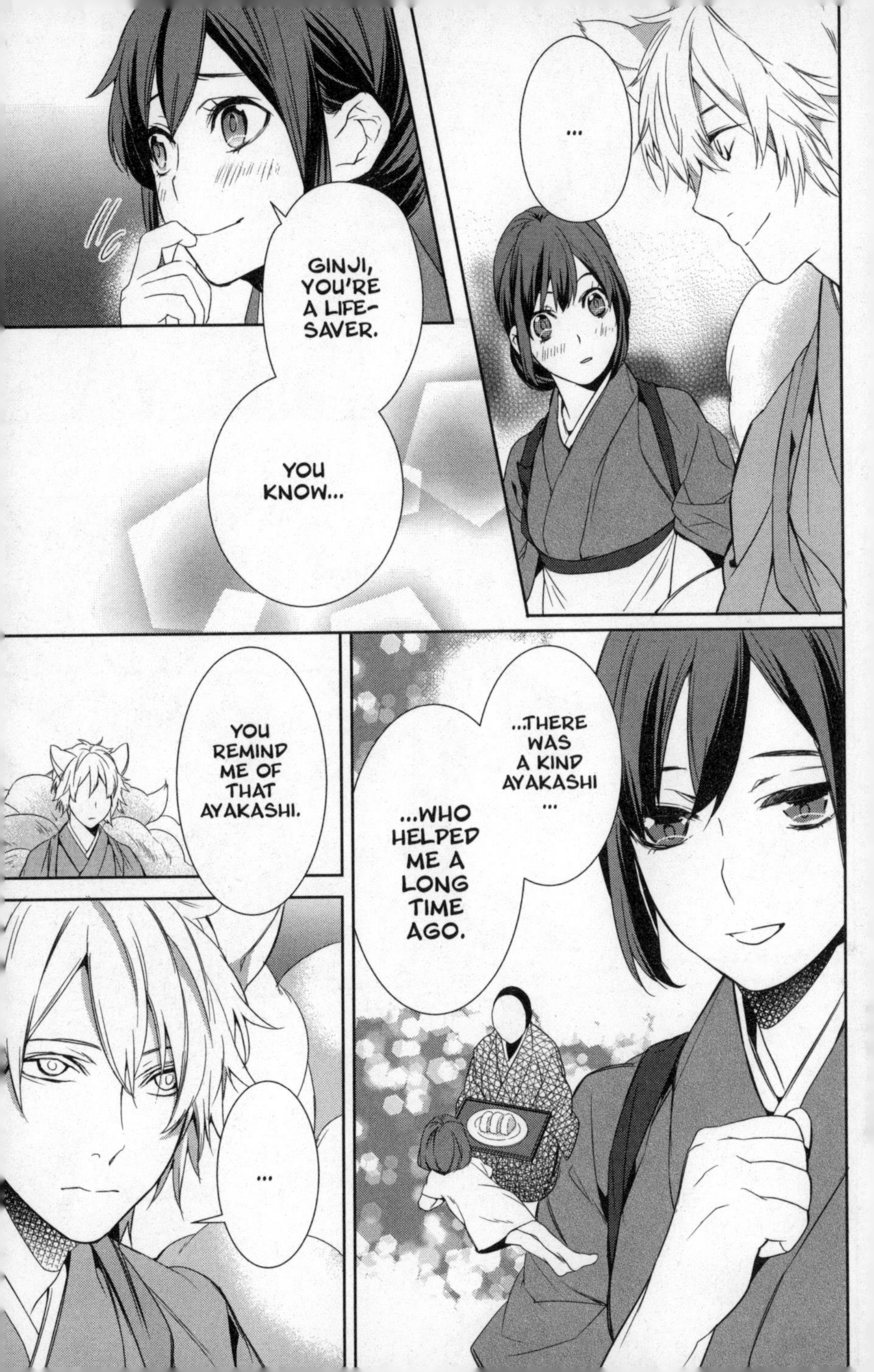
...
GINJI, YOU'RE A LIFE-SAVER.
YOU KNOW...
...THERE WAS A KIND AYAKASHI ...
...WHO HELPED ME A LONG TIME AGO.
YOU REMIND ME OF THAT AYAKASHI.
...

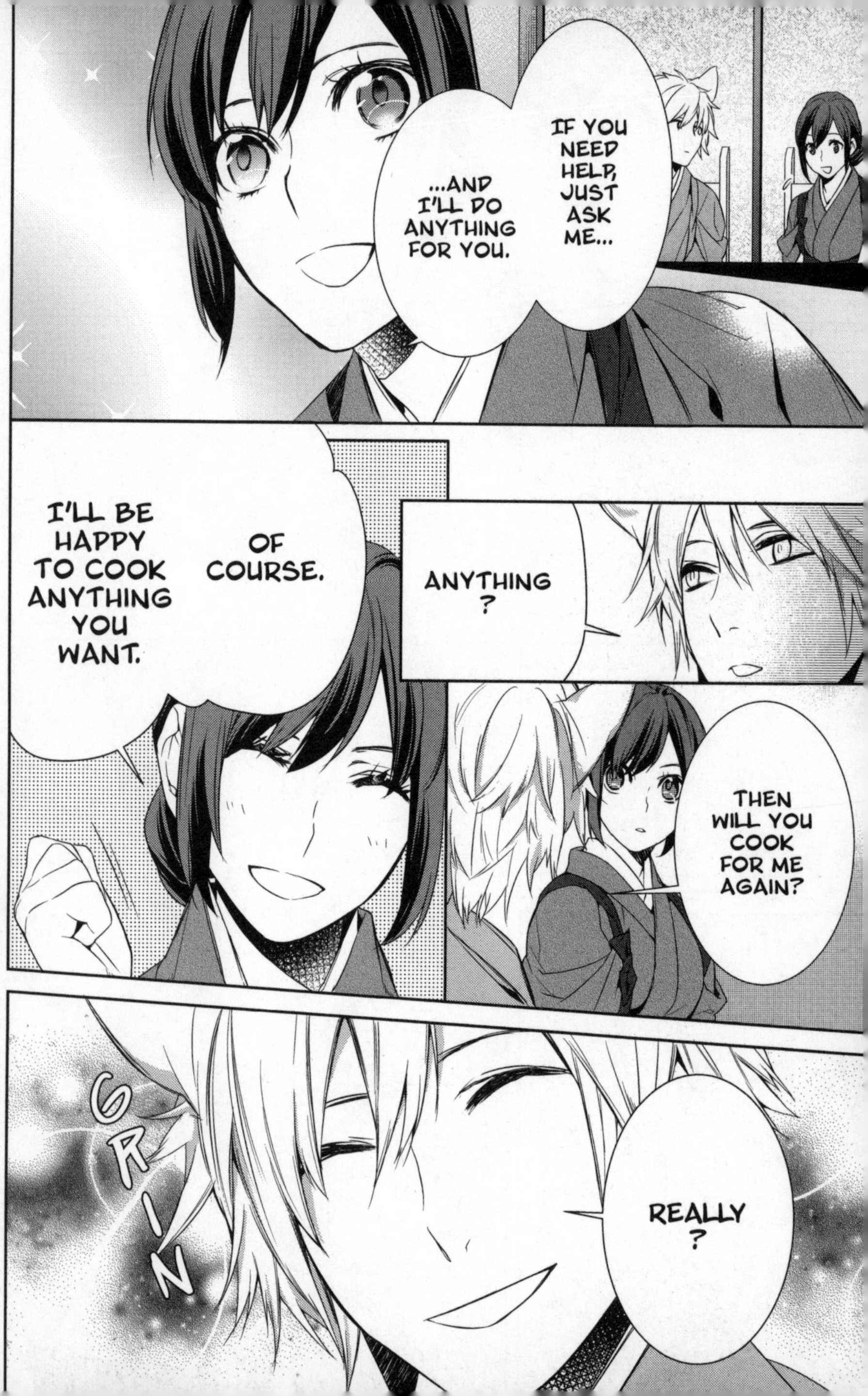
IF YOU NEED HELP, JUST ASK ME...
...AND I'LL DO ANYTHING FOR YOU.
ANYTHING?
THEN WILL YOU COOK FOR ME AGAIN?
OF COURSE.
I'LL BE HAPPY TO COOK ANYTHING YOU WANT.
REALLY?
GRIN

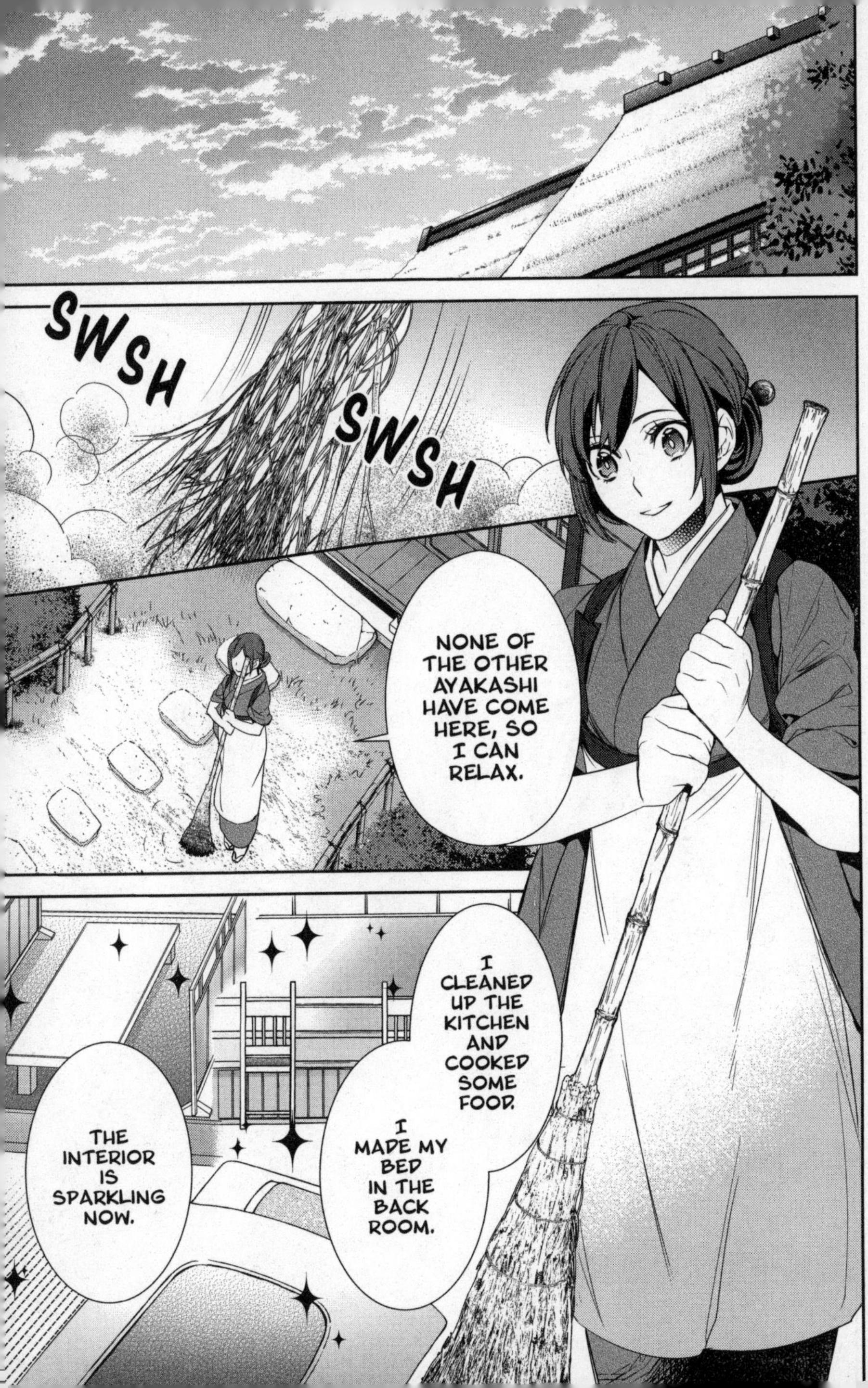
SWSH
SWSH
NONE OF THE OTHER AYAKASHI HAVE COME HERE, SO I CAN RELAX.
I CLEANED UP THE KITCHEN AND COOKED SOME FOOD.
I MADE MY BED IN THE BACK ROOM.
THE INTERIOR IS SPARKLING NOW.

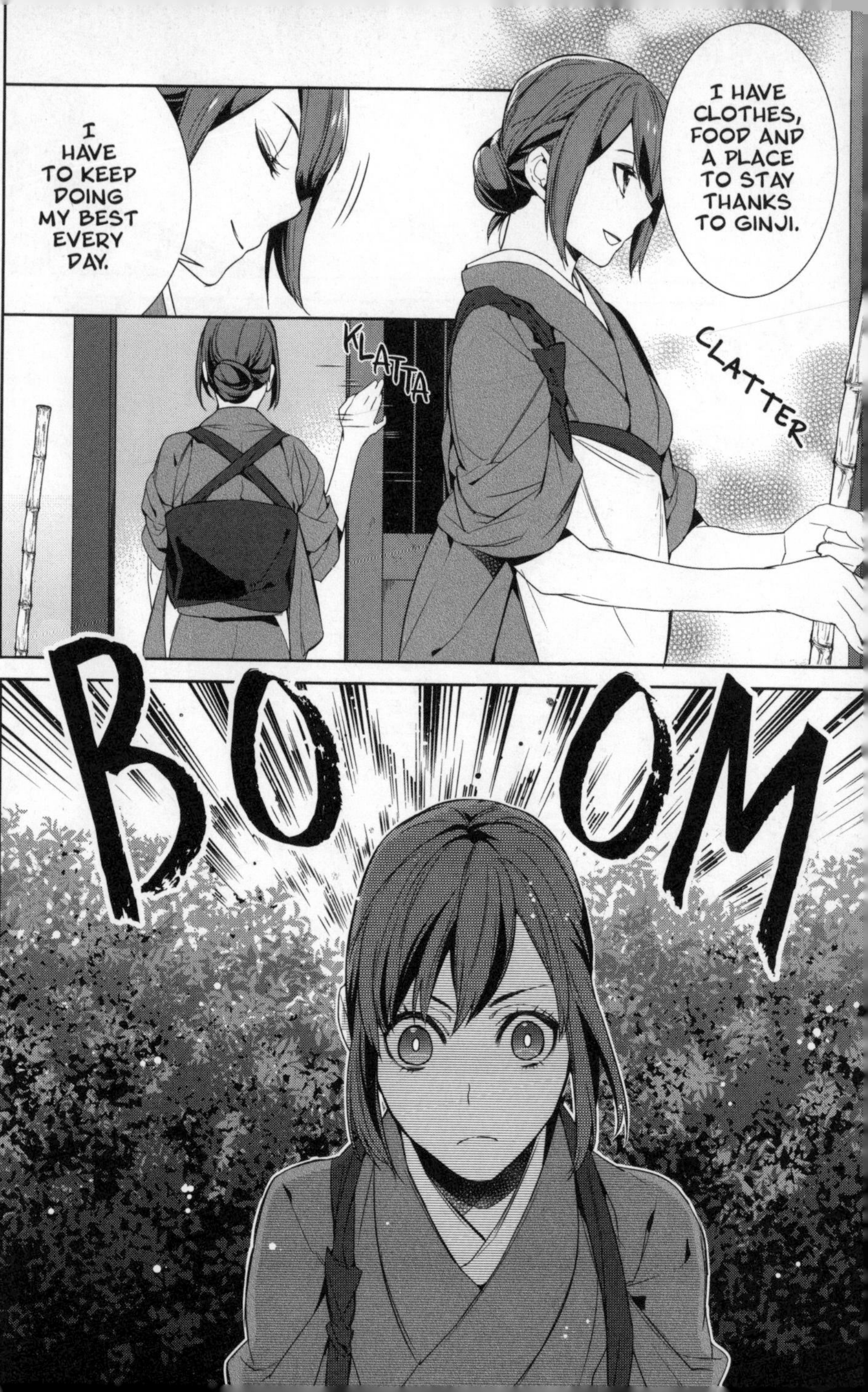
I HAVE CLOTHES, FOOD AND A PLACE TO STAY THANKS TO GINJI.
CLATTER
I HAVE TO KEEP DOING MY BEST EVERY DAY.
KLATTA
BOOM

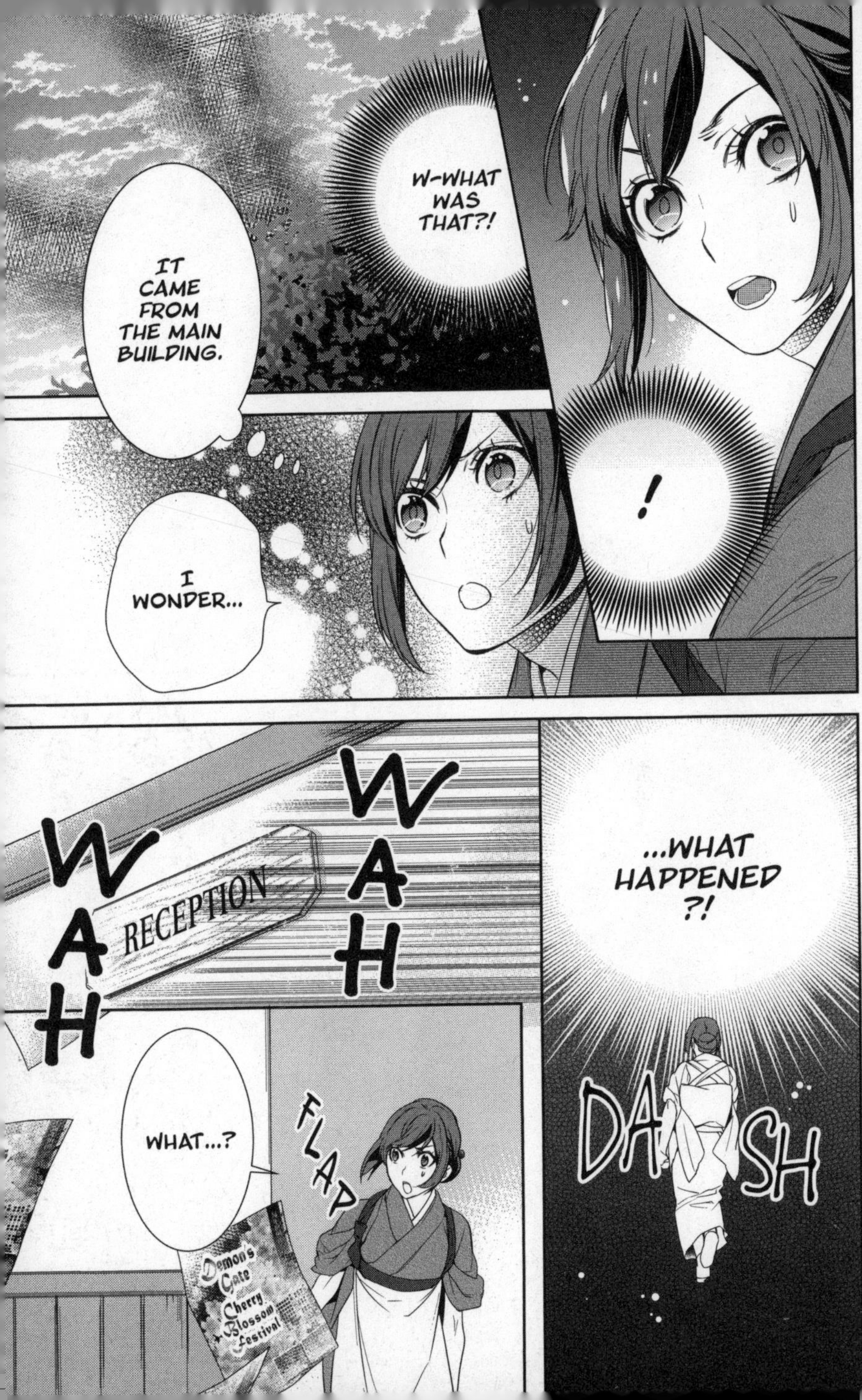
W-WHAT WAS THAT?!
!
IT CAME FROM THE MAIN BUILDING.
I WONDER...
...WHAT HAPPENED ?!
DASH
WAH
WAH
RECEPTION
FLAP
WHAT...?
Demon's Gate Cherry Blossom Festival

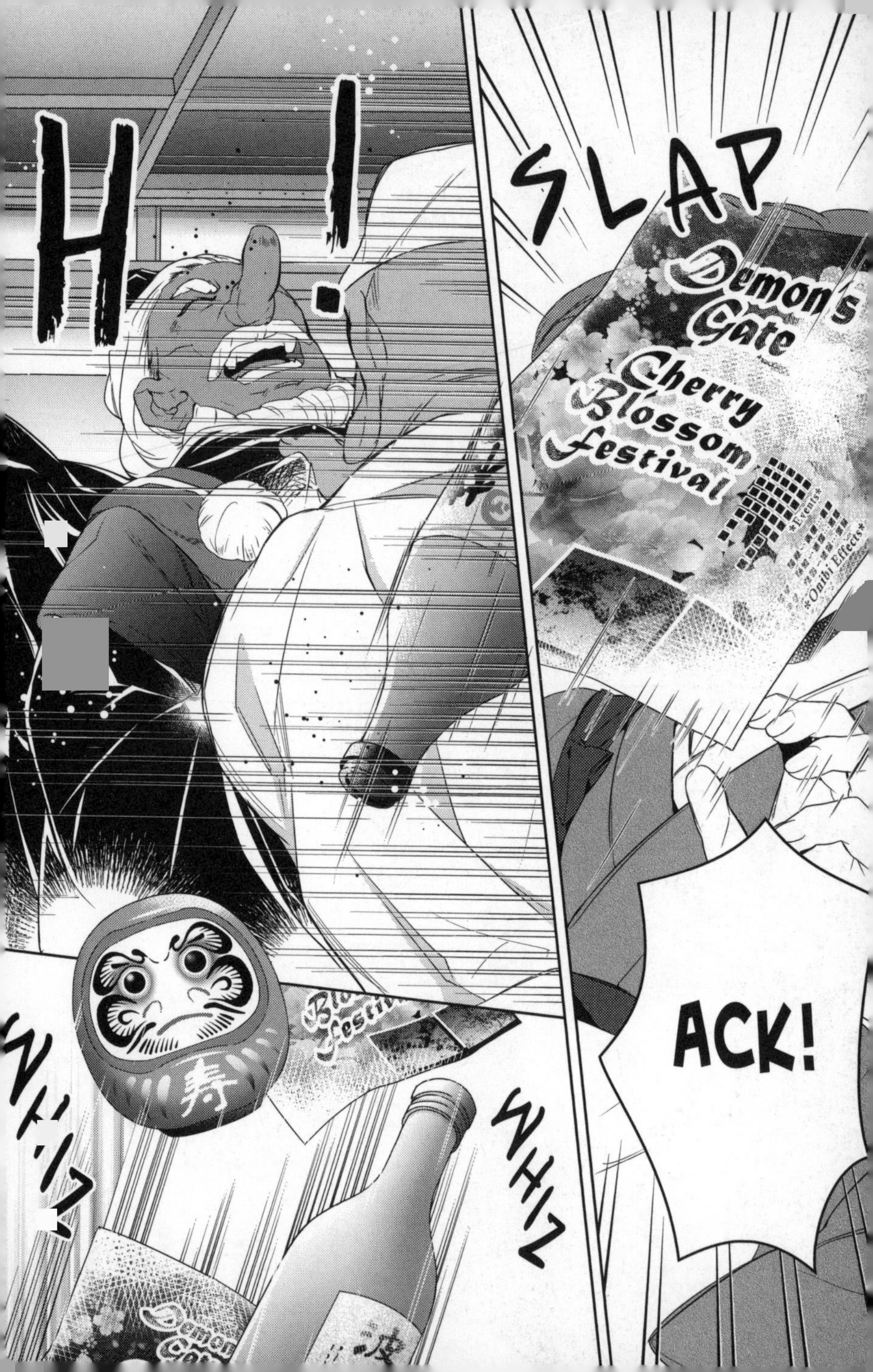
SLAP
Demon's Gate Cherry Blossom Festival
Events
Onibi Effects
ACK!
HI!
寿
WHIZ
WHIZ

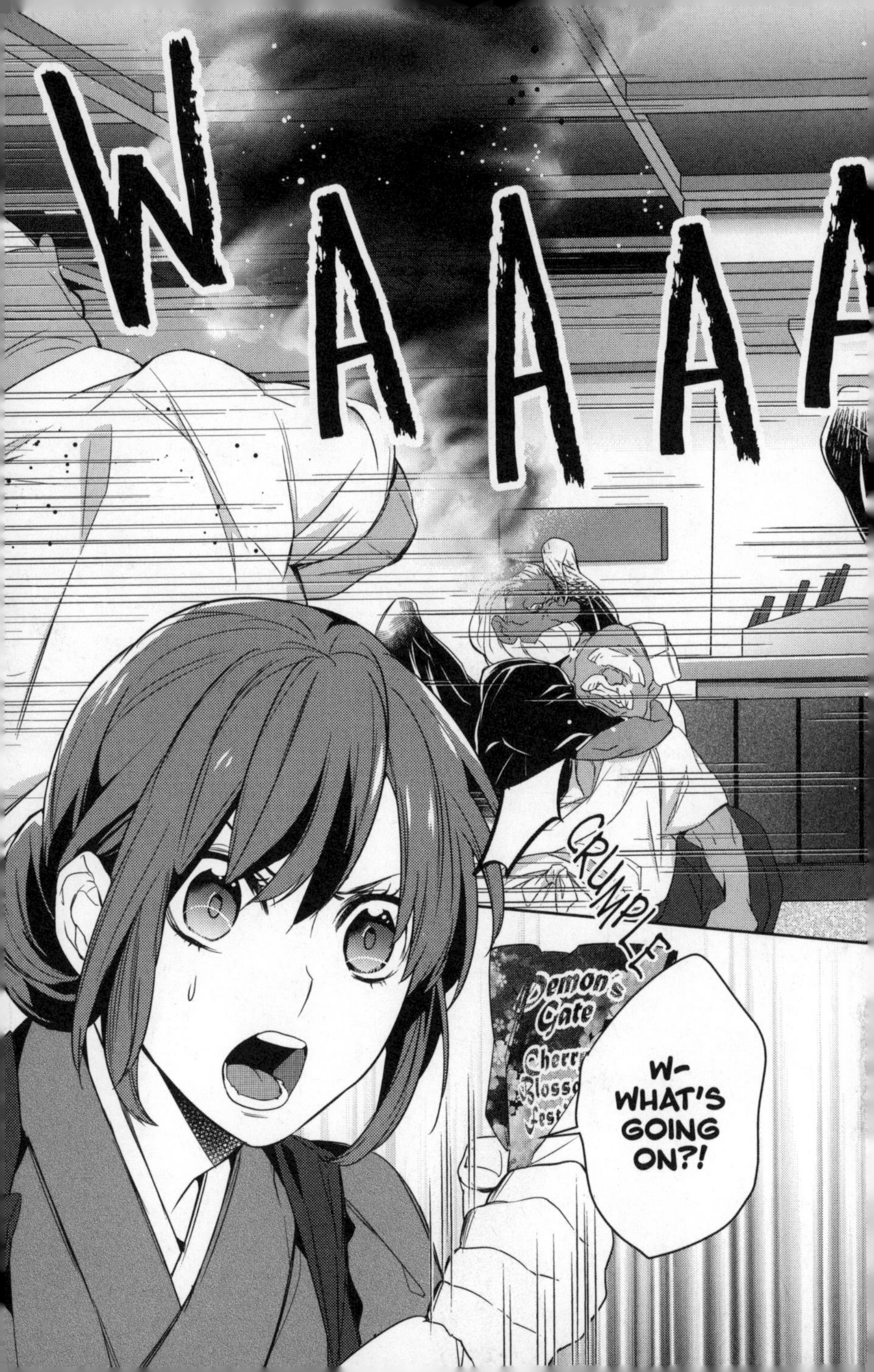
WAAAA
CRUMPLE
Demon's Gate
W-WHAT'S GOING ON?!

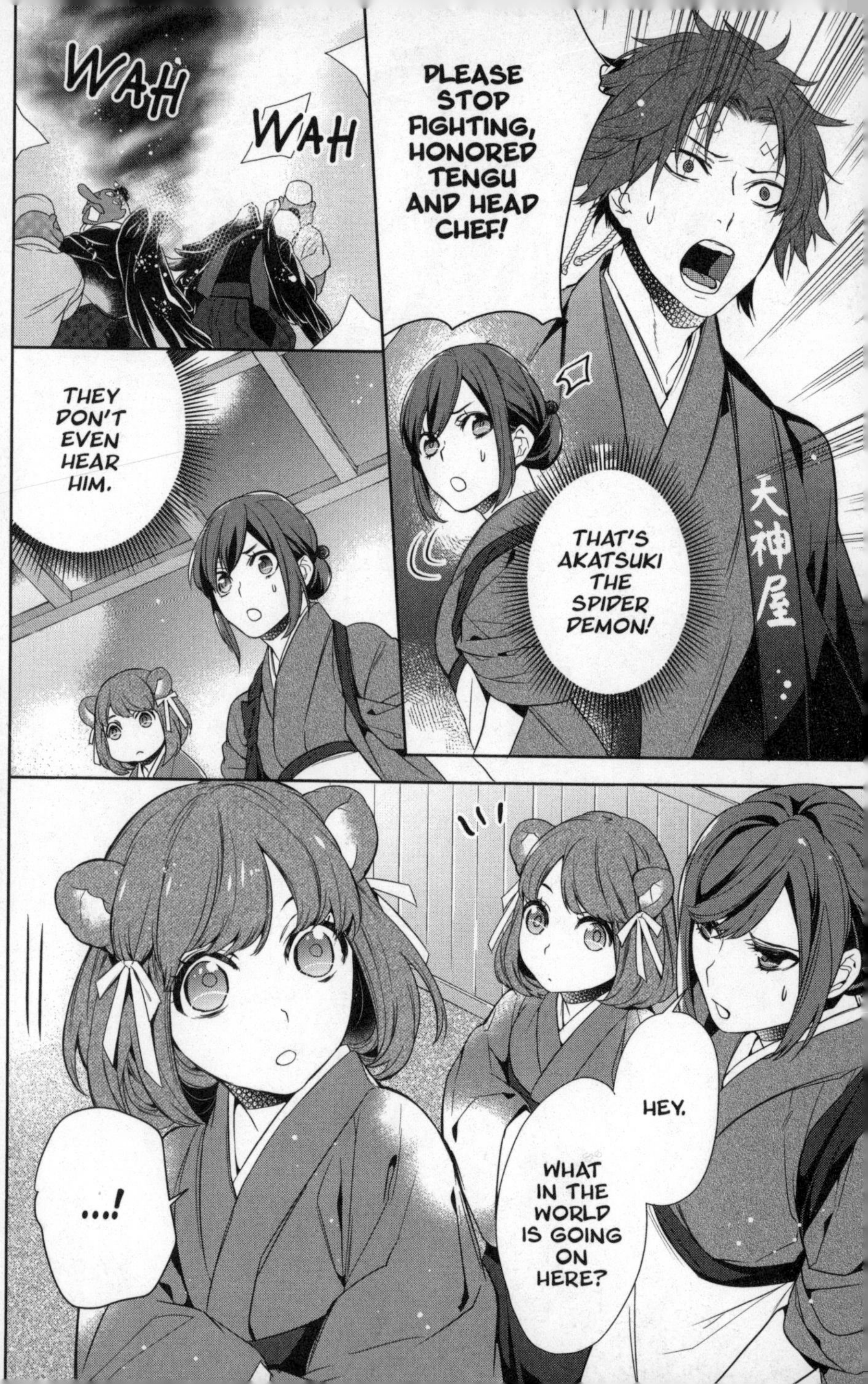
PLEASE STOP FIGHTING, HONORED TENGU AND HEAD CHEF!
WAH
WAH
天神屋
THAT'S AKATSUKI THE SPIDER DEMON!
THEY DON'T EVEN HEAR HIM.
HEY.
WHAT IN THE WORLD IS GOING ON HERE?
...!

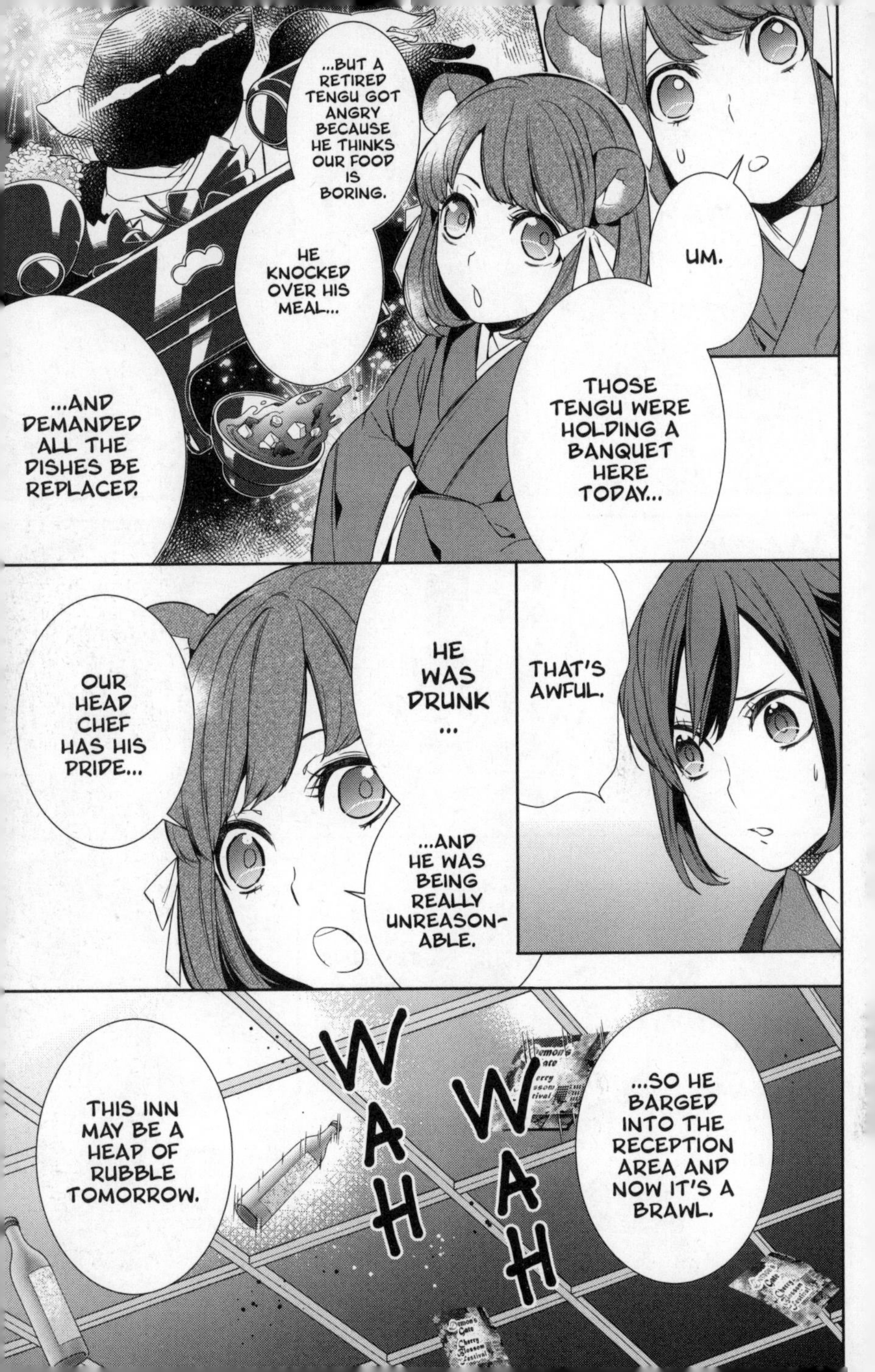
UM.
THOSE TENGU WERE HOLDING A BANQUET HERE TODAY...
...BUT A RETIRED TENGU GOT ANGRY BECAUSE HE THINKS OUR FOOD IS BORING.
HE KNOCKED OVER HIS MEAL...
...AND DEMANDED ALL THE DISHES BE REPLACED.
THAT'S AWFUL.
HE WAS DRUNK...
...AND HE WAS BEING REALLY UNREASON-ABLE.
OUR HEAD CHEF HAS HIS PRIDE...
...SO HE BARGED INTO THE RECEPTION AREA AND NOW IT'S A BRAWL.
WAH
WAH
THIS INN MAY BE A HEAP OF RUBBLE TOMORROW.

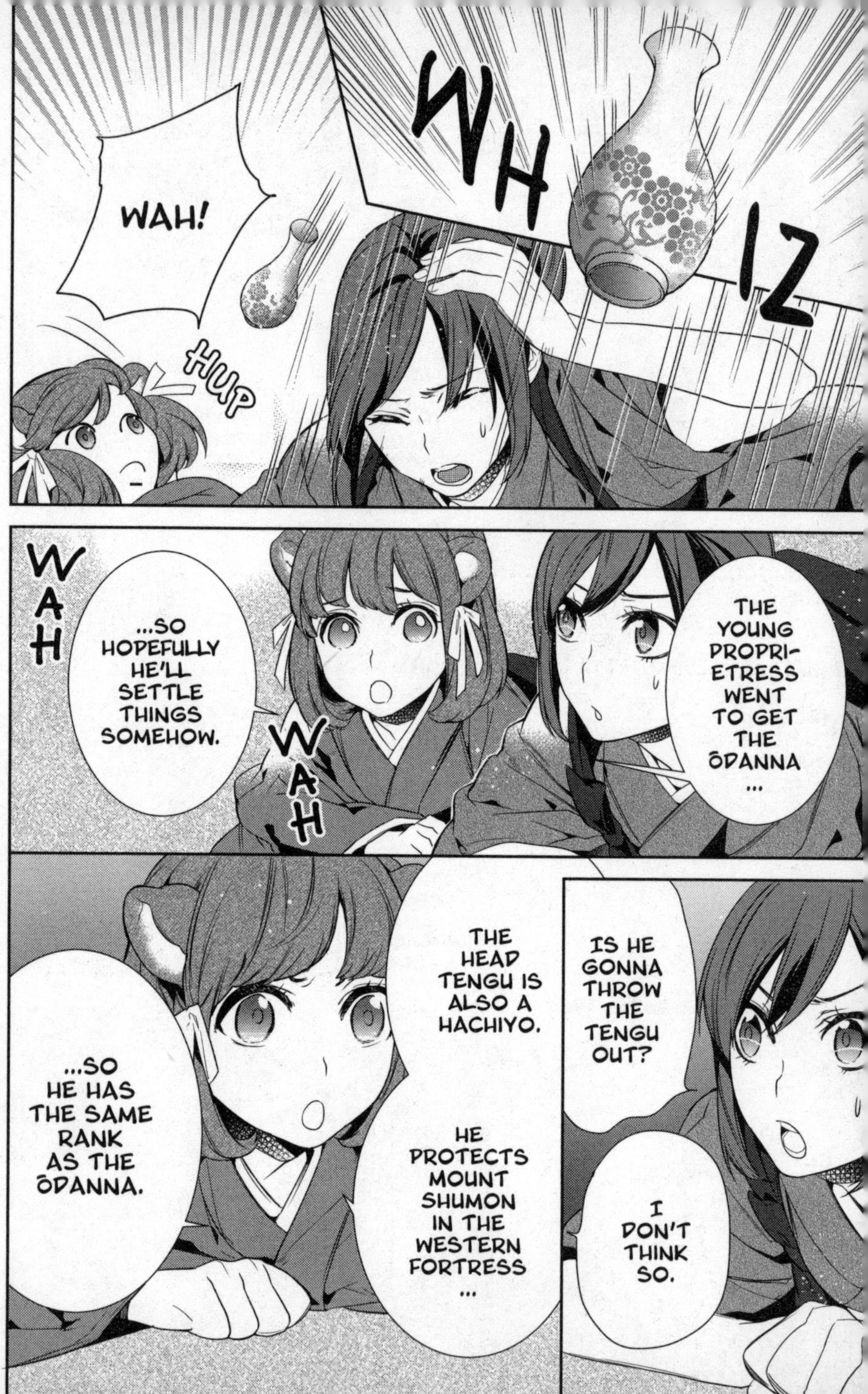
WHIZ
WAH!
HUP
THE YOUNG PROPRIETRESS WENT TO GET THE ŌDANNA ...
WAH WAH
...SO HOPEFULLY HE'LL SETTLE THINGS SOMEHOW.
WAH
IS HE GONNA THROW THE TENGU OUT?
I DON'T THINK SO.
THE HEAD TENGU IS ALSO A HACHIYO.
HE PROTECTS MOUNT SHUMON IN THE WESTERN FORTRESS ...
...SO HE HAS THE SAME RANK AS THE ŌDANNA.

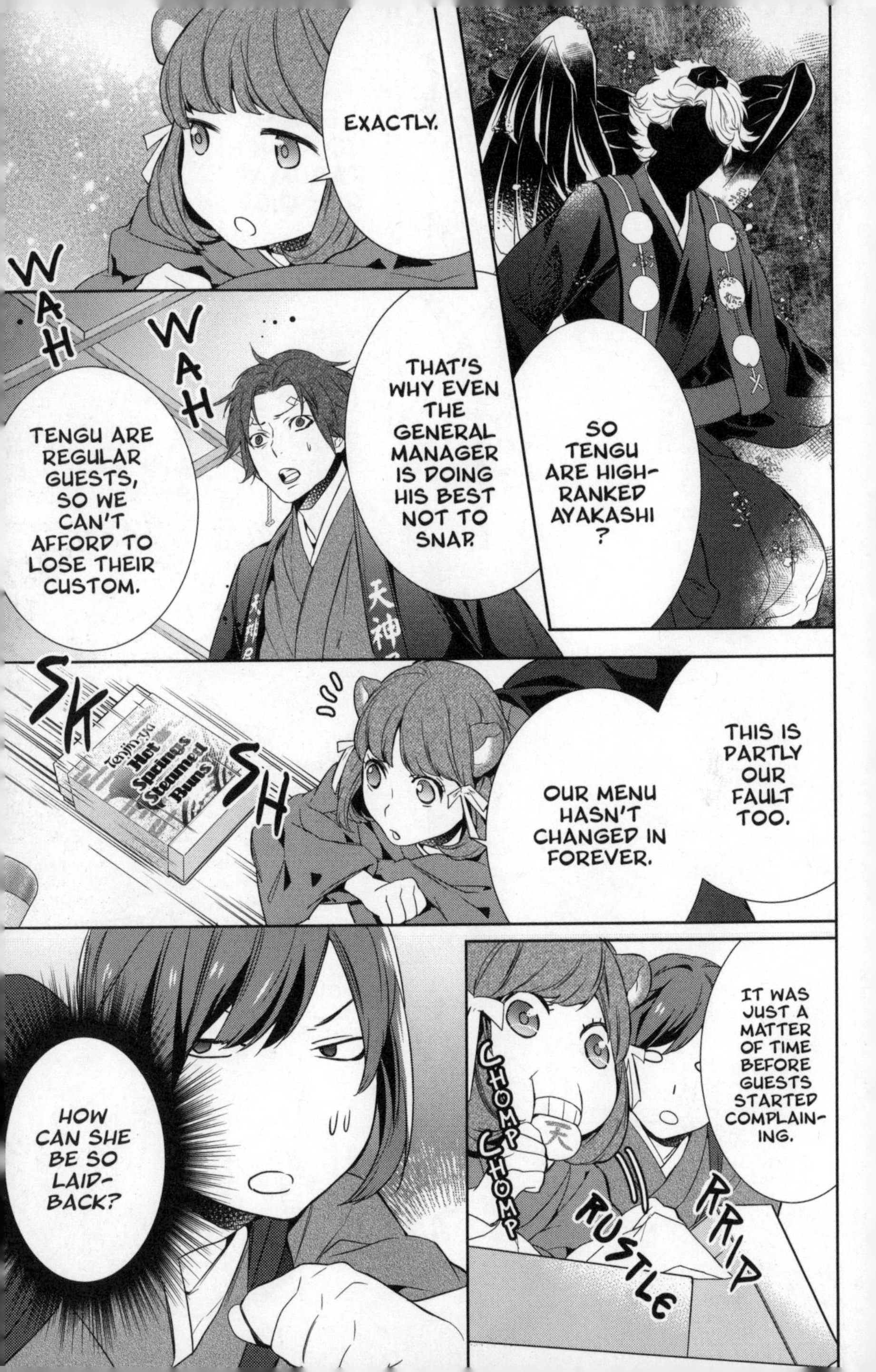
SO TENGU ARE HIGH-RANKED AYAKASHI?
EXACTLY.
WAH WAH
THAT'S WHY EVEN THE GENERAL MANAGER IS DOING HIS BEST NOT TO SNAP.
TENGU ARE REGULAR GUESTS, SO WE CAN'T AFFORD TO LOSE THEIR CUSTOM.
WAH WAH
THIS IS PARTLY OUR FAULT TOO.
OUR MENU HASN'T CHANGED IN FOREVER.
SK SH
Tenjin-ya Hot Springs Steamed Buns
IT WAS JUST A MATTER OF TIME BEFORE GUESTS STARTED COMPLAIN-ING.
RRIP
RUSTLE
CHOMP CHOMP
HOW CAN SHE BE SO LAID-BACK?

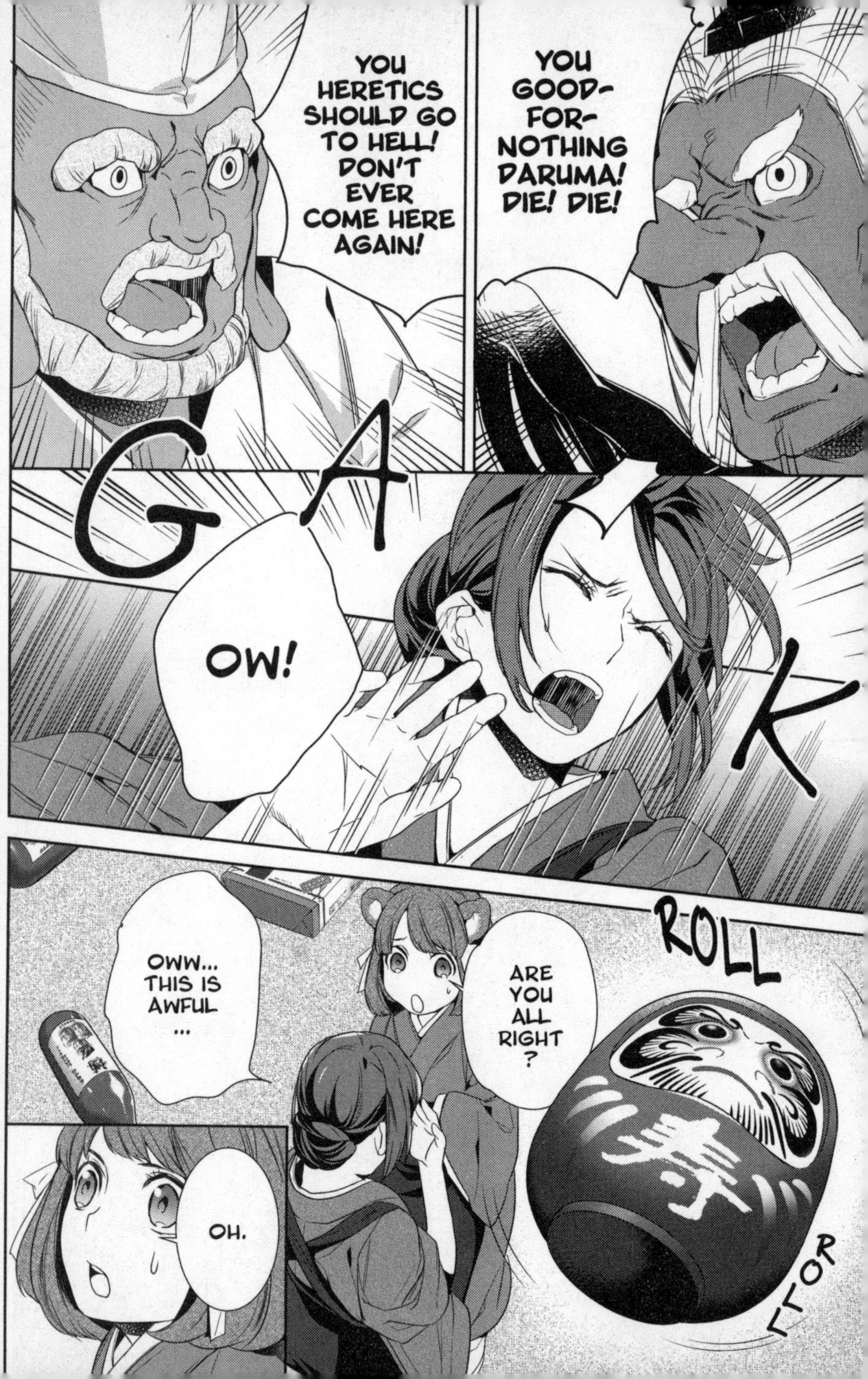
YOU GOOD-FOR-NOTHING DARUMA! DIE! DIE!
YOU HERETICS SHOULD GO TO HELL! DON'T EVER COME HERE AGAIN!
GAK
OW!
ROLL
ARE YOU ALL RIGHT?
OWW... THIS IS AWFUL...
ROLL
OH.

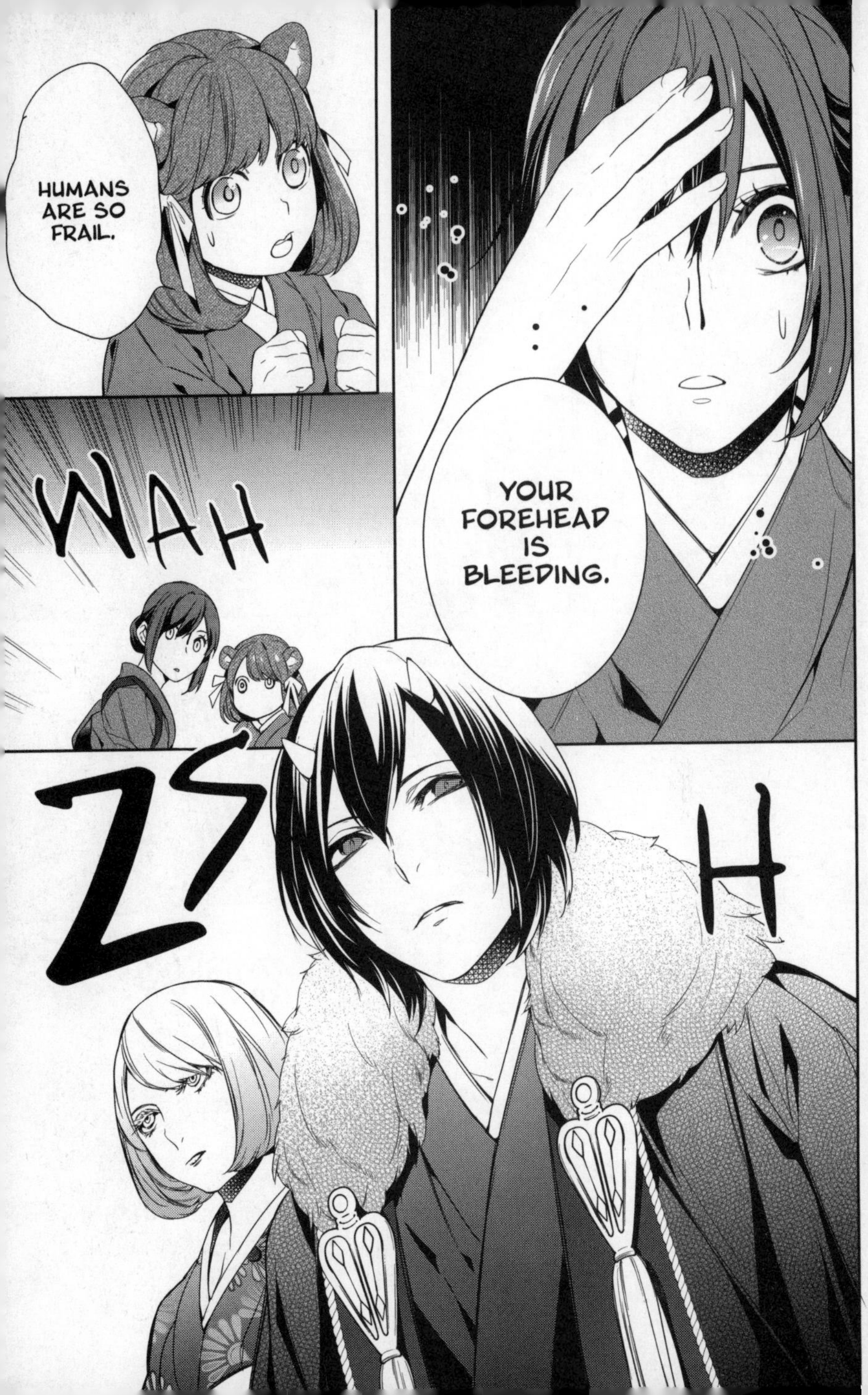
YOUR FOREHEAD IS BLEEDING.
HUMANS ARE SO FRAIL.
WAH
ZSH

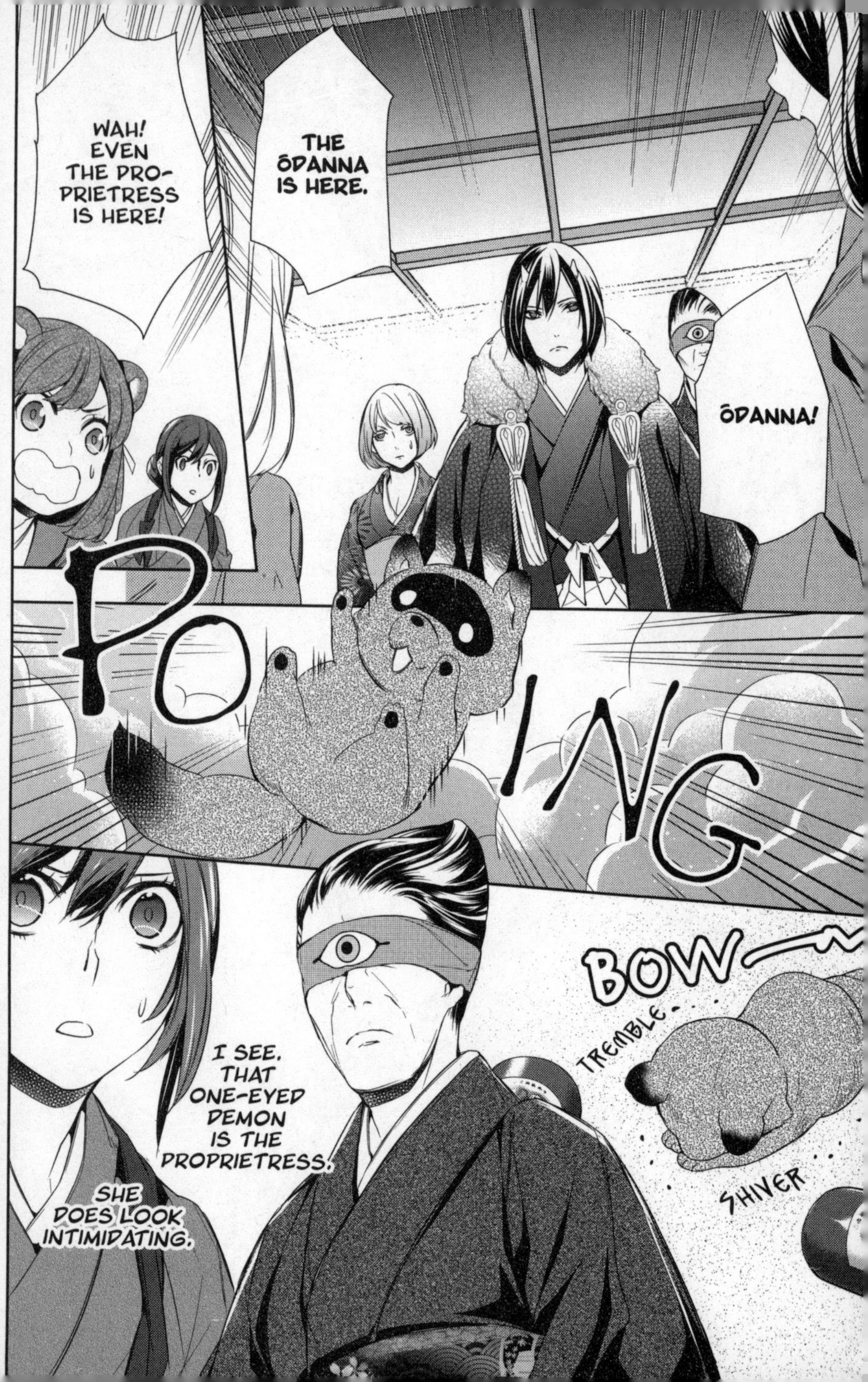
ŌDANNA!
THE ŌDANNA IS HERE.
WAH! EVEN THE PRO-PRIETRESS IS HERE!
POING
BOW
TREMBLE...
SHIVER
I SEE. THAT ONE-EYED DEMON IS THE PROPRIETRESS.
SHE DOES LOOK INTIMIDATING.

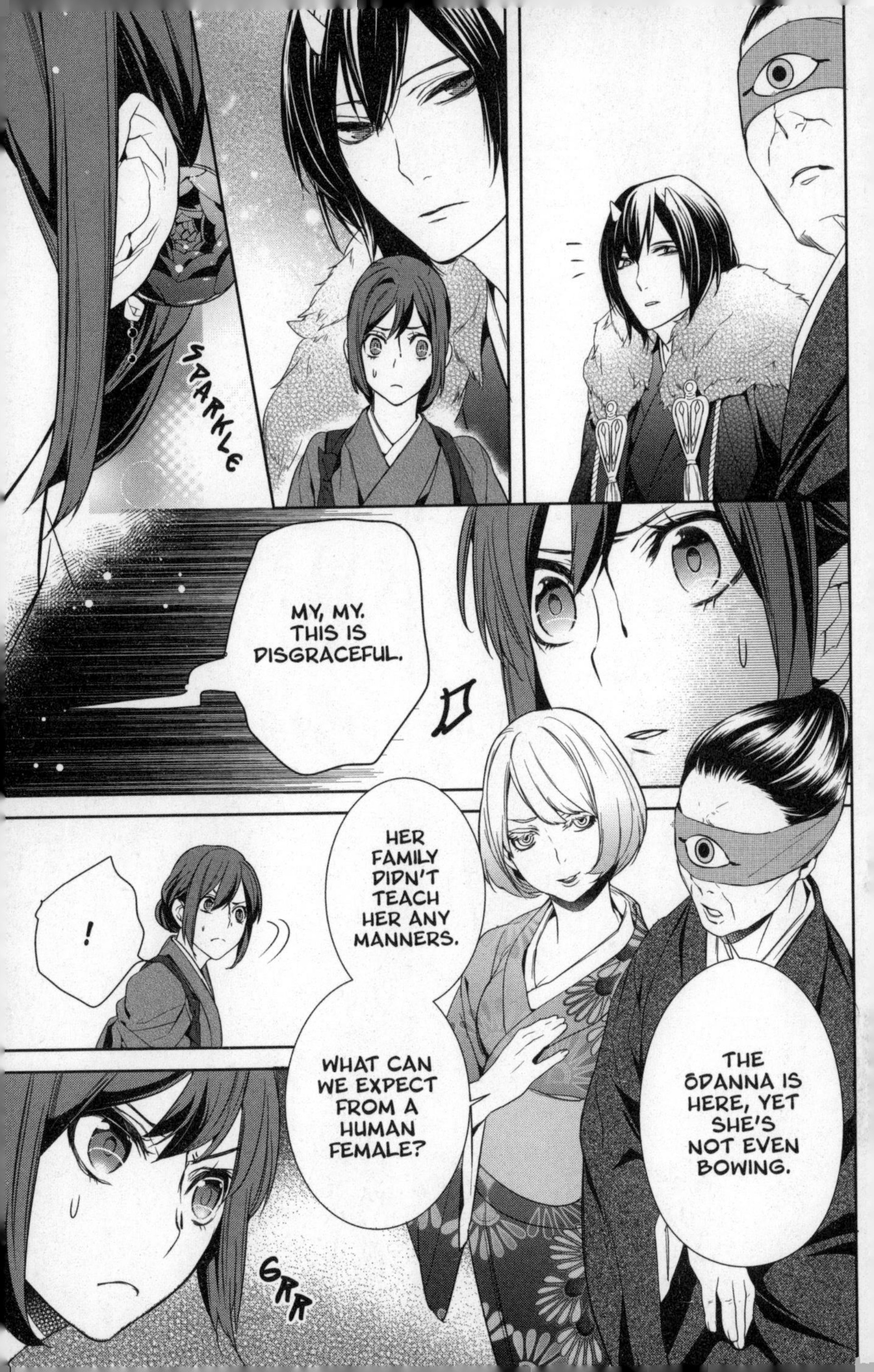
SPARKLE
MY, MY. THIS IS DISGRACEFUL.
THE ŌDANNA IS HERE, YET SHE'S NOT EVEN BOWING.
HER FAMILY DIDN'T TEACH HER ANY MANNERS.
WHAT CAN WE EXPECT FROM A HUMAN FEMALE?
!
GRR

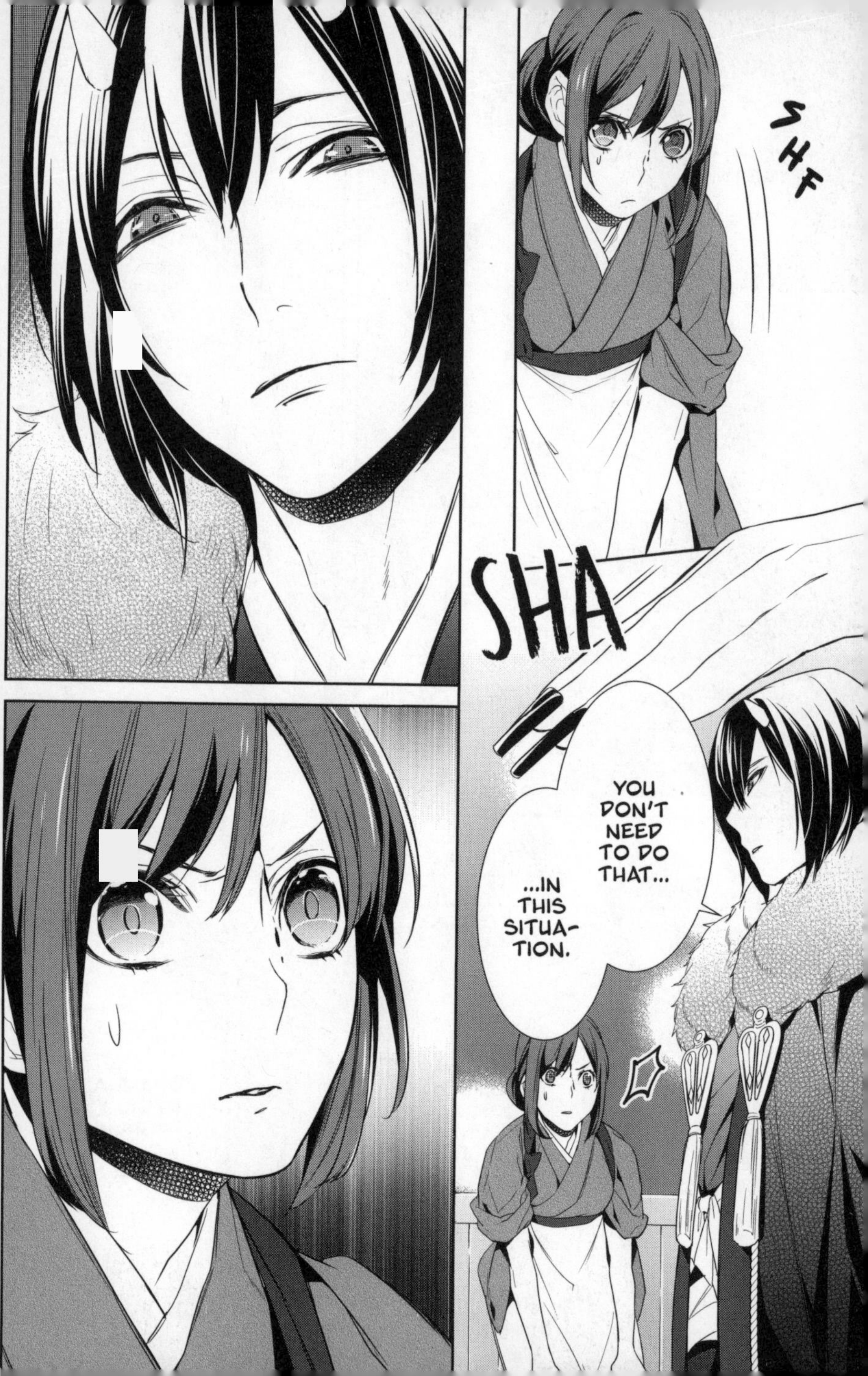
SHF
SHA
YOU DON'T NEED TO DO THAT...
...IN THIS SITUATION.

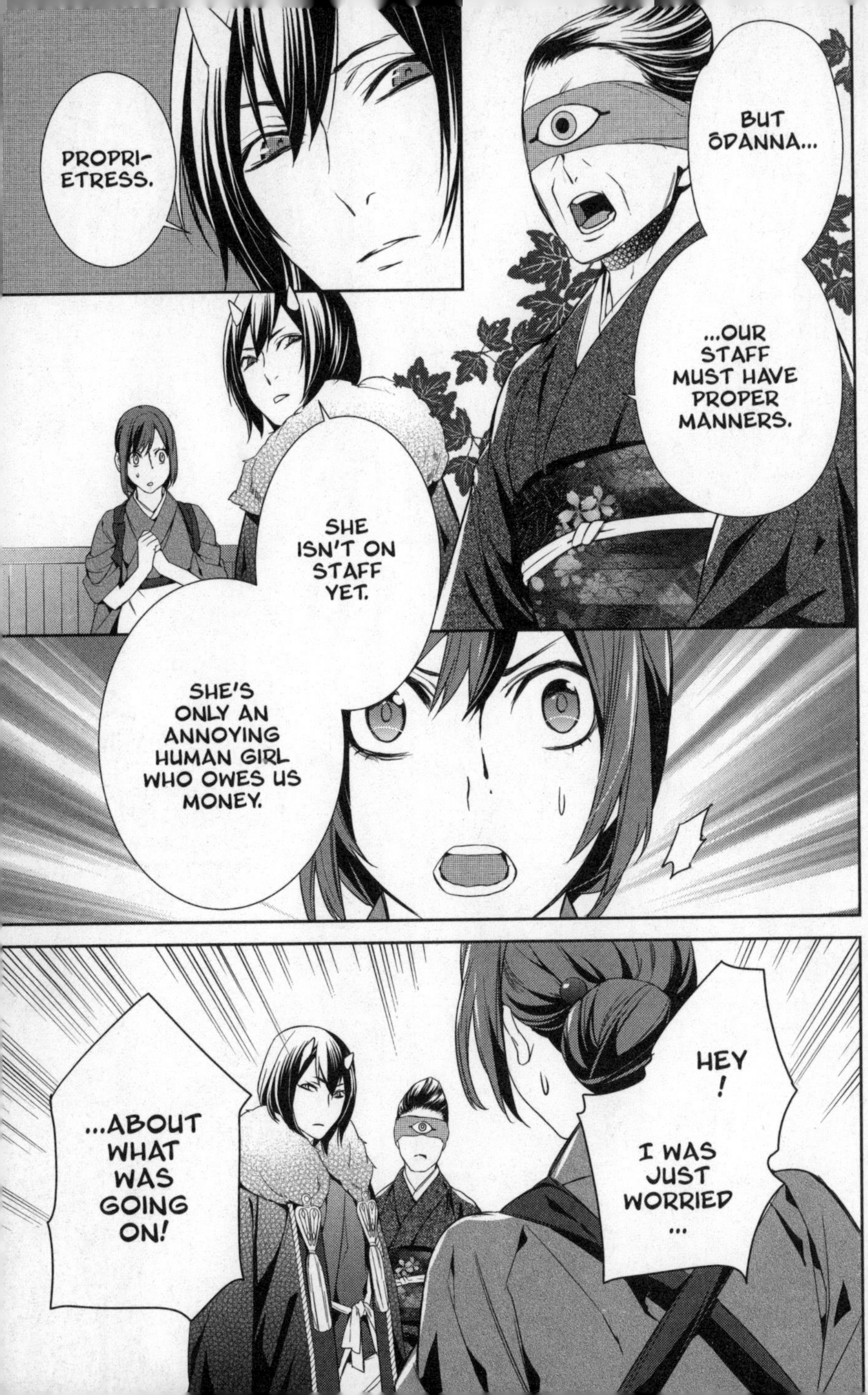
BUT ŌDANNA...
...OUR STAFF MUST HAVE PROPER MANNERS.
PROPRI-ETRESS.
SHE ISN'T ON STAFF YET.
SHE'S ONLY AN ANNOYING HUMAN GIRL WHO OWES US MONEY.
HEY!
I WAS JUST WORRIED...
...ABOUT WHAT WAS GOING ON!

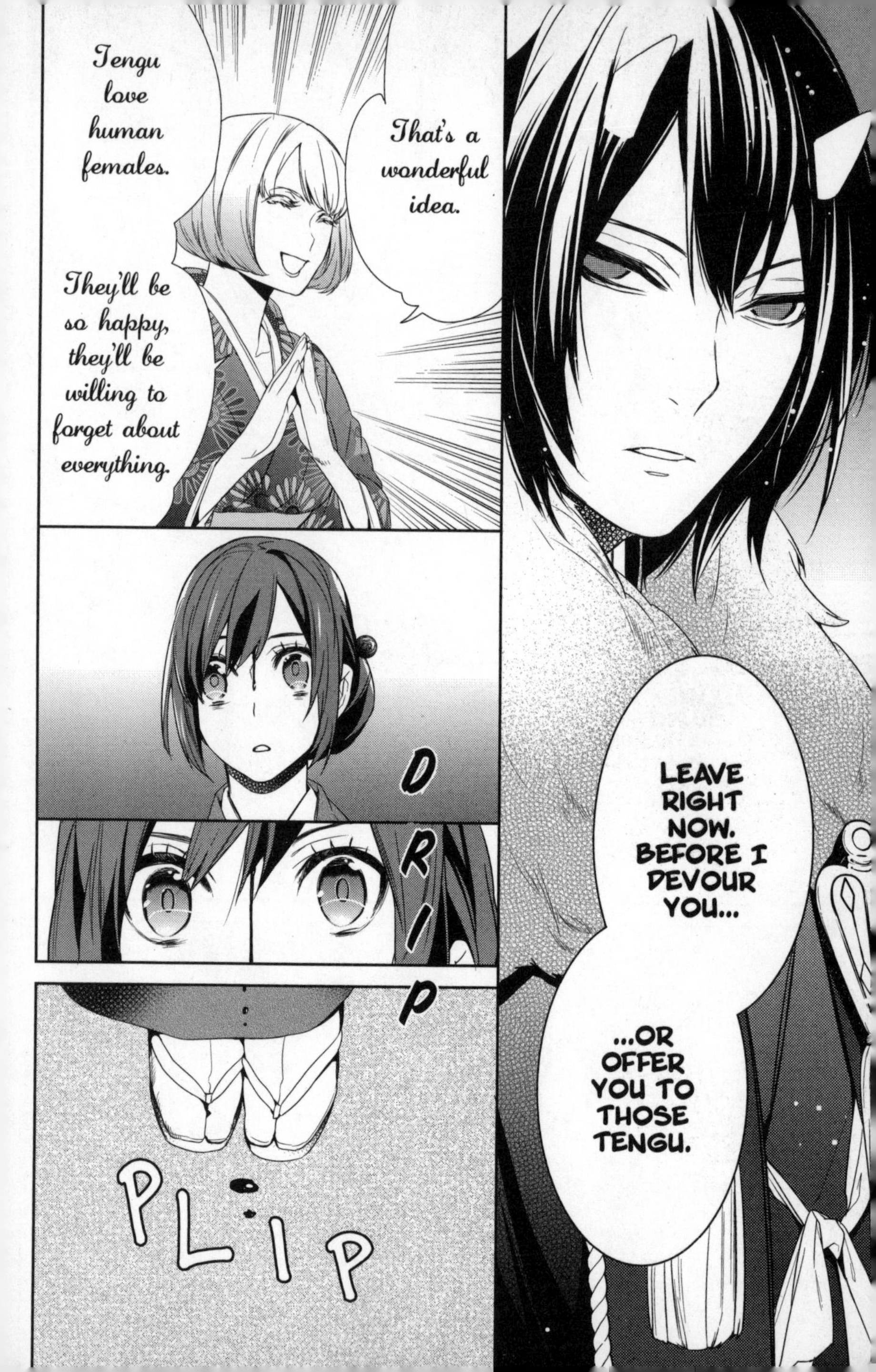
LEAVE RIGHT NOW. BEFORE I DEVOUR YOU...
...OR OFFER YOU TO THOSE TENGU.
That's a wonderful idea.
Tengu love human females.
They'll be so happy, they'll be willing to forget about everything.
DRIP
PLIP

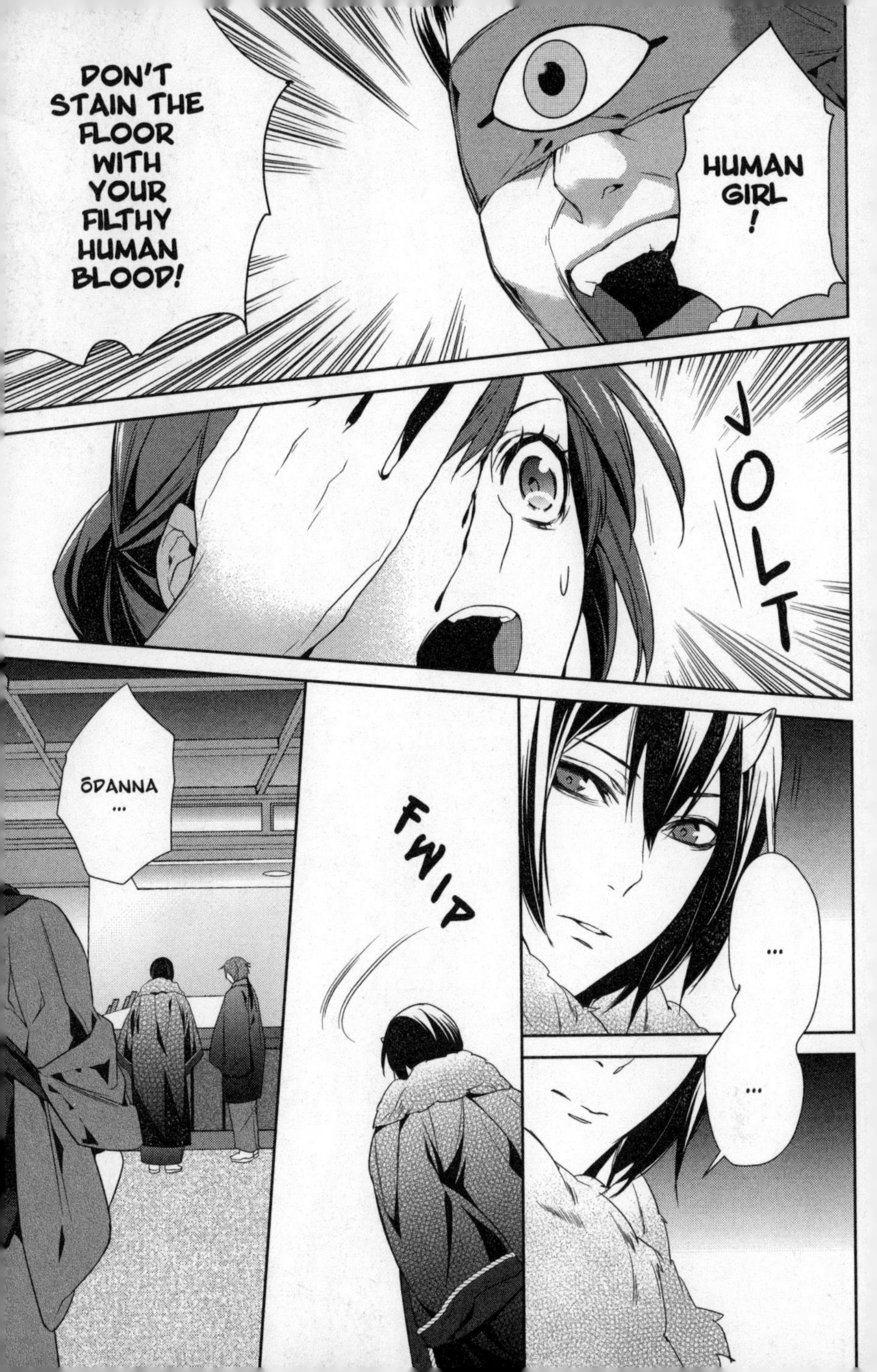
HUMAN GIRL!
DON'T STAIN THE FLOOR WITH YOUR FILTHY HUMAN BLOOD!
VOLT
...
...
FWIP
ŌDANNA ...

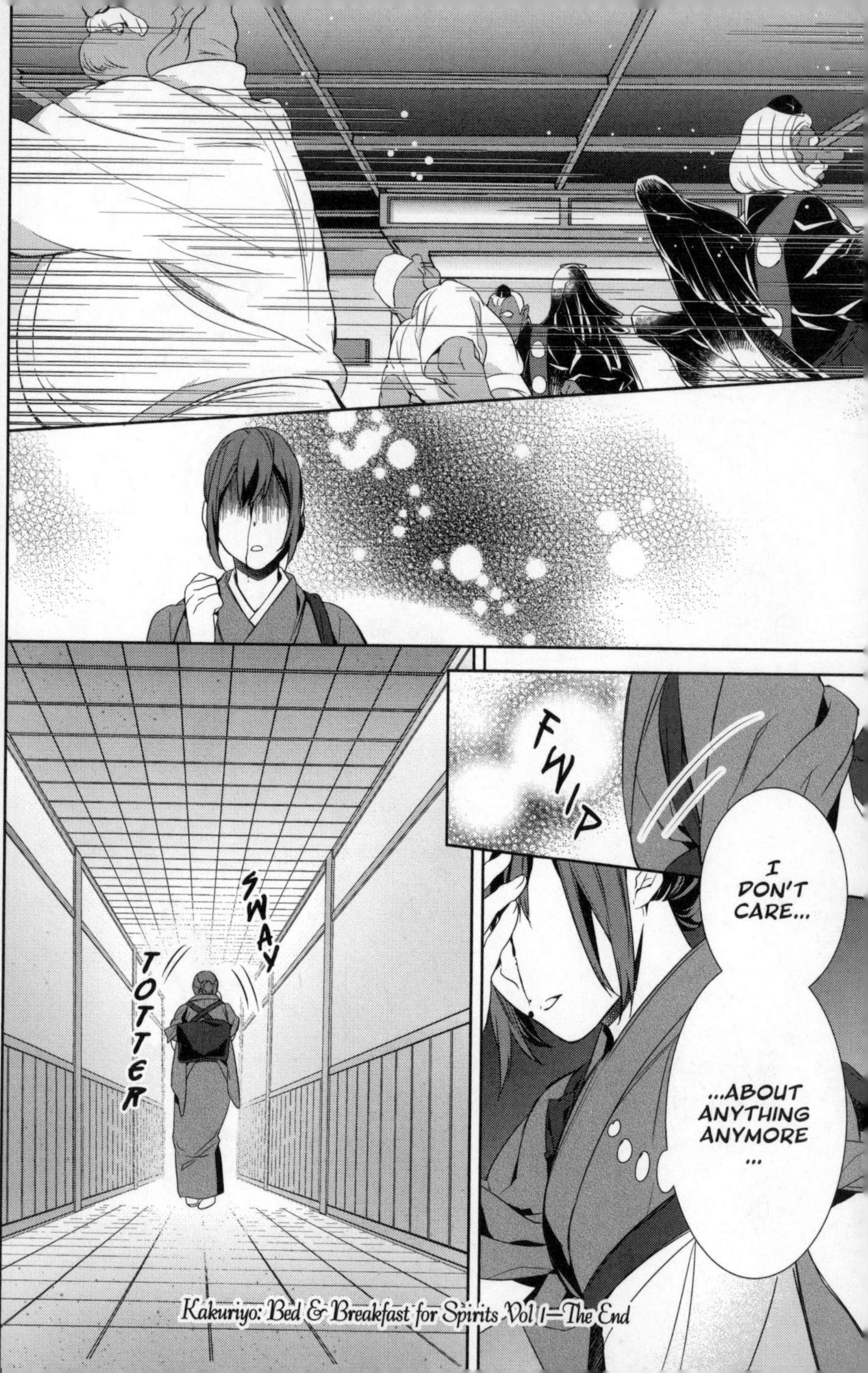
FWIP
I DON'T CARE...
...ABOUT ANYTHING ANYMORE ...
SWAY
TOTTER
Kakuriyo: Bed & Breakfast for Spirits Vol 1—The End

Kakuriyo
Bed & Breakfast
for Spirits

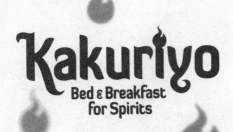

END NOTES

PAGE 66, PANEL 4
Noppera-bo
An ayakashi without eyes, nose or mouth.

PAGE 70, PANEL 2
Yukata
A casual summer kimono made of cotton. Japanese inns provide guests with yukata to wear as lounge and sleepwear.

PAGE 72, PANEL 1
100 million yen
About U.S. $1,000,000.

PAGE 91, PANEL 1
Nine-tailed fox
Kyubi in Japanese. A mythical Chinese fox ayakashi. The number of tails indicates their level of power, and the strongest have nine tails.

PAGE 98, PANEL 5
Octagon
The kanji and symbols in the octagon are icons of ancient Chinese fortune-telling called *hakke* (*bagua* in Chinese).

PANE 98, PANEL 2
Ogre god
Another way of reading the kanji for Kijin is *oni kami*, which can mean "ogre god" in Japanese.

PAGE 99, PANEL 5
Demon's gate
Kimon in Japanese. Ogres are believed to enter and leave from this direction, making it an unlucky direction.

PAGE 101, PANEL 1
One-eyed demon
Hitotsume in Japanese.

PAGE 5, PANEL 3
Ofuda
A strip of paper or a small wooden tablet that acts as a spell.

PAGE 16, PANEL 1
Kappa
A type of water ayakashi that mainly haunts rivers. Kappa look like children, are green or red, have plates on their heads, tortoise shells on their backs, webbed hands and a beak.

PAGE 24, PANEL 5
Torii
A torii is built at the entrance of a shrine. It's a shield that separates the enshrined god's precincts from the outside world.

PAGE 25, PANEL 1
Mask
The ayakashi is wearing a *noh* mask called a *hannya*. The mask expresses vengeful female spirits.

PAGE 44, PANEL 4
Ogres
Ogres or trolls are called *oni* in Japanese. They have one or two horns, and are traditionally red- or blue-skinned.

PAGE 50, PANEL 4
Hyottoko
A stock comic character mask with a polka-dot scarf and puckered mouth.

PAGE 65, PANEL 5
Spider demon
Tsuchigumo in Japanese. A huge ayakashi with the face of an ogre, body of a tiger and long spider legs.

PAGE 138, PANEL 3
Icicle Woman
Tsuraraonna in Japanese. Brought into being in winter by lonely men staring at the lovely shape of icicles. They melt if exposed to heat.

PAGE 143, PANEL 4
Omelet rice
Ketchup-flavored stir-fried rice wrapped in a thin omelet.

PAGE 145, PANEL 4
Kotodama
Literally "word spirit," the spiritual power that dwells in words. In Shinto, the words you speak are believed to affect reality.

PAGE 155, PANEL 3
Ponzu sauce
Soy sauce with citrus juice.

PAGE 160, PANEL 2
Shiso leaves
Also called perilla. An herb that tastes like a mix of mint and basil.

PAGE 164, PANEL 4
Kyushu soy sauce
Soy sauce made in Kyushu, the southern island of Japan, is sweeter than soy sauce made in other regions. The farther south you go, the sweeter the soy sauce.

PAGE 165, PANEL 1
Dejima
A man-made island in Nagasaki that was built in 1634 when Japan closed its borders to the outside world. It was the sole trading post with Portugal, then the Netherlands, until Japan opened up its borders in 1853.

PAGE 178, PANEL 1
Tengu
Winged mythical beings thought to be either gods or ayakashi. They are usually dressed as mountain priests and have prominent noses.

PAGE 101, PANEL 1
Snow Woman
Yukionna in Japanese. Female snow ayakashi who wear white funeral kimono. They kill men by either freezing them to death or sucking out their life force.

PAGE 101, PANEL 1
Hakutaku
A mythical Chinese animal with nine eyes and the body of a lion. They were believed to appear in the human world when a virtuous statesman was ruling the land.

PAGE 101, PANEL 2
Daruma
Round good-luck dolls made in the shape of the Buddhist monk Bodhidarma. They're usually red.

PAGE 101, PANEL 3
In charge of the guests' footwear
These staff put away the guests' footwear when they arrive at an inn and bring them out when guests leave the inn building.

PAGE 101, PANEL 3
Whirlwind
Kamaitachi in Japanese. Ayakashi who appear in whirlwinds and slash humans, although the humans aren't hurt and no blood is drawn.

PAGE 101, PANEL 3
Sea Woman
Nureonna in Japanese. Female ayakashi who appear on the seashore to devour humans.

PAGE 108, PANEL 4
The clock
The Japanese lunar calendar used the Japanese animal zodiac to count hours instead of Arabic numerals. The kanji on the outer circle lists the zodiac in turn, starting with the Rat at 12 o'clock. The kanji on the inner circle indicates the cardinal directions.

Kakuriyo
Bed & Breakfast for Spirits

1

SHOJO BEAT EDITION

Art by **Waco Ioka**
Original story by **Midori Yuma**
Character design by **Laruha**

English Translation & Adaptation **Tomo Kimura**
Touch-up Art & Lettering **Joanna Estep**
Design **Alice Lewis**
Editor **Pancha Diaz**

KAKURIYO NO YADOMESHI AYAKASHIOYADO NI YOMEIRI SHIMASU, Vol. 1
©Waco Ioka 2016
©Midori Yuma 2016
©Laruha 2016
First published in Japan in 2016 by KADOKAWA CORPORATION, Tokyo.
English translation rights arranged with KADOKAWA CORPORATION, Tokyo.

Printed in the U.S.A.

Published by VIZ Media, LLC
P.O. Box 77010
San Francisco, CA 94107

10 9 8 7 6 5 4 3 2 1
First printing, January 2019

PARENTAL ADVISORY
KAKURIYO: BED & BREAKFAST FOR SPIRITS is rated T for Teen and is recommended for ages 13 and up. This volume contains fantasy violence.

viz.com

shojobeat.com

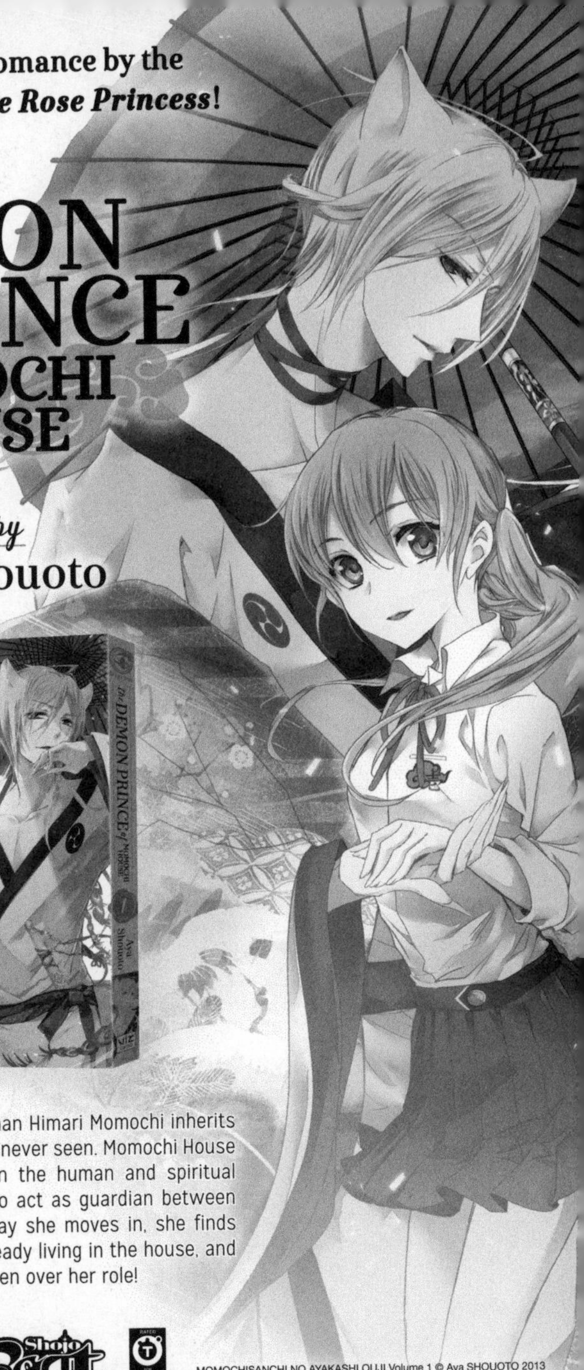

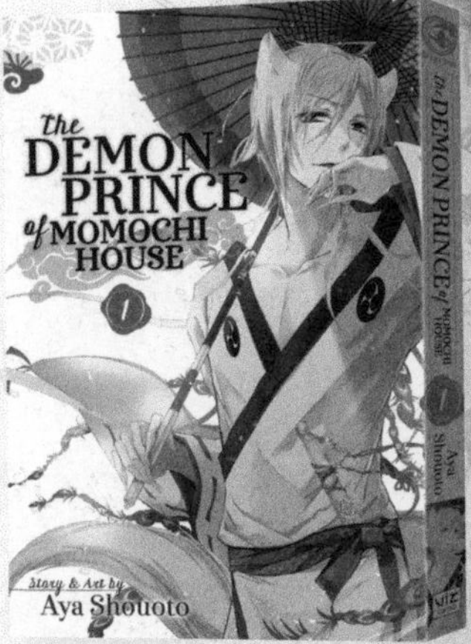
The DEMON PRINCE of MOMOCHI HOUSE
1
Story & Art by
Aya Shouoto
The DEMON PRINCE of MOMOCHI HOUSE 1
Aya Shouoto
VIZ

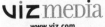

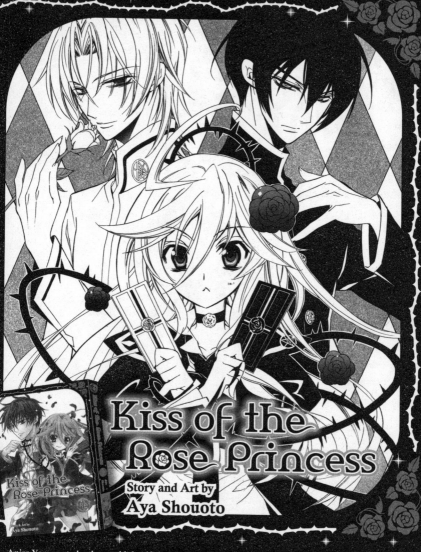

Kiss of the Rose Princess

Story and Art by Aya Shouoto

Anise Yamamoto has been told that if she ever removes the rose choker given to her by her father, a terrible punishment will befall her. Unfortunately she loses that choker when a bat-like being named Ninufa falls from the sky and hits her. Ninufa gives Anise four cards representing four knights whom she can summon with a kiss. But now that she has these gorgeous men at her beck and call, what exactly is her quest?!

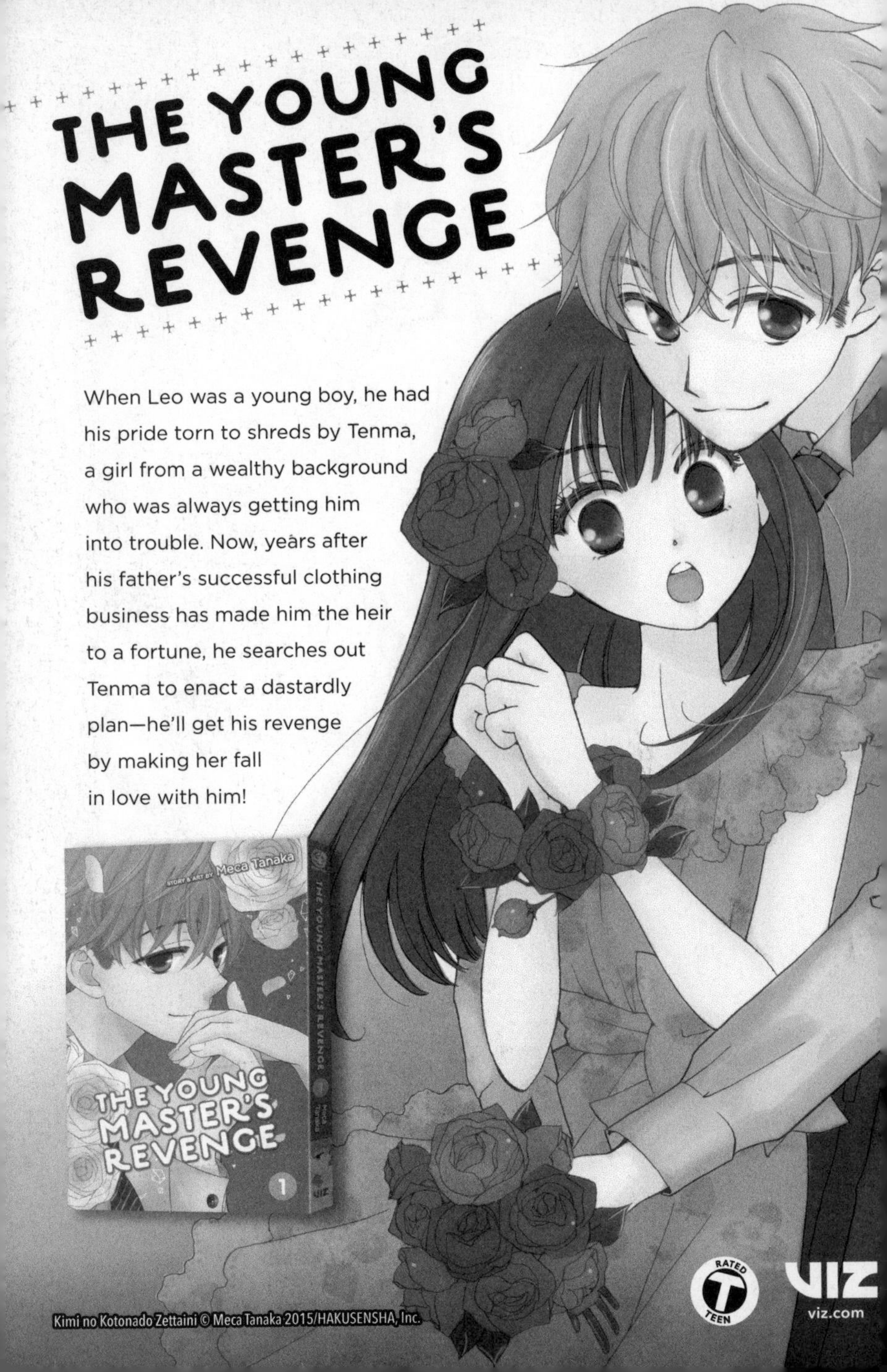
THE YOUNG MASTER'S REVENGE
When Leo was a young boy, he had his pride torn to shreds by Tenma, a girl from a wealthy background who was always getting him into trouble. Now, years after his father's successful clothing business has made him the heir to a fortune, he searches out Tenma to enact a dastardly plan—he'll get his revenge by making her fall in love with him!
STORY & ART BY Meca Tanaka
THE YOUNG MASTER'S REVENGE
1
THE YOUNG MASTER'S REVENGE
RATED T TEEN
VIZ
viz.com
Kimi no Kotonado Zettaini © Meca Tanaka 2015/HAKUSENSHA, Inc.

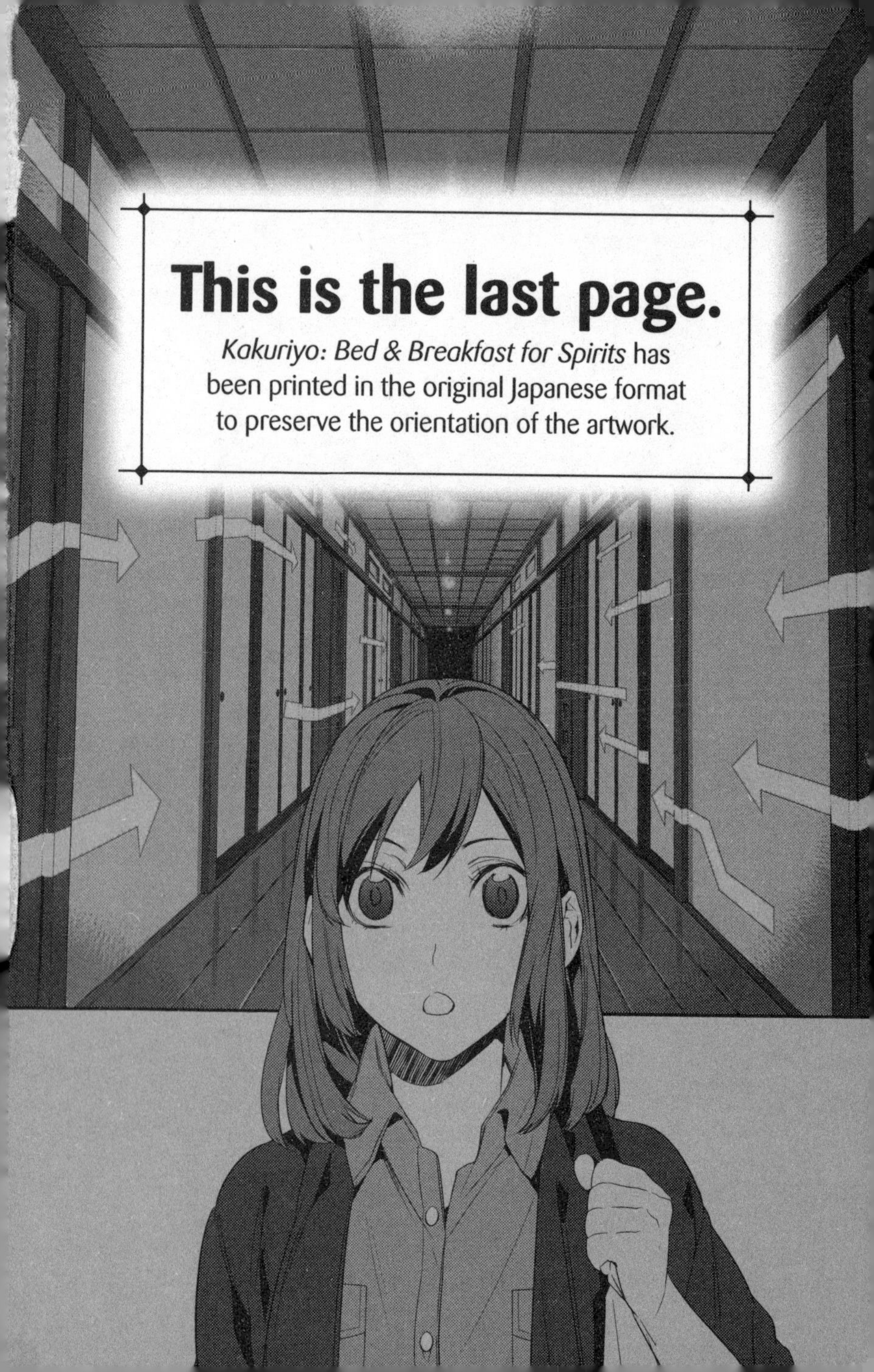
This is the last page.
Kakuriyo: Bed & Breakfast for Spirits has been printed in the original Japanese format to preserve the orientation of the artwork.